SCHAUM'S OUTLINE OF

THEORY AND PROBLEMS

of

COMPUTER GRAPHICS

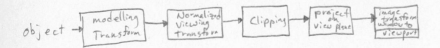

•

ROY A. PLASTOCK, Ph.D.
Associate Professor of Mathematics
New Jersey Institute of Technology

GORDON KALLEY, M.S.I.E.
Special Lecturer in Industrial Engineering
New Jersey Institute of Technology

•

SCHAUM'S OUTLINE SERIES
McGRAW-HILL BOOK COMPANY

New York   St. Louis   San Francisco   Auckland   Bogotá   Hamburg   London
Madrid   Mexico   Milan   Montreal   New Delhi   Panama   Paris
São Paulo   Singapore   Sydney   Tokyo   Toronto

ROY A. PLASTOCK, Ph.D., is an Associate Professor of Mathematics at New Jersey Institute of Technology. He is listed in *Who's Who in Frontier Science and Technology*. His special interests are computer graphics, computer vision, and artificial intelligence.

GORDON KALLEY, M.S.I.E., is a special lecturer in Industrial and Management Engineering at New Jersey Institute of Technology. He is listed in *Who's Who in Technology Today*. His particular interests are computer ergonomics, robotics, and artificial intelligence.

Schaum's Outline of Theory and Problems of
COMPUTER GRAPHICS

2 3 4 5 6 7 8 9 10 11 12 13 14 15 16 17 18 19 20 SHP SHP 8 9 8 7

ISBN 0-07-050326-5

Sponsoring Editor, John Aliano
Production Manager, Nick Monti
Editing Supervisor, Marthe Grice

Library of Congress Cataloging-in-Publication Data

Plastock, Roy A.
  Schaum's outline of computer graphics.

  Includes index.
  1. Computer graphics. I. Kalley, Gordon. II. Title.
III. Title: Computer graphics.
T385.P53   1986   006.6   85-23105
ISBN 0-07-050326-5

To Sharon and Adam, the sunshine of my life.

—Roy Plastock

In memory of James Hicks, who gave me my first Schaum's Outline.

—Gordon Kalley

Preface

From the display of text to the computer-aided design of bridges, from business graphics to dazzling computer art compositions, from video games to flight simulators for jet aircraft: The field of computer graphics and its application presents new vistas and challenges to those who believe in the promise of the computer as a tool for learning, discovery, and creativity.

Born from the merging of computer and television technologies, the field of computer graphics has, until recently, been explored only by those who have had access to the large computers and costly display devices required to generate computer graphic images. Now, through microelectronic technology, there are small, inexpensive microcomputers that are powerful enough to support high-level computer graphics applications. Thus the excitement of experimenting with computer graphics can be made accessible to a wide audience. The real difficulty, however, in learning computer graphics lies in the complex nature of the subject.

The study of computer graphics calls for an understanding of computer and display technologies and a solid grounding in two- and three-dimensional analytic geometry. This is to be combined with a knowledge of matrix operations, data structures, and algorithms. Finally, one must understand how all the pieces fit together. It is no wonder that after their initial enthusiasm, many students get bogged down in a myriad of details and so end their studies. Disheartened, they are left with the impression that the field will always remain complex and mysterious to them. It is the aim of this book to provide a path through the complexities of the subject and to provide the necessary technical and mathematical background required for the study of computer graphics.

In the tradition of the Schaum's Outline Series, this book presents complete explanations of the fundamental concepts and makes concrete the many details of computer graphics through the presentation of a large number of completely worked out illustrative examples.

Chapters 1 and 2 provide the technical information on how graphics systems work. Chapter 3 builds on this by describing the algorithms used for primitive raster operations and for displaying points, lines, and circles, and filling regions. Chapters 4 through 8 describe the mathematics and algorithms used for the display and manipulation of two- and three-dimensional geometric objects and pictures. Chapter 7 includes a complete discussion of parallel and perspective projection. In Chapter 9 we describe the tools used for building and designing complex two- and three-dimensional models and surfaces. Chapter 10 is devoted to the problem of realistically rendering images through the removal of hidden surfaces. Chapter 11 describes some applications of computer graphics and Chapter 12 provides an introduction to the GKS programming language. Two appendixes provide the requisite mathematical background, especially in two- and three-dimensional analytic geometry and matrix algebra.

The completeness of this book makes it suitable as a text or supplementary text for an introductory course in computer graphics. In addition, this Outline can be used effectively as a self-study tool. It is suggested that the operations and algorithms presented in the text be programmed so as to allow for experimentation with the basic ideas. It is the hope of the authors that this book will help make the tools of computer graphics accessible to a wide range of individuals. If this is the case, we would like to hear of your experiences (preferably even see them).

Finally, we wish to say thanks to our wives, Sharon and Wendi, for their patience and understanding while we were preparing this book. We also express our gratitude to the staff of McGraw-Hill and especially to John Aliano for his faith in this project.

ROY A. PLASTOCK
GORDON KALLEY

Caution

The reader should be alerted to the fact that within the field of computer graphics there are two different matrix notations that are used.

This book represents points by column vectors and applies transformations by left multiplying by the transformation matrix. We have chosen this notation because it is the standard used in mathematics and computer science texts and the majority of students have already encountered matrix operations in this form.

The other notation represents points by row vectors and applies transformations by right multiplying by the transformation matrix. It is used in much of the computer graphics literature.

To change from one notational style to another, it is necessary to take the transpose of the matrices that appear in any expression.

Contents

Chapter 1 GRAPHICS INPUT, STORAGE, AND COMMUNICATIONS **1**

1.1 Graphics Input Devices.. 1
1.2 Graphics Storage Devices... 11
1.3 Communications Devices 15
1.4 Processing Devices 17

Chapter 2 DISPLAY DEVICES.. **32**

2.1 Introduction.. 32
2.2 Common Display Devices... 32
2.3 Raster-Scan CRT 32
2.4 Other Output Devices 42

Chapter 3 SCAN CONVERSION **55**

3.1 Introduction.. 55
3.2 Scan-Converting a Point 56
3.3 Scan-Converting a Straight Line.................................... 56
3.4 Scan-Converting a Circle... 58
3.5 Scan-Converting an Ellipse 61
3.6 Scan-Converting Arcs and Sectors 64
3.7 Scan-Converting a Rectangle 65
3.8 Region Filling 65
3.9 Boundary Block Transfer (BITBLT) or Raster Operational Graphics...... 68
3.10 Side Effects of Scan Conversion.................................... 69

Chapter 4 TWO-DIMENSIONAL GRAPHICS TRANSFORMATIONS............ **80**

4.1 Introduction.. 80
4.2 Geometric Transformations... 80
4.3 Coordinate Transformations 82
4.4 Composite Transformations 85
4.5 Instance Transformations 86

Chapter 5 TWO-DIMENSIONAL VIEWING TRANSFORMATIONS AND CLIPPING **98**

5.1 Introduction.. 98
5.2 Viewing Transformations 98
5.3 Clipping and Shielding 99

CONTENTS

Chapter 6 THREE-DIMENSIONAL GRAPHICS TRANSFORMATIONS **115**

6.1 Introduction.. 115
6.2 Geometric Transformations 115
6.3 Coordinate Transformations................................. 117
6.4 Composite Transformations and Matrix Concatenation.................. 118
6.5 Instance Transformations 119

Chapter 7 MATHEMATICS OF PROJECTION............................. **127**

7.1 Introduction.. 127
7.2 The Various Kinds of Projection 127
7.3 Perspective Projection....................................... 127
7.4 Parallel Projection.. 130

Chapter 8 THREE-DIMENSIONAL VIEWING TRANSFORMATIONS AND CLIPPING **149**

8.1 Introduction.. 149
8.2 Three-Dimensional Viewing 149
8.3 Clipping.. 153
8.4 Viewing Transformations 156

Chapter 9 GEOMETRIC FORMS AND MODELS.......................... **170**

9.1 Introduction.. 170
9.2 Simple Geometric Forms 170
9.3 Wireframe Models.. 171
9.4 Curved Surfaces.. 172
9.5 Curve Design... 172
9.6 Polynomial Basis Functions................................. 173
9.7 The Problem of Interpolation................................ 175
9.8 The Problem of Approximation 177
9.9 Curved-Surface Design 179
9.10 Transforming Curves and Surfaces........................... 182
9.11 Quadric Surfaces 182

Chapter 10 HIDDEN SURFACES...................................... **190**

10.1 Introduction.. 190
10.2 Depth Comparisons... 190
10.3 Z-Buffer Algorithm (Depth Buffer Algorithm)..................... 192
10.4 Scan-Line Algorithms 193
10.5 The Painter's Algorithm 196
10.6 Subdivision Algorithms 199
10.7 Hidden-Line Elimination.................................... 202
10.8 Ray Tracing.. 202
10.9 The Rendering of Mathematical Surfaces 203

CONTENTS

Chapter 11   **COMPUTER GRAPHICS APPLICATIONS** **224**

     11.1 Introduction 224
     11.2 Computer Ergonomics 224
     11.3 Information Structures 226
     11.4 Fields of Application 229

Chapter 12   **INTRODUCTION TO GRAPHICS KERNEL SYSTEM** **244**

     12.1   Introduction 244
     12.2   GKS Primitives 244
     12.3   GKS Primitive Attributes 245
     12.4   GKS Window and Viewport 247
     12.5   GKS Clipping 249
     12.6   GKS Programmer Primitive Construction 249
     12.7   GKS Segments 249
     12.8   GKS Segment Transformations 250
     12.9   GKS Input 250
     12.10 Multiusers 250
     12.11 Implementation 250

Appendix 1   **MATHEMATICS FOR TWO-DIMENSIONAL COMPUTER GRAPHICS** .. **260**

     A1.1 Introduction 260
     A1.2 The Two-Dimensional Cartesian Coordinate System 260
     A1.3 The Polar Coordinate System 263
     A1.4 Vectors 264
     A1.5 Matrices 267
     A1.6 Functions and Transformations 269
     A1.7 Number Systems 271

Appendix 2   **MATHEMATICS FOR THREE-DIMENSIONAL COMPUTER GRAPHICS** **290**

     A2.1 Three-Dimensional Cartesian Coordinates 290
     A2.2 Curves and Surfaces in Three Dimensions 291
     A2.3 Vectors in Three Dimensions 295
     A2.4 Homogeneous Coordinates 298

ANSWERS TO SUPPLEMENTARY PROBLEMS **310**

INDEX **335**

Chapter 1

Graphics Input, Storage, and Communications

1.1 GRAPHICS INPUT DEVICES

Any device that allows information from outside the computer to be communicated to the computer is considered an *input device*. Since the central processing unit (CPU) of a digital computer can understand only discrete binary information, all computer input devices and circuitry must eventually communicate with the computer in this form. Many devices are capable of performing this task. Some common computer graphics input devices are:

Keyboard

Trackball

Joystick

Mouse

Paddle controls

Light pen

Magnetic tablet

Digitizing camera

Analog Devices versus Digital Devices

Input devices are of two basic types, *analog* and *digital*. This section provides a brief overview and explanation of how some of the more popular analog and digital devices work.

Humans perceive a continuous universe; digital devices sense a discrete universe consisting of discrete segments. For example, the temperature indicated by a digital thermometer may be observed to change from 73 to 74 degrees instantaneously. We know that the actual temperature did not suddenly jump from 73 to 74 degrees. Rather, there was a continuous warming of the air, and at some moment the temperature became closer to 74 than 73 degrees. If a more accurate digital thermometer were used such as one that could measure tenths of a degree, the exact temperature would still not be sensed. Instead, closer approximations would be given.

Figures 1-1(a) and 1-1(b) illustrate the differences in the way temperatures would be recorded by a

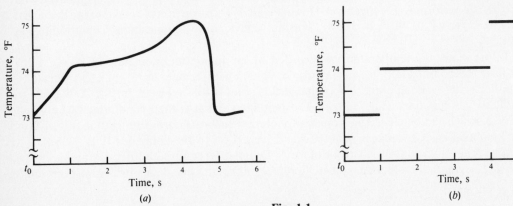

(a)   (b)

Fig. 1-1

1

continuous [Fig. 1-1(a)] and a discrete [Fig. 1-1(b)] device. Notice that while the temperature is actually changing continuously, the discrete device only records incremental changes of one or more degrees. The device capable of recording continuous changes is an analog device; the device which can sense only discrete changes is a digital device.

   Time is also perceived as continuous. (However, recent physics experiments have begun to challenge this concept.) Therefore, a digital device must take "snapshots" of the environment with sufficient rapidity if a high degree of accuracy is to be attained. When a computer takes a snapshot of the environment by obtaining a value from an input device, it is said to *strobe* the device. For example, Table 1-1 demonstrates the temperature readings that would be recorded 3.5 seconds (s) from time t_0 if a digital device accurate to one degree were used to record the temperatures shown in Fig. 1-1(a); the frequency of strobing ranges from once every 0.5 s to once every 5 s starting at t_0.

Table 1-1   Effects of Strobe Frequency on Accuracy

Frequency of Strobe	Observed Temperature at 3.5 s from t_0
0.5	75
1.0	75
2.0	74
3.0	74
4.0	73
5.0	73

Analog-to-Digital Conversion

   Since the computer is a discrete digital device, while most data in the world outside the computer is continuous, the data must be converted to enable the computer to use it. The conversion of continuous analog data to discrete digital data is called *analog-to-digital conversion*, or simply *A/D conversion*.

   The computer graphics programmer must have some knowledge of A/D conversion because many graphics input devices are analog devices and A/D conversion can affect the accuracy of data collected even while exhibiting a high degree of precision.

   Typically, A/D conversion is performed either by hardware devices incorporated in the computer's input circuitry or by means of firmware that directly interfaces with the computer's input circuitry. Many different circuits can perform A/D conversion. However, all A/D conversion systems must go through the steps shown in Figs. 1-2(a) through 1-2(e): sensing, conversion, amplification, conditioning, and quantization.

   Figure 1-2(a) shows the temperature as recorded by an analog thermometer. In Figure 1-2(b), these data have been converted to an electronic signal, with temperature changes reflected as changes in either voltage or amperage. The signal at this point is still too weak for the A/D converter to work with, so it is amplified [Fig. 1-2(c)]. The amplified signal is then conditioned to eliminate electronic noise, which can be picked up from many sources, such as fluorescent lighting [Fig. 1-2(d)]. Finally, the amplified analog signal is quantized and passed on to the computer [Fig. 1-2(e)].

   The frequency and duration of each strobe of the A/D converter can greatly affect the accuracy of the final recording. The graphics programmer must, therefore, make sure that data processing is coordinated with the A/D converter.

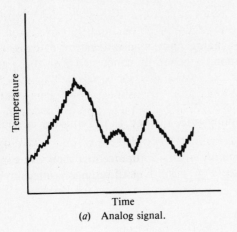

(a)　Analog signal.

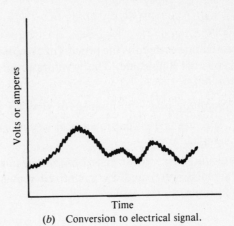

(b)　Conversion to electrical signal.

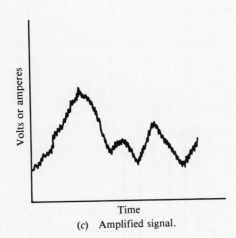

(c)　Amplified signal.

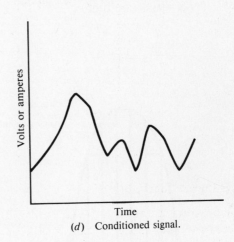

(d)　Conditioned signal.

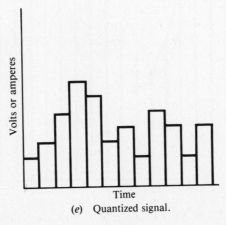

(e)　Quantized signal.

Fig. 1-2

Quantizing

Quantizing is defined as the process of dividing an analog input signal into a string of discrete outputs, each of constant amplitude. The graphics programmer is generally concerned with three aspects of quantization:

1. *Sampling rate*—the number of samples per second.
2. *Aperture time*—The reciprocal of the sampling rate, defined as the number of seconds per sample.
3. *Coding error* (also called *amplitude uncertainty*)—the difference between the conditioned signal $y = f(t)$ and the quantized signal (see Fig. 1-3). This difference is measured by the formula

$$\int_0^T F(t)\, dt - \sum_{i=0}^{N-1} F(i \cdot a)a \qquad (1.1)$$

where T = duration of the measurement

a = aperture time = $\dfrac{1}{s}$

$N = \dfrac{T}{a}$

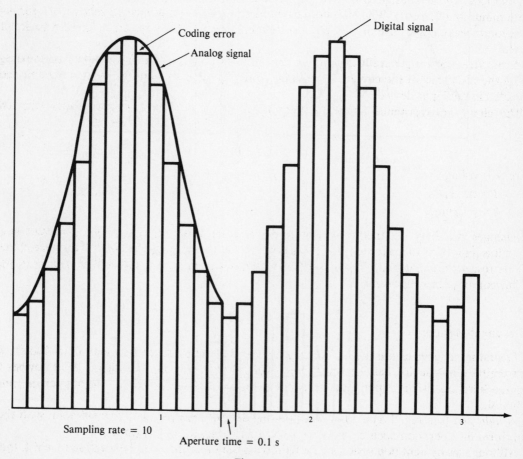

Sampling rate = 10

Aperture time = 0.1 s

Time, s

Fig. 1-3

Analog Input Devices

The joystick, trackball, mouse, and paddle controls are all transducers that convert a graphics system user's movements into changes in voltage. A *transducer* is a device that converts energy from one form to another.

The *paddle* control [Fig. 1-4(a)] is the simplest of the analog input devices. Like all variable resistors, the paddle control varies its resistance, thereby changing the voltage of the input circuit in relation to the movement of the paddle's control knob. Commonly, two paddle controls are used in graphics systems, one to control movement in the x direction and one to control movement in the y direction.

The *trackball* [Fig. 1-4(b)] mechanically combines two variable resistors in a single device, thus allowing the user to use one hand to enter both x and y information with a single device. The trackball is normally operated by rolling the ball with the palm of the hand.

The *mouse* [Fig. 1-4(c)] is very similar in design to the trackball. The mouse, like the trackball, combines two variable resistors in a single device. However, the mouse is normally operated by rolling the ball over the surface of a table. There is also a digital version of the mouse which counts light and dark lines in graph paper or any other surface with light and dark lines, thus eliminating the use of variable resistors. Because the digital mouse has no moving parts, it is far less susceptible to mechanical breakdown.

The *joystick* [Fig. 1-4(d)] again makes use of two variable resistors to specify x and y movement. Here the user pushes the handle to cause movement. The joystick may be designed with either of two basic methods. The first design consists of four switches (one for plus x, one for minus x, one for plus y, and one for minus y movement). When this design is used, the joystick sends relative movement information. The second design makes use of variable resistors and in principle works much like the trackball and mouse.

Analog transducers generally convert user movement into changes in either voltage or amperage by varying the resistance of the circuit. The change in resistance is accomplished with a variable resistor embedded in the input device.

The change in resistance alters the output voltage of the circuit in accordance with Ohm's law:

$$V = I * R \qquad\qquad (1.2)$$

where V = voltage
I = current
R = resistance

The changes in voltage are then passed on to the A/D converter. In designing a computer graphics system it is important to make sure that the acceptable range of voltages for the A/D converter and the variable resistor are matched. Failure to do so may result in damage to the A/D converter or precise but inaccurate data collection.

Digital Input Devices

Digital input devices are actually analog devices that collect input information in discrete form. Each digital input device has its own distinct method of operation. The digital input devices to be analyzed here are the light pens, the magnetic pens and tablets, the touch-sensitive screen, and the keyboard.

A *light pen* (see Fig. 1-5) is used as a pointing device. Typically the user will point with the pen to perform an operation such as drawing a line or rotating an object on a CRT.

Although many light pen systems emit light from the tip of the pen, the location to which the user is pointing is not found by light sensors in the CRT. Instead, the light pen senses the light emitted by the CRT.

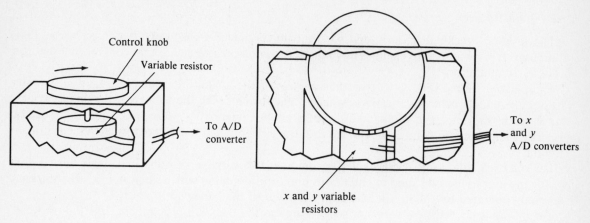

(a) Paddle control.   (b) Trackball.

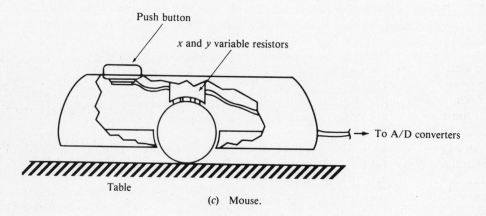

(c) Mouse.

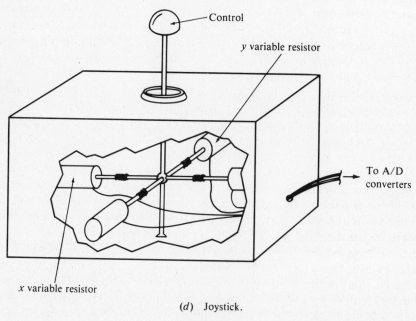

(d) Joystick.

Fig. 1-4

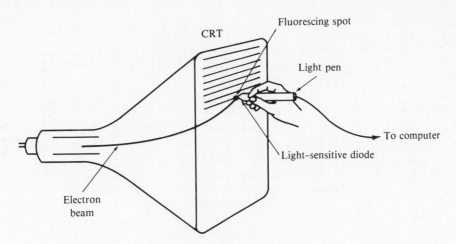

Fig. 1-5 Light pen system.

The location to which the user is pointing can be found by first keeping track of when the CRT's electron beam starts each refresh cycle. Then, the amount of time that passes before the light pen receives a pulse of light (indicating that the beam has just passed) is measured. When a noninterlaced CRT is used, the duration of each refresh cycle will normally be equal to the line frequency [60 hertz (Hz) in the United States and 50 Hz elsewhere].

As discussed in Chap. 2, the computer "perceives" the pixels' ouput to the CRT as a continuous line. Therefore, the percentage of the refresh cycle completed before the light pen receives a pulse should be equal to the percentage of the screen that has been written to; this, in turn, should be equal to the percentage of display memory that has been written. Because of overscan, however, the task of locating where the user is pointing becomes far more complex. The problem is further complicated when an interlaced CRT is used.

The computer does not have to actually time the period between the start of each refresh cycle and the time when a pulse is recorded by the pen because the computer is already keeping track of which portion of display memory is being written at any given moment. Therefore, the computer can easily locate where the user is pointing by storing the address of the byte which is being displayed at the time the light pen records a pulse (see Prob. 1.12).

A *magnetic pen* and *tablet* [see Fig. 1-6(*a*)] are composed of a two-dimensional wire grid and a radiowave-emitting stylus. The wire grid is a matrix antenna which locates the position of the stylus measuring the intensity of the radio signal received by each wire in the grid. By comparing the intensity of signal received by each wire in the grid the demultiplexing circuitry, you will be able to calculate the position of the stylus even when it lies between wires.

An *acoustic tablet* [see Fig. 1-6(*b*)] makes use of strip microphones located around the perimeter of the tablet. The stylus generates a series of small sparks when placed near the tablet. The acoustic tablet has been losing popularity, however, because it is too noisy (it generates a buzzing sound) and too susceptible to ambient noise. Capacitance tablets are also quite popular. The capacitance tablet operates the same way as the touch-sensitive screen described next.

There are three basic types of *touch-sensitive screens*. The first design incorporates a fine grid of wire pairs placed over the face of the display. When the user presses the screen, the capacitance of the wire pairs is altered, thus indicting the position of the user's finger [see Fig. 1-7(*a*)].

The second design utilizes a series of strain gauges located around the perimeter of a plate of glass or plastic placed over the display. When the user presses the plate, the material is deformed, thereby allowing the location of the user's finger to be calculated [see Fig. 1-7(*b*)].

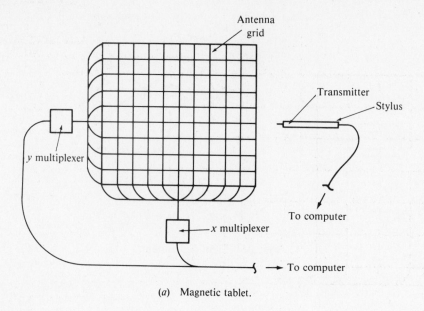

(*a*) Magnetic tablet.

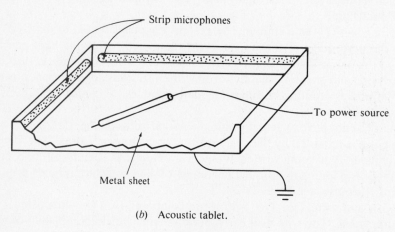

(*b*) Acoustic tablet.

Fig. 1-6

The most popular method of creating a touch-sensitive screen makes use of a series of infrared light-emitting diodes (LEDs) and sensors located around the perimeter of the display [see Fig. 1-7(*c*)]. When the user touches the screen, light beams are broken, indicating the location of the user's finger.

Touch-sensitive screens, although popular in concept, have been slow to be implemented because of technical problems. For example, in the first method, the wire grid covering the screen has been found to be too susceptible to wear. In the second method, the plate is too easily affected by changes in temperature (heat causes the plate to expand, thus causing strain) and mechanical fatigue. In the third method, designers have had trouble creating a sufficiently dense matrix of light beams. As a result, the user's finger is often placed either between the light beams or in a location in which only one beam is broken.

The *keyboard* is a common input device. A standard known as the American Standard Code for Information Interchange (ASCII) has been developed to allow computers to encode keyboard characters.

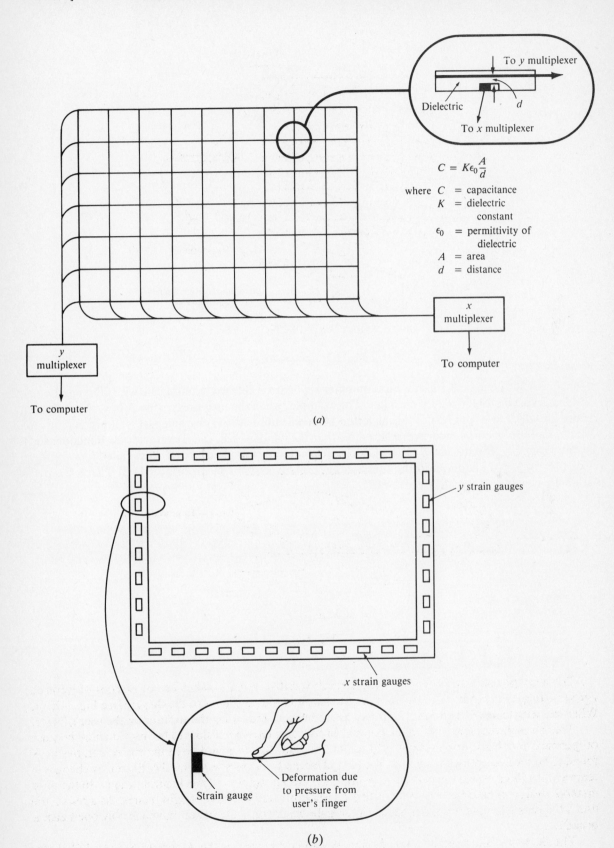

$$C = K\epsilon_0 \frac{A}{d}$$

where C = capacitance
K = dielectric constant
ϵ_0 = permittivity of dielectric
A = area
d = distance

(a)

(b)

Fig. 1-7

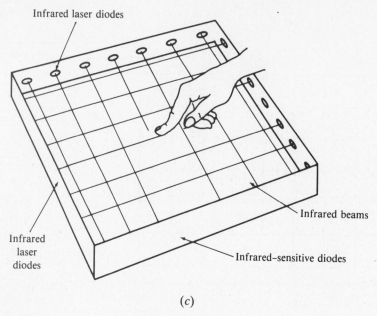

(c)

Fig. 1-7   (*continued*)

Using the ASCII standard, the graphics computer keyboard is able to communicate with the computer by sending a specific 7-bit code for each key. For example, when the user presses the A key, the computer generally will receive the ASCII for the letter "A" (the entire ASCII character set is shown in App. 3). Many graphics system keyboards produce more than the standard 128 ASCII character set. Functions such as Save Drawing, Rotate, and Remove Object are commonly found on "extra" keys called *function keys* [see Fig. 1-8(a)]. In addition to the function keys, many systems incorporate BITBLT (see Chap. 3) graphics symbols, as shown in Fig. 1-8(b).

(a)

Fig. 1-8

(*Photo by Boto*)

(*b*)

Fig. 1-8 (*continued*)

Digital Cameras and Digitizing Video Images

Images can be converted into digital form. The video image to computer transformation is usually accomplished in either of the following two ways. In the first method, a lens is used to focus light on a bank of light-sensitive diodes. When exposed to sufficiently high light intensity, a diode will jump into the "on" state. Since the array of light-sensitive diodes can be read by the computer as random-access memory (RAM), the image is "instantly" digitized.

The second method is almost the reverse of scan conversion (Chap. 3). The video signal generated by a video camera represents a series of scan lines. With the use of an A/D converter the signal is "chopped" into pixel-sized segments. (The level of each segment determines whether a pixel is on or off.) The resulting bit stream which now represents the image in digitized form is then stored in a buffer for later processing.

1.2 GRAPHICS STORAGE DEVICES

Most graphics system users want to store the images they have created. There are many storage devices currently available. Some common storage devices are floppy disks, hard disks, magnetic tape, paper tape, punched cards, video tape, and film. Each storage device has unique advantages and disadvantages. Therefore, the graphics user and the programmer should carefully examine the final application before selecting a storage device.

Graphics Storage Formats

Regardless of the storage medium selected, the graphics system designer will always use some combination of the following four basic storage formats:

1. The system can be designed to store only the image(s) created (image-only storage).
2. The system can be designed to store bit by bit exactly what is in display memory (display-memory storage).

3. The system can be designed to store the contents of display memory in compressed format (compressed-memory storage).

4. The system can be designed to store only the information that was used to create the image (information storage).

Image-Only Storage

In an image-only storage system the video image is retained on video tape or video disk or as a photograph. Storage of images in this fashion is relatively inexpensive. Both the storage medium and storage equipment are inexpensive. Once the image is stored, however, it is relatively difficult and expensive to restore it to the computer for further manipulation. For this reason, systems that store images only are seldom, if ever, used alone.

Display-Memory Storage

A storage system may be designed so that the bit pattern that represents the image is copied directly from display memory to the storage medium. Systems that store images by this method are very easy to develop because most computer operating systems contain utility programs that save blocks of the computer's memory. The programmer therefore needs only to issue a SAVE command and pass the starting and ending addresses of the display memory to the utility program. When the user desires to retrieve the image, it is copied from the storage medium to display memory. Any of the following storage media may be used: floppy disks, hard disks, paper tape, magnetic tape, or cards.

While this method saves on development time, it has two major drawbacks. First, storage of an image in this way is relatively time-consuming, requiring anywhere from 2 to 38 s. Studies on computer response time have revealed that in most situations users become agitated when response times exceed 2 s. The second drawback is that storing images in this manner requires a great deal of memory. One byte of display memory requires slightly more than 1 byte of storage medium. The reason for this is that extra memory is needed to direct the computer back to the part of the storage medium containing the image. For example, a 640×200 pixel display will require over 16K of memory. Thus only 60 images could be stored on a 1-megabyte hard-disk drive.

Compressed-Memory Storage

Storage time and space can be greatly reduced by storing images in compressed format. Compression takes advantages of repeated patterns in display memory. For example, examine the image shown in Fig. 1-9. Notice that this image contains contiguous regions of unlit and lit pixels. This means that the memory representing the image contains many identical bytes. (For further explanation of display memory refer to Chap. 2, "Display Devices.")

In noncompressed format, it takes 32×14 bits or 56 bytes to represent the image (Fig. 1-10). If the data are packed using 1 byte to represent the number of contiguous bytes and the following byte to represent the value of those bytes, the same image can be represented as shown in Fig. 1-11. It now takes only 15 bytes to represent the image.

Compression routines can be very complex, taking advantage of long series of replications. However, the more complex the packing routine, the longer it will take to code the image when storing and decode the image when retrieving. The graphics system designer must therefore compromise between (1) storage and retrieval speed and (2) memory usage.

The problem is further complicated when images to be saved contain no or few series of replicated bytes. For the display memory shown in Figs. 1-9 through 1-11, if no bytes were repeated, 56×2 or 112 bytes would be required to describe the image because 1 byte is needed to indicate the number of bytes to be repeated and 1 byte is needed to store the value of each byte in the series.

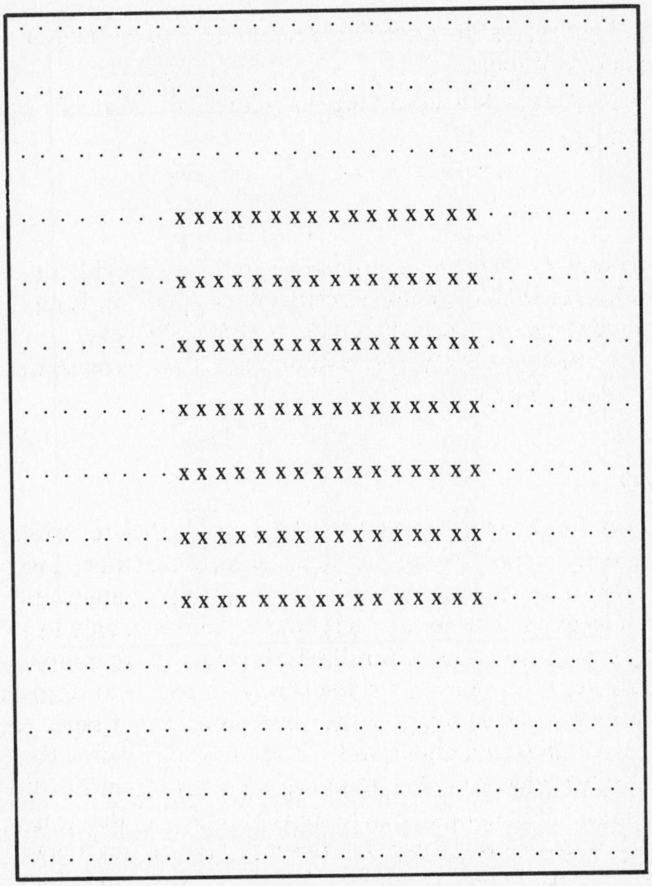

Fig. 1-9 32×14 pixel display.

Binary representation								Hexadecimal representation			
0000	0000	0000	0000	0000	0000	0000	0000	00	00	00	00
0000	0000	0000	0000	0000	0000	0000	0000	00	00	00	00
0000	0000	0000	0000	0000	0000	0000	0000	00	00	00	00
0000	0000	1111	1111	1111	1111	0000	0000	00	FF	FF	00
0000	0000	1111	1111	1111	1111	0000	0000	00	FF	FF	00
0000	0000	1111	1111	1111	1111	0000	0000	00	FF	FF	00
0000	0000	1111	1111	1111	1111	0000	0000	00	FF	FF	00
0000	0000	1111	1111	1111	1111	0000	0000	00	FF	FF	00
0000	0000	1111	1111	1111	1111	0000	0000	00	FF	FF	00
0000	0000	1111	1111	1111	1111	0000	0000	00	FF	FF	00
0000	0000	0000	0000	0000	0000	0000	0000	00	00	00	00
0000	0000	0000	0000	0000	0000	0000	0000	00	00	00	00
0000	0000	0000	0000	0000	0000	0000	0000	00	00	00	00
0000	0000	0000	0000	0000	0000	0000	0000	00	00	00	00

Fig. 1-10

Number of bytes to be repeated	Value of each byte in series
0D	00
02	FF
02	00
02	FF
02	00
02	FF
02	00
02	FF
02	00
02	FF
02	00
02	FF
02	00
02	FF
11	00

Fig. 1-11

Information Storage

A storage system that retains the information used to construct the image retains a series of commands that describe the image. Systems that store images in this format require a well-defined graphics language which clearly and consistently describes the objects that make up each image. System-design time is greatly increased when this method is used, unless a standard graphics language such as the graphics kernel system (GKS) is already in place. The saving of image construction information can result in saving of considerable time and memory if the image to be stored is composed entirely of standard objects.

Assuming that the image shown in Fig. 1-9 is a standard object, it could be described and stored as the following display list of graphics commands:

(Lower left coordinates)   (Upper right coordinates)

Box 8, 4, 23, 10

Fill 1

(Fill color/code number)

The use of 1-byte code to describe the graphics commands brings the required memory for storage down to 7 bytes: 2 bytes for the graphics commands and 5 bytes for the data which describe the box coordinates and fill color code number. A further advantage of this method is that when the image is retrieved it can easily be further manipulated and edited because all the information used to construct the image is retained.

However, if nonstandard objects are used—for example, odd-shaped curves—reconstruction of the image can become time-consuming and memory-intensive. When nonstandard objects are described, each point in the object must be stored separately. For example, if each point that made up the image above were described separately, 1344 bytes would be required to store it: $(32 \times 14 \text{ pixels}) \times (1$ byte to describe the x coordinate of each pixel + 1 byte to describe the y coordinate of each pixel + 1 byte to store the command to plot a point at the given x and y coordinates).

1.3 COMMUNICATIONS DEVICES

Computers generally transmit data to each other by use of either *parallel* or *serial* transmission methods.

Parallel Transmission

When a computer transmits data to another computer using the parallel method, 8 bits (1 byte) of data are sent at a time through eight wires connecting the two computers (see Fig. 1-12).

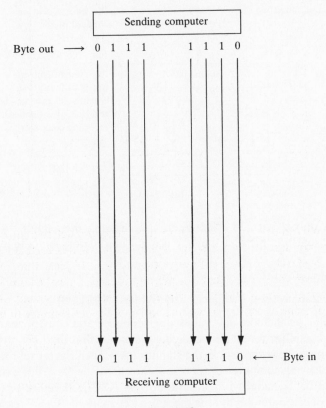

Fig. 1-12

While parallel transmission allows computers to communicate rapidly, there are some problems associated with this method. For example, the voltage representing ones and zeros is DC current, which is highly susceptible to line resistance. As a result, if the communicating computers are too far apart, the line signals will eventually be lost. Another problem associated with parallel transmission is called *echo*. Echo occurs every time a switch is rapidly turned off. When the switch is turned off, a slight backward current is set up. Depending on the distance between the communicating computers, the back current can either annihilate or reinforce the next signal. Either way, echo can cause faulty data to be received.

Serial Transmission

The serial transmission method allows computers to communicate over long distances by ordinary telephone lines. In this method, each byte is generally broken down into 1 start bit, 7 data bits, and 1 stop bit. Notice that only 7 bits are needed to send the information. This is because the ASCII

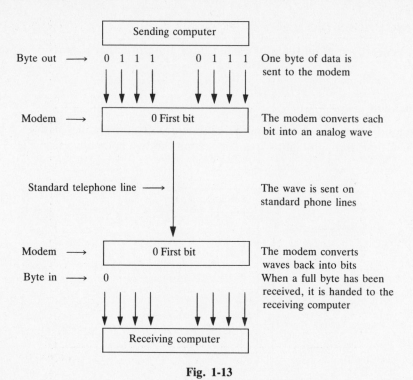

Fig. 1-13

character set contains only 2^7 or 128 characters, thus leaving the eighth bit unused. With serial transmission, data are sent one bit at a time by using a modulator-demodulator (*modem*) (see Fig. 1-13).

North American Presentation-Level Protocol-Level Syntax (NAPLPS)

The ASCII character set includes several escape-sequence and control characters. These characters allow the sending computer to tell the receiving computer that the next characters it will receive will have a special meaning. For example, in the standard ASCII character set the hexidecimal value 41 is understood by the receiving computer to represent the character "A." For expansion of the amount of information that can be exchanged beyond the normal ASCII character set, the following special scheme is used. On most computer keyboards there is a key marked "ESC" (escape) which is assigned the ASCII value 1B. With the use of software, escape can be used to alter the computer's interpretation of ASCII codes. Therefore, if the receiving computer first receives the hexidecimal value 1B (the ASCII value for escape), it will interpret the next value "41" as an escape character. Taking advantage of escape sequences, NAPLPS allows computers to communicate a wide variety of graphics commands and alternate BITBLT character sets.

The NAPLPS system also incorporates an ingenious method of encoding coordinate information which allows computers with different levels of resolution to communicate. First, NAPLPS uses a unit screen. That is, the coordinates of the lower left-hand corner of the display are assumed to be 0.0, 0.0 and the upper right-hand coordinates are assumed to be 1.0, 1.0 (see Fig. 1-14). Most computer displays have 4:3 aspect ratios, so the top 25 percent of the coordinates are generally discarded. Every pixel on the unit screen can be described as a fraction between 0.0 and 1.0. These fractions can be converted to binary form where each bit added to the right adds precision. The coordinate value is given by adding the values of the bits together. For example, the value received in Fig. 1-15 would be

$$1\left(\frac{1}{2}\right) + 1\left(\frac{1}{4}\right) + 0\left(\frac{1}{8}\right) + 1\left(\frac{1}{16}\right) + 1\left(\frac{1}{32}\right) + 0\left(\frac{1}{64}\right) + 1\left(\frac{1}{128}\right) + 1\left(\frac{1}{256}\right) = \frac{219}{256}$$

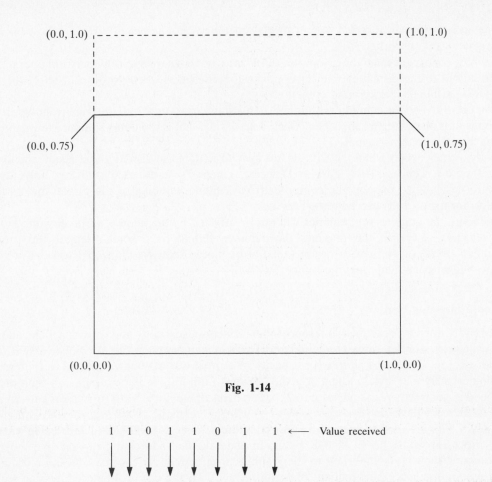

Fig. 1-14

Fig. 1-15

The resolution of the sending and the receiving computer need not be identical. The receiving computer can convert the coordinate values directly to pixel location by multiplying the value it receives by an appropriate power of 2 (left-shifting), which will convert the value received to an integer value equal to the correct pixel location. The remaining bits are discarded.

For example, assume that a graphics system capable of plotting $2^7 = 128$ horizontal pixels receives the data shown in Fig. 1-15. The binary value .11011011 would be multiplied by 2^7, giving 1101101.1. The ".1" would be discarded, leaving 1101101 binary, which equals 109 decimal. Notice that on both the sending and the receiving computer the point is located in the same relative location.

1.4 PROCESSING DEVICES

Single-Processor versus Coprocessor Systems

There are two basic hardware approaches commonly used when designing computer graphics systems. The first approach uses a single processor (i.e., a single CPU) to handle all the computer's functions and operations, including the output of display memory. The second method makes use of a second processor, often called a *display processing unit* (DPU), to handle the output of display memory. The two-processor method is usually resorted to when the main processor cannot handle the computer's functions and operations and also output display memory on a sufficiently regular basis to prevent dropping out, snow, or flicker.

Dropping out occurs when the computer's CPU does not have time to both perform operations and maintain output to the display device. Dropping out is indicated when portions or all of the display momentarily go blank (background color).

Snow occurs when the computer is not able to maintain operations and the display; however, in this case the result is many bright spots. The effect is similar to what is seen on a standard television that is receiving a weak broadcast signal.

Finally, *flicker* occurs when the CPU is too busy to update the display. As a result, the display is not refreshed often enough (see "Display Devices," Chap. 2). In the case of flicker, however, there is software designed to prevent the computer from sending anything to the display unless there is time to go through a full scan pattern.

In general, the graphics programmer will not be affected by the number of processors. However, before selecting a system the graphics programmer should have some idea of the processing requirements. Since two-processor systems tend to be more expensive than single-processor systems, hardware budget constraints may be a factor as well.

Processor Addressing Capacity

Most processors are described in terms of their addressing capacity and word size. The addressing capacity of a processor determines the number of bytes of memory the processor will be able to directly read and write to. The *direct addressing* capacity of a processor may be calculated as follows: direct addressing capacity $= 2^A$ bytes, where A is the address width in bits. For example, an 8-bit processor would be able to directly read and write to 2^8 or 256 bytes of memory. Most processors can expand the amount of memory they can read and write to by using a technique called *indirect addressing*. In this technique, 2 bytes are used to specify the desired address. Therefore, the total addressing capacity of an 8-bit processor would be 2^{16} or 64K bytes. In general, total addressing capacity $= 2^{2A}$ bytes.

Addressing capacity is important to the graphics programmer for two reasons: (1) most graphics systems require a considerable amount of memory, and (2), the use of 2-byte addressing will often increase the time required to read or write to memory by 40 percent. And because it is more complex, indirect addressing can increase development time.

Memory Pages

Ideally, then, the graphics programmer will prefer a processor with an address width wide enough that software, data, and display memory can all be stored in memory which is directly addressable by

Starting address	Ending address	Page number
00 00H	00 FFH	0
01 00H	01 FFH	1
02 00H	02 FFH	2
03 00H	03 FFH	3
04 00H	04 FFH	4
05 00H	05 FFH	5
06 00H	06 FFH	6
07 00H	07 FFH	7
08 00H	08 FFH	8
09 00H	09 FFH	9

Fig. 1-16

the computer. The area of memory that can be addressed directly is called the *zero page*. Each page of memory is 2 to the address width bytes long. Therefore, an 8-bit processor would have pages 256 (2^8) bytes long (see Fig. 1-16). Expansion beyond the memory made available with indirect addressing is possible by means of bank switching and other techniques. However, access to such memory is generally far too slow for graphics applications. This is because the additional memory must be treated as if it were a peripheral.

Word Size

A processor's word size determines the maximum number of commands in the processor's *instruction set*. The instruction set is a list of commands the processor recognizes, such as *move*, *add*, and *subtract* data. It also determines the number of bits the computer can operate on at a time and the number of decimal places the computer can accurately represent (*precision*).

The maximum number of instructions a processor can support is given by the formula maximum size of instruction set = 2^W instructions, where W is the word size in bits. Therefore, an 8-bit processor will be capable of supporting $2^8 = 256$ instructions. Unlike address width, there is no way to increase the size of the instruction set.

When dealing with display memory, you will find that word size can greatly affect the overall speed of a graphics system. The larger the word size, the more display memory that can be manipulated with a single instruction from the processor. For example, suppose that a 16×8 pixel figure is to be moved from one location to another in display memory. If it is assumed that each line of pixels in the figure fills 2 bytes, a 16-bit processor would move the pixels one word at a time, thus requiring eight MOVE commands (one per line). An 8-bit processor would be able to move only eight pixels at a time, thus requiring 16 MOVE commands.

Floating-point operations—operations that require decimal values to be computed—are far more time-consuming than integer operations, because a computer cannot deal directly with decimal numbers. For this reason, graphics programmers generally try to limit arithmetic to integer operations. However, the range of integer values a processor can operate on is limited by word size. The range of integer values is found as follows: integer range = $\pm 2^{(2*W-1)} - 1$, where W is the word size in bits. For example, an 8-bit processor can operate only on values between $-2^{15} - 1$ and $+2^{15} - 1$ (-32767 to 32767). It can be seen, then, that the word size of a processor can greatly affect the overall response time of a graphics system.

Clock Speed

At the heart of a computer system is its clock. A computer clock times and sequences all events within a computer. Clock speed does not, however, necessarily determine how rapidly a computer will perform operations. Some computers, for example, require several clock cycles to perform addition, while others can add in one or two cycles. For estimating the time it will take a system to complete a task, it is best to get data relating to the time to execute individual instructions in the task. Execution time data can usually be obtained from the manufacturer of the processor.

Solved Problems

1.1 (*a*) Define analog device, and give some examples of analog devices.

(*b*) Define digital device, and give some examples of digital devices.

SOLUTION

(*a*) An analog device is a continuous mechanism that represents information with continuous physical variations. For example, mercury thermometers and record players are all analog devices.

(*b*) A digital device is a discrete mechanism which represents all values with a specific number system. For example, digital watches and computers all process discrete information and use the binary number system.

1.2 Explain what accuracy means as related to input devices.

SOLUTION

Accuracy refers to the correctness of the data generated by the input device. For example, if the true temperature were 72.0031 degrees, an accurate digital thermometer precise to one degree would read 72 degrees.

1.3 Why is high precision misleading when combined with low accuracy?

SOLUTION

People tend to believe high-precision readings. Assume that we have a digital thermometer with eight-place precision that consistently gives readings 9 degrees higher than the actual temperature. It is precise but inaccurate. The user, however, would be inclined to believe the reading because of its precision. For example, assume that the true temperature is 75.089341 degrees but our thermometer (which is off by exactly nine degrees) reads 84.089341 degrees. Many people would be inclined to believe that the thermometer was correct.

1.4 If an A/D converter strobed the analog output of devices measuring the conditions shown in Figs. 1-17(*a*) through 1-17(*f*) for 1 microsecond (μs) once every 2 s, what readings would be recorded by a computer at 1, 2, 3, . . . , 8 s? (Assume that the A/D converter has one-unit precision and is accurate to one unit.)

SOLUTION

Time, s	(*a*) Degrees (°F)	(*b*) Feet/ second (ft/s)	(*c*) Volts (V)	(*d*) Feet (ft)	(*e*) Pounds per square inch (psi)	(*f*) Amperes (A)
0	2	6	2	1	7	2
1	2	6	2	1	7	2
2	3	4	3	2	4	3
3	3	4	3	2	4	3
4	2	3	4	5	3	6
5	2	3	4	5	3	6
6	4	1	2	2	3	7
7	4	1	2	2	3	7
8	4	0	2	1	3	7

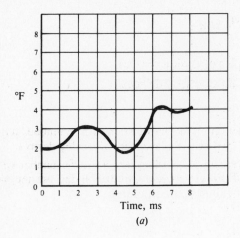

(a)

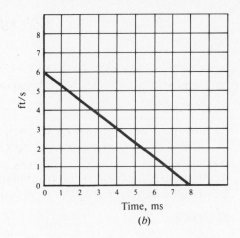

(b)

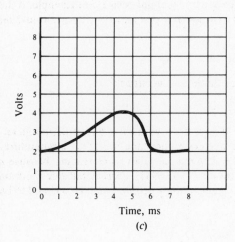

(c)

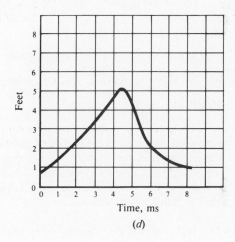

(d)

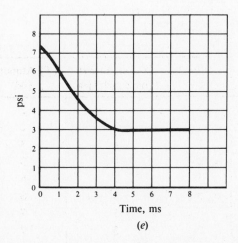

(e)

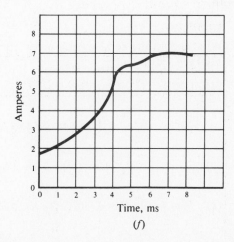

(f)

Fig. 1-17

1.5   What five steps are required for A/D conversion?

SOLUTION

1. Sensing
2. Conversion
3. Amplification
4. Conditioning
5. Quantization

1.6   Assume that a light pen traced the path shown in Fig. 1-18(*a*). How would Fig. 1-18(*a*) appear if the computer strobed only the light pen port at the indicated points?

SOLUTION

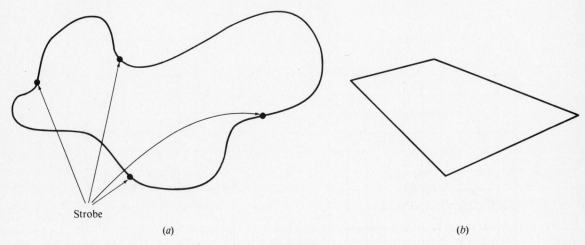

Strobe

(*a*)   (*b*)

Fig. 1-18

1.7   The following analog signals were entered into an A/D converter:

(*a*) $y = 12 \sin (t) + 3 \cos (2t)$

(*b*) $y = 12 \sin (5t) + 3 \cos (10t)$

(*c*) $y = 12 \sin (50t) + 3 \cos (100t)$

(*d*) $y = 12 \sin (500t) + 3 \cos (1000t)$

What would the total coding error after 1 s be if the A/D converter had a sampling rate of 120 Hz?

SOLUTION

(*a*) $$\int_0^1 [12 \sin (t) + 3 \cos (2t)] \, dt - \sum_{i=0}^{119} \frac{12 \sin (i/120) + 3 \cos [2(i/120)]}{120}$$

(*b*) $$\int_0^1 [12 \sin (5t) + 3 \cos (10t)] \, dt - \sum_{i=0}^{119} \frac{12 \sin [5(i/120)] + 3 \cos [10(i/120)]}{120}$$

(*c*) $$\int_0^1 [12 \sin (50t) + 3 \cos (100t)] \, dt - \sum_{i=0}^{119} \frac{12 \sin [50(i/120)] + 3 \cos [100(i/120)]}{120}$$

(*d*) $$\int_0^1 [12 \sin (500t) + 3 \cos (1000t)] \, dt - \sum_{i=0}^{119} \frac{12 \sin [500(i/120)] + 3 \cos (1000i/120)}{120}$$

Referring to formula (1.1), we have $T = 1\,s$, $s = 120$, so

$$a = \frac{1}{120} \quad \text{and} \quad N = \frac{T}{a} = 120$$

1.8 What three aspects of quantization are graphics programmers generally concerned with?

SOLUTION

Sampling rate, aperture time, and coding error.

1.9 If an A/D converter has a sampling rate of 600 Hz, what is the aperture time for the converter?

SOLUTION

The aperture time is defined as the reciprocal of the sampling rate. Therefore, the aperture time of the converter is $1/600\,s$.

1.10 Why are the heating coils in a toaster, an electric motor, and a light pen all considered transducers?

SOLUTION

A transducer is a device that converts energy from one form into another. Since the toaster coils convert electricity into heat, the motor converts electricity into mechanical motion, and the light pen converts light into electricity, they are all considered transducers.

1.11 What would be the output voltage of an analog circuit under these three sets of conditions?

(a) $I = 0.01\,A$, $R = 2\,\text{ohms}\,(\Omega)$

(b) $I = 0.03\,A$, $R = 7\,\Omega$

(c) $I = 0.08\,A$, $R = 1\,\Omega$

SOLUTION

Since $V = I * R$:

(a) $V = (0.08)(2) = 0.16\,V$

(b) $V = (0.03)(7) = 0.21\,V$

(c) $V = (0.08)(1) = 0.08\,V$

1.12 What steps are required to record the display location where a user is pointing to with a light pen?

SOLUTION

1. We define the following variables L and A where:
   $L = 1$ if electron beam is striking phosphors at the light pen's location
   $L = 0$ if electron beam is *not* striking phosphors at the light pen's location
   A = address of byte being displayed when electron beam passes light pen
2. If $L = 1$, then store A.

1.13   Why won't a light pen work with a liquid crystal display (LCD)?

SOLUTION

An LCD does not need to be refreshed. Since the display is not changed on a regular basis, there is nothing for the light pen to record. Furthermore, LCDs do not emit a brighter than usual (or darker than usual) burst the moment a pixel is turned on, so there is no way to distinguish which pixel is being turned on and which pixel is already turned on.

1.14   Why are most light pen systems designed to resolve areas the size of a character or larger?

SOLUTION

While it is very easy to locate the byte of display memory a light pen is pointing to (see Prob. 1.12), it is difficult to locate the exact pixel.

Light pen systems also often require several passes of the electron beam in the same area as the pen to reduce the frequency of errors.

1.15   How does a magnetic tablet system locate the coordinates of the stylus?

SOLUTION

The stylus used in a magnetic tablet system is a small radio transmitter. The tablet is composed of an array of radio receivers. By measuring the relative strength of the radio signals at each of the receivers, you can compute the location of the stylus.

1.16   What are the three major approaches used to design a touch-sensitive screen? How do they work?

SOLUTION

Touch-sensitive screens can be made by placing a grid of wires over the display which when pressed change the capacitance of the circuit [see Fig. 1-7(a)]. In another method a series of strain gauges are placed around the perimeter of the display. When the surface of the display is pressed, the display surface is slightly deformed, causing strain which is recorded by the strain gauges [see Fig. 1-7(b)]. The most popular method of creating a touch-sensitive screen works by creating a matrix of infrared beams across the surface of the display [see Fig. 1-7(c)]. When the user touches the display, the beams are broken, blocking light from hitting infrared sensors and thus indicating the location being touched.

1.17   What does ASCII stand for? Why was it developed?

SOLUTION

The acronym ASCII stands for American Standard Code for Information Interchange. The 7-bit ASCII code was developed so that there could be a standard method for communicating with computers.

1.18   What are some of the disadvantages of developing a specialized keyboard with commands printed on the function keys?

SOLUTION

Printing commands on function keys limit flexibility, since any future software changes will require a change of keyboards. Experience has shown that in most cases a removable template placed over function keys is just as effective but less limiting to future development.

1.19   For each of the following selection criteria, rank the media listed below (floppy disks, hard disks, etc.) in order of decreasing desirability: initial cost, cost per kilobyte, access time, cost of storage medium, expected life of storage device, expected life of storage medium, and storage capacity:

(a) Floppy disks   (d) Paper tape
(b) Hard disks   (e) Punched cards
(c) Magnetic tape   (f) Video tape

SOLUTION

(a) Initial cost   (b) Cost per kilobyte

1. Magnetic tape (cassette)   1. Video tape
2. Floppy disk   2. Hard disk
3. Video tape   3. Floppy disk
4. Hard disk   4. Magnetic tape
5. Paper tape   5. Punched cards
6. Punched cards   6. Paper tape
7. Magnetic tape (reel to reel)

(c) Access time   (d) Cost of storage medium

1. Hard disk   1. Magnetic tape
2. Floppy disk   2. Video tape
3. Magnetic tape   3. Floppy disk
4. Video tape   4. Punched cards
(*Note*: Paper tape and punched   5. Paper tape
    cards are not applicable.)   6. Hard disk

(e) Expected life of the storage device: the expected life of the device is largely a function of the quality of the vendor. In general, however, the fewer moving parts, the greater the life of the device. Therefore, magnetic tape drives usually last longer than the other devices.

(f) Expected life of storage medium   (g) Storage capacity

1. Punched cards   1. Video tape
2. Paper tape   2. Magnetic tape
3. Video tape   3. Hard disk
4. Magnetic tape   4. Floppy disk
5. Hard disk   5. Punched cards
6. Floppy disk   6. Paper tape

1.20 By what four basic methods may computer graphics images be stored for extended periods? Give an example of the type of storage medium that would be used.

SOLUTION

1. Store image only (video tape, film).
2. Store values in display memory "as is" (hard disk, floppy disk, magnetic tape, paper tape, punched cards).
3. Store values in display memory in compressed format (hard disk, floppy disk, magnetic tape, paper tape, punched cards).
4. Store image construction information (hard disk, floppy disk, magnetic tape, paper tape, punched cards).

1.21 (a) How many bytes are required to represent Fig. 1-19(a) in compressed format?

(b) How many bytes are required to represent Fig. 1-19(a) in noncompressed format?

(c) What values will be stored to represent the image in compressed format?

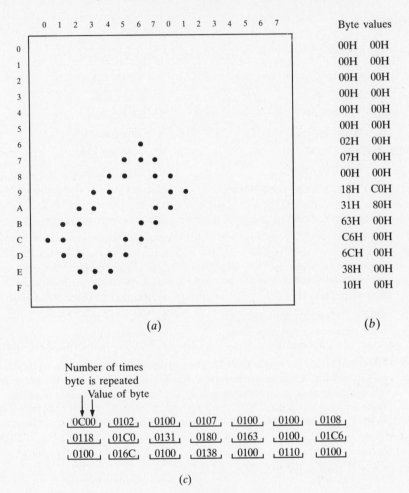

(a)   (b)

Number of times
byte is repeated
│ Value of byte
↓ ↓

0C00	0102	0100	0107	0100	0100	0108
0118	01C0	0131	0180	0163	0100	01C6
0100	016C	0100	0138	0100	0110	0100

(c)

Fig. 1-19

SOLUTION

The values of the bytes representing the image shown in Fig. 1-19(a) in display memory are listed in Fig. 1-19(b). For representation of the image in compressed format, 1 byte is assigned to represent the number of times a value is repeated. The next byte is assigned the value that is to be repeated. In this case the first 12 bytes of display memory contain the value 00H. Therefore, the packed-format representation of the first 12 bytes is 0C 00. The remaining image contains no repeated values in display memory. The complete list of values that would be stored are shown in Fig. 1-19(c).

(a) The number of bytes used to represent the image in compressed format can be found by counting the number of bytes listed in Fig. 1-19(c). Therefore, 42 bytes are required to represent Fig. 1-19(a) in compressed format.

(b) The number of bytes used to represent the image in noncompressed format is found by counting the number of bytes listed in Fig. 1-19(b). Therefore, 32 bytes are required to represent Fig. 1-19(a) in noncompressed format.

(c) The values that would be stored to represent the image in compressed format are shown in Fig. 1-19(c).

1.22 Explain why it takes more bytes to represent Fig. 1-19(*a*) in compressed format than noncompressed format.

SOLUTION

The compression algorithm requires 2 bytes to represent any series of repeated bytes, 1 byte to represent the number of bytes repeated, and 1 byte to represent the values that are to be repeated. In the case of Fig. 1-19(*a*); only 12 bytes are repeated; the remaining 20 bytes are unique. Therefore, while only 2 bytes are required to represent the first 12 bytes of display memory, 40 bytes are needed to represent the remaining 20 bytes.

1.23 (*a*) How could Fig. 1-19(*a*) be stored in only 23 bytes?

(*b*) What design trade-offs would have to be made?

SOLUTION

(*a*) In order to store Figure 1-19(*a*) in only 23 bytes, the compression algorithm must be made "smart" enough to realize that series of unique bytes should not be compressed. The compression algorithm could accomplish this by comparing the present byte with the next byte in display memory. If the two bytes are not equal, the algorithm could then stop attempting to compress the data.

(*b*) As compression algorithms become more complex, an increasing number of bytes must be added to identify the beginning and end of a run of identical bytes. Therefore, the complexity of the code required to compress the data increases rapidly along with the time it takes to compress and decompress the data. Furthermore, the amount of space required to mark the beginning and end of a run increases. There always exists, therefore, a chance that the compression algorithm may result in more rather than less space being required to store an image.

1.24 Compare the two common methods used to link two or more computers for communications purposes.

SOLUTION

The two common methods of linking computers are serial and parallel interfacing. Serial interfacing is relatively slow. It allows computers to send and receive data only 1 bit at a time (see Fig. 1-13). Parallel interfacing is much faster; it allows data to be sent a byte at a time (see Fig. 1-12). Parallel communications cannot take place over great distances because of voltage drop and echo. Serial communications, however, can take place over any distance.

1.25 Why is knowledge of the effects of line resistance important in parallel data communications?

SOLUTION

One factor that limits the distance over which parallel data communications can take place is the drop in DC voltage that occurs as a result of the resistance of the wire used to transmit the signal.

1.26 Why are only 7 data bits required to send ASCII data?

SOLUTION

The ASCII character set consists of only 128 or 2^7 characters. Therefore, only 7 bits are needed to describe the entire character set.

1.27 What is the acronym for the most common computer graphics communications standard? What does it stand for?

SOLUTION

The most common computer graphics communications standard is the North American Presentation-Level Protocol-Level Syntax (NAPLPS).

1.28 When the NAPLPS standard is used, how does the sending computer indicate to the receiving computer that the data it is receiving are not standard ASCII data?

SOLUTION

The NAPLPS standard is designed so that the receiving computer will constantly scan the incoming data for an escape (1BH). Upon receiving the escape value, the receiving computer will interpret the next value sent as an NAPLPS command.

1.29 Assume that a computer supporting a 512×200 pixel display is communicating with a computer which supports a 256×200 pixel display using the NAPLPS standard. The sending computer has a point plotted at screen coordinate (200, 100).

(*a*) What data will the sending computer transmit?

(*b*) How will the receiving computer convert the coordinates?

(*c*) At what screen coordinates will the receiving computer place the point?

SOLUTION

(*a*) The sending computer must first convert the screen x coordinate of the point to unit screen coordinate as follows:

$$x \text{ coordinate} = 200 \rightarrow x \text{ coordinate} = \frac{200}{512} = 0.390625$$

$$\underbrace{\qquad}_{\text{screen}} \qquad \underbrace{\qquad}_{\text{unit}}$$

The point is half-way down the physical screen. However, 25 percent of the unit screen is by convention not displayed (see Fig. 1-19). The unit screen y coordinate of the point is found as follows:

$$y \text{ coordinate} = 100 \rightarrow y \text{ coordinate} = \frac{100}{200} * 0.75 + 0.25$$

$$\underbrace{\qquad}_{\text{screen}} \qquad \underbrace{\qquad}_{\text{unit}}$$

$$= 0.625$$

NAPLPS sends all data in the form of binary decimals. Therefore, the sending computer will transmit the binary value .011001000 to represent the x coordinate and .101000000 to represent the y coordinate. The sending computer has 512-pixel resolution along the x axis; therefore, 9 bits are needed to represent all possible locations of the point.

(*b*) The receiving computer does not have the same resolution as the sending computer. All points can be represented on the receiving computer's screen with 8 bits. To convert the incoming data, the receiving computer left-shifts each group of coordinates eight times. Therefore, the converted x-coordinate value is

$$x \text{ coordinate} = 01100100 \text{ binary} = 100 \text{ decimal}$$

The converted y-coordinate value is also found by left-shifting eight times. However, the coordinate value was modified in order to find the placement of the point on the unit screen. To convert back (assuming that the receiving computer has the same aspect ratio as the sending computer), the receiving computer must subtract 0.25 from the value it receives and then divide by 0.75. Finally, the result is multiplied by the y resolution. Therefore, subtracting 0.25, we obtain

.101000000 binary	0.625 decimal
$-$.010000000 binary	$-$0.250 decimal
.011000000 binary	0.375 decimal

Division by 0.75 yields

$$\frac{0.375}{0.750} \text{ decimal} = 0.5 \text{ decimal}$$

$$\frac{.011000000}{.11000000} \text{ binary} = .100000000 \text{ binary}$$

and then multiplying by the y resolution,

$$200 * 0.5 \text{ decimal} = 100 \text{ decimal}$$
$$11001000 * .100000000 \text{ binary} = 01100100 \text{ binary}$$

(c)   Therefore

$$y \text{ coordinate} = 01100100 \text{ binary} = 100 \text{ decimal}$$
$$x \text{ coordinate} = 01100100 \text{ binary} = 100 \text{ decimal}$$

1.30   Why do computer graphics systems often use more than one processor?

SOLUTION

Computer graphics systems often require more than one processor because the calculations required for graphics can overload the main processor. When overloading occurs, the processor cannot update the display often enough to prevent flicker or snow.

1.31   What is display memory called in a system which has portions of memory reserved for graphics use only?

SOLUTION

A special area of memory dedicated to graphics only is called the *frame buffer*.

1.32   What is processor addressing capacity?

SOLUTION

Processor addressing capacity relates the maximum number of bytes to which a processor has access, as determined by the number of address lines (address width) the processor has.

1.33   What are the direct and indirect addressing capacities of processors with the address widths (a) 4, (b) 8, and (c) 16?

SOLUTION

The direct addressing capacity of a processor is found by calculating 2^A where A is the address width. Indirect addressing capacity is found by calculating 2^{2A}. Therefore

Direct Addressing Capacity	Indirect Addressing Capacity
(a) $2^4 = 16$	$2^{(2*4)} = 256$ bytes
(b) $2^8 = 256$	$2^{(2*8)} = 65536$ bytes
(c) $2^{16} = 65536$	$2^{(2*16)} = 4294967295$ bytes

1.34   What does one call the area of memory a processor can reach without indirect addressing? What importance does it hold for the computer graphics programmer?

SOLUTION

The page of memory a processor can reach with direct addressing is called the zero page. The zero page is important to the graphics programmer because no indirect addressing is required in order to read or write to that area of memory. Since indirect addressing takes longer than direct addressing, data in the zero page can be operated on more rapidly.

1.35 Define word size.

SOLUTION

Word size is the number of bits a processor will operate on at a time as determined by the size of the processor's internal registers.

1.36 What would be the maximum possible size of a computer's instruction set if it were based on a processor with a (*a*) 4-bit, (*b*) 8-bit, and (*c*) 16-bit word size?

SOLUTION

The maximum size of a computer's instruction set is equal to 2^W, where W is the word size in bits. Therefore, the maximum size of the instruction sets would be

(*a*) $2^4 = 16$ instructions

(*b*) $2^8 = 256$ instructions

(*c*) $2^{16} = 65536$ instructions

1.37 Good graphics programming avoids the use of floating-point operations whenever possible. Why?

SOLUTION

Floating-point operations require the computer to go through many steps that are not required if all values are handled as integers. Thus floating-point operations slow down the system.

1.38 Why is a computer's clock speed a poor measure for comparing the relative time it will take a computer to complete specific tasks?

SOLUTION

The clock speed is a poor comparative measure because different processors require different numbers of clock cycles to complete tasks. For example, computer A may have a clock speed twice as fast as computer B. However, computer A may require three clock cycles to perform an instruction, while computer B requires only one. As a result, it takes computer A longer than computer B to complete an instruction.

Supplementary Problems

1.39 Explain what precision means as related to input devices.

1.40 Why are Figs. 1-18(*a*) and 1-18(*b*) so different?

1.41 What would be the total coding error if the A/D converter in Prob. 1.7 had a sampling rate of 240 Hz?

1.42 A noninterlaced CRT has a refresh rate of 60 Hz. The computer hooked up to the CRT displays a 600×200 pixel memory map. Top and bottom vertical overscan are 10 and 14 percent, respectively, and left and right horizontal overscan are 20 and 10 percent, respectively. Calculate how many seconds from the start of a refresh cycle it will take for the electron beam to reach a light pen located at the following screen coordinates: (*a*) (137,80), (*b*) (580,190), and (*c*) (28,195).

1.43 Why is the actual time it takes an electron beam to reach the location of a light pen not required?

1.44 Why have acoustic tablet systems lost their popularity?

1.45 What are the basic attributes of graphics storage systems used to evaluate competing storage systems?

1.46 Assume that a 12-V, 1-A current is applied to a particular wire which exhibits 0.05-Ω resistance per foot. After how many feet will the voltage measured at the end of the wire fall to 1 V?

1.47 What is the standard format used for sending serial computer communications?

1.48 Why is the computer graphics programmer concerned with a processor's addressing capacity?

1.49 How is a computer's page size related to its addressing width?

1.50 How does processor word size affect computer graphics programming?

1.51 Give the range of integer values that could be manipulated directly by processors with the following word sizes: (*a*) 4, (*b*) 8, and (*c*) 16.

Chapter 2

Display Devices

2.1 INTRODUCTION

A computer is capable of sending its output to a wide variety of devices, many of which are designed for special purposes. For example, computers can be used to regulate air-fuel mixtures in internal combustion engines or control temperatures in a building. We will concern ourselves, however, with only special- and general-purpose devices that are capable of producing graphical output and the basic principles involved in converting a model stored in a computer's memory into an image on that computer's display.

2.2 COMMON DISPLAY DEVICES

The most commonly used computer output devices that are capable of producing graphical output are:

Raster-scan cathode ray tube (CRT)

Memory-tube displays

Plasma displays

Liquid crystal displays (LCDs)

Plotters

Printers

Of these, the raster-scan CRT is by far the most popular. The popularity of the raster-scan CRT is due more to its relative cost and availability than to any technological superiority.

2.3 RASTER-SCAN CRT

CRT Components

The most common type of computer output device capable of displaying graphical output in use today is the raster-scan CRT. Raster-scan CRTs are used in common television sets. The majority of this chapter is dedicated to their use.

Although complete comprehension of the raster-scan CRT's internal operations is unnecessary, a basic understanding will assist you greatly in graphics programming. Also, since the computer is a *digital device* and the CRT is an *analog device*, grasping the concepts behind this interface from the graphics programmers' point of view will make understanding devices such as plasma panels, LCDs, and storage-tube CRTs relatively simple. You may recall that a digital device is a device that represents all quantities as discrete values. An analog device is a device that represents all quantities as continuous values.

Figure 2-1 illustrates a basic raster-scan CRT and its major components: the electron gun, the control electrode, the focusing electrode, the deflection yoke, and the phosphorus-coated screen.

1. *Electron gun*—consisting of a series of components (primarily a heater and a cathode) which together cause electrons to congregate at the end of the electron gun. The electrons are then accelerated by application of an electric field.

2. *Control electrode*—used to regulate the flow of electrons. The control electrode is connected to an amplifier which, in turn, is connected to the output circuitry of the computer, thus allowing the computer to control when the electron beam is turned off and on.

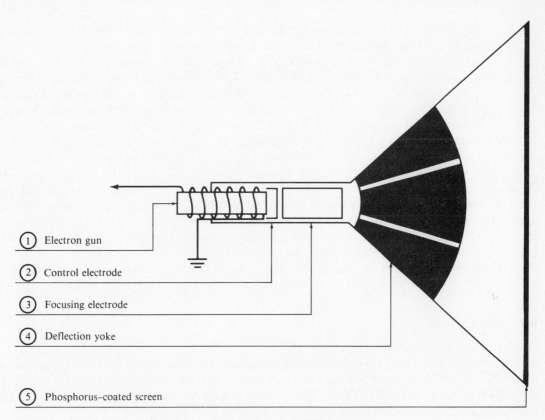

Fig. 2-1 Major raster-scan CRT components.

3. *Focusing electrode*—used to create a clear picture by focusing the electrons into a narrow beam. The focusing electrode serves this purpose by exerting an electromagnetic force on the electrons in the electron beam. The effect of the focusing electrode on the electron beam resembles that of a glass lens on light waves.

4. *Deflection yoke*—used to control the direction of the electron beam. The deflection yoke creates an electric or magnetic field which will bend the electron beam as it passes through the field. In a conventional CRT the yoke is connected to a *sweep* or *scan generator*. The scan generator sends out an oscillating sawtooth current (see Fig. 2-2) that, in turn, causes the deflection yoke to apply a varying magnetic field to the electron beam's path. The oscillating voltage potential causes the electron beam to move across the CRT's screen in a regular pattern.

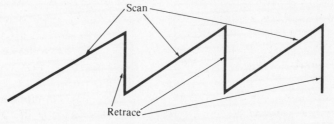

Fig. 2-2 Example of signal from a scan generator.

5. *Phosphorus-coated screen*—phosphorus coating on the inside front surface of every CRT. This surface is coated with special crystals called *phosphors*, which have a unique property that allows the entire system to work. Phosphors glow when they are hit by a high-energy electron beam. They continue to glow for a distinct period of time (the exact time and color is unique to

each type of phosphor) after being exposed to the electron beam. The glow given off by the phosphor during exposure to the electron beam is known as *fluorescence*, the continuing glow given off after the beam is removed is known as *phosphorescence*, and the duration of phosphorescence is known as the phosphor's *persistence*. All phosphors have a limited life, which is a function of both the amount of time it is exposed to the electron beam and the intensity of the electron beam. Once a phosphor will no longer be fluorescent it is said to be "burned." Graphics programmers should, therefore, try to limit the intensity and duration of images displayed on CRTs to avoid damage.

Raster Scan

The term "raster" is a synonym for the term "matrix." Therefore, a raster-scan CRT scans a matrix with an electron beam. The rate at which the electron beam scans the surface of the CRT is often directly related to the frequency of the local line voltage. Therefore, in areas such as the United States where 60-cycle line voltage is used, the electron beam will usually scan across the entire face of the CRT 60 times per second. In Europe, 50-cycle power is provided. Therefore, most European CRTs are designed to have the electron beam scan the entire surface of the CRT at 50 Hz.

Refresh and Flicker

Each time the electron beam goes through a complete cycle of raster or scan lines, the CRT is said to be "refreshed." It is very important that the persistence of the phosphor used and the refresh rate be matched. Otherwise, an image on the CRT may appear to flash rapidly on and off. When flashing of this type does occur, it is called *flicker*. Fortunately, few people can perceive visual changes that last less than $\frac{1}{30}$ s because they are under the average visual perceptual threshold. The perceptual threshold exists because humans, like computers, can process only a finite amount of information within any given time period. The programmer may consider changes below the visual threshold as being similar to changes that take place in less than one computer clock cycle; in both cases the computer and a human will be unable to detect changes.

Interlacing

Since the perceptual threshold is greater than the frequency of standard line voltage, a technique called *interlacing* is often used (see Fig. 2-3). Again, the refresh rate and the persistence of the

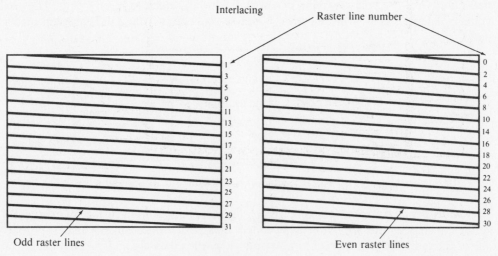

Fig. 2-3

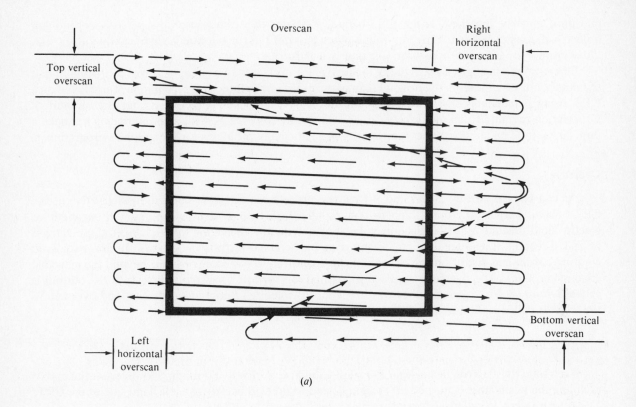

Overscan

Right horizontal overscan

Top vertical overscan

Left horizontal overscan

Bottom vertical overscan

(a)

Blanking

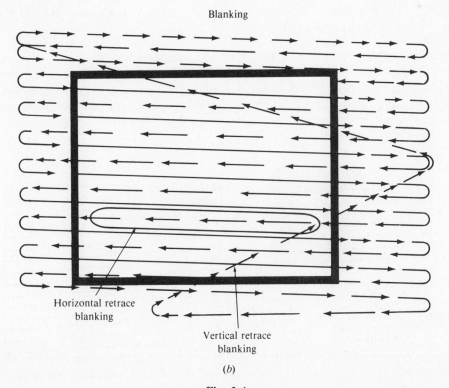

Horizontal retrace blanking

Vertical retrace blanking

(b)

Fig. 2-4

phosphor must be matched. If the refresh rate is greater than the phosphor's persistence, moving objects will tend to become blurred. On the other hand, if the refresh rate is significantly longer than the phosphor's persistence, the user will perceive flicker.

Often an interlacing is used to break the raster-line cycle into two sweep patterns consisting of half the number of raster lines in the original scan pattern. When the interlacing technique is employed on a CRT using a medium-persistence phosphor, not only can flicker be reduced, but the amount of information required to fill the display can be reduced by 50 percent. Although interlacing has been a popular method on standard television sets, it presents many problems for the graphics programmer.

Overscan

As can be seen in Fig. 2-4(a) and 2-4(b), the raster lines extend beyond the visible edge of the CRT. This is because there is a limit to how rapidly the sweep generator can alter the magnetic or electric field created by the deflection yoke. Further, as the deflection yoke changes the electrons beam's direction, it also tends to create annoying borders and distorts the picture. In order to avoid creating border and distortion the electron beam is allowed to run some distance beyond the viewable edge of the CRT. The overscan on the top is called *top vertical overscan*, overscan to the bottom is called *bottom vertical overscan*, overscan to the left is called *left horizontal overscan*, and overscan to the right is called *right horizontal overscan* [see Fig. 2-4(a)].

Blanking

Each time the electron beam scans from left to right it is in WRITE mode. However, at the end of each line the beam must be turned off (blanked) and redirected back to the left-hand side of the CRT. The return sweep is called *horizontal retrace blanking* [see Fig. 2-4(b)].

Vertical retrace blanking refers to the shutting off of the electron beam as its returns from the bottom of the display at the end of a cycle to the upper left-hand corner to start a new cycle.

Spot Size

Every time the electron beam is turned on during its journey across the display area, a "spot" of light is created. The spot size is primarily a function of the diameter of the electron beam and the size of the phosphorous crystals coating the screen. To obtain the most pleasing image from a CRT, the spot size should be just large enough to slightly overlap or be close to the eight spots surrounding it. If the spot size is too small, the images on the display will appear "grainy"—too large—and the images will appear "fuzzy" (see Fig. 2-5).

Note: If these spots are exactly the right size, the viewer will perceive a filled square.

Fig. 2-5

Plotting a Point

The CRT is a two-dimensional plane on which point locations are typically described through the use of a Cartesian coordinate system. When using this system, we tend to think of the bottom edge of the CRT as the x axis, the leftmost edge as the y axis and the lower left-hand corner as the origin, as in a right-handed Cartesian coordinate system [see Fig. 2-6(a)]. However, due to memory organization

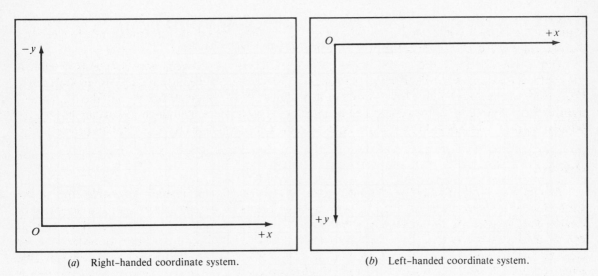

(a)   Right-handed coordinate system.   (b)   Left-handed coordinate system.

Fig. 2-6

most computer systems are based on a left-handed Cartesian coordinate system and use the upper left-hand corner as the origin [see Fig. 2-6(b)].

There is also a difference between the way we would assume the coordinates of a point are found and the way they are actually found by a computer. The graphics computer "perceives" the memory map and the CRT as one long straight line. This means the computer is "blind" to horizontal retrace blanking (see Fig. 2-7).

Most graphics computers see their memory map as a series of bytes, each byte composed of 8 bits. The majority of monochromatic (single-color) systems assign 1 bit in the memory map to one pixel on the display. There are four steps involved in converting Cartesian coordinates (the coordinate system we are used to working with) into a form the computer can understand. These four steps are:

1. Locate the starting address corresponding to the line on which the point is to appear.

2. Locate the address of the byte in which the point will be represented.

3. Locate the bit which will represent the correct pixel (i.e., compute the value for the byte that will correctly represent the point).

4. Logically OR the calculated value with the present value of the byte (see Example 1, step 4).

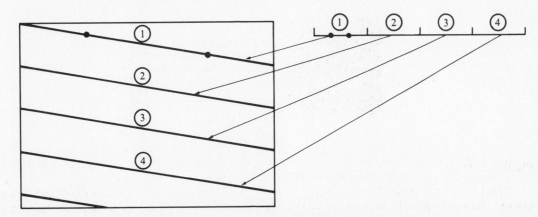

Fig. 2-7   The way we perceive a CRT (matrix perception) vs. the way a computer perceives a CRT (linear perception).

EXAMPLE 1. Plot the point $x = 15$, $y = 2$ to the 8×16 display shown in (Fig. 2-8).

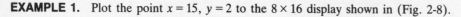

Display coordinates and memory-map display locations

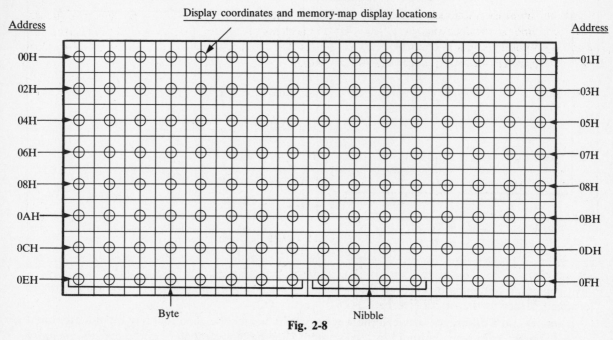

Fig. 2-8

Figure 2-8 represents a 16-byte memory map (or frame buffer if the memory is reserved with hardware) starting at address 00H and the associated pixel locations on a CRT.

Step 1. Use the y value to locate the starting address of the line that is to contain the point. In this case the starting address of the line that will contain the point is $0010 = 02H$.

Step 2. Find x modulo 8. Note that this is the same as dividing the x value by 8 (the number of bits per byte) and saving the remainder. Add the integer portion to the starting address found in step 1. (*Note*: If $x = 0$, proceed to step 3.) [*Remember*: To expedite calculations, division should be avoided. Instead of dividing by 8, right-shift the register containing the x value three times ($8H = 1111$; shifting right three times, we obtain 0001.111). The integer portion is 0001. This is added to the binary value found in step 1 $(0010 + 0001 = 0011 = 03H)$.]

Step 3. Compute the correct value to be ORed with the present value of byte 03H. The remainder from step 2 was 7 (i.e., when the three right shifts were performed, the binary value 0.111 was left over, which is stored as 0111). This means that we would like to set the seventh bit, counting from the most significant bit, equal to 0. [See Fig. 2-9, which shows most significant bits (MSBs) and least significant bits (LSBs).]

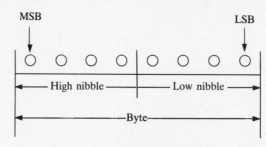

Fig. 2-9

Step 4. OR the value calculated in step 3 (00000010) with the current value of the byte found in steps 1 and 2 (03H). In this case byte 03H has a value of 00H (00000000 binary).

$$
\begin{array}{ll}
& 00000000\text{---present value of byte 03H} \\
\text{OR} & 00000010\text{---value found in steps 1 to 3} \\
\hline
& 00000010\text{---result of OR operation}
\end{array}
$$

The result of the OR operation (00000010) is then stored in the byte found in steps 1 and 2.

Lookup Tables

When memory is mapped to the CRT, it is often "out of sequence." That is, the address of the last byte on a line is not necessarily one less than the address of the first byte on the next line (see Fig. 2-10). Computer designers are often able to decrease the cost and complexity of hardware of graphics systems by using out-of-sequence memory mapping.

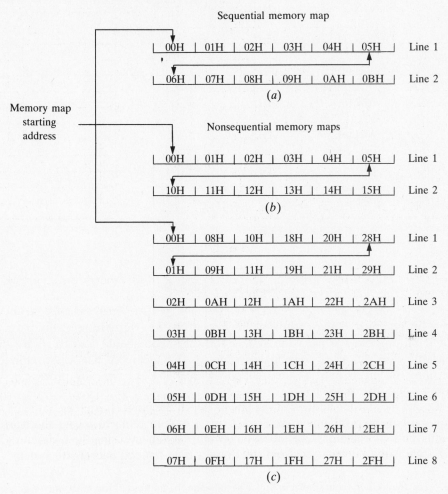

Fig. 2-10

A lookup table is an array of numbers that may be referred to by subscript, thus avoiding the recalculation of values each time a number in a table must be referred to. In computer graphics, lookup tables are used to store the starting addresses of each line and the values corresponding to the placement of pixels within a byte. Thus, if the memory and screen of a computer system were organized as shown in Fig. 2-11, a lookup table could be set up such that the first element in the array called WIN would contain the starting address of the first line, the second array element would hold the starting address of the second line, and so on.

Plotting a Point Using Lookup Tables

The following four steps describe how a point may be placed on the CRT of any monochromatic computer system on which the user has access to the frame buffer (display memory on microcomputer systems). However, at this level all x, y coordinates should be within the range of addresses reserved by

Array element	=	starting address		of display line
		(Hexadecimal)	(Decimal)	
WIN (1)	=	01H	1	1
WIN (2)	=	03H	3	2
WIN (3)	=	05H	5	3
WIN (4)	=	07H	7	4
WIN (5)	=	09H	9	5
WIN (6)	=	02H	2	6
WIN (7)	=	04H	4	7
WIN (8)	=	06H	6	8
WIN (9)	=	08H	8	9
WIN (10)	=	0AH	10	10

Fig. 2-11 Lookup table.

the computer for graphics. Failure to do so may result in the overwriting of the parts of memory storing your data, program, or even the system software. You should also be aware that you are working in a left-handed Cartesian coordinate system and that factors such as aspect ratio (discussed in the next section), scaling (Chap. 4), and clipping (Chap. 5) are typically processed prior to the placement of a point on the CRT.

Step 1. Locate the starting address of the line on which the point is to apear. If the computer does not use sequential memory mapping, you must use a lookup table to locate the starting address associated with the y coordinate. Remember, however, that you are using the computer's left-handed coordinate system, which is reversed from the normal right-handed coordinate system.

EXAMPLE 2.   Use the lookup table shown in Fig. 2-11 to locate the address of the following y values: (a) 1, (b) 5, and (c) 10. To find the starting address corresponding to the y values, use y as the subscript value in the array WIN (I): (a) WIN (01) = 01H, (b) WIN (05) = 09H, and (c) WIN (10) = 0AH.

Step 2. Locate the address of the byte in which the point will be represented. The byte that will represent the x coordinate is found by right-shifting the byte containing the x value three times. (This is equivalent to dividing the x value by 8.) The result of the three right shifts is then added to the value found in step 1. (*Note*: On rare occasions the bytes on each line are also "out of sequence." If this is the case, a lookup table must be used to locate the correct value for each byte on a line.)

Step 3. Locate the bit which will represent the correct pixel (i.e., compute the value for the byte that will represent the point). You must now calculate the correct value of the byte in steps 1 and 2. Just as computers vary in terms of sequential and nonsequential memory mapping, there are differences in the way individual bits within each byte are used to represent pixels to be displayed. We will assume that direct correspondence is used (see Fig. 2-12). Table 2-1 lists this relationship. If you know the value of the remainder from step 2, you may now use either of two methods to find the correct value to OR with the byte found in steps 1 and 2: (a) shift the byte storing the value 10000000 binary right N times (where N = the value of the remainder), or (b) use a lookup table containing eight

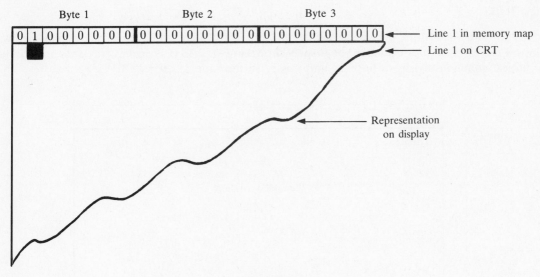

Byte 1   Byte 2   Byte 3

| 0 | 1 | 0 | 0 | 0 | 0 | 0 | 0 | 0 | 0 | 0 | 0 | 0 | 0 | 0 | 0 | 0 | 0 | 0 | 0 | 0 | 0 | 0 | 0 |

← Line 1 in memory map
← Line 1 on CRT

← Representation
on display

Fig. 2-12

Table 2-1

Value of remainder	Correct value of byte in		
	Binary	Decimal	Hexadecimal
	10000000	128	80H
1	01000000	64	40H
2	00100000	32	20H
3	00010000	16	10H
4	00001000	8	08H
5	00000100	4	04H
6	00000010	2	02H
7	00000001	1	01H

elements (one for each pixel position—the lookup table would contain the values shown in Table 2-1). Your choice of method a or b should be determined by reading the hardware specifications for your computer. Compare the time required to use both methods a and b. Implement whichever method is shorter.

Step 4. Logically OR the value found in step 3 with the present value of the byte found in steps 1 and 2. The OR function is used to prevent erasure of any bits previously written to the byte. The result of the OR may now be placed in the byte found in steps 1 and 2. The correct pixel should light.

Other Memory-Mapping Schemes

Occasionally computer designers use other memory-mapping schemes. One method is to design the memory map such that it will be easy to enter characters on the screen. If this is the case you may still have to develop a lookup table; however, your goal will be to locate the address of the correct character block rather than the correct starting address of the line. The x coordinate will usually change according to the number of bytes used to define a character. Usually, when this type of memory-mapping scheme is used, a formula can be substituted for the steps shown in the prior section. The graphics programmer need only eliminate the divisions and multiplications in the formula and replace them with right and left shifts.

Aspect Ratio

Aspect ratio is an output device's width-height ratio. Most standard CRTs have a display area with an aspect ratio of 4 : 3. For example, the display shown in Fig. 2-13 is 12 inches (in) wide and 9 in tall. The largest common divisor of both 12 and 9 is 3, so the ratio $12 : 9 = 4 : 3$.

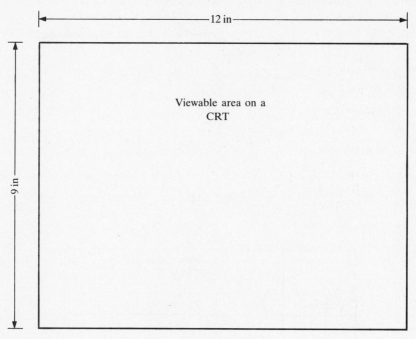

Viewable area on a
CRT

Fig. 2-13

Resolution

The graphics programmer must also consider the resolution of the system. *Resolution* is normally described in terms of the number of pixels. For example, if a system can produce 512 pixels in the horizontal direction and 384 pixels in the vertical, the device would be described as having a 512×384 pixel display.

Squareness and Fit

Squareness is the ability of a system to accurately reproduce a square model in the computer's memory as a square on the display with no manipulation other than uniformly scaling the model to the memory map (by dividing both the x and y coordinates by the same integer). If the aspect ratio and resolution are not equal, it is often impossible to do this scaling without the use of floating-point division.

Fit is how well model data will fit in the memory map without scaling (multiplying or dividing) (see Prob. 2.56). In fitting model data to the memory map it is best to work within the boundaries of the memory map. The most effective fit is one that will allow the data to be scaled by multiplying or dividing by a power of 2. The use of power of 2 division and multiplication will allow fitting to be done with right and left shifts only.

2.4   OTHER OUTPUT DEVICES

Often special applications require the use of an output device other than a CRT. The following section briefly describes how many of the more popular alternatives to the CRT operate.

Plasma Displays and Related Technologies

Plasma or gas discharge displays (see Fig. 2-14) are actually nothing more than an array of small fluorescent gas lights. Related technologies can use fluorescent solids or liquids. Such technologies have become increasingly popular because they involve the use of one of the few "flat" types of display, which can be mass-produced and offer fairly high resolution. Furthermore, plasma and related displays do not have to be refreshed; that is, once a pixel is displayed on the screen, it will remain lit until it is intentionally turned off. The basic components of a plasma and related displays are as follows:

1. *Cathodes*—fine wires attached to a glass plate which delivers negative voltage to the gas cells on the vertical axis.

2. *Fluorescent cells*—small pockets of gas liquids or solids are excited when a voltage is applied. In the excited state the substance emits light.

3. *Anodes*—fine wires attached to a glass plate supply positive voltage along the horizontal axis.

4. *Glass plates*—plates that act as capacitors in DC plasma displays and maintain voltage to ensure that a cell will continue to glow after the cell has received a single burst of power. To remain lit, alternating-current plasma displays must supply a background voltage.

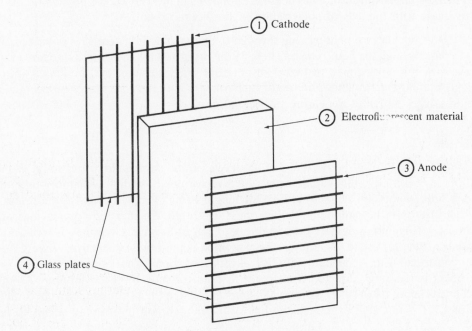

Fig. 2-14   Electrofluorescent display.

Liquid Crystal Displays

Unlike most other types of display, liquid crystal displays (LCDs) (see Fig. 2-15) depend on an outside light source. This is because LCDs work by polarizing ambient light. Liquid crystal displays can be viewed only from a limited angle. To observe this, hold a calculator that uses an LCD at arm's length in front of you. Next, turn the calculator slowly back and forth along its vertical axis. You should observe the numbers on the display "fading" as the calculator display makes a greater angle with your line of sight.

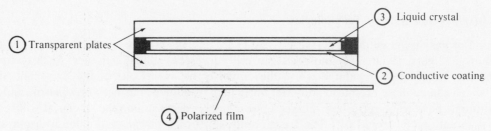

Fig. 2-15 Liquid crystal cell.

Liquid crystal displays are also temperature-dependent (operating temperatures are typically between 0 and 70 degrees Celsius (°C)) and relatively sluggish (making animation very difficult). Therefore, the use of LCDs is rather restricted. On the positive side, LCDs are "flat" and require very little power to operate. The basic components of an LCD are as follows:

1. *Glass or plastic plate*—contains liquid crystal and serves as a bonding surface for a conductive coating.

2. *Conductive coating*—acts as a conductor so that a voltage can be applied across the liquid crystal.

3. *Liquid crystal*—a substance which will polarize light when a voltage is applied to it.

4. *Polarized film*—a transparent sheet that polarizes light. The axis of polarization is set 90° out of phase with the axis of polarization of the liquid crystal.

The LCD works because light passing through the polarized film (item 4) is polarized. When light attempts to pass through the liquid crystal (item 3) the ray is annihilated; thus a dark area is perceived. To observe how this works, take two pairs of polaroid sunglasses and put the lenses on top of each other. Next, keeping the two lenses on top of each other, rotate the glasses with respect to each other. You should notice the lenses appearing to become darker.

Vector Devices

The simplest image or *primitive* that can be drawn on the devices discussed so far is a point. The simplest image or primitive that can be drawn on a vector device such as a memory-tube display or a plotter is a line (points are defined as lines of length zero). Vector devices require less computer memory because only the endpoints of lines must be stored. Further memory savings are realized because most vector output devices have memory. Therefore, once something is written to them, it does not have to be refreshed. A noteworthy exception is the *random accessor vector CRT*, which is similar in construction to a conventional CRT except that there is no sweep generator. Instead, the electron beam is randomly directed from point to point directly by the computer. As the beam is moved, a line is left in its wake. A major problem occurs when the list of endpoints becomes too long. The vector CRT is not able to refresh the line often enough and the display begins to flicker.

Memory-Tube Displays

From the graphics programmer's point of view, memory-tube displays and plotters are quite similar. Both are vector devices; that is, the simplest primitive is a line rather than a point. The principal components of a memory-tube display are as follows (Fig. 2-16):

1. *Flooding gun*—an electron gun designed to flood the entire screen with electrons. This charges the collector plate (see item 3).

2. *Writing gun system*—used in a memory-tube display and basically the same as the electron gun used in a conventional CRT. It consists of a series of components (primarily a heater, a cathode, a focusing electrode, and a deflection yoke) which together cause electrons to

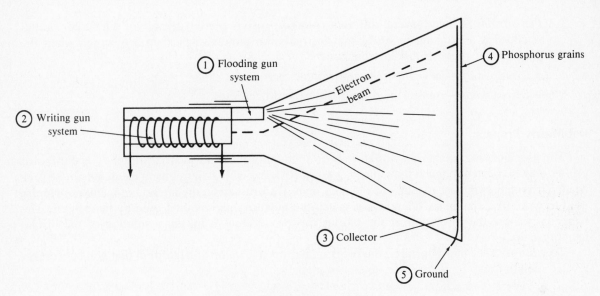

Fig. 2-16   Memory-tube display.

congregate at the end of the gun. The electrons are then accelerated by applying an electric field.

3. *Collector*—already partly energized by the flooding gun, stores the charge generated by the writing gun. The electrons stored on the collector provide a background charge. The background charge from the flooding gun supplies enough energy so that the phosphors will continue to phosphoresce indefinitely after they are hit by the writing gun.

4. *Phosphorus grains*—used in a memory-tube display and similar to those used in a standard CRT except that they have a much longer persistence.

5. *Ground*—used to discharge the collector. When the collector is discharged, the background voltage will drop to zero and the entire screen will be erased.

Plotters

There are several types of plotter available today. Basically all plotters behave like slow vector devices from the graphics programmer's point of view.

Flatbed Plotter

1. *Pen*—an actual pen that draws on the plotted paper.
2. *Write-move mechanism*—used to lift and lower the pen.
3. *Pen cartridge*—holds several different-colored pens. A plotter capable of multicolor output usually has a program in read-only memory (ROM) that instructs the plotter to pick up a new pen when the programmer requests a color change.
4. *x Driver motor*—moves the pen horizontally across the paper.
5. *y Driver motor*—moves the pen vertically across the paper.

Drum Plotter

1. *Pen*—an actual pen that draws on the plotted paper.
2. *Write-move mechanism*—used to lift and lower the pen.

3. *Pen cartridge*—holds several different-colored pens. A plotter capable of multicolor output usually has a program in ROM that instructs the plotter to pick up a new pen when the programmer requests a color change.

4. *x Driver motor*—moves the pen horizontally across the paper.

5. *y Driver motor*—rotates the drum forward and backward.

Dot-Matrix Printers

The graphics programmer may often want to send output to a dot-matrix printer. The dot-matrix printer may be viewed in much the same way as a CRT; that is, it assigns bits to elements on the print head. This requires the use of a unique memory map. Unfortunately, the method of memory mapping used to write to a system's CRT may not match the memory map method used by the printer. This happens because the resolution of the plotter can be different from the resolution of the display memory map.

To write to a dot-matrix printer, the programmer must develop an algorithm that will convert the display memory map to the printer's memory map.

Character Printers and Computers with Only Character Output Capability

When using equipment that was not designed to output graphics, the programmer must create a memory map. This can be done by setting up a two-dimensional array. Table 2-2 lists the commands that could be used to set up a memory map on a device that can output an 80-character × 24-line display.

Once the memory map is defined, the programmer only needs to scale the graphics data to fit the array.

Table 2-2

Language	Command
FORTRAN	DIMENSION WIN (80, 24)
BASIC	DIM W$ (80, 24)
PASCAL	WINDOW: ARRAY [80, 24] OF CHAR;
COBOL	03 VARIABLE OCCURS 80 TIMES
	05 VARIABLE OCCURS 24 TIMES

Solved Problems

2.1   What is the function of the control electrode in a CRT?

SOLUTION

The control electrode is used to turn the electron beam on and off.

2.2   What is the function of the electron gun in a CRT?

SOLUTION

The electron gun creates a source of electrons which are focused into a narrow beam directed at the face of the CRT.

2.3   What causes the electron beam to move across the screen in a regular pattern in a raster-scan CRT?

SOLUTION

The deflection yoke which is connected to the sweep generator creates a fluctuating electric or magnetic potential. The change in potential causes the electron beam to be deflected.

2.4   What coats the inside front surface of a CRT and glows when exposed to a high-energy electron beam?

SOLUTION

Phosphors coat the inside front surface of a CRT.

2.5   True or false: Fluorescence is the term used to describe the light given off by a phosphor after it has been exposed to a high-energy electron beam. Explain your answer.

SOLUTION

False. Phosphorescence is the term used to describe the light given off by a phosphor after it has been exposed to a high-energy electron beam. Fluorescence is the term used to describe the light given off by a phosphor while it is being exposed to an electron beam.

2.6   What is persistence?

SOLUTION

Persistence is the term used to describe the duration of phosphorescence exhibited by a phosphor.

2.7   How does a computer control the shutting off and on of the electron beam?

SOLUTION

The computer's video output is connected to a signal amplifier which, in turn, is connected to the control electrode. This allows the computer to control when the CRT's electron beam is turned on or off.

2.8   Why is the electron beam allowed to overscan?

SOLUTION

The electron beam is allowed to overscan to avoid the creation of a border and to avoid picture distortion on the top, bottom, or both sides of the screen. The distortion occurs because the yoke and scan generator cannot instantly change the direction of the electron beam.

2.9   If you lived in an area that supplied 70-cycle power, your CRT would most likely refresh how many times per second and trace how many raster lines on the screen each cycle?

SOLUTION

Since the sweep generator is directly regulated by the frequency of its power source, the screen would refresh 70 times per second. The number of scan lines generated is independent of the power source frequency and would therefore be unaffected.

2.10 What is the technique called which involves splitting a raster-scan pattern into two separate patterns?

SOLUTION

Interlacing is the technique which involves splitting the scan pattern into two separate patterns.

2.11   Draw a diagram showing the location of left and right horizontal overscan and top and bottom vertical overscan.

SOLUTION

See Fig. 2-4.

2.12   What do you call the path an electron beam takes when returning to the left side of the CRT?

SOLUTION

The path the electron beam takes when returning to the left side of the CRT is called the horizontal retrace.

2.13   What do you call the path an electron beam takes at the end of each refresh cycle?

SOLUTION

The path the electron beam takes when at the end of each refresh cycle is called the vertical retrace.

2.14   What do you call the technique of turning off the electron beam while it is either horizontally or vertically retracing?

SOLUTION

The technique of turning the electron beam off while retracing is called retrace blanking.

2.15   What type of coordinate system do computers use to locate points? What type of coordinate system do we normally use?

SOLUTION

Most computer graphics systems internally locate a point with respect to a left-handed Cartesian coordinate system, while we normally work in a right-handed Cartesian coordinate system.

2.16   Add the following binary numbers in both hexadecimal and binary: $0010 + 1011$.

SOLUTION

$$
\begin{array}{r}
0010 = 02\text{H} \\
+\,1011 = 0\text{BH} \\
\hline
1101 = 0\text{DH}
\end{array}
$$

2.17   Subtract the following numbers in both hexadecimal and binary: $1110 - 1101$.

SOLUTION

$$
\begin{array}{r}
1110 = 0\text{EH} \\
-\,1101 = 0\text{DH} \\
\hline
0001 = 01\text{H}
\end{array}
$$

2.18   Multiply the binary value 0111 by 2. Perform the calculation in both hexadecimal and binary.

SOLUTION

$$
\begin{array}{r}
0111 = 07\text{H} \\
*\,0010 = 02\text{H} \\
\hline
0000 \\
0111 \\
0000 \\
0000 \\
\hline
0001110 = 0\text{EH}
\end{array}
$$

2.19 Divide the binary value 1100 by 2 and then by 8.

SOLUTION

Dividing by 2 is the same as a single right shift in binary. Therefore, 1100/0011 = 0110. Dividing by 8 is the same as three right shifts in binary. Therefore, 1100/1000 = 0001.1.

2.20 OR the following binary values. Show your work in hexadecimal and binary: (*a*) 1010 OR 0101, (*b*) 1100 OR 1111, (*c*) 1111 OR 1111, and (*d*) 0000 OR 1111.

SOLUTION

$$
\begin{array}{llll}
(a) & \begin{array}{r} 1010 = 0AH \\ OR \;\; 0101 = 05H \\ \hline 1111 = 0FH \end{array} &
(b) & \begin{array}{r} 1100 = 0CH \\ OR \;\; 1111 = 0FH \\ \hline 1111 = 0FH \end{array} \\[3em]
(c) & \begin{array}{r} 1111 = 0FH \\ OR \;\; 1111 = 0FH \\ \hline 1111 = 0FH \end{array} &
(d) & \begin{array}{r} 0000 = 00H \\ OR \;\; 1111 = 0FH \\ \hline 1111 = 0FH \end{array}
\end{array}
$$

2.21 Using the memory map shown in Example 1, show the steps required to light the pixel: (5, 3) decimal.

SOLUTION

1. Locate the starting address of the line that is to represent the y coordinate. In this case, line 3 starts at address 04H (0100 binary).

2. Right-shift the equivalent binary-value of the x coordinate three times (this is the same as dividing by 8). Next add the integer portion of this result to the result in step 1:

    5 decimal = 00000101 binary

    Right-shifting three times yields 00000000.101 binary. Add the integer portion of this to the result in step 1.

    $$
    \begin{array}{l}
    00000100 = 04H\text{---from step 1} \\
    \underline{+00000000 = 00H}\text{---}x \text{ integer value after right shifts} \\
    00000100 = 04H\text{---address of byte that will represent pixel}
    \end{array}
    $$

3. The remainder from step 2, .101, would actually be stored as 0101, which is 05H. This tells us that we want to light the sixth pixel counting from the MSB as 0:

    $$
    \begin{array}{cc}
    \text{MSB} & \text{LSB} \\
    \downarrow & \downarrow \\
    \multicolumn{2}{c}{00000100} \\
    \multicolumn{2}{c}{\uparrow}
    \end{array}
    $$

    Bit to be turned on

4. OR the result in step 3 (00001000) with the present value of the byte found in steps 1 and 2, and place the result in the address found in steps 1 and 2:

    $$
    \begin{array}{l}
    00000000 = 00H\text{---value stored at address 04H} \\
    \underline{OR \;\; 00001000 = 05H}\text{---value found in step 3} \\
    00001000 = 05H\text{---value to be stored at address}
    \end{array}
    $$

2.22 Using the memory map shown in Fig. 2-17, plot the screen coordinates (50, 10).

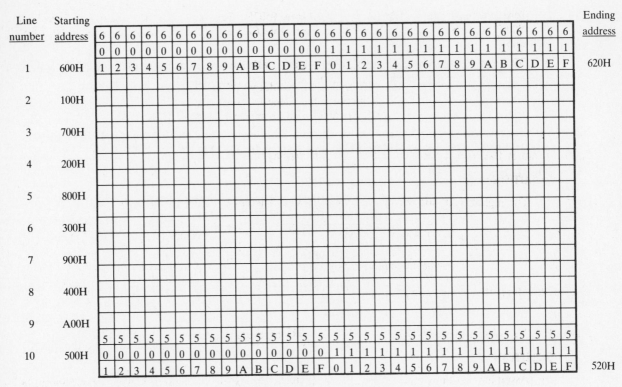

Fig. 2-17 Sample memory map.

SOLUTION

1. Because the memory is not sequential, a lookup table (Table 2-3) must be developed. Since $y = 10$, from the table the first point is located on the line starting at address 0500H.

2. Right-shift the x value three times, and add the integer portion to the result of step 1:

$$50 \text{ decimal} = 3AH = 00111010 \text{ binary}$$

Three right shifts yield 00000111.01. The integer portion is 00000111 = 07H. Add this result to the address found in step 1. The address which will represent the point is

$$\begin{array}{r} 0500\text{H} \\ +0007\text{H} \\ \hline 0507\text{H} \end{array}$$

Table 2-3

Line number	Address
1	0600H
2	0100H
3	0700H
4	0200H
5	0800H
6	0300H
7	0900H
8	0400H
9	0A00H
10	0500H

3. Compute the value to be ORed with address 0507H. The remainder from step 2 is 2 decimal (000000010 binary). According to the lookup table (Table 2-1), the value to be ORed is 00100000 binary.

4. OR the value found in step 3 (00100000 binary) with the byte found in steps 1 and 2.

$$
\begin{array}{ll}
& 00000000 \text{ value of address 0507H} \\
\text{OR } & \underline{00100000} \text{ value found in step 4} \\
& 00100000 \text{ value to be stored at address 0507H}
\end{array}
$$

2.23 What is the aspect ratio of a $12\,\text{in} \times 16\,\text{in}$ display?

SOLUTION

The highest common divisor for 12 and 16 is 4. Therefore, divide 12 and 16 by 4:

$$3 = \frac{12}{4} \quad\quad\quad 4 = \frac{16}{4}$$

where 12 is the CRT width, 16 is the CRT height, and 4 is the highest common divisor.

Therefore, the aspect ratio is $3:4$.

2.24 Fit the coordinates (900, 1000) to a 512×384 memory map.

SOLUTION

Assuming that these are the largest values to be fit, the coordinates must be scaled so that they are in the range of values allowed in the memory map. In this case, we must divide by $2^2 = 4$:

$$\frac{900}{4} = 225 \quad\quad \frac{1000}{4} = 250$$

2.25 What are some of the more popular alternatives to the raster-scan CRT?

SOLUTION

Plasma displays, LCDs, memory-tube displays, and random-access CRTs.

2.26 What are the major components of a plasma display?

SOLUTION

The major components of a plasma display are the cathodes, anodes, gas cells, and glass plates.

2.27 What are the major components of an LCD?

SOLUTION

The major components of an LCD are the conductive coating, the transparent plate, the liquid crystal, and the polarized film.

2.28 What are the major components of a memory-tube CRT?

SOLUTION

The major components of a memory-tube CRT are the write gun, the flooding gun, the collector, the phosphorus-coated screen, and the collector ground.

2.29 What are the differences between raster-scan CRTs and random-access or vector CRTs?

SOLUTION

Random-access CRTs do not follow a regular scanning pattern. Instead, the electron beam is directed from one point to another in the order in which the points were originally plotted. This method allows the random-access CRT to present much better animation than a raster-scan CRT. Memory requirements are also reduced because a coordinate list is stored rather than a memory map.

2.30 What is a major problem with random-access CRT application?

SOLUTION

When the coordinate data list becomes too long, the display will begin to flicker.

2.31 What type of display device are plotters similar to?

SOLUTION

Memory tube.

2.32 What are the major components of a flatbed plotter?

SOLUTION

The pen, the write-move device, and the x and y driver motors.

2.33 What is the major difference between a flatbed plotter and a drum plotter?

SOLUTION

The drum plotter moves the paper to change the y axis. The flatbed plotter moves the pen.

2.34 Plot the coordinate $(30, 25)$ on a dot-matrix printer.

SOLUTION

Most dot-matrix printers are designed to print characters. Therefore, we must first locate the correct character block. In most cases each character block will be presented by a series of 8 bytes :

Byte 1 00000000	Byte 5 00000000
Byte 2 00000000	Byte 6 00000000
Byte 3 00000000	Byte 7 00000000
Byte 4 00000000	Byte 8 00000000

Since each character block represents an 8×8 pixel area, we can position the printer as follows:

1. Divide the y value by 8. In this case $25/8 = 3$, with a remainder of 1. Since each group of eight lines represents one line of characters, 3 line feeds are issued.

2. Divide the x value by 8. In this case $30/8 = 3$ with a remainder of 6. The print head should thus be moved to the third character position.

3. Use the remainder from step 1 to find the correct byte to represent the coordinate. In this case, the remainder from $25/8$ was 1. The second byte in the character block will represent the point.

4. Use the remainder from step 2 to find the correct hexadecimal value to represent the coordinate. (*Note*: In this case the remainder was 6. Therefore, the sixth bit from the MSB must be set to 1. The byte should be set to 00000100 or 04H. The correct bit can be set to 1 by using the lookup table shown in Table 2-1.)

5. OR the value found in step 3 with the value found in 4, and issue the print command.

2.35 Plot an *x* at coordinate (20, 41) on a 24-line × 80-character device.

SOLUTION

1. Create a memory map. Since the device can only reproduce characters, we must create our own memory map. This may be done by initializing an 80 × 24 element array to a single blank.
2. Set array element *x, y* to "x." In this case the element is 20, 41.
3. Print the entire array, for example:

BASIC	FORTRAN
10 DIM X$(80, 24)	DIMENSION MAP (80, 24)
20 FOR Y = 1 to 24	DATA BLANK/' '/FILL 'X'
30 FOR X = 1 to 80	DO 10Y = 1, 24
40 X$(X, Y) = " "	DO 10X = 1, 80
50 NEXT X	10 MAP(X, Y) = BLANK
60 NEXT Y	
70 X$(20, 41) = "x"	MAP(20, 41) = FILL
80 FOR Y = 1 to 24	DO 20Y = 1, 24
90 FOR X = 1 to 80	WRITE(X, 20)(MAP(X, Y), X = 1, 80)
100 PRINT X$(X, Y);	20 FORMAT (80I1)
110 NEXT X	STOP
120 NEXT Y	END
130 END	

Supplementary Problems

2.36 Draw a diagram of a CRT and label its five major components.

2.37 What does the acronym CRT stand for?

2.38 Is a CRT an analog or a digital device? Explain.

2.39 What are the two methods in which an electron beam can be bent?

2.40 What two variables contribute to the life of a phosphor?

2.41 If a thin horizontal line, of only one raster line thickness, were drawn on a CRT that employed interlacing, it would appear to flicker. Why?

2.42 Top vertical overscan is 10 percent of CRT height, bottom vertical overscan is 8 percent of CRT height, and left and right horizontal overscan are 10 and 20 percent, respectively, of CRT width. How much additional computer memory would be required if provisions were not made to shut off the data flow from a 512 × 290 pixel display memory?

2.43 Ideally, most American CRT designers would like to use a phosphor with a persistence of exactly 1/30 s. Why?

2.44 What would be the approximate spot size in inches of 7-in-high 525-line raster-scan CRT that has a total vertical overscan of 20 percent? (Assume that pixels are square.)

2.45 All raster-scan CRTs tend to have some flicker. The strobe effect resulting from this flicker can be observed by moving your hand rapidly back and forth in front of a common television in a darkened room. Why are most people not aware of CRT flicker?

2.46 What does the acronym LSB mean?

2.47   The MSB represents 2 to what power in a computer's memory?

2.48   The LSB represents 2 to what power in a computer's memory?

2.49   Add the following numbers in hexadecimal and binary: (*a*) $1100 + 0011$, (*b*) $1111 + 1111$, and (*c*) $0110 + 0011$.

2.50   Subtract the following numbers in hexadecimal and binary: (*a*) $1010 - 0011$, (*b*) $1011 - 0001$, and (*c*) $1111 - 0001$.

2.51   Multiply the binary value 1010 by 8. Perform the calculations in both hexadecimal and binary.

2.52   Divide the binary value 0111 by 2 and then by 8.

2.53   Using the memory map shown in Example 1, show the steps required to light the pixel: (2, 14) decimal.

2.54   Using the memory map shown in Fig. 2-17, plot the screen coordinates (25, 8).

2.55   Give the aspect ratio of the following displays: (*a*) 15×10, (*b*) 4×4, and (*c*) 24×18.

2.56   Fit the coordinates (900, 520) to a 512×384 memory map.

2.57   What are some advantages of plasma displays over raster-scan CRTs?

2.58   What are some of the primary advantages of an LCD?

2.59   What are some disadvantages of an LCD?

2.60   What are the major advantages of a memory-tube display?

2.61   What are major disadvantages of a memory-tube display?

Chapter 3

Scan Conversion

3.1 INTRODUCTION

As discussed in Chap. 2, "Display Devices," the video output circuitry of a computer is capable of converting binary values stored in its display memory into pixel-on, pixel-off information that can be used by a raster output device to display a point. This ability allows graphics computers to display models composed of discrete dots (see Fig. 3-1).

While almost any model can be reproduced with a sufficiently dense matrix of dots (*pointillism*), most human operators generally think in terms of more complex graphic objects such as points, lines,

Fig. 3-1 Image generated by a dot matrix printer.

circles, and ellipses. Since the inception of computer graphics, many algorithms have been developed to provide human users with fast, memory-efficient routines that generate higher-level objects of this kind. However, regardless of what routines are developed, the computer can produce images on raster devices only by turning the appropriate pixels on or off. The process of representing continuous graphics objects as a collection of discrete pixels is called *scan conversion*.

Many scan-conversion algorithms are implemented in computer hardware or firmware. However, if a specific graphics computer does not have the hardware or firmware necessary to perform a particular scan-conversion algorithm, the scan-conversion algorithm can be implemented in software. The most commonly used graphics objects are the line, the sector, the arc, the ellipse, the rectangle, and the polygon.

In this chapter it is assumed that all objects lie within the boundaries of the display device coordinate system. In practice it is often necessary to apply a viewing transformation (Chap. 5) to accomplish this.

3.2 SCAN-CONVERTING A POINT

Each pixel on the graphics display does not represent a mathematical point. Rather, it represents a region which theoretically can contain an infinite number of points. Scan-converting a point involves illuminating the pixel that contains the point. For example, display coordinate points $P_1(2\frac{1}{3}, 1\frac{3}{4})$ and $P_2(2\frac{2}{3}, 1\frac{1}{4})$ in Fig. 3.2(a) would both be represented by pixel $(2, 1)$. In general, a point $P(x, y)$ is represented by the integer part of x and the integer part of y, that is, pixel $[(\text{INT}(x), \text{INT}(y)]$. In practice, the actual process of plotting a point is performed as described in Chap. 2, Sec. 2.3, under "Plotting a Point."

3.3 SCAN-CONVERTING A STRAIGHT LINE

A straight line may be defined by two endpoints and an equation [see Fig. 3-2(b)]. In Fig. 3-2(b) the two endpoints are described by (x_1, y_1) and (x_2, y_2). The equation of the line is used to describe the x, y coordinates of all the points that lie between these two endpoints. Using the equation of a straight line, $y = mx + b$ where $m = \Delta y/\Delta x$ and $b = $ the y intercept, we can find values of y by incrementing x from $x = x_1$ to $x = x_2$. By scan-converting these calculated x, y values, we represent the line as a sequence of pixels.

While this method of scan-converting a straight line is adequate for many graphics applications, interactive graphics systems require a much faster response than the method described above can provide. Interactive graphics is a graphics system in which the user dynamically controls the presentation of graphics models on a computer display.

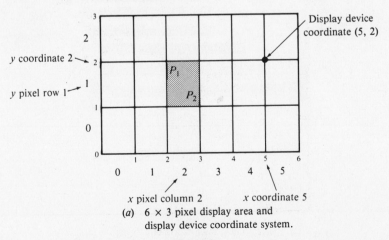

(a) 6 × 3 pixel display area and
display device coordinate system.

Fig. 3-2

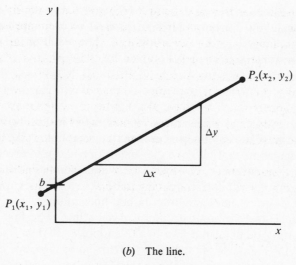

(b) The line.

Fig. 3-2 (*continued*)

Bresenham's Line Algorithm

Bresenham's line algorithm is an efficient method for scan-converting straight lines in that it uses only integer addition, subtraction, and multiplication by 2. As described in Chap. 2, the computer can perform the operations of integer addition and subtraction very rapidly. The computer is also time-efficient when performing integer multiplication and division by powers of 2.

The method works as follows. Assume that you would like to scan-convert the line shown in Fig. 3-3. The best approximation of the true line is described by those pixels in the raster that fall the least distance from the true line. Call the distance to those pixels lying immediately above the true line t_i and the distance to those directly below it s_i. Bresenham's algorithm identifies the decision variable, $d_i = s_i - t_i$. When d_i is less than zero, the closest pixel in the raster will be the pixel below the true line. Conversely, when d_i is greater than or equal to zero, the pixel immediately above the true line is closest.

To implement the algorithm, all that remains is to calculate and update the various values of d_i as follows. Following Prob. 3-23(a), we scan convert points P_1 and P_2 so that x_1, x_2, y_1, y_2 are integers. Set $d_2 = 2dy - dx$, where $dx = x_2 - x_1$, $dy = y_2 - y_1$. Thereafter, if $d_i \geq 0$, then x and y are incremented: $x_{i+1} = x_i + 1$, $y_{i+1} = y_i + 1$, and $d_{i+1} = d_i + 2(dy - dx)$. If $d_i < 0$, then only x is incremented: $x_{i+1} = x_i + 1$ and $d_{i+1} = d_i + 2dy$. See Prob. 3.4. This technique provides an efficient

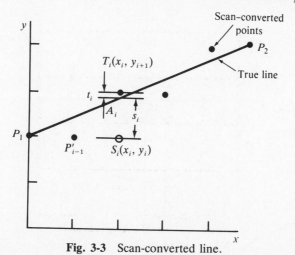

Fig. 3-3 Scan-converted line.

method for scan-converting lines whose slopes are less than 45°. For straight lines whose slopes are greater than 45 and less than 90°, the coordinates (x, y) must be exchanged prior to passing them to the routine and must be exchanged again prior to plotting. The result of the exchange will cause just y or both x and y to be incremented at each step (see Prob. 3.21).

Dashed Lines

Although dashed-line routines are not always implemented in hardware or firmware, they are commonly used in both business and engineering graphics applications. A dashed line is simply a series of consecutive short line segments that all have the same slope and y-intercept value. Generally, the line segments all have the same length; however, some applications, such as center lines, require multiple line segment lengths. As with the straight line, interactive graphics systems demand a very fast response from the computer when implementing dashed-line routines.

Either of two approaches may be used to plot a dashed line. The first approach draws a solid straight line from the starting point of the line to the endpoint. It then goes back and creates the illusion of dashes by changing segments of the line to the current background color at regular intervals. This method is slightly inefficient.

The second method computes the endpoints of a visible segment and then calls the line routine to draw that segment. The endpoints of the next segment are found, and the next segment is drawn. This process continues until the entire dashed line has been drawn. While drawing a dashed line by this method is a bit slower than drawing a solid line because floating-point division must be used to find the endpoints of each segment, time is saved when the routine skips over "blank" segments.

3.4 SCAN-CONVERTING A CIRCLE

A circle is a symmetrical figure. Any circle-generating algorithm can take advantage of the circle's symmetry to plot eight points for each value that the algorithm calculates. Eight-way symmetry is used by reflecting each calculated point around each 45° axis. For example, if point 1 in Fig. 3-4 were calculated with a circle algorithm, seven more points could be found by reflection. The reflection is accomplished by reversing the x, y coordinates as in point 2, reversing the x, y coordinates and reflecting about the y axis as in point 3, reflecting about the y axis as in point 4, switching the signs of x and y as in point 5, reversing the x, y coordinates, reflecting about the y axis and reflecting about the x

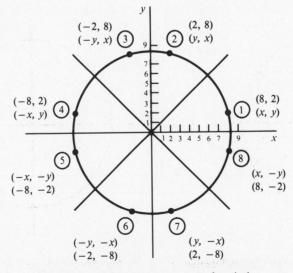

Fig. 3-4 Eight-way symmetry of a circle.

axis as in point 6, reversing the x, y coordinates and reflecting about the y axis as in point 7, and reflecting about the x axis as in point 8.

To summarize:

$$P_1 = (x, y) \qquad P_5 = (-x, -y)$$
$$P_2 = (y, x) \qquad P_6 = (-y, -x)$$
$$P_3 = (-y, x) \qquad P_7 = (y, -x)$$
$$P_4 = (-x, y) \qquad P_8 = (x, -y)$$

Defining a Circle

There are two standard methods of mathematically defining a circle centered at the origin. The first method defines a circle with the second-order polynomial equation (see Fig. 3-5).

$$y^2 = r^2 - x^2$$

where x = the x coordinate

y = the y coordinate

r = the circle radius

With this method, each x coordinate in the sector, from 90 to 45°, is found by stepping x from 0 to $r/\sqrt{2}$, and each y coordinate is found by evaluating $\sqrt{r^2 - x^2}$ for each step of x. This is a very inefficient method, however, because for each point both x and r must be squared and subtracted from each other; then the square root of the result must be found.

The second method of defining a circle makes use of trigonometric functions (see Fig. 3-6):

$$x = r \cos \theta \qquad y = r \sin \theta$$

where θ = current angle

r = circle radius

x = x coordinate

y = y coordinate

By this method, θ is stepped from θ to $\pi/4$, and each value of x and y is calculated. However, computation of the values of $\sin \theta$ and $\cos \theta$ is even more time-consuming than the calculations required by the first method.

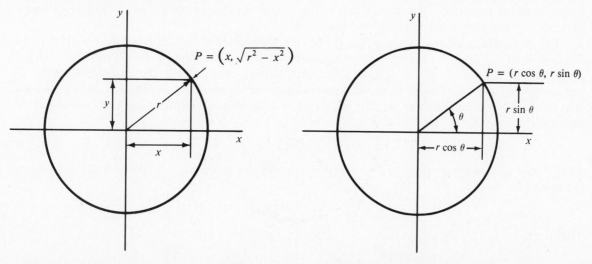

Fig. 3-5 Circle defined with a second-degree polynomial equation.

Fig. 3-6 Circle defined with trigonometric functions.

Bresenham's Circle Algorithm

If a circle is to be plotted efficiently, the use of trigonometric and power functions must be avoided. And as with the generation of a straight line, it is also desirable to perform the calculations necessary to find the scan-converted points with only integer addition, subtraction, and multiplication by powers of 2. *Bresenham's circle algorithm* allows these goals to be met.

Scan-converting a circle using Bresenham's algorithm works as follows. If the eight-way symmetry of a circle is used to generate a circle, points will only have to be generated through a 45° angle. And, if points are generated from 90 to 45°, moves will be made only in the $+x$ and $-y$ directions (see Fig. 3-7).

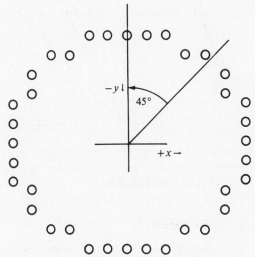

Fig. 3-7 Circle scan-converted with Bresenham's algorithm.

The best approximation of the true circle will be described by those pixels in the raster that fall the least distance from the true circle. Examine Figs. 3-8(a) and 3-8(b). Notice that if points are generated from 90 and 45°, each new point closest to the true circle can be found by taking either of two actions: (1) move in the x direction one unit or (2) move in the x direction one unit and move in the negative y direction one unit. Therefore, a method of selecting between these two choices is all that is necessary to find the points closest to the true circle.

The process is as follows. Assume that the last scan-converted pixel is P_1 [see Fig. 3-8(b)]. Let the distance from the origin to the true circle squared minus the distance to point P_3 squared $= D(S_i)$. Then let the distance from the origin to the true circle squared minus the distance to point P_2 squared $= D(T_i)$. As the only possible valid moves are to move either one step in the x direction or one step in the x direction and one step in the negative y direction, the following expressions can be developed:

$$D(S_i) = (x_{i-1} + 1)^2 + y_{i-1}^2 - r^2 \qquad D(T_i) = (x_{i-1} + 1)^2 + (y_{i-1} - 1)^2 - r^2$$

Since $D(S_i)$ will always be positive and $D(T_i)$ will always be negative, a decision variable d may be defined as follows:

$$d_i = D(S_i) + D(T_i)$$

Therefore

$$d_i = (x_{i-1} + 1)^2 + y_{i-1}^2 - r^2 + (x_{i-1} + 1)^2 + (y_{i-1} - 1)^2 - r^2$$

From this equation we can derive [see Prob. 3.23(b)]

$$d_1 = 3 - 2r$$

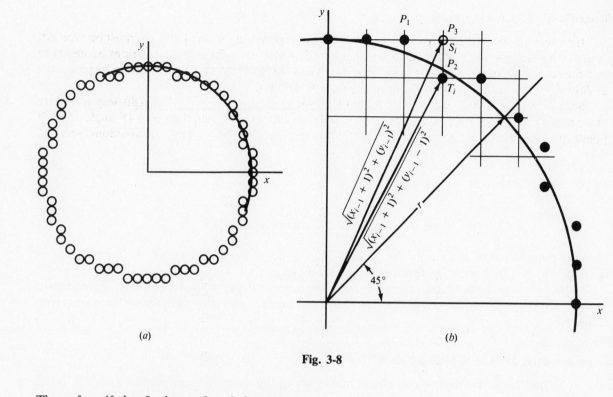

Fig. 3-8

Thereafter, if $d_i > 0$, then only x is incremented:

$$x_{i+1} = x_i + 1 \qquad d_{i+1} = d_i + 4x_i + 6$$

and if $d \leq 0$, then x and y are incremented:

$$x_{i+1} = x_i + 1 \qquad y_{i+1} = y_i - 1 \qquad d_{i+1} = d_i + 4(x_i - y_i) + 10$$

3.5 SCAN-CONVERTING AN ELLIPSE

The ellipse, like the circle, shows symmetry. In the case of an ellipse, however, symmetry is four- rather than eight-way. There are two methods of mathematically defining an ellipse.

Polynomial Method of Defining an Ellipse

The polynomial method of defining an ellipse (Fig. 3-9) is given by the expression

$$\frac{(x - h)^2}{a^2} + \frac{(y - k)^2}{b^2} = 1$$

where (h, k) = ellipse center

a = length of major axis

b = length of minor axis

When the polynomial method is used to define an ellipse, the value of x is incremented from h to a. For each step of x, each value of y is found by evaluating the expression

$$y = b\sqrt{1 - \frac{x - h^2}{a^2}} + k$$

This method is very inefficient, however, because the squares of a and $(x - h)$ must be found; then

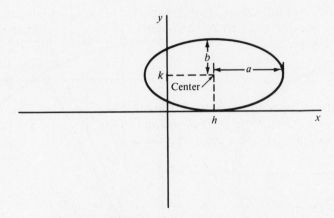

Fig. 3-9 Polynomial description of an ellipse.

floating-point division of $(x - h)^2$ by a^2 and floating-point multiplication of the square root of $[1 - (x - h)^2/a^2]$ by b must be performed (see Prob. 3.8).

Routines have been found that will scan-convert general polynomial equations, including the ellipse. However, these routines are logic intensive and thus are very slow methods for scan-converting ellipses.

Trigonometric Method of Defining an Ellipse

A second method of defining an ellipse makes use of trigonometric relationships (see Fig. 3-10). The following equations define an ellipse trigonometrically:

$$x = a * \cos(\theta) + h \qquad \text{and} \qquad y = b * \sin(\theta) + k$$

where (x, y) = the current coordinates

a = length of major axis

b = length of minor axis

θ = current angle

(h, k) = ellipse center

For generation of an ellipse using the trigonometric method, the value of θ is varied from 0 to $\pi/2$ radians (rad). The remaining points are found by symmetry. While this method is also inefficient and thus generally too slow for interactive applications, a lookup table containing the values for $\sin(\theta)$ and $\cos(\theta)$ with θ ranging from 0 to $\pi/2$ rad can be used. This method would have been considered

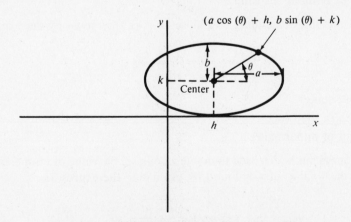

Fig. 3-10 Trigonometric description of an ellipse.

unacceptable at one time because of the relatively high cost of the computer memory used to store the values of θ. However, because the cost of computer memory has plummeted in recent years, this method is now quite acceptable.

Ellipse Axis Rotation

Since the ellipse shows fourway symmetry, it can easily be rotated 90°. The new equation is found by trading a and b, the values which describe the major and minor axes. When the polynomial method is used, the equations used to describe the ellipse become

$$\frac{(x-h)^2}{b^2} + \frac{(y-k)^2}{a^2} = 1$$

where (h, k) = ellipse center
$\quad a$ = length of major axis
$\quad b$ = length of minor axis

When the trigonometric is used, the equations used to describe the ellipse become

$$x = b * \cos(\theta) + h \qquad \text{and} \qquad y = a * \sin(\theta) + k$$

where (x, y) = current coordinates
$\quad a$ = length of major axis
$\quad b$ = length of minor axis
$\quad \theta$ = current angle
$\quad (h, k)$ = ellipse center

Assume that you would like to rotate the ellipse through an angle other than 90 degrees. It can be seen from Fig. 3-11 that rotation of the ellipse may be accomplished by rotating the x and y axis α degrees. When this is done, the equations describing the x, y coordinates of each scan-converted point become

$$x = a \cos(\theta) - b \sin(\theta + \alpha) + h \qquad y = b \sin(\theta) + a \cos(\theta + \alpha) + k$$

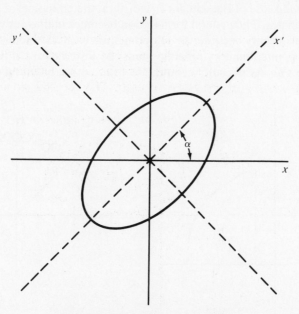

Fig. 3-11   Rotation of an ellipse.

3.6 SCAN-CONVERTING ARCS AND SECTORS

Arcs

An arc [Fig. 3-12(a)] may be generated by using either the polynomial or the trigonometric method. When the trigonometric method is used, the starting value is set equal to θ_1 and the ending value is set equal to θ_2 [see Figs. 3-12(a) and 3-12(b)]. The rest of the steps are similar to those used when scan-converting a circle, except that symmetry is not used.

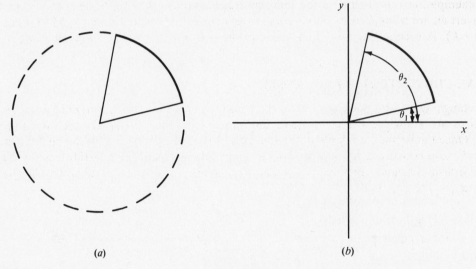

(a)   (b)

Fig. 3-12

When the polynomial method is used, the value of x is varied from x_1 to x_2 and the values of y are found by evaluating the expression $\sqrt{r^2 - x^2}$ (Fig. 3-13).

From the graphics programmer's point of view, arcs would appear to be nothing more than portions of circles. However, problems occur if algorithms such as Bresenham's circle algorithm are used in drawing an arc. In the case of Bresenham's algorithm, the endpoints of an arc must be specified in terms of the x, y coordinates. The general formulation becomes inefficient when endpoints must be found (see Fig. 3-14). This occurs because the endpoints for each 45° increment of the arc must be found. Each of the eight points found by reflection must be tested to see if the point is between the specified endpoints of the arc. As a result, a routine to draw an arc based on Bresenham's algorithm

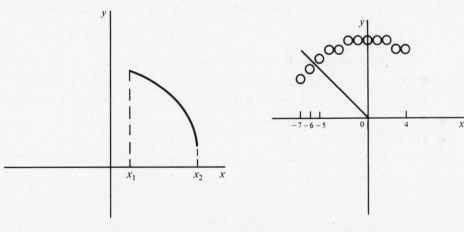

Fig. 3-13   **Fig. 3-14**

must take the time to calculate and test every point on the circle's perimeter. There is always the danger that the endpoints will be missed when a method like this is used. If the endpoints are missed, the routine can become caught in an infinite loop.

Sectors

A sector is scan-converted by using any of the three methods of scan converting an arc and then scan-converting two lines from the center of the arc to the endpoints of the arc.

For example, assume that a sector whose center is at point (h, k) is to be scan-converted. First, scan-convert an arc from θ_1 to θ_2. Next, a line would be scan-converted from (h, k) to $(r \cos(\theta_1) + h, r \sin(\theta_1) + k)$. A second line would be scan-converted from (h, k) to $(r \cos(\theta_2) + h, r \sin(\theta_2) + k)$.

3.7 SCAN-CONVERTING A RECTANGLE

A rectangle whose sides are parallel to the coordinate axes may be constructed if the locations of two vertices are known [see Fig. 3-15(a)]. The remaining corner points are then derived [see Fig. 3-15(b)]. Once the vertices are known, the four sets of coordinates are sent to the line routine and the rectangle is scan-converted. In the case of the rectangle shown in Figs. 3-15(a) and 3-15(b), lines would be drawn as follows: line (x_1, y_1) to (x_1, y_2); line (x_1, y_2) to (x_2, y_2); line (x_2, y_2) to (x_2, y_1); and line (x_2, y_1) to (x_1, y_1).

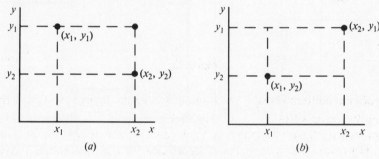

Fig. 3-15

3.8 REGION FILLING

Region filling is the process of "coloring in" a definite area or region. Regions may be described at the pixel or geometric level. At the pixel level, we describe a region either as the totality of pixels that comprise it or in terms of the bounding pixels that outline it (see Fig. 3-16). In the first case the region

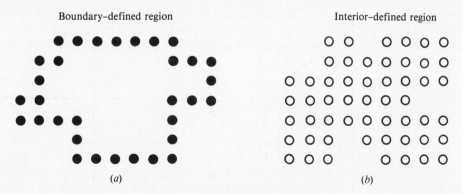

Fig. 3-16

is called *interior-defined* and the collection of algorithms used for filling such a region are collectively called *flood-fill algorithms*. The other type of region is called a *boundary-defined region* and the accompanying algorithms are called *boundary-fill algorithms*. At the geometric level a region is described in terms of objects such as lines, polygons, circles, and so on.

Flood Filling

When flood filling is used, the user will generally provide an initial pixel called a *seed*. From the seed the algorithm will inspect each of the surrounding eight pixels to determine whether the extent has been reached [see Fig. 3-17(*a*)]. The process is repeated until all pixels inside the region have been inspected (see Prob. 3.14).

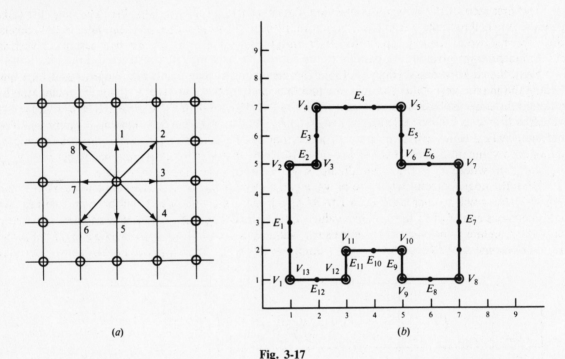

(*a*)   (*b*)

Fig. 3-17

Boundary Filling

In boundary filling, the user will also provide a seed (starting pixel). The boundary-fill algorithm, then, one by one, inspects each pixel to the left and right of the seed. When the left- and rightmost boundary pixels are hit, a run or line of pixels is drawn. Next, the boundary-fill algorithm inspects each pixel above and below the line just drawn. Again, when the boundary pixels are hit, a line is drawn. The process is continued until all pixels inspected are shown to be boundary pixels (see Prob. 3.13).

Geometrically Defined Regions

Flood-fill and boundary-fill algorithms assume that the pixels of an area are already stored in display memory. If polygons are described in terms of their vertices, as is the case in three-dimensional modeling, the process of filling the polygon by first scan-converting the edges to get the boundary pixels and then applying a boundary-fill algorithm is usually inefficient. The following polygon scan-conversion algorithm is designed to take advantage of both scan line and edge coherences (Chap. 10, Sec. 10.4, under "Types of Coherence") to produce an effective method of scan-converting polygons.

To apply the polygon scan-conversion algorithm (Prob. 3.30), it is assumed that the vertex list describing the polygon is in order and that the polygon has already been scaled to the viewport and window (Chap. 5). For Fig. 3-17(b), for example, it will be assumed that the matrix describing the polygon is stored as

Vertex	1	2	3	4	5	6	7	8	9	10	11	12	13
x	1	1	2	2	5	5	7	7	5	5	3	3	1
y	1	5	5	7	7	5	5	1	1	2	2	1	1

The first step of the polygon conversion algorithm is to create an edge list. The edge list (EL) contains one cell for each y scan line. Therefore, if the vertical resolution of a computer is 1024 pixels, the edge list would contain space for 1024 entries. [For Fig. 3-17(b), we will assume a vertical resolution of eight pixels.]

Next, the edge list entry values are found by computing the reciprocal of the slope of each edge and finding the maximum y value for the edge and the minimum x value. These values are sorted one by one into the edge list by minimum y value. For Fig. 3-17(b), there are 13 vertices; therefore, there are 12 edges (see Table 3-1). In Table 3-1, edges 2, 4, 6, 8, 10, and 12 are horizontal. Therefore, filling between vertical edges will account for them, so they need not be included in the edge list. Sorting by minimum y value into the edge list yields Table 3-2. Note that each edge list entry need only store y_{max}, x_A, and $1/m$ where x_A is the x coordinate of y_{min} and m is the slope of the edge.

With the edge list completed, the polygon can now be filled by stepping y in increments of 1. For Fig. 3-17(b), y will be increased from 1 to 8. As y is increased by 1, edges will become "active." An edge becomes active when the scan line value y equals the edge's cell number. The edge remains active until the scan line value y equals the edge's y_{max} value. For example, when $y = 1$, edges E_1, E_7, E_9, and E_{11} will become active (i.e., the line $y = 1$ intersects edges E_1, E_7, E_9, and E_{11}). The active edges are

Table 3-1

Edge	y_{min}	y_{max}	x_A coord. of y_{min}	x_A coord. of y_{max}	$1/m$
E_1	1	5	1	1	0
E_2	5	5	1	2	—
E_3	5	7	2	2	0
E_4	7	7	2	5	—
E_5	5	7	5	5	0
E_6	5	5	5	7	—
E_7	1	5	7	7	0
E_8	1	1	5	7	—
E_9	1	2	5	5	0
E_{10}	2	2	3	5	—
E_{11}	1	2	3	3	0
E_{12}	1	1	1	3	—

Table 3-2

EL	Edge number
Cell 8	—
Cell 7	—
Cell 6	—
Cell 5	3, 5
Cell 4	—
Cell 3	—
Cell 2	—
Cell 1	1, 7, 9, 11

then sorted by the x_A value to form the active edge list. In Fig. 3-17(b), the active edges would be sorted as follows: order of sorted active edges E_1, E_{11}, E_9, E_7. (*Note*: Examine Table 3-1.)

The actual fill is performed by filling the pixels, one scan line at a time between edge pairs. To demonstrate examine Table 3-2, where $E_1(x_A, y) = (1, 1)$, $E_{11}(x_A, y) = (3, 1)$, $E_9(x_A, y) = (5, 1)$, and $E_7(x_A, y) = (7, 1)$. Note that in this example the pixels between and including $E_1(x_A, y)$ and $E_{11}(x_A, y)$ would be filled and the pixels between and including $E_9(x_A, y)$ and $E_7(x_A, y)$ would be filled.

After the pixels are filled, the edges whose y_{max} value equals the current value of y are removed from the active edge list. The x_A values for the remaining edges are incremented by $1/m$ (i.e., $x_A = x_A + 1/m$, and y is incremented by 1. The new edges that become active are added to the active edge list and the process is repeated until y equals the maximum cell number.

It should be noted that a special problem can occur when the current y scan coordinate is equal to the y coordinate of one of the vertices. In such cases the polygon will not be properly filled because the edges will be counted twice at the vertex. In our example this occurs at $y = 1, 2, 5$, and 7. If edges E_{12} and E_8 were included in the edge list table, the algorithm would attempt to fill the pixels "between" and including $(1, 1)$ and $(1, 1)$, leaving pixel $(1, 2)$ unlit, and so on. To avoid this, when a vertex lies directly on a scan line, the minimum x value is increased by $1/m$ to give $x + 1/m$, and the entry into the edge table is made at cell number $y_{min} + 1$. In Fig. 3-17(b), the value of y is greater than the y maximum, so the entry for that edge is dropped, thus eliminating the horizontal edges E_2, E_4, E_6, E_8, E_{10}, and E_{12} from the edge list. This is why horizontal lines are not included in the edge list.

3.9 BOUNDARY BLOCK TRANSFER (BITBLT) OR RASTER OPERATIONAL GRAPHICS

Graphics models may often be stored as a block of the computer's display memory. This is often the case with alphanumeric characters (see Fig. 3-18).

It is useful to be able to move a section of display memory after it is defined without having to scan-convert again; BITBLT graphics allow such operations to be performed. In addition, BITBLT has been found to be useful for comparing models, filling regions, and performing many other commonly used graphics operations at speeds much faster than conventional scan conversion methods would allow. As BITBLT is still in its infancy, we will discuss the use of BITBLT only for transformations.

Character	Binary representation	Hexadecimal representation
● ● ● ● ● ●	1 1 1 1　1 1 0 0	F C
●　　　　　●	1 0 0 0　0 0 1 0	8 3
●　　　　　●	1 0 0 0　0 0 1 0	8 3
● ● ● ● ● ●	1 1 1 1　1 1 0 0	F C
●　　　　　●	1 0 0 0　0 0 1 0	8 3
●　　　　　●	1 0 0 0　0 0 1 0	8 3
●　　　　　●	1 0 0 0　0 0 1 0	8 3
● ● ● ● ● ●	1 1 1 1　1 1 0 0	F C

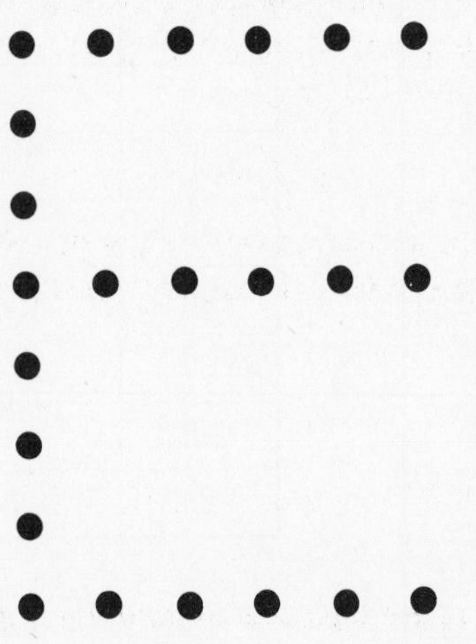

Fig. 3-18

BITBLT Transformations

Suppose that a portion of the sequential memory map (see Fig. 3-19) is to be copied to another portion of display memory. The copy is performed by simply reproducing the values stored in locations 01H through 08H to the desired area of display memory. Thus graphics objects can be moved about on the display without scan-converting. While BITBLT graphics are very fast and often useful in animation applications, the smallest area that can be directly manipulated is 1 byte (eight pixels).

Address	Character	Binary representation	Hexadecimal representation
01 H	○ ○ ○ ○ ○	0 1 1 1 1 1 0 0	7 C
02 H	○ ○	1 0 0 0 0 0 1 0	8 2
03 H	○	1 0 0 0 0 0 0 0	8 0
04 H	○	1 0 0 0 0 0 0 0	8 0
05 H	○	1 0 0 0 0 0 0 0	8 0
06 H	○	1 0 0 0 0 0 0 0	8 0
07 H	○ ○	1 0 0 0 0 0 1 0	8 2
08 H	○ ○ ○ ○ ○	0 1 1 1 1 1 0 0	7 3

Fig. 3-19

An Alternate Character Set with BITBLT

Alternate character sets can be generated by using BITBLT methods. Typically, an alternate character set is stored in a range of memory. A lookup table is then used to locate the specific series of addresses that represent the character associated with the key the user presses (see Probs. 3.16 and 3.28).

3.10 SIDE EFFECTS OF SCAN CONVERSION

The computer graphics software designer, like all designers, is faced with many design trade-offs. No one solution is correct for all applications. The following section discusses the four most common design trade-offs faced by computer graphics software designers when working with raster devices: aliasing, unequal intensity, overstrike, and the "picket fence" problem.

Aliasing

The term "aliasing" refers to the plotting of a point in a location other than its true location in order to fit the point into the raster. For example, the true location of the point shown in Fig. 3-20 is given by the equation

$$y = mx + b$$

where $b = 1$
$\quad m = 0.5$
$\quad x = 3$

Solving for y, the true point is $(3, 2.5)$. However, the raster does not contain fractional locations, so the point is plotted at the alias location $(3, 3)$ (see Fig. 3-20).

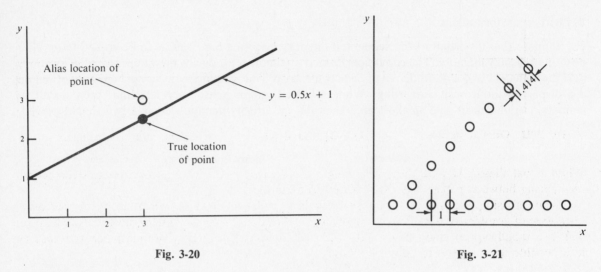

Fig. 3-20   Fig. 3-21

Unequal Intensity

The unequal-intensity problem occurs because human perception of light is dependent on both the density and the intensity of a light source. Thus, on a raster display with perfect squareness, a diagonal line of pixels will appear dimmer than a horizontal or vertical line (see Fig. 3-21). As can be seen in Fig. 3-21, the pixels on the horizontal line are placed one unit apart, while the pixels on the diagonal line are approximately 1.414 units apart. This difference in density produces the perceived difference in brightness. Software designers can respond to this problem in one of three ways:

1. If speed of scan conversion is of primary importance, the unequal intensity problem can be ignored.
2. The unequal intensity of the lines can be corrected by increasing the number of pixels used to generate the diagonal line.
3. The unequal-intensity problem can be corrected by increasing the intensity of pixels plotted on the diagonal.

Overstrike

Overstrike occurs when the same pixel is written to more than once. In most applications, overstrike will have little effect on the output of a raster computer graphics system. Usually the only consequence is that the speed of output is slightly degraded because time is spent in scan-converting the same point two or more times.

However, when the graphics system is sending its output to a photographic medium, such as a slide or transparency, the overstrike amounts to a double, triple, or more exposures of the same portion of film. As a result, the pixel appears with greater intensity on the slide. This effect may be prevented by checking each pixel to see whether it has already been written to prior to writing a new point. Here, the computer graphics software designer must decide whether a separate scan-conversion routine should be written to handle photographic applications.

The Picket Fence Problem

The picket fence problem occurs when a user attempts to scan-convert an object that will not fit exactly into the raster (see Fig. 3-22).

The computer graphics software designer must decide whether to use local or global aliasing. With local aliasing, the distances between pickets in the picket fence will be kept as close to their true relative distances as possible. However, the overall length of the fence will be distorted (see Fig. 3-23).

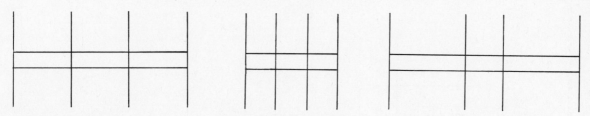

Fig. 3-22 Original picture.   **Fig. 3-23** Local aliasing.   **Fig. 3-24** Global aliasing.

When global aliasing is used, the overall length of the picket fence will be approximately correct but the spacing between pickets will be distorted (see Fig. 3-24).

While aliasing presents a thorny problem for graphics system designers, the ever increasing resolution of graphics systems is slowly evolving a "back door" solution to the problem. That is, pixel density is rapidly approaching the resolution of the human eye at normal viewing distance, thus making it impossible for a person to perceive aliasing.

Solved Problems

3.1 The endpoints of a given line are $(0, 0)$ and $(6, 18)$. Compute each value of y as x steps from 0 to 6 and plot the results.

SOLUTION

An equation for the line was not given. Therefore, the equation of the line must be found. The equation of the line ($y = mx + b$) is found as follows. First the slope is found:

$$m = \frac{\Delta y}{\Delta x} = \frac{y_2 - y_1}{x_2 - x_1} = \frac{18 - 0}{6 - 0} = \frac{18}{6} = 3$$

Next, the y intercept b_1 is found by plugging y_1 and x_1 into the equation $y = 3x + b$: $0 = 3(0) + b$. Therefore, $b = 0$, so the equation for the line is $y = 3x$ (see Fig. 3-25).

3.2 What steps are required to plot a line using the slope method?

SOLUTION

1. Compute dx: $dx = x_2 - x_1$.
2. Compute dy: $dy = y_2 - y_1$.
3. Compute m: $m = dy/dx$.
4. Compute b: $b = y_1 - m * x_1$.
5. Set (x, y) equal to the lower left-hand endpoint and set x_{end} equal to the largest value of x. If $dx < 0$, then $x = x_2$, $y = y_2$, and $x_{end} = x_1$. If $dx > 0$, then $x = x_1$, $y = y_1$, and $x_{end} = x_2$.
6. Test to determine whether the entire line has been drawn. If $x > x_{end}$, stop.
7. Plot a point at the current (x, y) coordinates.
8. Increment x: $x = x + 1$.
9. Compute the next value of y from the equation $y = mx + b$.
10. Go to step 6.

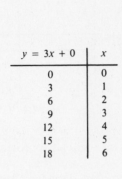

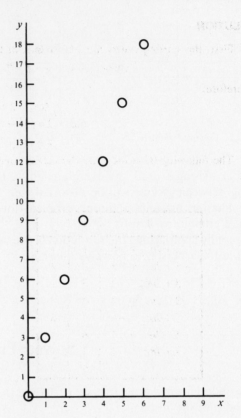

Fig. 3-25

3.3   What steps are required to plot a line whose slope is between 0 and 45° using Bresenham's method?

SOLUTION

1. Compute the initial values:

$$
\begin{aligned}
dx &= x_2 - x_1 & Inc_2 &= 2 * (dy - dx)\\
dy &= y_2 - y_1 & d &= Inc_1 - dx\\
Inc_1 &= 2 * dy
\end{aligned}
$$

2. Set (x, y) equal to the lower left-hand endpoint and x_{end} equal to the largest value of x. If $dx < 0$, then $x = x_2$, $y = y_2$, $x_{\text{end}} = x_1$. If $dx > 0$, then $x = x_1$, $y = y_1$, $x_{\text{end}} = x_2$.

3. Plot a point at the current (x, y) coordinates.

4. Test to see whether the entire line has been drawn. If $x > x_{\text{end}}$, stop.

5. Compute the location of the next pixel. If $d < 0$, then $d = d + Inc_1$. If $d \geq 0$, then $d = d + Inc_2$, and then $y = y + 1$.

6. Increment x: $x = x + 1$.

7. Plot a point at the current (x, y) coordinates.

8. Go to step 4.

3.4   Indicate which raster locations would be chosen by Bresenham's algorithm when scan-converting a line from screen coordinate $(1, 1)$ to screen coordinate $(8, 5)$.

SOLUTION

First, the starting values must be found. In this case

$$dx = x_2 - x_1 = 8 - 1 = 7 \qquad dy = y_2 - y_1 = 5 - 1 = 4$$

Therefore:

$$Inc_1 = 2 * dy = 2 * 4 = 8$$
$$Inc_2 = 2 * (dy - dx) = 2 * (4 - 7) = -6$$
$$d = Inc_1 - dx = 8 - 7 = 1$$

The following table indicates the values computed by the algorithm (see also Fig. 3-26).

d	x	y
$1 + Inc_2 = -5$	1	1
$-5 + Inc_1 = 3$	2	2
$3 + Inc_2 = -3$	3	2
$-3 + Inc_1 = 5$	4	3
$5 + Inc_2 = -1$	5	3
$-1 + Inc_1 = 7$	6	4
$7 + Inc_2 = 1$	7	4
	8	5

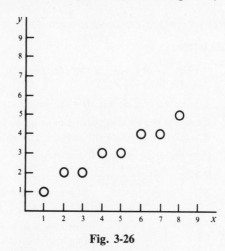

Fig. 3-26

3.5 What steps are required to generate a circle using the polynomial method?

SOLUTION

1. Set the initial variables: r = circle radius; (h, k) = coordinates of the circle center; $x = 0$; i = step size; $x_{end} = r/\sqrt{2}$.
2. Test to determine whether the entire circle has been scan-converted. If $x > x_{end}$, stop.
3. Compute the value of the y coordinate, where $y = \sqrt{r^2 - x^2}$.
4. Plot the eight points, found by symmetry with respect to the center (h, k), at the current (x, y) coordinates:

Plot $(x + h, y + k)$	Plot $(-x + h, -y + k)$
Plot $(y + h, x + k)$	Plot $(-y + h, -x + k)$
Plot $(-y + h, x + k)$	Plot $(y + h, -x + k)$
Plot $(-x + h, y + k)$	Plot $(x + h, -y + k)$

5. Increment x: $x = x + i$.
6. Go to step 2.

3.6 What steps are required to scan-convert a circle using the trigonometric method?

SOLUTION

1. Set the initial variables: r = circle radius; (h, k) = coordinates of the circle center; i = step size; $\theta_{end} = (22/7)/4$ [$(22/7)/4 = \pi/4$ radians = 90°]; $\theta = 0$.
2. Test to determine whether the entire circle has been scan-converted. If $\theta > \theta_{end}$, stop.
3. Compute the value of the x and y coordinates:

$$x = r * \cos(\theta) \qquad y = r * \sin(\theta)$$

4. Plot the eight points, found by symmetry with respect to the center (h, k), at the current (x, y) coordinates:

Plot $(x + h, y + k)$ Plot $(-x + h, -y + k)$

Plot $(y + h, x + k)$ Plot $(-y + h, -x + k)$

Plot $(-y + h, x + k)$ Plot $(y + h, -x + k)$

Plot $(-x + h, y + k)$ Plot $(x + h, -y + k)$

5. Increment θ: $\theta = \theta + i$.

6. Go to step 2.

3.7 What steps are required to scan-convert a circle using Bresenham's algorithm?

SOLUTION

1. Set the initial values of the variables: $(h, k) =$ coordinates of circle center; $x = 0$; $y =$ circle radius r; and $d = 3 - 2 * r$.

2. Test to determine whether the entire circle has been scan-converted. If $x > y$, stop.

3. Compute the location of the next pixel. If $d < 0$, then $d = d + 4 * x + 6$ and $x = x + 1$. If $d \geq 0$, then $d = d + 4 * (x - y) + 10$, $x = x + 1$, and $y = y - 1$.

4. Plot the eight points, found by symmetry with respect to the center (h, k), at the current (x, y) coordinates:

Plot $(x + h, y + k)$ Plot $(-x + h, -y + k)$

Plot $(y + h, x + k)$ Plot $(-y + h, -x + k)$

Plot $(-y + h, x + k)$ Plot $(y + h, -x + k)$

Plot $(-x + h, y + k)$ Plot $(x + h, -y + k)$

5. Go to step 2.

3.8 What steps are required to generate an ellipse using the polynomial method?

SOLUTION

1. Set the initial variables: $a =$ length of major axis; $b =$ length of minor axis; $(h, k) =$ coordinates of ellipse center; $x = 0$; $i =$ step size; $x_{end} = a$.

2. Test to determine whether the entire ellipse has been scan-converted. If $x > x_{end}$, stop.

3. Compute the value of the y coordinate:

$$y = b\sqrt{1 - \frac{x^2}{a^2}}$$

4. Plot the four points, found by symmetry, at the current (x, y) coordinates:

Plot $(x + h, y + k)$ Plot $(-x + h, -y + k)$

Plot $(-x + h, y + k)$ Plot $(x + h, -y + k)$

5. Increment x: $x = x + i$.

6. Go to step 2.

3.9 What steps are required to scan-convert an ellipse using the trigonometric method?

SOLUTION

1. Set the initial variables: $a =$ length of major axis; $b =$ length of minor axis; $(h, k) =$ coordinates of ellipse center; $i =$ counter step size; $\theta_{end} = 11/7 = \pi/2$; $\theta = 0$.

2. Test to determine whether the entire ellipse has been scan-converted. If $\theta > \theta_{end}$, stop.

3. Compute the values of the x and y coordinates:

$$x = a * \cos(\theta) \qquad y = b * \sin(\theta)$$

4. Plot the four points, found by symmetry, at the current (x, y) coordinates:

Plot $(x + h, y + k)$	Plot $(-x + h, -y + k)$
Plot $(-x + h, y + k)$	Plot $(x + h, -y + k)$

5. Increment θ: $\theta = \theta + i$.
6. Go to step 2.

3.10 What steps are required to scan-convert an arc using the trigonometric method?

SOLUTION

1. Set the initial variables: $a = $ major axis; $b = $ minor axis; $(h, k) = $ coordinates of arc center; $i = $ step size; $\theta = $ starting angle; $\theta_1 = $ ending angle.
2. Test to determine whether the entire arc has been scan-converted. If $\theta > \theta_1$, stop.
3. Compute the values of the x and y coordinates:

$$x = a * \cos(\theta) + h \qquad y = a * \sin(\theta) + k$$

4. Plot the points at the current (x, y) coordinates: Plot (x, y).
5. Increment θ: $\theta = \theta + i$.
6. Go to step 2.

(Note: For the arc of a circle $a = b = $ circle radius r.)

3.11 What steps are required to generate an arc of a circle using the polynomial method?

SOLUTION

1. Set the initial variables: $r = $ radius; $(h, k) = $ coordinates of arc center; $x = x$ coordinate of start of arc; $x_1 = x$ coordinate of end of arc; $i = $ counter step size.
2. Test to determine whether the entire arc has been scan-converted. If $x > x_1$, stop.
3. Compute the value of the y coordinate:

$$y = \sqrt{r^2 - x^2}$$

4. Plot at the current (x, y) coordinates:

$$\text{Plot } (x_1 + h, y + k)$$

5. Increment x: $x = x + i$.
6. Go to step 2.

3.12 What steps are required to scan-convert a rectangle whose sides are parallel to the coordinate axes?

SOLUTION

1. Set initial variables: $(x_1, y_1) = $ coordinates of first point specified; $(x_2, y_2) = $ coordinates of second point specified.
2. Plot the rectangle:

Plot (x_1, y_1)	to	(x_2, y_1)
Plot (x_2, y_1)	to	(x_2, y_2)

Plot (x_2, y_2)	to	(x_1, y_2)
Plot (x_1, y_2)	to	(x_2, y_1)

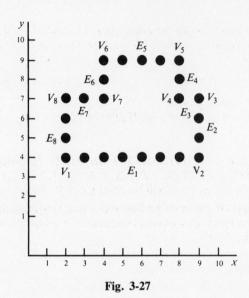

Fig. 3-27

3.13 The coordinates of the vertices of a polygon are shown in Fig. 3-27. (*a*) Write the edge list for the polygon. (*b*) State which edges will be active on scan lines $y = 6$, 7, 8, 9, and 10. What are the current values of y_{max}, x_A, and $1/m$ for each edge?

SOLUTION

(*a*) Figure 3-27 has 10 scan lines; therefore the edge list will consist of 10 cells. The edges in the edge list (EL) are those whose minimum y value equals the cell number. Horizontal edges are not included.

EL	Edge Number	EL	Edge Number
Cell 10	—	Cell 5	—
9	—	5	8, 2
8	—	3	—
7	6, 4	2	—
6	—	1	—

(*b*) An edge becomes active when the scan line value y equals the edge's cell number. The edge remains active until the scan line value y equals the edge's y_{max} value. Therefore, the active edge list for $y = 6$, 7, 8, 9, and 10 appears as follows.

At $y = 6$,

y_{max}	x_A	$1/m$
7	2	0

y_{max}	x_A	$1/m$
7	9	0

At $y = 7$, $y = y_{max}$ for both edges E_8 and E_2 so they are removed from the active edge list. Also at $y = 7$, the edges in cell 7 become active.

y_{max}	x_A	$1/m$
9	4	0

y_{max}	x_A	$1/m$
9	8	0

At $y = 8$, the active edges remain the same. At $y = 9$, edges E_2 and E_4 are removed from the active edge list and no new edges are activated. Therefore the active edge list is empty. At $y = 10$, the active edge list remains empty.

3.14 How would a flood-fill algorithm fill the region shown in Fig. 3-28?

SOLUTION

1. Assume that a seed is given at coordinate 3, 3. The flood-fill algorithm will inspect the eight points surrounding the seed (4, 4; 3, 4; 2, 4; 2, 3; 2, 2; 3, 2; 4, 2; 4, 3). Since none of the points surrounding the seed is on a border, each point will be filled (see Fig. 3-29).

2. Each of the eight points found in step 1 becomes a new seed, and the points surrounding each new seed are inspected and filled. This process continues until all the points surrounding all the seeds run into a border (see Fig. 3-30).

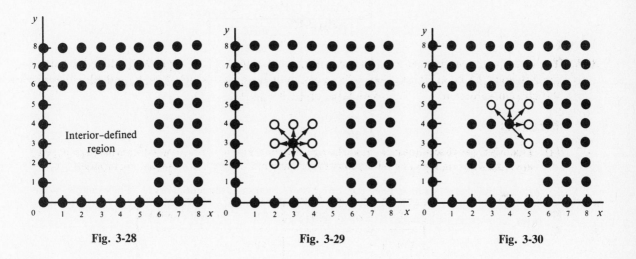

Fig. 3-28   Fig. 3-29   Fig. 3-30

3.15 What steps are required to fill a region using the boundary-fill method?

SOLUTION

1. A seed point is passed to the boundary-fill algorithm.

2. Each byte to the right and left of the seed is inspected to determine whether a boundary has been hit.

3. When the bytes containing the left and right boundary points (indicated by different values from the bytes set to the background color) are found, a line is drawn from the left-hand point to the right-hand point.

4. The pixel above and below the seed row are inspected to see whether they contain boundary points and lines are drawn from boundary to boundary in each of these rows. This process continues until all the pixels examined are found to be on the boundary.

3.16 What steps are required to set up an alternate character set using the BITBLT method?

SOLUTION

1. Assuming each character is to be stored in an 8-bit by 8-byte matrix, fill in the appropriate pixels to form each character as shown in Fig. 3-31.

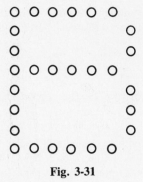

Fig. 3-31

2. Convert the pixels to their binary equivalent. Then convert the binary values to hexadecimal:

Binary	Hexadecimal
11111100	FCH
10000010	82H
10000010	82H
11111100	FCH
10000010	82H
10000010	82H
10000010	82H
11111100	FCH

3. After all the characters have been converted, store them in a sequential array. (For example, if the alternate character set is to be in a font different from the one provided with your computer, load the 8 bytes representing the character A first, B second, etc.)

3.17 What are the four major adverse side effects of scan conversion?

SOLUTION

The four major adverse effects of scan conversion are aliasing, unequal intensity of diagonal lines, overstriking in photographic applications, and local or global aliasing.

3.18 How can the effects of aliasing be minimized?

SOLUTION

In the case of local and global aliasing, nothing can be done. The designer can compensate only by remaining consistent. When aliasing occurs, the designer compensates by adding pixels to the object that will smooth out aliased lines (see Fig. 3-32).

3.19 How can a designer eliminate overstrike?

SOLUTION

Overstrike can be eliminated by checking each pixel before writing to it. If the pixel has already been written to, no point will be written.

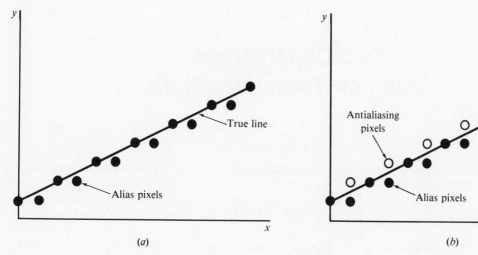

Fig. 3-32

Supplementary Problems

3.20 Given the following equations, find the corresponding values of y for each value of x ($x = 2, 7, 1$): (a) $y = 4x + 3$, (b) $y = 1x + 0$, (c) $y = -3x - 4$, and (d) $y = -2x + 1$.

3.21 What steps are required to plot a line whose slope is between 45 and 90° using Bresenham's method?

3.22 What steps are required to plot a dashed line?

3.23 (a) Show that the decision variables of Bresenham's line algorithm agree with the definition $d_i = s_i - t_i$. (b) Show for Bresenham's circle algorithm that $d_1 = 3 - 2r$ by reducing $d = D(S_i) + D(T_i)$.

3.24 Show graphically that an ellipse has four-way symmetry by plotting four points on the ellipse:

$$x = a * \cos(\theta) + h \qquad y = b * \sin(\theta) + k$$

where $a = 2$
       $b = 1$
       $h = 0$
       $k = 0$
       $\theta = \pi/4, 3\pi/4, 5\pi/4, 7\pi/4$

3.25 How must Prob. 3.9 be modified if an ellipse is to be rotated (a) $\pi/4$, (b) $\pi/9$, and (c) $\pi/2$ radians?

3.26 What steps are required to scan-convert a sector using the trigonometric method?

3.27 What steps must be added to a fill algorithm if a region is to be filled with a pattern?

3.28 What steps would be required to display the alternate character set developed in Prob. 3.16?

3.29 Why is it important for the designer to remain consistent when choosing either local or global aliasing?

3.30 What steps are required to scan-convert a polygonal area?

Chapter 4

Two-Dimensional
Graphics Transformations

4.1 INTRODUCTION

Fundamental to all computer graphics systems is the ability to simulate both the movement and the manipulation of objects in the plane. These processes are described in terms of translations, rotations, scalings, and reflections. Our object is to describe these operations in mathematical form suitable for computer processing and show how they are used to achieve the ends of object manipulation and motion.

There are two complementary points of view for describing object movement. The first is that the object itself is moved relative to a stationary coordinate system or background. The mathematical statement of this viewpoint is described by *geometric transformations* applied to each point of the object. The second point of view holds that the object is held stationary while the coordinate system is moved relative to the object. This effect is attained through the application of *coordinate transformations*. An example involves the motion of an automobile against a scenic background. We can simulate this by moving the car while keeping the backdrop fixed (a geometric transformation). We can also keep the automobile fixed while moving the backdrop scenery (a coordinate transformation). In some situations, both methods are employed.

Coordinate transformations play an important role in the *instancing* of an object—the placement of objects, each of which is defined in its own coordinate system, into an overall picture or design defined with respect to a master coordinate system.

4.2 GEOMETRIC TRANSFORMATIONS

Let us impose a coordinate system on a plane. An object *Obj* in the plane can be considered as a set of points. Every object point P has coordinates (x, y), and so the object is the sum total of all its coordinate points (Fig. 4-1). If the object is moved to a new position, it can be regarded as a new object *Obj'*, all of whose coordinate points P' can be obtained from the original points P by the application of a geometric transformation.

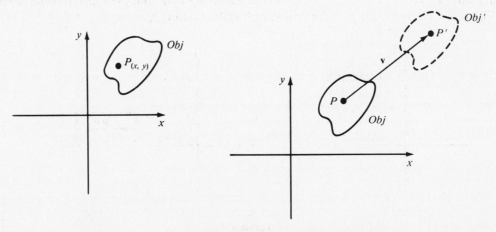

Fig. 4-1   Fig. 4-2

Translation

In *translation*, an object is displaced a given distance and direction from its original position. If the displacement is given by the vector $\mathbf{v} = t_x\mathbf{I} + t_y\mathbf{J}$, the new object point $P'(x', y')$ can be found by applying the transformation $T_\mathbf{v}$ to $P(x, y)$ (see Fig. 4-2).

$$P' = T_\mathbf{v}(P)$$

where $x' = x + t_x$ and $y' = y + t_y$.

Rotation about the Origin

In *rotation*, the object is rotated $\theta°$ about the origin. The convention is that the direction of rotation is counterclockwise if θ is a positive angle and clockwise if θ is a negative angle (see Fig. 4-3). The transformation of rotation R_θ is

$$P' = R_\theta(P)$$

where $x' = x \cos(\theta) - y \sin(\theta)$ and $y' = x \sin(\theta) + y \cos(\theta)$.

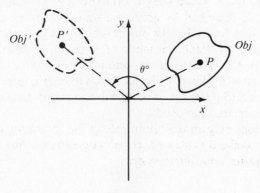

Fig. 4-3

Scaling with Respect to the Origin

Scaling is the process of expanding or compressing the dimensions of an object. Positive scaling constants s_x and s_y are used to describe changes in length with respect to the x direction and y direction, respectively. A scaling constant greater than one indicates an expansion of length, and less than one, compression of length. The scaling transformation S_{s_x,s_y} is given by $P' = S_{s_x,s_y}(P)$ where $x' = s_x \cdot x$ and $y' = s_y \cdot y$. Notice that after a scaling transformation is performed, the new object is located at a different position relative to the origin. In fact, in a scaling transformation the only point that remains fixed is the origin. Figure 4-4 shows scaling transformation with scaling factors $s_x = 2$ and $s_y = \frac{1}{2}$.

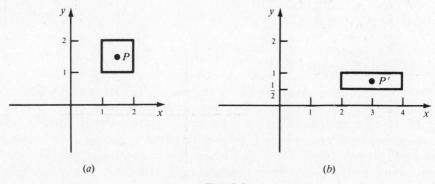

(a)　　　　　　　　　　　　　　　(b)

Fig. 4-4

If both scaling constants have the same value s, the scaling transformation is said to be *homogeneous*. Furthermore, if $s > 1$, it is a *magnification* and for $s < 1$, a *reduction*.

Mirror Reflection about an Axis

If either the x or y axis is treated as a mirror, the object has a mirror image or reflection. Since the reflection P' of an object point P is located the same distance from the mirror as P (Fig. 4-5), the mirror reflection transformation M_x about the x axis is given by

$$P' = M_x(P)$$

where $x' = x$ and $y' = -y$.

Similarly, the mirror reflection about the y axis is

$$P' = M_y(P)$$

where $x' = -x$ and $y' = y$.

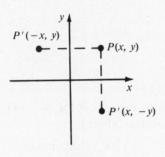

Fig. 4-5

Inverse Geometric Transformations

Each geometric transformation has an inverse (see App. 1) which is described by the opposite operation performed by the transformation.

Translation: $T_v^{-1} = T_{-v}$, or translation in the opposite direction

Rotation: $R_\theta^{-1} = R_{-\theta}$, or rotation in the opposite direction

Scaling: $S_{s_x,s_y}^{-1} = S_{1/s_x,1/s_y}$

Mirror reflection: $M_x^{-1} = M_x$ and $M_y^{-1} = M_y$

4.3 COORDINATE TRANSFORMATIONS

Suppose that we have two coordinate systems in the plane. The first system is located at origin O and has coordinate axes xy. The second coordinate system is located at origin O' and has coordinate axes $x'y'$ (Fig. 4-6). Now each point in the plane has two coordinate descriptions: (x, y) or (x', y'), depending on which coordinate system is used. If we think of the second system $x'y'$ as arising from a transformation applied to the first system xy, we say that a *coordinate transformation* has been applied. We can describe this transformation by determining how the (x', y') coordinates of a point P are related to the (x, y) coordinates of the same point.

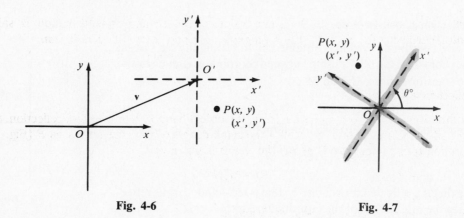

Fig. 4-6   Fig. 4-7

Translation

If the xy coordinate system is displaced to a new position, where the direction and distance of the displacement is given by the vector $\mathbf{v} = t_x\mathbf{I} + t_y\mathbf{J}$, the coordinates of a point in both systems are related by the translation transformation $\bar{T}_\mathbf{v}$:

$$(x', y') = \bar{T}_\mathbf{v}(x, y)$$

where $x' = x - t_x$ and $y' = y - t_y$.

Rotation about the Origin

The xy system is rotated $\theta°$ about the origin (see Fig. 4-7). Then the coordinates of a point in both systems are related by the rotation transformation $\bar{R}_\theta$:

$$(x', y') = \bar{R}_\theta(x, y)$$

where $x' = x \cos(\theta) + y \sin(\theta)$ and $y' = -x \sin(\theta) + y \cos(\theta)$.

Scaling with Respect to the Origin

Suppose that a new coordinate system is formed by leaving the origin and coordinate axes unchanged, but introducing different units of measurement along the x and y axes. If the new units are obtained from the old units by a scaling of s_x units along the x axis and s_y units along the y axis, the coordinates in the new system are related to coordinates in the old system through the scaling transformation $\bar{S}_{s_x,s_y}$:

$$(x', y') = \bar{S}_{s_x,x_y}(x, y)$$

where $x' = 1/s_x \cdot x$ and $y' = 1/s_y \cdot y$. Figure 4-8 shows coordinate scaling transformation using scaling factors $s_x = 2$ and $s_y = \frac{1}{2}$.

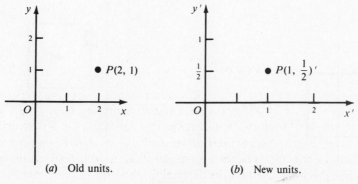

(a) Old units.   (b) New units.

Fig. 4-8

Mirror Reflection about an Axis

If the new coordinate system is obtained by reflecting the old system about either x or y axis, the relationship between coordinates is given by the coordinate transformations $\bar{M}_x$ and $\bar{M}_y$:

$$(x', y') = \bar{M}_x(x, y)$$

where $x' = x$ and $y' = -y$. For reflection about the y axis (Fig. 4-9)

$$(x', y') = \bar{M}_y(x, y)$$

where $x' = -x$ and $y' = y$.

Notice that the reflected coordinate system is left-handed; thus reflection changes the orientation of the coordinate system.

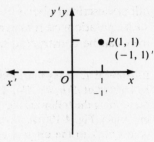

Fig. 4-9

Inverse Coordinate Transformations

Each coordinate transformation has an inverse (see App. 1) which can be found by applying the opposite transformation:

Translation: $\bar{T}_v^{-1} = \bar{T}_{-v}$, translation in the opposite direction

Rotation: $\bar{R}_\theta^{-1} = \bar{R}_{-\theta}$, rotation in the opposite direction

Scaling: $\bar{S}_{s_x, s_y}^{-1} = \bar{S}_{1/s_x, 1/s_y}$

Mirror reflection: $\bar{M}_x = \bar{M}_x$ and $\bar{M}_y = \bar{M}_y$

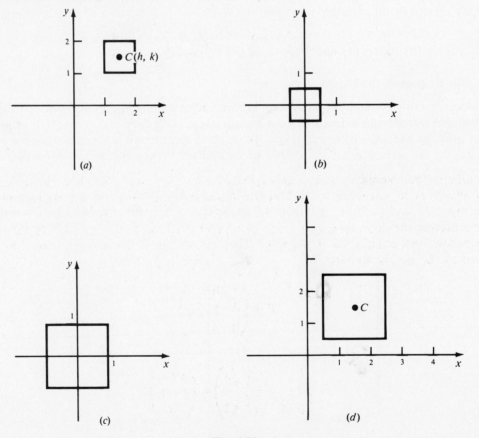

Fig. 4-10

4.4 COMPOSITE TRANSFORMATIONS

More complex geometric and coordinate transformations can be built from the basic transformations described above by using the process of *composition of functions* (see App. 1). For example, such operations as rotation about a point other than the origin or reflection about lines other than the axes can be constructed from the basic transformations.

EXAMPLE 1. Magnification of an object while keeping its center fixed (see Fig. 4-10). Let the geometric center be located at $C(h, k)$ [Fig. 4-10(a)]. Choosing a magnification factor $s > 1$, we construct the transformation by performing the following sequence of the transformations: (1) translate the object so that its center coincides with the origin [Fig. 4-10(b)], (2) scale the object with respect to the origin [Fig. 4-10(c)], and (3) translate the scaled object back to the original position [Fig. 4-10(d)].

The required transformation $S_{s,C}$ can be formed by composition $S_{s,C} = T_{\mathbf{v}}^{-1} \cdot S_{s,s} \cdot T_{\mathbf{v}}$ where $\mathbf{v} = -h\mathbf{I} - k\mathbf{J}$. By using composition, we can build more general scaling, rotation, and reflection transformations. For these transformations, we shall use the following notations: (1) $S_{s_x,s_y,P}$—scaling with respect to a fixed point P; (2) $R_{\theta,P}$—rotation about a point P; and (3) M_L—reflection about a line L.

The matrix descriptions of these transformations can be found in Probs. 4.4, 4.7, and 4.10.

Matrix Description of the Basic Transformations

The transformations of rotation, scaling, and reflection can be represented as matrix functions:

Geometric Transformations   **Coordinate Transformations**

$$R_\theta = \begin{pmatrix} \cos(\theta) & -\sin(\theta) \\ \sin(\theta) & \cos(\theta) \end{pmatrix} \qquad \bar{R}_\theta = \begin{pmatrix} \cos(\theta) & \sin(\theta) \\ -\sin(\theta) & \cos(\theta) \end{pmatrix}$$

Rotation (around the origin)

$$S_{s_x,s_y} = \begin{pmatrix} s_x & 0 \\ 0 & s_y \end{pmatrix} \qquad \bar{S}_{s_x,s_y} = \begin{pmatrix} \dfrac{1}{s_x} & 0 \\ 0 & \dfrac{1}{s_y} \end{pmatrix}$$

Scaling

$$M_x = \begin{pmatrix} 1 & 0 \\ 0 & -1 \end{pmatrix} \qquad \bar{M}_x = \begin{pmatrix} 1 & 0 \\ 0 & -1 \end{pmatrix}$$

x: Mirror Reflection

$$M_y = \begin{pmatrix} -1 & 0 \\ 1 & 1 \end{pmatrix} \qquad \bar{M}_y = \begin{pmatrix} -1 & 0 \\ 0 & 1 \end{pmatrix}$$

y: Mirror Reflection

The translation transformation cannot be expressed as a 2×2 matrix function. However, a certain artifice allows us to introduce a 3×3 matrix function which performs the translation transformation.

We represent the coordinate pair (x, y) of a point P by the triple $(x, y, 1)$. This is simply the homogeneous representation of P (App. 1). Then translation in the direction $\mathbf{v} = t_x\mathbf{I} + t_y\mathbf{J}$ can be expressed by the matrix function

$$T_{\mathbf{v}} = \begin{pmatrix} 1 & 0 & t_x \\ 0 & 1 & t_y \\ 0 & 0 & 1 \end{pmatrix}$$

Translation

Then

$$\begin{pmatrix} 1 & 0 & t_x \\ 0 & 1 & t_y \\ 0 & 0 & 1 \end{pmatrix} \begin{pmatrix} x \\ y \\ 1 \end{pmatrix} = \begin{pmatrix} x + t_x \\ y + t_y \\ 1 \end{pmatrix}$$

From this we extract the coordinate pair $(x + t_x, y + t_y)$.

Concatenation of Matrices

The advantage of introducing a matrix form for translation is that we can now build complex transformations by multiplying the basic matrix transformations. This process is sometimes called *concatenation of matrices*. Here, we are using the fact that the composition of matrix functions is equivalent to matrix multiplication (App. 1). We must be able to represent the basic transformations as 3×3 *homogeneous coordinate matrices* (App. 2) so as to be compatible (from the point of view of matrix multiplication) with the matrix of translation. This is accomplished by augmenting the 2×2 matrices with a third column $\begin{pmatrix} 0 \\ 0 \\ 1 \end{pmatrix}$ and a third row (0 0 1). That is

$$\begin{pmatrix} a & b & 0 \\ c & d & 0 \\ 0 & 0 & 1 \end{pmatrix}$$

EXAMPLE 2.   Express as a matrix the transformation which magnifies an object about its center $C(h, k)$. From Example 1, the required transformation $S_{s,C}$ can be written as

$$S_{s,C} = T_\mathbf{v}^{-1} \cdot S_{s,s} \cdot T_\mathbf{v}$$

$$= \begin{pmatrix} 1 & 0 & h \\ 0 & 1 & k \\ 0 & 0 & 1 \end{pmatrix} \begin{pmatrix} s & 0 & 0 \\ 0 & s & 0 \\ 0 & 0 & 1 \end{pmatrix} \begin{pmatrix} 1 & 0 & -h \\ 0 & 1 & -k \\ 0 & 0 & 1 \end{pmatrix} = \begin{pmatrix} s & 0 & -sh + h \\ 0 & s & -sk + k \\ 0 & 0 & 1 \end{pmatrix}$$

4.5   INSTANCE TRANSFORMATIONS

Quite often a picture or design is composed of many objects used several times each. In turn, these objects may also be composed of other symbols and objects. We suppose that each object is defined, independently of the picture, in its own *object coordinate space*. We wish to place these objects together to form the picture or at least part of the picture, called a *subpicture*. We can accomplish this by defining a transformation of coordinates, called an *instance transformation*, which converts object coordinates to picture coordinates so as to place or create an *instance* (image) of the object in the picture coordinate system.

The *instance transformation* $N_{\text{picture, object}}$ is formed as a composition or concatenation of scaling, rotation, and translation operations, usually performed in this order (although any order can be used):

$$N_{\text{picture, object}} = T_\mathbf{v} \cdot R_{\theta,P} \cdot S_{a,b,P}$$

With the use of different instance transformations, the same object can be placed in different positions, sizes, and orientations within a subpicture. For intance, Fig. 4-11(*a*) is placed in the picture coordinate system of Fig. 4-11(*b*) by using the instance transformations $N_{\text{picture, object}}$.

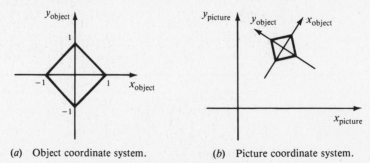

(*a*)   Object coordinate system.   (*b*)   Picture coordinate system.

Fig. 4-11

Nested Instances and Multilevel Structures

A subpicture or picture may exhibit a multilevel or nested structure by being composed of objects which are, in turn, composed of still other objects, and so on. Separate instance transformations must then be applied at each level of the picture structure for the subpicture display.

EXAMPLE 3. A picture of an apple tree contains branches, and an apple hangs on each branch. Suppose that each branch and apple is described in its own coordinate system [Figs. 4-12(a) and 4-12(b)]. Then a subpicture call to place an instance of this branch in the picture of the tree requires an additional subpicture call to place an instance of the apple into the branch coordinate system.

We can perform each instance transformation separately, that is, instance the apple in the branch coordinate system and then instance both branch and apple from the branch coordinate system to the picture coordinate system. However, it is much more efficient to transform the apple directly into picture coordinates. [See Fig. 4-12(c).] This is accomplished by defining the *current transformation matrix* $C_{\text{picture, object}}$ to be the composition of the nested instance transformations from apple coordinates to branch coordinates and then from branch coordinates to picture coordinates:

$$C_{\text{picture, apple}} = N_{\text{picture, branch}} \cdot N_{\text{branch, apple}}$$

Since the branch subpicture is only one level below the picture

$$C_{\text{picture, branch}} = N_{\text{picture, branch}}$$

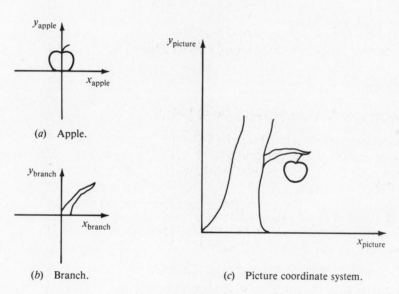

(a) Apple.

(b) Branch.

(c) Picture coordinate system.

Fig. 4-12

Solved Problems

4.1   Derive the transformation that rotates an object point $\theta°$ about the origin. Write the matrix representation for this rotation.

SOLUTION

Refer to Fig. 4-13. Definition of the trigonometric functions sin and cos yields

$$x' = r \cos (\theta + \phi) \qquad y' = r \sin (\theta + \phi)$$

and

$$x = r \cos \phi \qquad y = r \sin \phi$$

Using trigonometric identities, we obtain

$$r \cos (\theta + \phi) = r(\cos \theta \cos \phi - \sin \theta \sin \phi) = x \cos \theta - y \sin \theta$$

and

$$r \sin (\theta + \phi) = r(\sin \theta \cos \phi + \cos \theta \sin \phi) = x \sin \theta + y \cos \theta$$

or

$$x' = x \cos \theta - y \sin \theta \qquad y' = x \sin \theta + y \cos \theta$$

Writing $P' = \begin{pmatrix} x' \\ y' \end{pmatrix}$, $P = \begin{pmatrix} x \\ y \end{pmatrix}$, and

$$R_\theta = \begin{pmatrix} \cos \theta & -\sin \theta \\ \sin \theta & \cos \theta \end{pmatrix}$$

we can now write $P' = R_\theta \cdot P$.

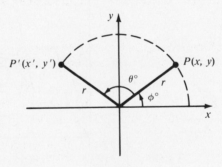

Fig. 4-13

4.2   (a)   Find the matrix that represents rotation of an object by $30°$ about the origin.

(b)   What are the new coordinates of the point $P(2, -4)$ after the rotation?

SOLUTION

(a)   From Prob. 4.1:

$$R_{30°} = \begin{pmatrix} \cos 30° & -\sin 30° \\ \sin 30° & \cos 30° \end{pmatrix} = \begin{pmatrix} \dfrac{\sqrt{3}}{2} & -\dfrac{1}{2} \\ \dfrac{1}{2} & \dfrac{\sqrt{3}}{2} \end{pmatrix}$$

(b)   So the new coordinates can be found by multiplying:

$$\begin{pmatrix} \dfrac{\sqrt{3}}{2} & -\dfrac{1}{2} \\ \dfrac{1}{2} & \dfrac{\sqrt{3}}{2} \end{pmatrix} \begin{pmatrix} 2 \\ -4 \end{pmatrix} = \begin{pmatrix} \sqrt{3} + 2 \\ 1 - 2\sqrt{3} \end{pmatrix}$$

4.3 Describe the transformation that rotates an object point, $Q(x, y)$, θ degrees about a fixed center of rotation $P(h, k)$ (Fig. 4-14).

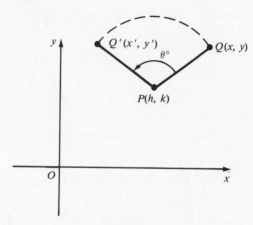

Fig. 4-14

SOLUTION

We determine the transformation $R_{\theta,P}$ in three steps: (1) translate so that the center of rotation P is at the origin, (2) perform a rotation of θ degrees about the origin, and (3) translate the origin back to P. Using $\mathbf{v} = -h\mathbf{I} - k\mathbf{J}$ as the translation vector, we build $R_{\theta,P}$ by composition of transformations:

$$R_{\theta,O'} = T_{-\mathbf{v}} \cdot R_{\theta} \cdot T_{\mathbf{v}}$$

4.4 Write the general form of the matrix for rotation about a point $P(h, k)$.

SOLUTION

Following Prob. 4.3, we write $R_{\theta,P} = T_{-\mathbf{v}} \cdot R_{\theta} \cdot T_{\mathbf{v}}$, where $\mathbf{v} = -h\mathbf{I} - k\mathbf{J}$. Using the 3×3 homogeneous coordinate form for the rotation and translation matrices, we have

$$R_{\theta,P} = \begin{pmatrix} 1 & 0 & h \\ 0 & 1 & k \\ 0 & 0 & 1 \end{pmatrix} \begin{pmatrix} \cos(\theta) & -\sin(\theta) & 0 \\ \sin(\theta) & \cos(\theta) & 0 \\ 0 & 0 & 1 \end{pmatrix} \begin{pmatrix} 1 & 0 & -h \\ 0 & 1 & -k \\ 0 & 0 & 1 \end{pmatrix}$$

$$= \begin{pmatrix} \cos(\theta) & -\sin(\theta) & [-h\cos(\theta) + k\sin(\theta) + h] \\ \sin(\theta) & \cos(\theta) & [-h\sin(\theta) - k\cos(\theta) + k] \\ 0 & 0 & 1 \end{pmatrix}$$

4.5 Perform a 45° rotation of triangle $A(0, 0)$, $B(1, 1)$, $C(5, 2)$ (*a*) about the origin and (*b*) about $P(-1, -1)$.

SOLUTION

We represent the triangle by a matrix formed from the homogeneous coordinates of the vertices:

$$\begin{matrix} & A & B & C \\ & \begin{pmatrix} 0 & 1 & 5 \\ 0 & 1 & 2 \\ 1 & 1 & 1 \end{pmatrix} \end{matrix}$$

(*a*) The matrix of rotation is

$$R_{45°} = \begin{pmatrix} \cos 45° & -\sin 45° & 0 \\ \sin 45° & \cos 45° & 0 \\ 0 & 0 & 1 \end{pmatrix} = \begin{pmatrix} \dfrac{\sqrt{2}}{2} & -\dfrac{\sqrt{2}}{2} & 0 \\ \dfrac{\sqrt{2}}{2} & \dfrac{\sqrt{2}}{2} & 0 \\ 0 & 0 & 1 \end{pmatrix}$$

So the coordinates $A'B'C'$ of the rotated triangle ABC can be found as

$$[A'B'C] = R_{45°} \cdot [ABC] = \begin{pmatrix} \frac{\sqrt{2}}{2} & -\frac{\sqrt{2}}{2} & 0 \\ \frac{\sqrt{2}}{2} & \frac{\sqrt{2}}{2} & 0 \\ 0 & 0 & 1 \end{pmatrix} \begin{pmatrix} 0 & 1 & 5 \\ 0 & 1 & 2 \\ 1 & 1 & 1 \end{pmatrix} = \begin{matrix} A' & B' & C' \\ \begin{pmatrix} 0 & 0 & \frac{3\sqrt{2}}{2} \\ 0 & 2 & \frac{7\sqrt{2}}{2} \\ 1 & 1 & 1 \end{pmatrix} \end{matrix}$$

Thus $A' = (0,0)$, $B' = (0,2)$, and $C' = (\frac{3}{2}\sqrt{2}, \frac{7}{2}\sqrt{2})$.

(b) From Prob. 4.4, the rotation matrix is given by $R_{45°,P} = T_{-v} \cdot R_{45°} \cdot T_v$, where $v = I + J$. So

$$R_{45°,P} = \begin{pmatrix} 1 & 0 & -1 \\ 0 & 1 & -1 \\ 0 & 0 & 1 \end{pmatrix} \begin{pmatrix} \frac{\sqrt{2}}{2} & -\frac{\sqrt{2}}{2} & 0 \\ \frac{\sqrt{2}}{2} & \frac{\sqrt{2}}{2} & 0 \\ 0 & 0 & 1 \end{pmatrix} \begin{pmatrix} 1 & 0 & 1 \\ 0 & 1 & 1 \\ 0 & 0 & 1 \end{pmatrix} = \begin{pmatrix} \frac{\sqrt{2}}{2} & -\frac{\sqrt{2}}{2} & -1 \\ \frac{\sqrt{2}}{2} & \frac{\sqrt{2}}{2} & (\sqrt{2}-1) \\ 0 & 0 & 1 \end{pmatrix}$$

Now

$$[A'B'C'] = R_{45°,P} \cdot [ABC]$$

$$= \begin{pmatrix} \frac{\sqrt{2}}{2} & -\frac{\sqrt{2}}{2} & -1 \\ \frac{\sqrt{2}}{2} & \frac{\sqrt{2}}{2} & (\sqrt{2}-1) \\ 0 & 0 & 1 \end{pmatrix} \begin{pmatrix} 0 & 1 & 5 \\ 0 & 1 & 2 \\ 1 & 1 & 1 \end{pmatrix} = \begin{pmatrix} -1 & -1 & (3\sqrt{2}-1) \\ (\sqrt{2}-1) & (2\sqrt{2}-1) & (\frac{9}{2}\sqrt{2}-1) \\ 1 & 1 & 1 \end{pmatrix}$$

So $A' = (-1, \sqrt{2}-1)$, $B' = (-1, 2\sqrt{2}-1)$, and $C' = (3\sqrt{2}-1, \frac{9}{2}\sqrt{2}-1)$.

4.6 Find the transformation that scales (with respect to the origin) by (a) a units in the X direction, (b) b units in the Y direction, and (c) simultaneously a units in the X direction and b units in the Y direction.

SOLUTION

(a) The scaling transformation applied to a point $P(x, y)$ produces the point (ax, y). We can write this in matrix form as $S_{a,1} \cdot P$, or

$$\begin{pmatrix} a & 0 \\ 0 & 1 \end{pmatrix} \begin{pmatrix} x \\ y \end{pmatrix} = \begin{pmatrix} ax \\ y \end{pmatrix}$$

(b) As in part (a), the required transformation can be written in matrix form as $S_{1,b} \cdot P$. So

$$\begin{pmatrix} 1 & 0 \\ 0 & b \end{pmatrix} \begin{pmatrix} x \\ y \end{pmatrix} = \begin{pmatrix} x \\ by \end{pmatrix}$$

(c) Scaling in both directions is described by the transformation $x' = ax$ and $y' = by$. Writing this in matrix form as $S_{a,b} \cdot P$, we have

$$\begin{pmatrix} a & 0 \\ 0 & b \end{pmatrix} \begin{pmatrix} x \\ y \end{pmatrix} = \begin{pmatrix} ax \\ by \end{pmatrix}$$

4.7 Write the general form of a scaling matrix with respect to a fixed point $P(h, k)$.

SOLUTION

Following the same general procedure as in Probs. 4.3 and 4.4, we write the required transformation with $\mathbf{v} = -h\mathbf{I} - k\mathbf{J}$ as

$$S_{a,b,P} = T_{-\mathbf{v}} \cdot S_{a,b} \cdot T_{\mathbf{v}}$$

$$= \begin{pmatrix} 1 & 0 & h \\ 0 & 1 & k \\ 0 & 0 & 1 \end{pmatrix} \begin{pmatrix} a & 0 & 0 \\ 0 & b & 0 \\ 0 & 0 & 1 \end{pmatrix} \begin{pmatrix} 1 & 0 & -h \\ 0 & 1 & -k \\ 0 & 0 & 1 \end{pmatrix}$$

$$= \begin{pmatrix} a & 0 & -ah + h \\ 0 & b & -bk + k \\ 0 & 0 & 1 \end{pmatrix}$$

4.8 Magnify the triangle with vertices $A(0, 0)$, $B(1, 1)$, and $C(5, 2)$ to twice its size while keeping $C(5, 2)$ fixed.

SOLUTION

From Prob. 4.7, we can write the required transformation with $\mathbf{v} = -5\mathbf{I} - 2\mathbf{J}$ as

$$S_{2,2,C} = T_{-\mathbf{v}} \cdot S_{2,2} \cdot T_{\mathbf{v}}$$

$$= \begin{pmatrix} 1 & 0 & 5 \\ 0 & 1 & 2 \\ 0 & 0 & 1 \end{pmatrix} \begin{pmatrix} 2 & 0 & 0 \\ 0 & 2 & 0 \\ 0 & 0 & 1 \end{pmatrix} \begin{pmatrix} 1 & 0 & -5 \\ 0 & 1 & -2 \\ 0 & 0 & 1 \end{pmatrix} = \begin{pmatrix} 2 & 0 & -5 \\ 0 & 2 & -2 \\ 0 & 0 & 1 \end{pmatrix}$$

Representing a point P with coordinates (x, y) by the column vector $\begin{pmatrix} x \\ y \\ 1 \end{pmatrix}$, we have

$$S_{2,2,C} \cdot A = \begin{pmatrix} 2 & 0 & -5 \\ 0 & 2 & -2 \\ 0 & 0 & 1 \end{pmatrix} \begin{pmatrix} 0 \\ 0 \\ 1 \end{pmatrix} = \begin{pmatrix} -5 \\ -2 \\ 1 \end{pmatrix}$$

$$S_{2,2,C} \cdot B = \begin{pmatrix} 2 & 0 & -5 \\ 0 & 2 & -2 \\ 0 & 0 & 1 \end{pmatrix} \begin{pmatrix} 1 \\ 1 \\ 1 \end{pmatrix} = \begin{pmatrix} -3 \\ 0 \\ 1 \end{pmatrix}$$

$$S_{2,2,C} \cdot C = \begin{pmatrix} 2 & 0 & -5 \\ 0 & 2 & -2 \\ 0 & 0 & 1 \end{pmatrix} \begin{pmatrix} 5 \\ 2 \\ 1 \end{pmatrix} = \begin{pmatrix} 5 \\ 2 \\ 1 \end{pmatrix}$$

So $A' = (-5, -2)$, $B' = (-3, 0)$, and $C' = (5, 2)$. Note that since the triangle ABC is completely determined by its vertices, we could have saved much writing by representing the vertices using a 3×3 matrix

$$[ABC] = \begin{pmatrix} 0 & 1 & 5 \\ 0 & 1 & 2 \\ 1 & 1 & 1 \end{pmatrix}$$

and applying $S_{2,2,C}$ to this. So

$$S_{2,2,C} \cdot [ABC] = \begin{pmatrix} 2 & 0 & -5 \\ 0 & 2 & -2 \\ 0 & 0 & 1 \end{pmatrix} \begin{pmatrix} 0 & 1 & 5 \\ 0 & 1 & 2 \\ 1 & 1 & 1 \end{pmatrix} = \begin{pmatrix} -5 & -3 & 5 \\ -2 & 0 & 2 \\ 1 & 1 & 1 \end{pmatrix} = [A'B'C']$$

4.9   Describe the transformation M_L which reflects an object about a line L.

SOLUTION

Let line L in Fig. 4-15 have a y intercept $(0, b)$ and an angle of inclination θ degrees (with respect to the x axis). We reduce the description to known transformations:

1. Translate $(0, b)$ to the origin.
2. Rotate by $-\theta$ degrees so that line L aligns with the x axis.
3. Mirror-reflect about the x axis.
4. Rotate back by θ degrees.
5. Translate the origin back to the point $(0, b)$.

In transformation notation, we have

$$M_L = T_{-\mathbf{v}} \cdot R_\theta \cdot M_x \cdot R_{-\theta} \cdot T_{\mathbf{v}}$$

where $\mathbf{v} = -b\mathbf{J}$.

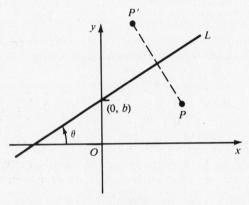

Fig. 4-15

4.10   Find the form of the matrix for reflection about a line L with slope m and y intercept $(0, b)$.

SOLUTION

Following Prob. 4.9 and applying the fact that the angle of inclination of a line is related to its slope m by the equation $\tan(\theta) = m$, we have with $\mathbf{v} = -b\mathbf{J}$,

$$M_L = T_{-\mathbf{v}} \cdot R_\theta \cdot M_x \cdot R_{-\theta} \cdot T_{\mathbf{v}},$$

$$= \begin{pmatrix} 1 & 0 & 0 \\ 0 & 1 & b \\ 0 & 0 & 1 \end{pmatrix} \begin{pmatrix} \cos(\theta) & -\sin(\theta) & 0 \\ \sin(\theta) & \cos(\theta) & 0 \\ 0 & 0 & 1 \end{pmatrix} \begin{pmatrix} 1 & 0 & 0 \\ 0 & -1 & 0 \\ 0 & 0 & 1 \end{pmatrix} \cdot \begin{pmatrix} \cos(\theta) & \sin(\theta) & 0 \\ -\sin(\theta) & \cos(\theta) & 0 \\ 0 & 0 & 1 \end{pmatrix} \begin{pmatrix} 1 & 0 & 0 \\ 0 & 1 & -b \\ 0 & 0 & 1 \end{pmatrix}$$

Now if $\tan(\theta) = m$, standard trigonometry yields $\sin(\theta) = m/\sqrt{m^2 + 1}$ and $\cos(\theta) = 1/\sqrt{m^2 + 1}$. Substituting these values for $\sin(\theta)$ and $\cos(\theta)$ after matrix multiplication, we have

$$M_L = \begin{pmatrix} \dfrac{1 - m^2}{m^2 + 1} & \dfrac{2m}{m^2 + 1} & \dfrac{-2bm}{m^2 + 1} \\ \dfrac{2m}{m^2 + 1} & \dfrac{m^2 - 1}{m^2 + 1} & \dfrac{2b}{m^2 + 1} \\ 0 & 0 & 1 \end{pmatrix}$$

4.11　Reflect the diamond-shaped polygon whose vertices are $A(-1, 0)$, $B(0, -2)$, $C(1, 0)$, and $D(0, 2)$ about (a) the horizontal line $y = 2$, (b) the vertical line $x = 2$, and (c) the line $y = x + 2$.

SOLUTION

We represent the vertices of the polygon by the homogeneous coordinate matrix

$$V = \begin{pmatrix} -1 & 0 & 1 & 0 \\ 0 & -2 & 0 & 2 \\ 1 & 1 & 1 & 1 \end{pmatrix}$$

From Prob. 4.9, the reflection matrix can be written as

$$M_L = T_{-v} \cdot R_\theta \cdot M_x \cdot R_{-\theta} \cdot T_v$$

(a)　The line $y = 2$ has y intercept $(0, 2)$ and makes an angle of 0 degrees with the x axis. So with $\theta = 0$ and $v = -2J$, the transformation matrix is

$$M_L = \begin{pmatrix} 1 & 0 & 0 \\ 0 & 1 & 2 \\ 0 & 0 & 1 \end{pmatrix} \begin{pmatrix} 1 & 0 & 0 \\ 0 & 1 & 0 \\ 0 & 0 & 1 \end{pmatrix} \begin{pmatrix} 1 & 0 & 0 \\ 0 & -1 & 0 \\ 0 & 0 & 1 \end{pmatrix} \begin{pmatrix} 1 & 0 & 0 \\ 0 & 1 & 0 \\ 0 & 0 & 1 \end{pmatrix} \begin{pmatrix} 1 & 0 & 0 \\ 0 & 1 & -2 \\ 0 & 0 & 1 \end{pmatrix} = \begin{pmatrix} 1 & 0 & 0 \\ 0 & -1 & 4 \\ 0 & 0 & 1 \end{pmatrix}$$

This same matrix could have been obtained directly by using the results of Prob. 4.10 with slope $m = 0$ and y intercept $b = 0$. To reflect the polygon, we set

$$M_L \cdot V = \begin{pmatrix} 1 & 0 & 0 \\ 0 & -1 & 4 \\ 0 & 0 & 1 \end{pmatrix} \begin{pmatrix} -1 & 0 & 1 & 0 \\ 0 & -2 & 0 & 2 \\ 1 & 1 & 1 & 1 \end{pmatrix} = \begin{array}{cccc} A' & B' & C' & D' \\ \begin{pmatrix} -1 & 0 & 1 & 0 \\ 4 & 6 & 4 & 2 \\ 1 & 1 & 1 & 1 \end{pmatrix} \end{array}$$

Converting from homogeneous coordinates, $A' = (-1, 4)$, $B' = (0, 6)$, $C' = (1, 4)$, and $D' = (0, 2)$.

(b)　The vertical line $x = 2$ has no y intercept and an infinite slope! We can use M_y, reflection about the y axis, to write the desired reflection by (1) translating the given line two units over to the y axis, (2) reflect about the y axis, and (3) translate back two units. So with $v = -2I$,

$$M_L = T_{-v} \cdot M_y \cdot T_v,$$

$$= \begin{pmatrix} 1 & 0 & 2 \\ 0 & 1 & 0 \\ 0 & 0 & 1 \end{pmatrix} \begin{pmatrix} -1 & 0 & 0 \\ 0 & 1 & 0 \\ 0 & 0 & 1 \end{pmatrix} \begin{pmatrix} 1 & 0 & -2 \\ 0 & 1 & 0 \\ 0 & 0 & 1 \end{pmatrix} = \begin{pmatrix} -1 & 0 & 4 \\ 0 & 1 & 0 \\ 0 & 0 & 1 \end{pmatrix}$$

Finally

$$M_L \cdot V = \begin{pmatrix} -1 & 0 & 4 \\ 0 & 1 & 0 \\ 0 & 0 & 1 \end{pmatrix} \begin{pmatrix} -1 & 0 & 1 & 0 \\ 0 & -2 & 0 & 2 \\ 1 & 1 & 1 & 1 \end{pmatrix} = \begin{pmatrix} 5 & 4 & 3 & 4 \\ 0 & -2 & 0 & 2 \\ 1 & 1 & 1 & 1 \end{pmatrix}$$

or $A' = (5, 0)$, $B' = (4, -2)$, $C' = (3, 0)$, and $D' = (4, 2)$.

(c)　The line $y = x + 2$ has slope 1 and a y intercept $(0, 2)$. From Prob. 4.10, with $m = 1$ and $b = 2$, we find

$$M_L = \begin{pmatrix} 0 & 1 & -2 \\ 1 & 0 & 2 \\ 0 & 0 & 1 \end{pmatrix}$$

The required coordinates A', B', C', and D' can now be found.

$$M_L \cdot V = \begin{pmatrix} 0 & 1 & -2 \\ 1 & 0 & 2 \\ 0 & 0 & 1 \end{pmatrix} \begin{pmatrix} -1 & 0 & 1 & 0 \\ 0 & -2 & 0 & 2 \\ 1 & 1 & 1 & 1 \end{pmatrix} = \begin{pmatrix} -2 & -4 & -2 & 0 \\ 1 & 2 & 3 & 2 \\ 1 & 1 & 1 & 1 \end{pmatrix}$$

So $A' = (-2, 1)$, $B' = (-4, 2)$, $C' = (-2, 3)$, and $D' = (0, 2)$.

4.12 The matrix $\begin{pmatrix} 1 & a \\ b & 1 \end{pmatrix}$ defines a transformation called a *shearing*. The special case when $b = 0$ is called *shearing in the x direction*. When $a = 0$, we have *shearing in the y direction*. Illustrate the effect of these shearing transformations on the square $A(0,0)$, $B(1,0)$, $C(1,1)$, and $D(0,1)$ when $a = 2$ and $b = 3$.

SOLUTION

Figure 4-16(a) shows the original square, Fig. 4-16(b) shows shearing in the x direction, Fig. 4-16(c) shows shearing in the y direction, and Fig. 4-16(d) shows shearing in both directions.

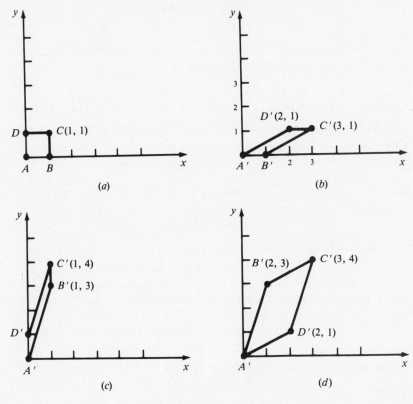

Fig. 4-16

4.13 An observer standing at the origin sees a point $P(1, 1)$. If the point is translated one unit in the direction $\mathbf{v} = \mathbf{I}$, its new coordinate position is $P'(2, 1)$. Suppose instead that the observer stepped back one unit along the x axis. What would be the apparent coordinates of P with respect to the observer?

SOLUTION

The problem can be set up as a transformation of coordinate systems. If we translate the origin O in the direction $\mathbf{v} = -\mathbf{I}$ (to a new position at O') the coordinates of P in this system can be found by the translation $\bar{T}_{\mathbf{v}}$:

$$\bar{T}_{\mathbf{v}} \cdot P = \begin{pmatrix} 1 & 0 & 1 \\ 0 & 1 & 0 \\ 0 & 0 & 1 \end{pmatrix} \begin{pmatrix} 1 \\ 1 \\ 1 \end{pmatrix} = \begin{pmatrix} 2 \\ 1 \\ 1 \end{pmatrix}$$

So the new coordinates are $(2, 1)'$. This has the following interpretation: a displacement of one unit in a given direction can be achieved by either moving the object forward or stepping back from it.

4.14 An object is defined with respect to a coordinate system whose units are measured in feet. If an observer's coordinate system uses inches as the basic unit, what is the coordinate transformation used to describe object coordinates in the observer's coordinate system?

SOLUTION

Since there are 12 in to a foot, the required transformation can be described by a coordinate scaling transformation with $s = \frac{1}{12}$ or

$$\bar{S}_{1/12} = \begin{pmatrix} \dfrac{1}{1/12} & 0 \\ 0 & \dfrac{1}{1/12} \end{pmatrix} = \begin{pmatrix} 12 & 0 \\ 0 & 12 \end{pmatrix}$$

and so

$$\bar{S}_{1/12} \cdot \begin{pmatrix} x \\ y \end{pmatrix} = \begin{pmatrix} 12 & 0 \\ 0 & 12 \end{pmatrix} \begin{pmatrix} x \\ y \end{pmatrix} = \begin{pmatrix} 12x \\ 12y \end{pmatrix}$$

4.15 Find the equation of the circle $(x')^2 + (y')^2 = 1$ in terms of xy coordinates, assuming that the $x'y'$ coordinate system results from a scaling of a units in the x direction and b units in the y direction.

SOLUTION

From the equations for a coordinate scaling transformation (see pp. 83 and 85), we find

$$x' = \frac{1}{a} \cdot x \qquad y' = \frac{1}{a} \cdot y$$

Substituting, we have

$$\left(\frac{x}{a}\right)^2 + \left(\frac{y}{b}\right)^2 = 1$$

Notice that as a result of scaling, the equation of the circle is transformed to the equation of an ellipse in the xy coordinate system.

4.16 Find the equation of the line $y' = mx' + b$ in xy coordinates if the $x'y'$ coordinate system results from a 90° rotation of the xy coordinate system.

SOLUTION

The rotation coordinate transformation equations can be written as

$$x' = x \cos(90°) + y \sin(90°) = y \qquad y' = -x \sin(90°) + y \cos(90°) = -x$$

Substituting, we find $-x = my + b$. Solving for y, we have $y = (-1/m)x - b/m$.

4.17 Find the instance transformation which places a half-size copy of the square $A(0, 0), B(1, 0), C(1, 1), D(0, 1)$ [Fig. 4-17(a)] into a master picture coordinate system so that the center of the square is at $(-1, -1)$ [Fig. 4-17(b)].

SOLUTION

The center of the square $ABCD$ is at $P(\frac{1}{2}, \frac{1}{2})$. We shall first apply a scaling transformation while keeping P fixed (see Prob. 4.7). Then we shall apply a translation that moves the center P to P' $(-1, -1)$. Taking $t_x = (-1) - (\frac{1}{2}) = -\frac{3}{2}$ and similarly $t_y = -\frac{3}{2}$ (so $\mathbf{v} = -\frac{3}{2}\mathbf{I} + -\frac{3}{2}\mathbf{J}$), we obtain

$$N_{\text{picture, square}} = T_{\mathbf{v}} \cdot S_{1/2,1/2,P} = \begin{pmatrix} 1 & 0 & -\frac{3}{2} \\ 0 & 1 & -\frac{3}{2} \\ 0 & 0 & 1 \end{pmatrix} \begin{pmatrix} \frac{1}{2} & 0 & \frac{1}{4} \\ 0 & \frac{1}{2} & \frac{1}{4} \\ 0 & 0 & 1 \end{pmatrix} = \begin{pmatrix} \frac{1}{2} & 0 & -\frac{5}{4} \\ 0 & \frac{1}{2} & -\frac{5}{4} \\ 0 & 0 & 1 \end{pmatrix}$$

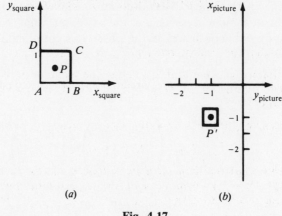

Fig. 4-17

4.18 Write the current transformation that creates the design in Fig. 4-19 from the symbols in Fig. 4-18.

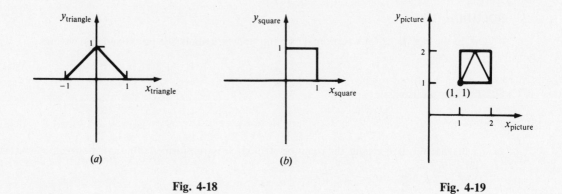

Fig. 4-18   Fig. 4-19

SOLUTION

First we create an instance of the triangle [Fig. 4-18(a)] in the square [Fig. 4-18(b)]. Since the base of the triangle must be halved while keeping the height fixed at one unit, the appropriate instance transformation is the scaling $N_{\text{square, triangle}} = S_{1/2,1}$.

The instance transformation needed to place the square at the desired position in the picture coordinate system (Fig. 4-19) is a translation in the direction $\mathbf{v} = \mathbf{I} + \mathbf{J}$.

$$N_{\text{picture, square}} = T_{\mathbf{v}}$$

Then the current transformation for placing the triangle into the picture is

$$C_{\text{picture, triangle}} = N_{\text{picture, square}} \cdot N_{\text{square, triangle}}$$

and the current transformation to place the square into the picture is

$$C_{\text{picture, square}} = N_{\text{picture, square}}$$

Supplementary Problems

4.19　What is the relationship between the rotations R_θ, $R_{-\theta}$, and R_θ^{-1}?

4.20　Describe the transformations used in magnification and reduction with respect to the origin. Find the new coordinates of the triangle $A(0, 0)$, $B(1, 1)$, $C(5, 2)$ after it has been (a) magnified to twice its size and (b) reduced to half its size.

4.21　Show that reflection about the line $y = x$ is attained by reversing coordinates. That is,

$$M_L(x, y) = (y, x)$$

4.22　Show that the order in which transformations are performed is important by the transformation of triangle $A(1, 0)$, $B(0, 1)$, $C(1, 1)$, by (a) rotating 45° about the origin and then translating in the direction of vector **I**, and (b) translating and then rotating.

4.23　An object point $P(x, y)$ is translated in the direction $\mathbf{v} = a\mathbf{I} + b\mathbf{J}$ and simultaneously an observer moves in the direction **v**. Show that there is no apparent motion (from the point of view of the observer) of the object point.

4.24　Find the form of a mathematical equation defining a curve in $x'y'$ coordinates after it is transformed to xy coordinates.

Chapter 5

Two-Dimensional Viewing Transformations and Clipping

5.1 INTRODUCTION

Displaying an image of a picture involves mapping the coordinates of the points and lines that form the picture into the appropriate coordinates on the device or workstation where the image is to be displayed. This is done through the use of coordinate transformations known as *viewing transformations*. We use the following names for the various coordinate systems:

The *world coordinate system* (WCS) is the right-handed Cartesian coordinate system in whose coordinates we describe the picture that is to be displayed. The *physical device coordinate system* (PDCS) is the coordinate system that corresponds to the device or workstation where the image of the picture or model is to be displayed.

Since there is such a wide variety of display devices (see Chap. 2), each with its own physical coordinate system, it is convenient to introduce a logical or virtual display surface with a standardized coordinate system.

The *normalized device coordinate system* (NDCS) is a right-handed coordinate system in which the display area of the virtual display device corresponds to the unit (1×1) square whose lower left-hand corner is at the origin of the coordinate system.

5.2 VIEWING TRANSFORMATIONS

The viewing transformation which maps picture coordinates in the WCS to display coordinates in the PDCS is formed by the following transformations: *normalization transformation* (N) maps world coordinates to normalized device coordinates, and *workstation transformation* (W) maps normalized device coordinates to physical device coordinates. The *viewing transformation* (V) is given as $V = W \cdot N$.

Windows and Viewports

In calculating these transformations, we are faced with the problem that the WCS is theoretically infinite in extent (actually, it is limited by the floating-point range of the computer being used), while the device display area is finite. To perform a viewing transformation, we deal with a finite region in the WCS called a *window*. The window can be mapped directly onto the display area of the device or onto a subregion of the display called a *viewport*. (Note that viewport defines the physical location of the display area within the physical raster. By contrast, window assigns the scale for objects appearing within the viewport.) The normalization transformation maps a window described in world coordinate (WC) space to a viewport in normalized device coordinate (NDC) space.

For windows and viewports represented by rectangular regions whose sides are aligned with the x and y axes, the required transformations can be written as matrices (see Fig. 5-1):

$$N \ \text{(or } W) = \begin{pmatrix} s_x & 0 & (-s_x \cdot xw_{min} + xv_{min}) \\ 0 & s_y & (-s_y \cdot yw_{min} + yv_{min}) \\ 0 & 0 & 1 \end{pmatrix}$$

where
$$s_x = \frac{xv_{max} - xv_{min}}{xw_{max} - xw_{min}} \quad \text{and} \quad s_y = \frac{yv_{max} - yv_{min}}{yw_{max} - yw_{min}}$$

and xv, yv refer to viewport coordinates and xw, yw refer to window coordinates.

98

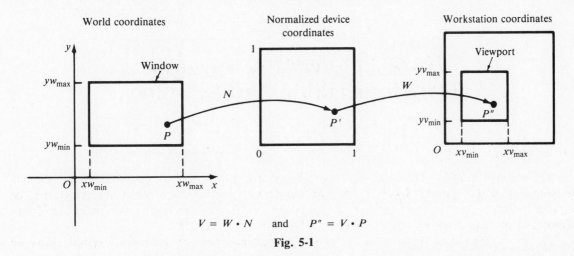

$$V = W \cdot N \quad \text{and} \quad P'' = V \cdot P$$

Fig. 5-1

By using the appropriate coordinate transformations, we can create viewing transformations for rotated rectangular windows and even nonrectangular windows and viewports (see Prob. 5.5).

Aspect Ratio

Since the viewing transformation involves scaling, undesirable distortions may be introduced whenever $s_x \neq s_y$. For example, circles within the window may be displayed as ellipses and squares as rectangles. In considering how these distortions may be avoided, the concept of *aspect ratio* is needed.

The *aspect ratio* of a rectangular window or viewport is defined by

$$a = \frac{x_{max} - x_{min}}{y_{max} - y_{min}}$$

If the aspect ratio a_w of the window equals the aspect ratio a_v of the viewport, then $s_x = s_y$, and no distortion (other than uniform magnification or compression) occurs. If $a_w \neq a_v$, then distortion occurs. If desired, in this case we can describe a region within the viewport, a *subviewport*, whose aspect ratio is that of the window. We can then redefine the viewing transformation so that the window is transformed onto the subviewport (see Fig. 5-2).

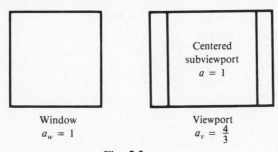

Window
$a_w = 1$

Centered
subviewport
$a = 1$

Viewport
$a_v = \frac{4}{3}$

Fig. 5-2

5.3 CLIPPING AND SHIELDING

Quite often we wish to display only a portion of the total picture (see Fig. 5-3).

In this case a window is used to select that portion of the picture which is to be viewed (much like clipping or cutting out a picture from a magazine). This is known as *clipping*. The process of clipping determines which elements of the picture lie inside the window and so are visible (i.e., displayed). The reverse of clipping is *shielding*—covering up a portion of the picture so that it is not visible.

The algorithm selected for clipping depends on the geometric shape of the clipping window.

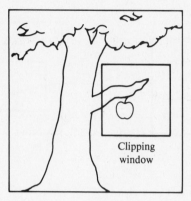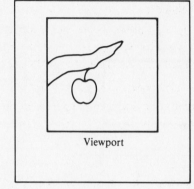

Fig. 5-3

Rectangular Clipping Windows

We shall assume that our window is a rectangle whose sides are aligned with the coordinate axes. The *x extent* is measured from x_{min} to x_{max}, and the *y extent* is measured from y_{min} to y_{max}.

Point Clipping

A point $P(x, y)$ is inside the window (visible) if *all* the following inequalities are true:

$$x \leq x_{max} \qquad y \leq y_{max}$$
$$x \geq x_{min} \qquad y \geq y_{min}$$

If any of these inequalities is false, point P is outside the window and is not displayed.

Any object can be considered as the totality of its points and so clipped accordingly. However, this disregards the inherent structure of objects such as lines and polygons for which more efficient algorithms can be developed.

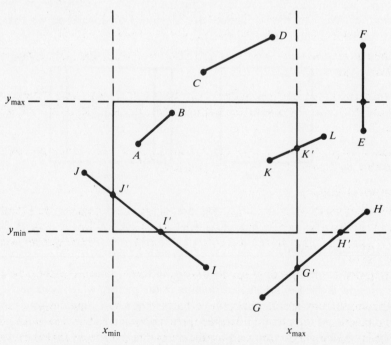

Fig. 5-4

Line Segment Clipping

We divide the line clipping process into two phases: (1) identify those lines which intersect the window and so need to be clipped and (2) perform the clipping.

All line segments fall into one of the following *clipping categories*:

1. *Visible*—both endpoints of the line segment lie within the window.
2. *Not visible*—the line segment definitely lies outside the window. This will occur if the line segment from (x_1, y_1) to (x_2, y_2) satisfies any one of the following four inequalities:

$$x_1, x_2 > x_{max} \qquad y_1, y_2 > y_{max}$$
$$x_1, x_2 < x_{min} \qquad y_1, y_2 < y_{min}$$

3. *Clipping candidate*—the line is in neither category 1 nor 2.

In Fig. 5-4, line segment AB is in category 1 (visible); line segments CD and EF are in category 2 (not visible); and line segments GH, IJ, and KL are in category 3 (clipping candidate).

The Cohen-Sutherland algorithm provides an efficient procedure for finding the category of a line segment. The algorithm proceeds in two steps:

1. Assign a 4-bit code to each endpoint of the line segment. The code is determined according to which of the following nine regions of the plane the endpoint lies in

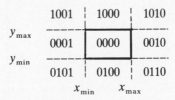

Starting from the leftmost bit, each bit of the code is set to true (1) or false (0) according to the scheme

Bit 1 ≡ endpoint is above the window = sign $(y - y_{max})$
Bit 2 ≡ endpoint is below the window = sign $(y_{min} - y)$
Bit 3 ≡ endpoint is to the right of the window = sign $(x - x_{max})$
Bit 4 ≡ endpoint is to the left of the window = sign $(x_{min} - x)$

We use the convention that sign $a = 1$ if a is positive, 0 otherwise. Of course, a point with code 0000 is inside the window.

2. The line segment is visible if both endpoint codes are 0000, not visible if the logical AND of the codes is not 0000, and a candidate for clipping if the logical AND of the endpoint codes is 0000. (See Prob. 5.8.)

We now decide whether the lines in category 3 either intersect the window and so are to be clipped or don't intersect the window and so are not displayed.

Line Intersections and Clipping

We determine the intersection points of the lines in category 3 (clipping candidate) with the boundaries of the window. These intersection points then subdivide the line segment into several smaller line segments which can belong only to category 1 (visible) or category 2 (not visible). The segment in category 1 will be the clipped line segment.

The intersection points are found by solving the equations representing the line segment and the boundary lines.

For rectangular windows whose sides are parallel to the coordinate axes, we need not check the given line segment for intersections with every one of the four boundary lines. The Cohen-Sutherland algorithm finds the appropriate boundary line(s) to check by observing that those boundary lines that are candidates for intersection are the ones for which the endpoints of the given line segment must be "pushed across" so as to change the 1s in the endpoint code to 0s. Thus (see Fig. 5-5)

If bit 1 is 1, intersect with line $y = y_{max}$.

If bit 2 is 1, intersect with line $y = y_{min}$.

If bit 3 is 1, intersect with line $x = x_{max}$.

If bit 4 is 1, intersect with line $x = x_{min}$.

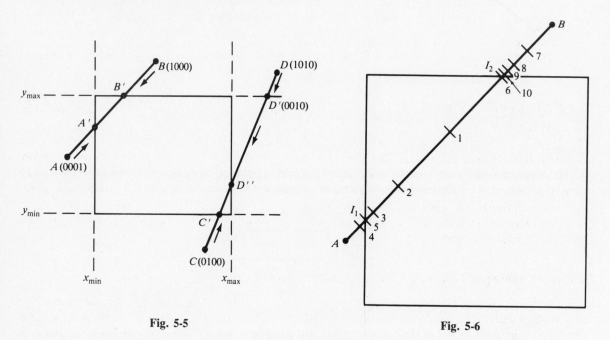

Fig. 5-5   Fig. 5-6

Midpoint Subdivision

An alternative to finding intersection points by equation solving is based on the bisection method of numerical analysis. The line segment is divided at its midpoint into two smaller line segments. The clipping categories of the two new line segments are then determined. Each segment in category 3 is divided again into smaller segments and categorized. The bisection and categorization process continues until all segments are in category 1 (visible) or category 2 (invisible). The midpoint coordinates (x_m, y_m) of a line segment joining $P_1(x_1, y_1)$ to $P_2(x_2, y_2)$ are given by

$$x_m = \frac{x_1 + x_2}{2} \qquad y_m = \frac{y_1 + y_2}{2}$$

In Fig. 5-6, 10 bisections determine the intersections I_1 and I_2.

If clipping is done against a viewport in physical device coordinates, the midpoint subdivision process proceeds until the line segments become smaller than the precision of the display. If the maximum number of pixels in a line is M, the bisection method will yield a pixel-sized line segment in N subdivisions, where $2^N = M$ or $N = \log_2 M$. For example, a 512×512 raster display needs at most $N = \log_2 512 = 9$ subdivisions.

Convex Polygonal Clipping Windows

A polygon is called *convex* if the line joining any two interior points of the polygon lies completely inside the polygon (see Fig. 5-7).

By convention, a polygon with vertices $P_1, \ldots, P_N$ (and edges $P_{i-1}P_i$ and $P_N P_1$) is said to be *positively oriented* if a tour of the vertices in the given order produces a counterclockwise circuit.

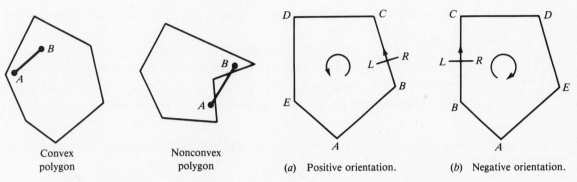

Fig. 5-7   Fig. 5-8

Equivalently, the left hand of a person standing along any directed edge $\overline{P_{i-1}P_i}$ or $\overline{P_N P_1}$ would be pointing inside the polygon [see orientations in Figs. 5-8(a) and 5-8(b)].

Let $A(x_1, y_1)$ and $B(x_2, y_2)$ be the endpoints of a directed line segment. A point $P(x, y)$ will be to the *left* of the line segment if the expression $C = (x_2 - x_1)(y - y_1) - (y_2 - y_1)(x - x_1)$ is positive (see Prob. 5.12). We say that the point is to the *right* of the line segment if this quantity is negative. If a point P is to the right of any one edge of a positively oriented, convex polygon, it is outside the polygon. If it is to the left of *every* edge of the polygon, it is inside the polygon.

This observation forms the basis for clipping any polygon, convex or nonconvex, against a convex polygonal clipping window.

Polygon Clipping and the Sutherland-Hodgman Algorithm

Let $P_1, \ldots, P_N$ be the vertex list of the polygon to be clipped. Let edge E, determined by endpoints A and B, be any edge of the positively oriented, convex clipping polygon. We clip each edge of the polygon in turn against the edge E of the clipping polygon, forming a new polygon whose vertices are determined as follows.

Consider the edge $\overline{P_{i-1}P_i}$:

1. If both P_{i-1} and P_i are to the left of the edge, vertex P_i is placed on the *vertex output list* of the clipped polygon [Fig. 5-9(a)].

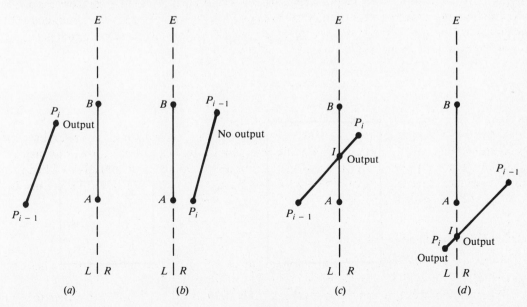

Fig. 5-9

2. If both P_{i-1} and P_i are to the right of the edge, nothing is placed on the vertex output list [Fig. 5-9(b)].

3. If P_{i-1} is to the left and P_i is to the right of the edge E, the intersection point I of line segment $\overline{P_{i-1}P_i}$ with the extended edge E is calculated and placed on the vertex output list [Fig. 5-9(c)].

4. If P_{i-1} is to the right and P_i is to the left of edge E, the intersection point I of the line segment $\overline{P_{i-1}P_i}$ with the extended edge E is calculated. Both I and P_i are placed on the vertex output list [Fig. 5-9(d)].

The algorithm proceeds in stages by passing each clipped polygon to the next edge of the window and clipping. See Probs. 5.13 and 5.14.

Solved Problems

5.1 Find the general form of the transformation N which maps a rectangular window with x extent xw_{min} to xw_{max} in the x direction and y extent yw_{min} to yw_{max} in the y direction onto a rectangular viewport with x extent xv_{min} to xv_{max} and y extent yv_{min} to yv_{max} (see Fig. 5-10).

SOLUTION

We form N by composing (1) a translation taking (xw_{min}, yw_{min}) to (xv_{min}, yv_{min}) and (2) a scaling about the point $L(xv_{min}, yv_{min})$ with

$$s_x = \frac{\text{viewport } x \text{ extent}}{\text{window } x \text{ extent}} = \frac{xv_{max} - xv_{min}}{xw_{max} - xw_{min}} \quad \text{and} \quad s_y = \frac{\text{viewport } y \text{ extent}}{\text{window } y \text{ extent}} = \frac{yv_{max} - yv_{min}}{yw_{max} - yw_{min}}$$

So $N = S_{s_x, s_y, L} \cdot T_v$ (where $v = a\mathbf{I} + b\mathbf{J}$ with $a = xv_{min} - xw_{min}$, $b = yv_{min} - yw_{min}$). In matrix form (Chap. 4, Prob. 4.7):

$$N = \begin{pmatrix} s_x & 0 & (-s_x \cdot xv_{min} + xv_{min}) \\ 0 & s_y & (-s_y \cdot yv_{min} + yv_{min}) \\ 0 & 0 & 1 \end{pmatrix} \cdot \begin{pmatrix} 1 & 0 & (xv_{min} - xw_{min}) \\ 0 & 1 & (yv_{min} - yw_{min}) \\ 0 & 0 & 1 \end{pmatrix}$$

$$= \begin{pmatrix} s_x & 0 & (-s_x \cdot xw_{min} + xv_{min}) \\ 0 & s_y & (-s_y \cdot yw_{min} + yv_{min}) \\ 0 & 0 & 1 \end{pmatrix}$$

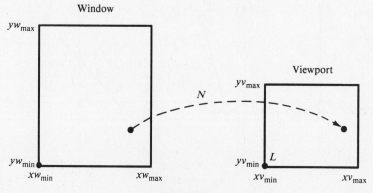

Fig. 5-10

5.2 Find the normalization transformation that maps a window whose lower left corner is at $(1, 1)$ and upper right corner is at $(3, 5)$ onto (a) a viewport that is the entire normalized device screen and (b) a viewport that has lower left corner at $(0, 0)$ and upper right corner $(\frac{1}{2}, \frac{1}{2})$.

SOLUTION

From Prob. 5.1, we need only identify the appropriate parameters.

(a) The window parameters are $xw_{min} = 1, xw_{max} = 3, yw_{min} = 1$, and $yw_{max} = 5$. The viewport parameters are $xv_{min} = 0, xv_{max} = 1, yv_{min} = 0$, and $yv_{max} = 1$. Then $s_x = \frac{1}{2}, s_y = \frac{1}{4}$, and

$$N = \begin{pmatrix} \frac{1}{2} & 0 & -\frac{1}{2} \\ 0 & \frac{1}{4} & -\frac{1}{4} \\ 0 & 0 & 1 \end{pmatrix}$$

(b) The window parameters are the same as in (a). The viewport parameters are now $xv_{min} = 0$, $xv_{max} = \frac{1}{2}, yv_{min} = 0, yv_{max} = \frac{1}{2}$. Then $s_x = \frac{1}{4}, s_y = \frac{1}{8}$, and

$$N = \begin{pmatrix} \frac{1}{4} & 0 & -\frac{1}{4} \\ 0 & \frac{1}{8} & -\frac{1}{8} \\ 0 & 0 & 1 \end{pmatrix}$$

5.3 Find the complete viewing transformation that maps a window in world coordinates with x-extent 1 to 10 and y extent 1 to 10 onto a viewport with x extent $\frac{1}{4}$ to $\frac{3}{4}$ and y extent 0 to $\frac{1}{2}$ in normalized device space, and then maps a window with x extent $\frac{1}{4}$ to $\frac{1}{2}$ and y extent $\frac{1}{4}$ to $\frac{1}{2}$ in the normalized device space into a viewport with x extent 1 to 10 and y extent 1 to 10 on the physical display device.

SOLUTION

From Prob. 5.1, the parameters for the normalization transformation are $xw_{min} = 1, xw_{max} = 10$, $yw_{min} = 1, yw_{max} = 10$, and $xv_{min} = \frac{1}{4}, xv_{max} = \frac{3}{4}, yv_{min} = 0$, and $yv_{max} = \frac{1}{2}$. Then

$$s_x = \frac{1/2}{9} = \frac{1}{18} \qquad s_y = \frac{1/2}{9} = \frac{1}{18}$$

and

$$N = \begin{pmatrix} \frac{1}{18} & 0 & \frac{7}{36} \\ 0 & \frac{1}{18} & -\frac{1}{18} \\ 0 & 0 & 1 \end{pmatrix}$$

The parameters for the workstation transformation are $xw_{min} = \frac{1}{4}, xw_{max} = \frac{1}{2}, yw_{min} = \frac{1}{4}, yw_{max} = \frac{1}{2}$, and $xv_{min} = 1, xv_{max} = 10, yv_{min} = 1$, and $yv_{max} = 10$. Then

$$s_x = \frac{9}{1/4} = 36 \qquad s_y = \frac{9}{1/4} = 36$$

and

$$W = \begin{pmatrix} 36 & 0 & -8 \\ 0 & 36 & -8 \\ 0 & 0 & 1 \end{pmatrix}$$

The complete viewing transformation is

$$V = W \cdot N$$

$$= \begin{pmatrix} 36 & 0 & -8 \\ 0 & 36 & -8 \\ 0 & 0 & 1 \end{pmatrix} \begin{pmatrix} \frac{1}{18} & 0 & \frac{7}{36} \\ 0 & \frac{1}{18} & -\frac{1}{8} \\ 0 & 0 & 1 \end{pmatrix} = \begin{pmatrix} 2 & 0 & -1 \\ 0 & 2 & -10 \\ 0 & 0 & 1 \end{pmatrix}$$

5.4   Find a normalization transformation from the window whose lower left corner is at $(0, 0)$ and upper right corner is at $(4, 3)$ onto the normalized device screen so that aspect ratios are preserved.

SOLUTION

The window aspect ratio is $a_w = \frac{4}{3}$. Unless otherwise indicated, we shall choose a viewport that is as large as possible with respect to the normalized device screen. To this end, we choose the x extent from 0 to 1 and the y extent from 0 to $\frac{3}{4}$. So

$$a_v = \frac{1}{3/4} = \frac{4}{3}$$

As in Prob. 5.2, with parameters $xw_{min} = 0$, $xw_{max} = 4$, $yw_{min} = 0$, $yw_{max} = 3$ and $xv_{min} = 0$, $xv_{max} = 1$, $yv_{min} = 0$, $yv_{max} = 1$,

$$N = \begin{pmatrix} \frac{1}{4} & 0 & 0 \\ 0 & \frac{1}{4} & 0 \\ 0 & 0 & 1 \end{pmatrix}$$

5.5   Find the normalization transformation N which uses the rectangle $A(1, 1)$, $B(5, 3)$, $C(4, 5)$, $D(0, 3)$ as a window [Fig. 5-11(a)] and the normalized device screen as a viewport [Fig. 5-11(b)].

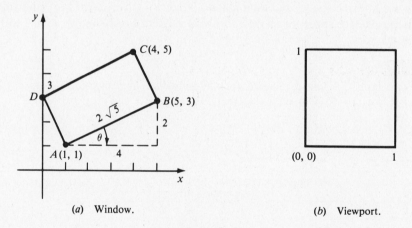

(a)   Window.   (b)   Viewport.

Fig. 5-11

SOLUTION

We will first rotate the rectangle about A so that it is aligned with the coordinate axes. Next, as in Prob. 5.1, we calculate s_x and s_y and finally we compose the rotation and the transformation N (from Prob. 5.1) to find the required normalization transformation N_R.

The slope of the line segment $\overline{AB}$ is

$$m = \frac{3 - 1}{5 - 1} = \frac{1}{2}$$

Looking at Fig. 5-11, we see that $-\theta$ will be the direction of the rotation. The angle θ is determined from the slope of a line (App. 1) by the equation $\tan \theta = \frac{1}{2}$. Then

$$\sin \theta = \frac{1}{\sqrt{5}}, \quad \text{and so} \quad \sin(-\theta) = -\frac{1}{\sqrt{5}}, \quad \cos \theta = \frac{2}{\sqrt{5}}, \quad \cos(-\theta) = \frac{2}{\sqrt{5}}$$

The rotation matrix about $A(1, 1)$ is then (Chap. 4, Prob. 4.3):

$$R_{-\theta,A} = \begin{pmatrix} \dfrac{2}{\sqrt{5}} & \dfrac{1}{\sqrt{5}} & \left(1 - \dfrac{3}{\sqrt{5}}\right) \\ -\dfrac{1}{\sqrt{5}} & \dfrac{2}{\sqrt{5}} & \left(1 - \dfrac{1}{\sqrt{5}}\right) \\ 0 & 0 & 1 \end{pmatrix}$$

The x extent of the rotated window is the length of $\overline{AB}$. Similarly, the y extent is the length of $\overline{AD}$. Using the distance formula (App. 1) to calculate these lengths yields

$$d(A, B) = \sqrt{2^2 + 4^2} = \sqrt{20} = 2\sqrt{5} \qquad d(A, D) = \sqrt{1^2 + 2^2} = \sqrt{5}$$

Also, the x extent of the normalized device screen is 1, as is the y extent. Calculating s_x and s_y,

$$s_x = \frac{\text{viewport } x \text{ extent}}{\text{window } x \text{ extent}} = \frac{1}{2\sqrt{5}} \qquad s_y = \frac{\text{viewport } y \text{ extent}}{\text{window } y \text{ extent}} = \frac{1}{\sqrt{5}}$$

So

$$N = \begin{pmatrix} \dfrac{1}{2\sqrt{5}} & 0 & -\dfrac{1}{2\sqrt{5}} \\ 0 & -\dfrac{1}{\sqrt{5}} & -\dfrac{1}{\sqrt{5}} \\ 0 & 0 & 1 \end{pmatrix}$$

The normalization transformation is then

$$N_R = N \cdot R_{-\theta,A}$$

$$= \begin{pmatrix} \frac{1}{5} & \frac{1}{10} & -\frac{1}{10} \\ -\frac{1}{5} & \frac{2}{5} & -\frac{1}{5} \\ 0 & 0 & 1 \end{pmatrix}$$

5.6 Let R be the rectangular window whose lower left-hand corner is at $L(-3, 1)$ and upper right-hand corner is at $R(2, 6)$. For the endpoint codes for the points in Fig. 5-12.

SOLUTION

The endpoint codes for point (x, y) are set according to the scheme

Bit 1 = sign $(y - y_{max})$ = sign $(y - 6)$ Bit 3 = sign $(x - x_{max})$ = sign $(x - 2)$
Bit 2 = sign $(y_{min} - y)$ = sign $(1 - y)$ Bit 4 = sign $(x_{min} - x)$ = sign $(-3 - x)$

Here

$$\text{Sign } a = \begin{cases} 1 \text{ if } a \text{ is positive or zero} \\ 0 \text{ otherwise} \end{cases}$$

So

$$A(-4, 2) \to 0001 \qquad F(1, 2) \to 0000$$
$$B(-1, 7) \to 1000 \qquad G(1, -2) \to 0100$$
$$C(-1, 5) \to 0000 \qquad H(3, 3) \to 0010$$
$$D(3, 8) \to 1010 \qquad I(-4, 7) \to 1001$$
$$E(-2, 3) \to 0000 \qquad J(-2, 10) \to 1000$$

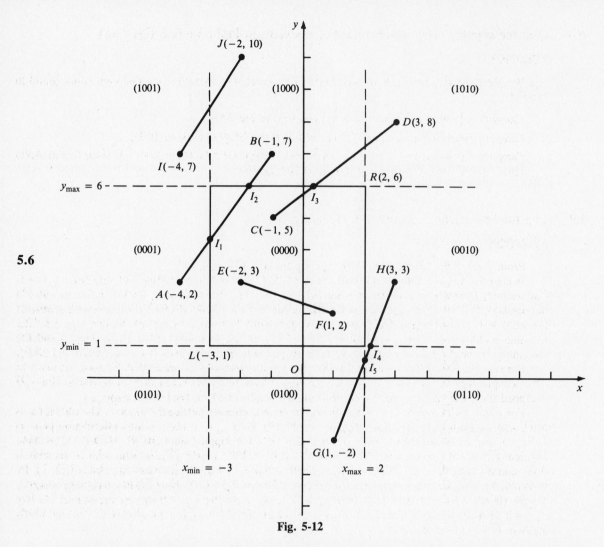

Fig. 5-12

5.7   Clipping against rectangular windows whose sides are aligned with the x and y axes involves computing intersections with vertical and horizontal lines. Find the intersection of a line segment $\overline{P_1P_2}$ [joining $P_1(x_1, y_1)$ to $P_2(x_2, y_2)$] with (a) the vertical line $x = a$ and (b) the horizontal line $y = b$.

SOLUTION

We write the equation of $\overline{P_1P_2}$ in parametric form (App. 1, Prob. 23):

$$x = x_1 + t(x_2 - x_1),\ 0 \le t \le 1 \tag{5.1}$$
$$y = y_1 + t(y_2 - y_1) \tag{5.2}$$

(a)   Since $x = a$, we substitute this into equation (5.1) and find $t = (a - x_1)/(x_2 - x_1)$. Then, substituting this value into equation (5.2), we find that the intersection point is $x_I = a$ and

$$y_I = y_1 + \left(\frac{a - x_1}{x_2 - x_1}\right)(y_2 - y_1)$$

(b)   Substituting $y = b$ into equation (5.2), we find $t = (b - y_1)/(y_2 - y_1)$. When this is placed into equation (5.1), the intersection point is $y_I = b$ and

$$x_I = x_1 + \left(\frac{b - y_1}{y_2 - y_1}\right)(x_2 - x_1)$$

5.8 Find the clipping categories for the line segments in Prob. 5.6 (see Fig. 5-12).

SOLUTION

We place the line segments in their appropriate categories by testing the endpoint codes found in Prob. 5.6.

Category 1 (visible): $\overline{EF}$ since both endpoint codes are 0000.

Category 2 (not visible): $\overline{IJ}$ since (1001) AND (1000) = 1000 (which is not 0000).

Category 3 (candidates for clipping): $\overline{AB}$ since (0001) AND (1000) = 0000, $\overline{CD}$ since (0000) AND (1010) = 0000, and $\overline{GH}$ since (0100) AND (0010) = 0000.

5.9 Clip the line segments in Prob. 5.6 (see Fig. 5-12).

SOLUTION

From Prob. 5.8, the candidates for clipping are $\overline{AB}$, $\overline{CD}$, and $\overline{GH}$.

In *clipping $\overline{AB}$*, the code for A is 0001. To push the 1 to 0, we clip against the boundary line $x_{\min} = -3$. The resulting intersection point (from Prob. 5.7) is $I_1(-3, 3\frac{2}{3})$. The code for I_1 is 0000, and so we clip (do not display) $\overline{AI_1}$. The clipping category for $\overline{I_1B}$ is 3 since (0000) AND (1000) is (0000). Now B is outside the window (i.e., its code is 1000), so we push the 1 to a 0 by clipping against the line $y_{\max} = 6$. The resulting intersection is $I_2(-1\frac{3}{5}, 6)$ (Prob. 5.7). The code for I_2 is 0000. Thus $\overline{BI_2}$ is clipped and the remaining segment $\overline{I_1I_2}$ is displayed since both endpoints lie in the window (i.e., their codes are 0000).

For *clipping $\overline{CD}$*, we start with D since it is outside the window. Its code is 1010. We push the first 1 to a 0 by clipping against the line $y_{\max} = 6$. The resulting intersection I_3 is $(\frac{1}{3}, 6)$ and its code is 0000. Thus $\overline{I_3D}$ is clipped and the remaining segment $\overline{CI_3}$ has both endpoints coded 0000 and so it is displayed.

For *clipping $\overline{GH}$*, we can start with either G or H since both are outside the window. The code for G is 0100, and we push the 1 to a 0 by clipping against the line $y_{\min} = 1$. The resulting intersection point is $I_4(2\frac{1}{5}, 1)$, and its code is 0010. Thus $\overline{GI_4}$ is a candidate for clipping since (0100) AND (0010) = 0000. Segment $\overline{I_4H}$ is not displayed since (0010) AND (0010) = 0010. To clip $\overline{GI_4}$, we start with G. Its code is 0100, and we push the 1 to a 0 by clipping against the line $x_{\max} = 2$. The intersection point is $I_5(2, \frac{1}{2})$. Its code is 0100. Thus $\overline{GI_5}$ is not displayed since (0100) AND (0100) = 0100. Now $\overline{I_4I_5}$ lies in clipping category 3 since (0010) AND (0100) = 0000. Starting with I_4, we push the 1 to a 0 by clipping against the line $x_{\max} = 2$. However, since I_5 already lies on $x_{\max} = 2$, we conclude that $\overline{I_4I_5}$ is not displayed. Thus the whole segment $\overline{GH}$ is not displayed.

5.10 Clip line segment $\overline{CD}$ of Prob. 5.6 by using the midpoint subdivision process.

SOLUTION

The midpoint subdivision process is based on repeated bisections. To avoid continuing indefinitely, we agree to say that a point (x_1, y_1) lies on any of the boundary lines of the rectangle, say, boundary line $x = x_{\max}$, for example, if $-\text{TOL} \le x_1 - x_{\max} \le \text{TOL}$. Here TOL is a prescribed tolerance, some small number, that is set before the process begins.

To clip $\overline{CD}$, we determine that it is in category 3. For this problem we arbitrarily choose TOL = 0.1. We find the midpoint of $\overline{CD}$ to be $M_1(1, 6.5)$. Its code is 1000.

So $\overline{M_1D}$ is not displayed since (1000) AND (1010) = 1000. We further subdivide $\overline{CM_1}$ since (0000) AND (1000) = 0000. The midpoint of $\overline{CM_1}$ is $M_2(0, 3.5)$; the code for M_2 is 0000. Thus $\overline{CM_2}$ is displayed since both endpoints are 0000 and $\overline{M_2M_1}$ is a candidate for clipping. The midpoint of $\overline{M_2M_1}$ is $M_3(0.5, 5)$, and its code is 0000. Thus $\overline{M_2M_3}$ is displayed and $\overline{M_3M_1}$ is subdivided. The midpoint of $\overline{M_3M_1}$ is $M_4(0.75, 5.75)$, whose code is 0000. So $\overline{M_3M_4}$ is displayed and $\overline{M_4M_1}$ is subdivided. The midpoint is $M_5(0.875, 6.125)$, whose code is 1000; thus $\overline{M_5M_1}$ is not displayed and $\overline{M_4M_5}$ is subdivided. The midpoint is $M_6(0.8125, 5.9375)$, whose code is 0000. However, since $y_1 = 5.9375$ lies within the tolerance 0.1 of the boundary line $y_{\max} = 6$—that is, $6 - 5.9375 = 0.0625 < 0.1$, we agree that M_6 lies on the boundary line $y_{\max} = 6$. Thus $\overline{M_4M_6}$ is displayed and $\overline{M_6M_5}$ is not displayed. So the original line segment $\overline{CD}$ is clipped at M_6 and the process stops.

5.11 In displaying a clipped picture, we have the choice of clipping against the window and then applying the window transformation or applying the window transformation and then clipping against the viewport. Are both processes equivalent?

SOLUTION

Since the window transformation is an affine transformation (App. 1, Probs. A1.35 and A1.36), it preserves lines and the inside-outside relationship between objects. Thus the two processes are mathematically equivalent.

In general, however, clipping before transforming is more efficient in that only visible lines need be transformed. A possible exception is, for example, the case when the window is a rotated rectangle and the viewport an aligned rectangle. In this case, the much more coplex Sutherland-Hodgman algorithm must be used to clip against the rotated window, whereas the simpler Cohen-Sutherland algorithm can be used to clip against the viewport.

5.12 How can we determine whether a point $P(x, y)$ lies to the left or to the right of a line segment joining the points $A(x_1, y_1)$ and $B(x_2, y_2)$?

SOLUTION

Refer to Fig. 5-13. Form the vectors $\mathbf{AB}$ and $\mathbf{AP}$. If the point P is to the left of $\mathbf{AB}$, then by the definition of the cross product of two vectors (App. 2) the vector $\mathbf{AB} \times \mathbf{AP}$ points in the direction of the vector $\mathbf{K}$ perpendicular to the xy plane (see Fig. 5-13). If it lies to the right, the cross product points in the direction $-\mathbf{K}$.

Now
$$\mathbf{AB} = (x_2 - x_1)\mathbf{I} + (y_2 - y_1)\mathbf{J} \qquad \mathbf{AP} = (x - x_1)\mathbf{I} + (y - y_1)\mathbf{J}$$

So
$$\mathbf{AB} \times \mathbf{AP} = [(x_2 - x_1)(y - y_1) - (y_2 - y_1)(x - x_1)]\mathbf{K}$$

Then the direction of this cross product is determined by the number

$$\bar{C} = (x_2 - x_1)(y - y_1) - (y_2 - y_1)(x - x_1)$$

If $\bar{C}$ is positive, P lies to the left of $\mathbf{AB}$. If $\bar{C}$ is negative, then P lies to the right of $\mathbf{AB}$.

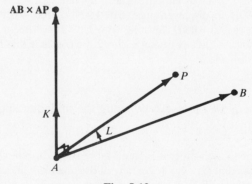

Fig. 5-13

5.13 Draw a flowchart illustrating the logic of the Sutherland-Hodgman algorithm.

SOLUTION

The algorithm inputs the vertices of a polygon one at a time. For each input vertex, either zero, one, or two output vertices will be generated depending on the relationship of the input vertices to the clipping edge E.

We denote by P the input vertex, S the previous input vertex, and F the first arriving input vertex. The vertex or vertices to be output are determined according to the logic illustrated in the flowchart in Fig. 5-14. Recall that a polygon with n vertices $P_1, P_2, \ldots, P_n$ has n edges $\overline{P_1P_2}, \ldots, \overline{P_{n-1}P_n}$ and the edge $\overline{P_nP_1}$ closing the polygon. In order to avoid the need to duplicate the input of P as the final input vertex (and a corresponding mechanism to duplicate the final output vertex to close the polygon), the closing logic shown in the flowchart in Fig. 5-15 is called after processing the final input vertex P.

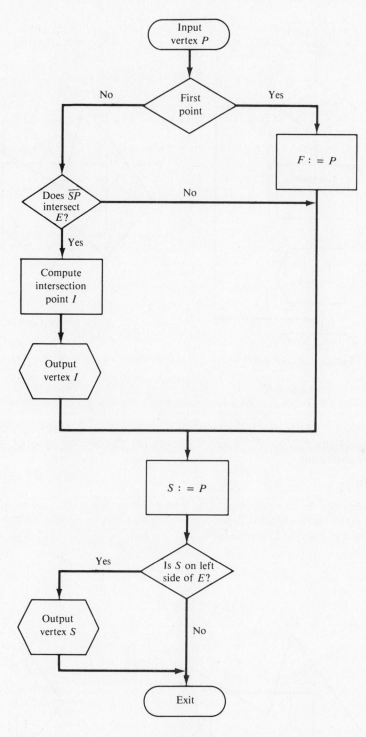

Fig. 5-14

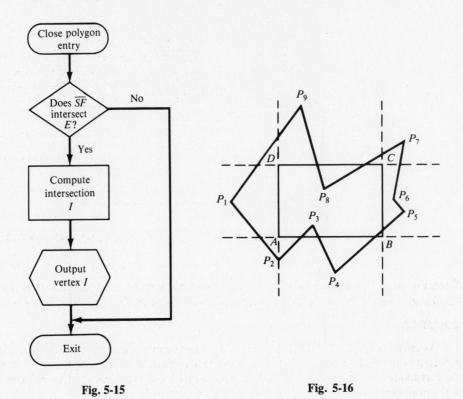

Fig. 5-15   Fig. 5-16

5.14 Clip the polygon $P_1, \ldots, P_9$ in Fig. 5-16 against the window $ABCD$ using the Sutherland-Hodgman algorithm.

SOLUTION

At each stage the new output polygon, whose vertices are determined by applying the Sutherland-Hodgman algorithm (Prob. 5.13), is passed on to the next clipping edge of the window $ABCD$. The results are illustrated in Figs. 5-17 through 5-20.

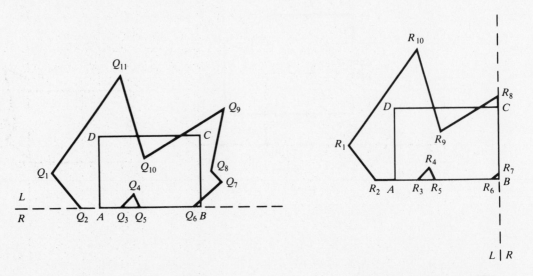

Fig. 5-17 Clip against $\overline{AB}$.   **Fig. 5-18** Clip against $\overline{BC}$.

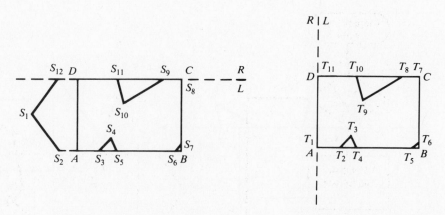

Fig. 5-19   Clip against $\overline{CD}$.   **Fig. 5-20**   Clip against $\overline{DA}$.

5.15   Describe how the Sutherland-Hodgman algorithm can be modified to produce shielding or blanking. Use the window and polygon of Prob. 5.14 to illustrate the process.

SOLUTION

As in the original algorithm, there are zero, one, or two output vertices depending on the relative positions of the input vertices with respect to the clipping edge. By interchanging the words left and right in the decision process for outputting vertices, we can produce the required shielded polygon with respect to a given window edge. The other changes in the process are:

1.   There is no closing of the output vertices; that is, the edge joining the last output vertex to the first output vertex is not drawn. (The output is what is known as a *polyline*.)

2.   At each stage the original polygon is input to be shielded (see Figs. 5-21 through 5-24) against the given edge (as opposed to the original clipping algorithm where the output of one clipping stage becomes the input to the next clipping stage).

The final shielded region is the union of the outputs at each shielding stage (see Fig. 5-25).

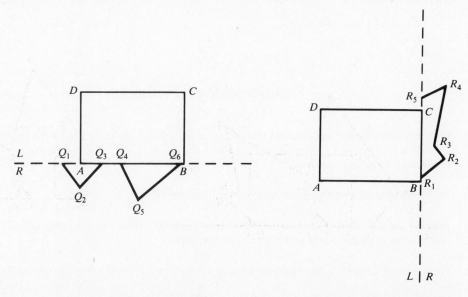

Fig. 5-21   Shield against $\overline{AB}$.   **Fig. 5-22**   Shield against $\overline{BC}$.

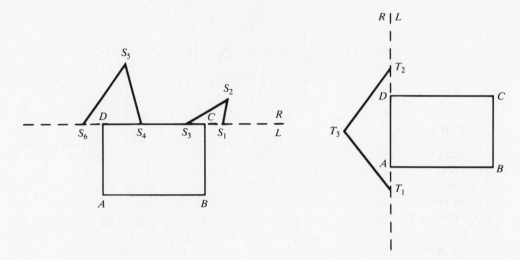

Fig. 5-23   Shield against $\overline{CD}$.   **Fig. 5-24**   Shield against $\overline{AD}$.

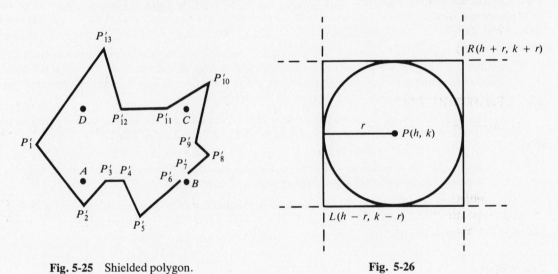

Fig. 5-25   Shielded polygon.   **Fig. 5-26**

Supplementary Problems

5.16   Find the workstation transformation that maps the normalized device screen onto a physical device whose x extent is 0 to 199 and y extent is 0 to 639 where the origin is located at the (*a*) lower left corner and (*b*) upper left corner of the device.

5.17   Show that for a viewing transformation, $s_x = s_y$ if and only if $a_w = a_v$.

5.18   Find the normalization transformation which uses a circle of radius five units and center $(1, 1)$ as a window and a circle of radius $\frac{1}{2}$ and center $(\frac{1}{2}, \frac{1}{2})$ as a viewport.

5.19   Describe how clipping a line against a circular window (or viewport) might proceed. Refer to Fig. 5-26.

5.20   Use the Sutherland-Hodgman algorithm to clip the line segment joining $P_1(-1, 2)$ to $P_2(6, 4)$ against the rotated window in Prob. 5.5.

Chapter 6

Three-Dimensional Graphics Transformations

6.1 INTRODUCTION

Manipulation, viewing, and construction of three-dimensional graphic images requires the use of three-dimensional geometric and coordinate transformations. These transformations are formed by composing the basic transformations of translation, scaling, and rotation. Each of these transformations can be represented as a matrix transformation. This permits more complex transformations to be built up by use of matrix multiplication or concatenation.

As with two-dimensional transformations, two complementary points of view are adopted: either the object or picture is manipulated directly through the use of geometric transformations, or the object remains stationary and the viewer's coordinate system is changed by using coordinate transformations. In addition, the construction of complex objects and pictures is facilitated by the use of instance transformations, which combine both points of view. The transformations and concepts introduced here are direct generalizations of those introduced in Chap. 4 for two-dimensional transformations.

6.2 GEOMETRIC TRANSFORMATIONS

With respect to some three-dimensional coordinate systems, an object Obj is considered as a set of points:

$$Obj = \{P(x, y, z)\}$$

If the object is moved to a new position, we can regard it as a new object Obj' all of whose coordinate points $P'(x', y', z')$ can be obtained from the original coordinate points $P(x, y, z)$ of Obj through the application of a geometric transformation.

Translation

An object is displaced a given distance and direction from its original position. The direction and displacement of the translation is prescribed by a vector

$$\mathbf{V} = a\mathbf{I} + b\mathbf{J} + c\mathbf{K}$$

The new coordinates of a translated point can be calculated by using the transformation

$$T_v: \begin{cases} x' = x + a \\ y' = y + b \\ z' = z + c \end{cases}$$

(see Fig. 6-1). In order to represent this transformation as a matrix transformation, we need to use homogeneous coordinates (App. 2). The required homogeneous matrix transformation can then be expressed as

$$\begin{pmatrix} x' \\ y' \\ z' \\ 1 \end{pmatrix} = \begin{pmatrix} 1 & 0 & 0 & a \\ 0 & 1 & 0 & b \\ 0 & 0 & 1 & c \\ 0 & 0 & 0 & 1 \end{pmatrix} \begin{pmatrix} x \\ y \\ z \\ 1 \end{pmatrix}$$

115

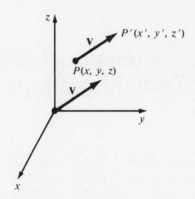

Fig. 6-1

Scaling

The process of scaling changes the dimensions of an object. The scale factor s determines whether the scaling is a magnification, $s > 1$, or a reduction, $s < 1$.

Scaling with respect to the origin, where the origin remains fixed, is effected by the transformation

$$S_{s_x, s_y, s_z}: \begin{cases} x' = s_x \cdot x \\ y' = s_y \cdot y \\ z' = s_z \cdot z \end{cases}$$

In matrix form this is

$$S_{s_x, s_y, s_z} = \begin{pmatrix} s_x & 0 & 0 \\ 0 & s_y & 0 \\ 0 & 0 & s_z \end{pmatrix}$$

Rotation

Rotation in three dimensions is considerably more complex than rotation in two dimensions. In two dimensions, a rotation is prescribed by an angle of rotation θ and a center of rotation P. Three-dimensional rotations require the prescription of an angle of rotation and an axis of rotation. The *canonical* rotations are defined when one of the positive x, y, or z coordinate axes is chosen as the axis of rotation. Then the construction of the rotation transformation proceeds just like that of a rotation in two dimensions about the origin (see Fig. 6-2).

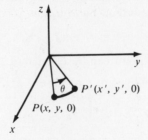

Fig. 6-2

Rotation about the z Axis

From Chap. 4 we know that

$$R_{\theta, \mathbf{K}}: \begin{cases} x' = x \cos \theta - y \sin \theta \\ y' = x \sin \theta + y \cos \theta \\ z' = z \end{cases}$$

Rotation about the y Axis

An analogous derivation leads to

$$R_{\theta,\mathbf{J}}:\begin{cases} x' = x\cos\theta + z\sin\theta \\ y' = y \\ z' = -x\sin\theta + z\cos\theta \end{cases}$$

Rotation about the x Axis

Similarly:

$$R_{\theta,\mathbf{I}}:\begin{cases} x' = x \\ y' = y\cos\theta - z\sin\theta \\ z' = y\sin\theta + z\cos\theta \end{cases}$$

Note that the direction of a positive angle of rotation is chosen in accordance to the right-hand rule with respect to the axis of rotation (App. 2).

The corresponding matrix transformations are

$$R_{\theta,\mathbf{K}} = \begin{pmatrix} \cos\theta & -\sin\theta & 0 \\ \sin\theta & \cos\theta & 0 \\ 0 & 0 & 1 \end{pmatrix}$$

$$R_{\theta,\mathbf{J}} = \begin{pmatrix} \cos\theta & 0 & \sin\theta \\ 0 & 1 & 0 \\ -\sin\theta & 0 & \cos\theta \end{pmatrix}$$

$$R_{\theta,\mathbf{I}} = \begin{pmatrix} 1 & 0 & 0 \\ 0 & \cos\theta & -\sin\theta \\ 0 & \sin\theta & \cos\theta \end{pmatrix}$$

The general case of rotation about an axis L can be built up from these canonical rotations using matrix multiplication (Prob. 6.3).

6.3 COORDINATE TRANSFORMATIONS

We can also achieve the effects of translation, scaling, and rotation by moving the observer who views the object and by keeping the object stationary. This type of transformation is called a *coordinate transformation*. We first attach a coordinate system to the observer and then move the observer and the attached coordinate system. Next, we recalculate the coordinates of the observed object with respect

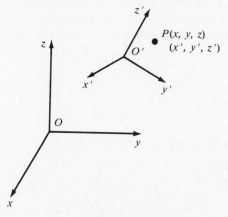

Fig. 6-3

to this new observer coordinate system. The new coordinate values will be exactly the same as if the observer had remained stationary and the object had moved, corresponding to a geometric transformation (see Fig. 6-3).

If the displacement of the observer coordinate system to a new position is prescribed by a vector $\mathbf{V} = a\mathbf{I} + b\mathbf{J} + c\mathbf{K}$, a point $P(x, y, z)$ in the original coordinate system has coordinates $P(x', y', z')$ in the new coordinate system, and

$$\bar{T}_v: \begin{cases} x' = x - a \\ y' = y - b \\ z' = z - c \end{cases}$$

The derivation of this transformation is completely analogous to that of the two-dimensional transformation (see Chap. 4).

Similar derivations hold for coordinate scaling and coordinate rotation transformations.

As in the two-dimensional case, we summarize the relationships between the matrix forms of the coordinate transformations and the geometric transformations:

Coordinate Transformations $\leftarrow$ $\rightarrow$ **Geometric Transformations**

	Coordinate Transformations	Geometric Transformations
Translation	$\bar{T}_v$	T_{-v}
Rotation	$\bar{R}_\theta$	$R_{-\theta}$
Scaling	$\bar{S}_{s_x, s_y, s_z}$	$S_{1/s_x, 1/s_y, 1/s_z}$

Inverse geometric and coordinate transformations are constructed by performing the reverse operation. Thus, for coordinate transformations (and similarly for geometric transformations):

$$\bar{T}_v^{-1} = \bar{T}_{-v} \qquad \bar{R}_\theta^{-1} = \bar{R}_{-\theta} \qquad \bar{S}_{s_x, s_y, s_z} = \bar{S}_{1/s_x, 1/s_y, 1/s_z}$$

6.4 COMPOSITE TRANSFORMATIONS AND MATRIX CONCATENATION

More complex geometric and coordinate transformations are formed through the process of *composition of functions*. For matrix functions, however, the process of composition is equivalent to matrix multiplication or concatenation. In Probs. 6.2, 6.3, 6.5, and 6.11, the following transformations are constructed:

1. $A_{V,N}$ = aligning a vector $\mathbf{V}$ with a vector $\mathbf{N}$.
2. $R_{\theta, L}$ = rotation about an axis L. The axis is prescribed by giving a direction vector $\mathbf{V}$ and a point P through which the axis passes.
3. $S_{s_x, s_y, s_z, P}$ = scaling with respect to an arbitrary point P.

In order to build these more complex transformations through matrix concatenation, we must be able to multiply translation matrices with rotation and scaling matrices. This necessitates the use of homogeneous coordinates and 4×4 matrices (App. 2). The standard 3×3 matrices of rotation and scaling can be represented as 4×4 homogeneous matrices by adjoining an extra row and column as follows:

$$\begin{pmatrix} a & b & c & 0 \\ d & e & f & 0 \\ g & h & i & 0 \\ 0 & 0 & 0 & 1 \end{pmatrix}$$

These transformations are then applied to points $P(x, y, z)$ having the homogeneous form:

$$\begin{pmatrix} x \\ y \\ z \\ 1 \end{pmatrix}$$

EXAMPLE 1. The matrix of rotation about the y axis has the homogeneous 4×4 form:

$$R_{\theta,\mathbf{J}} = \begin{pmatrix} \cos\theta & 0 & \sin\theta & 0 \\ 0 & 1 & 0 & 0 \\ -\sin\theta & 0 & \cos\theta & 0 \\ 0 & 0 & 0 & 1 \end{pmatrix}$$

6.5 INSTANCE TRANSFORMATIONS

If an object or picture is created and described in coordinates with respect to its own object coordinate space, we can place an instance or copy of it within a larger picture that is described in an independent picture coordinate space by the use of three-dimensional coordinate transformations. In this case, the transformations are referred to as *instance transformations*. The concepts and construction of three-dimensional instance transformations and the current transformation matrix are completely analogous to the two-dimensional cases described in Chap. 4.

Solved Problems

6.1 Define *tilting* as a rotation about the x axis followed by a rotation about the y axis: (*a*) find the tilting matrix; (*b*) does the order of performing the rotation matter?

SOLUTION

(*a*) We can find the required transformation T by composing (concatenating) two rotation matrices:

$$T = R_{\theta_y,\mathbf{J}} \cdot R_{\theta_x,\mathbf{I}}$$

$$= \begin{pmatrix} \cos\theta_y & 0 & \sin\theta_y & 0 \\ 0 & 1 & 0 & 0 \\ -\sin\theta_y & 0 & \cos\theta_y & 0 \\ 0 & 0 & 0 & 1 \end{pmatrix} \cdot \begin{pmatrix} 1 & 0 & 0 & 0 \\ 0 & \cos\theta_x & -\sin\theta_x & 0 \\ 0 & \sin\theta_x & \cos\theta_x & 0 \\ 0 & 0 & 0 & 1 \end{pmatrix}$$

$$= \begin{pmatrix} \cos\theta_y & \sin\theta_y \cdot \sin\theta_x & \sin\theta_y \cdot \cos\theta_x & 0 \\ 0 & \cos\theta_x & -\sin\theta_x & 0 \\ -\sin\theta_y & \cos\theta_y \cdot \sin\theta_x & \cos\theta_y \cdot \cos\theta_x & 0 \\ 0 & 0 & 0 & 1 \end{pmatrix}$$

(*b*) We multiply $R_{\theta_x,\mathbf{I}} \cdot R_{\theta_y,\mathbf{J}}$ to obtain the matrix

$$\begin{pmatrix} \cos\theta_y & 0 & \sin\theta_y & 0 \\ \sin\theta_x \cdot \sin\theta_y & \cos\theta_x & -\sin\theta_x \cdot \cos\theta_y & 0 \\ -\cos\theta_x \cdot \sin\theta_y & \sin\theta_x & \cos\theta_x \cdot \cos\theta_y & 0 \\ 0 & 0 & 0 & 1 \end{pmatrix}$$

This is not the same matrix as in part *a*; thus the order of rotation matters.

6.2 Find a transformation $A_{\mathbf{V}}$ which aligns a given vector $\mathbf{V}$ with the vector $\mathbf{K}$ along the positive z axis.

SOLUTION

See Fig. 6-4(*a*). Let $\mathbf{V} = a\mathbf{I} + b\mathbf{J} + c\mathbf{K}$. We perform the alignment through the following sequence of transformations [Figs. 6-4(*b*) and 6-4(*c*)]:

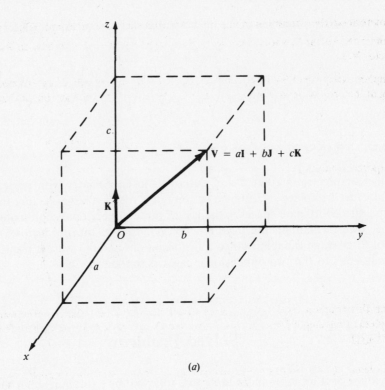

(a)

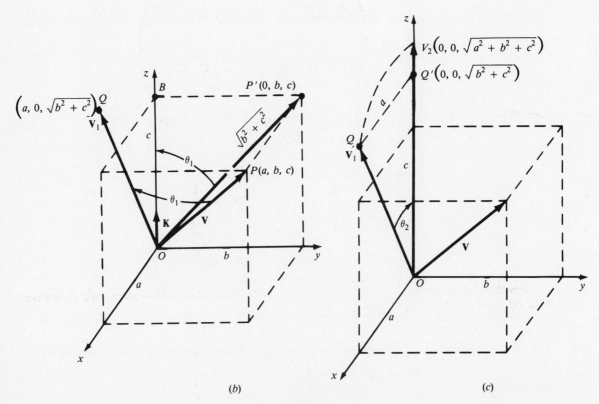

(b)   (c)

Fig. 6-4

1. Rotate about the x axis by an angle θ_1 so that $\mathbf{V}$ rotates into the upper half of the xz plane (as the vector $\mathbf{V}_1$).
2. Rotate the vector $\mathbf{V}_1$ about the y axis by an angle $-\theta_2$ so that $\mathbf{V}_1$ rotates to the positive z axis (as the vector $\mathbf{V}_2$).

Implementing step 1 from Fig. 6-4(b), we observe that the required angle of rotation θ_1 can be found by looking at the projection of $\mathbf{V}$ onto the yz plane. (We assume that b and c are not both zero.) From triangle $OP'B$:

$$\sin \theta_1 = \frac{b}{\sqrt{b^2 + c^2}} \qquad \cos \theta_1 = \frac{c}{\sqrt{b^2 + c^2}}$$

The required rotation is

$$R_{\theta_1,\mathbf{I}} = \begin{pmatrix} 1 & 0 & 0 & 0 \\ 0 & \dfrac{c}{\sqrt{b^2 + c^2}} & -\dfrac{b}{\sqrt{b^2 + c^2}} & 0 \\ 0 & \dfrac{b}{\sqrt{b^2 + c^2}} & \dfrac{c}{\sqrt{b^2 + c^2}} & 0 \\ 0 & 0 & 0 & 1 \end{pmatrix}$$

Applying this rotation to the vector $\mathbf{V}$ produces the vector $\mathbf{V}_1$ with the components $(a, 0, \sqrt{b^2 + c^2})$.

Implementing step 2 from Fig. 6-4(c), we see that a rotation of $-\theta_2$ degrees is required, and so from triangle OQQ':

$$\sin (-\theta_2) = -\sin \theta_2 = -\frac{a}{\sqrt{a^2 + b^2 + c^2}} \qquad \text{and} \qquad \cos (-\theta_2) = \cos \theta_2 = \frac{\sqrt{b^2 + c^2}}{\sqrt{a^2 + b^2 + c^2}}$$

Then

$$R_{-\theta_2,\mathbf{J}} = \begin{pmatrix} \dfrac{\sqrt{b^2 + c^2}}{\sqrt{a^2 + b^2 + c^2}} & 0 & \dfrac{-a}{\sqrt{a^2 + b^2 + c^2}} & 0 \\ 0 & 1 & 0 & 0 \\ \dfrac{a}{\sqrt{a^2 + b^2 + c^2}} & 0 & \dfrac{\sqrt{b^2 + c^2}}{\sqrt{a^2 + b^2 + c^2}} & 0 \\ 0 & 0 & 0 & 1 \end{pmatrix}$$

Since $|\mathbf{V}| = \sqrt{a^2 + b^2 + c^2}$, and introducing the notation $\lambda = \sqrt{b^2 + c^2}$, we find

$$A_{\mathbf{V}} = R_{-\theta_2,\mathbf{J}} \cdot R_{\theta_1,\mathbf{I}}$$

$$= \begin{pmatrix} \dfrac{\lambda}{|\mathbf{V}|} & \dfrac{-ab}{\lambda|\mathbf{V}|} & \dfrac{-ac}{\lambda|\mathbf{V}|} & 0 \\ 0 & \dfrac{c}{\lambda} & \dfrac{-b}{\lambda} & 0 \\ \dfrac{a}{|\mathbf{V}|} & \dfrac{b}{|\mathbf{V}|} & \dfrac{c}{|\mathbf{V}|} & 0 \\ 0 & 0 & 0 & 1 \end{pmatrix}$$

If both b and c are zero, then $\mathbf{V} = a\mathbf{I}$, and so $\lambda = 0$. In this case, only a $\pm 90°$ rotation about the y axis is required. So if $\lambda = 0$, it follows that

$$A_{\mathbf{V}} = R_{-\theta_2,\mathbf{J}} = \begin{pmatrix} 0 & 0 & \dfrac{-a}{|a|} & 0 \\ 0 & 1 & 0 & 0 \\ \dfrac{a}{|a|} & 0 & 0 & 0 \\ 0 & 0 & 0 & 1 \end{pmatrix}$$

In the same manner we calculate the inverse transformation that aligns the vector $\mathbf{K}$ with the vector $\mathbf{V}$.

$$A_{\mathbf{V}}^{-1} = (R_{-\theta_2, \mathbf{J}} \cdot R_{\theta_1, \mathbf{I}})^{-1} = R_{\theta_1, \mathbf{I}}^{-1} \cdot R_{-\theta_2, \mathbf{J}}^{-1} = R_{-\theta_1, \mathbf{I}} \cdot R_{\theta_2, \mathbf{J}}$$

$$= \begin{pmatrix} \dfrac{\lambda}{|\mathbf{V}|} & 0 & \dfrac{a}{|\mathbf{V}|} & 0 \\[2mm] \dfrac{-ab}{\lambda|\mathbf{V}|} & \dfrac{c}{\lambda} & \dfrac{b}{|\mathbf{V}|} & 0 \\[2mm] \dfrac{-ac}{\lambda|\mathbf{V}|} & -\dfrac{b}{\lambda} & \dfrac{c}{|\mathbf{V}|} & 0 \\[2mm] 0 & 0 & 0 & 1 \end{pmatrix}$$

6.3   Let an axis of rotation L be specified by a direction vector $\mathbf{V}$ and a location point P. Find the transformation for a rotation of $\theta°$ about L. Refer to Fig. 6-5.

SOLUTION

We can find the required transformation by the following steps:

1. Translate P to the origin.
2. Align $\mathbf{V}$ with the vector $\mathbf{K}$.
3. Rotate by θ^0 about $\mathbf{K}$.
4. Reverse steps 2 and 1.

So

$$R_{\theta, L} = T_{-P}^{-1} \cdot A_{\mathbf{V}}^{-1} \cdot R_{\theta, \mathbf{K}} \cdot A_{\mathbf{V}} \cdot T_{-P}$$

Here, $A_{\mathbf{V}}$ is the transformation described in Prob. 6.2.

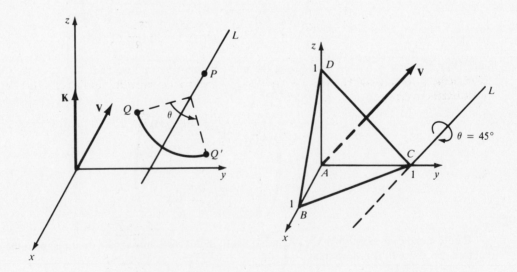

Fig. 6-5   Fig. 6-6

6.4   The pyramid defined by the coordinates $A(0, 0, 0)$, $B(1, 0, 0)$, $C(0, 1, 0)$, and $D(0, 0, 1)$ is rotated 45° about the line L that has the direction $\mathbf{V} = \mathbf{J} + \mathbf{K}$ and passing through point $C(0, 1, 0)$ (Fig. 6-6). Find the coordinates of the rotated figure.

SOLUTION

From Prob. 6.3, the rotation matrix $R_{\theta,L}$ can be found by concatenating the matrices

$$R_{\theta,L} = T_{-P}^{-1} \cdot A_{\mathbf{V}}^{-1} \cdot R_{\theta,\mathbf{K}} \cdot A_{\mathbf{V}} \cdot T_{-P}$$

With $P = (0, 1, 0)$, then

$$T_{-P} = \begin{pmatrix} 1 & 0 & 0 & 0 \\ 0 & 1 & 0 & -1 \\ 0 & 0 & 1 & 0 \\ 0 & 0 & 0 & 1 \end{pmatrix}$$

Now $\mathbf{V} = \mathbf{J} + \mathbf{K}$. So from Prob. 6.2, with $a = 0$, $b = 1$, $c = 1$, we find $\lambda = \sqrt{2}$, $|\mathbf{V}| = \sqrt{2}$, and

$$A_{\mathbf{V}} = \begin{pmatrix} 1 & 0 & 0 & 0 \\ 0 & \dfrac{1}{\sqrt{2}} & \dfrac{-1}{\sqrt{2}} & 0 \\ 0 & \dfrac{1}{\sqrt{2}} & \dfrac{1}{\sqrt{2}} & 0 \\ 0 & 0 & 0 & 1 \end{pmatrix} \qquad A_{\mathbf{V}}^{-1} = \begin{pmatrix} 1 & 0 & 0 & 0 \\ 0 & \dfrac{1}{\sqrt{2}} & \dfrac{1}{\sqrt{2}} & 0 \\ 0 & \dfrac{-1}{\sqrt{2}} & \dfrac{1}{\sqrt{2}} & 0 \\ 0 & 0 & 0 & 1 \end{pmatrix}$$

Also

$$R_{45°,\mathbf{K}} = \begin{pmatrix} \dfrac{1}{\sqrt{2}} & \dfrac{-1}{\sqrt{2}} & 0 & 0 \\ \dfrac{1}{\sqrt{2}} & \dfrac{1}{\sqrt{2}} & 0 & 0 \\ 0 & 0 & 1 & 0 \\ 0 & 0 & 0 & 1 \end{pmatrix} \qquad T_{-P}^{-1} = \begin{pmatrix} 1 & 0 & 0 & 0 \\ 0 & 1 & 0 & 1 \\ 0 & 0 & 1 & 0 \\ 0 & 0 & 0 & 1 \end{pmatrix}$$

Then

$$R_{\theta,L} = \begin{pmatrix} \dfrac{\sqrt{2}}{2} & -\dfrac{1}{2} & \dfrac{1}{2} & \dfrac{1}{2} \\ \dfrac{1}{2} & \dfrac{2+\sqrt{2}}{4} & \dfrac{2-\sqrt{2}}{4} & \dfrac{2-\sqrt{2}}{4} \\ -\dfrac{1}{2} & \dfrac{2-\sqrt{2}}{4} & \dfrac{2+\sqrt{2}}{4} & \dfrac{\sqrt{2}-2}{4} \\ 0 & 0 & 0 & 1 \end{pmatrix}$$

To find the coordinates of the rotated figure, we apply the rotation matrix $R_{\theta,L}$ to the matrix of homogeneous coordinates of the vertices A, B, C, and D.

$$C = (ABCD) = \begin{pmatrix} 0 & 1 & 0 & 0 \\ 0 & 0 & 1 & 0 \\ 0 & 0 & 0 & 1 \\ 1 & 1 & 1 & 1 \end{pmatrix}$$

So

$$R_{\theta,L} \cdot C = \begin{pmatrix} \dfrac{1}{2} & \dfrac{1+\sqrt{2}}{2} & 0 & 1 \\ \dfrac{2-\sqrt{2}}{4} & \dfrac{4-\sqrt{2}}{4} & 1 & \dfrac{2-\sqrt{2}}{2} \\ \dfrac{\sqrt{2}-2}{4} & \dfrac{\sqrt{2}-4}{4} & 0 & \dfrac{\sqrt{2}}{2} \\ 1 & 1 & 1 & 1 \end{pmatrix}$$

The rotated coordinates are (Fig. 6-7)

$$A' = \left(\dfrac{1}{2}, \dfrac{2-\sqrt{2}}{4}, \dfrac{\sqrt{2}-2}{4}\right) \qquad\qquad C' = (0, 1, 0)$$

$$B' = \left(\dfrac{1+\sqrt{2}}{2}, \dfrac{4-\sqrt{2}}{4}, \dfrac{\sqrt{2}-4}{4}\right) \qquad D' = \left(1, \dfrac{2-\sqrt{2}}{2}, \dfrac{\sqrt{2}}{2}\right)$$

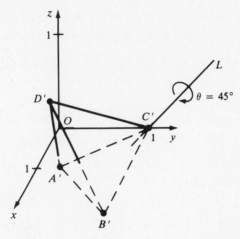

Fig. 6-7

6.5   Find a transformation $A_{V,N}$ which aligns a vector **V** with a vector **N**.

SOLUTION

We form the transformation in two steps: First, align vector **V** with vector **K**, and second, align vector **K** with vector **N**. So from Prob. 6.2,

$$A_{V,N} = A_N \cdot A_V$$

Referring to Prob. 6.8, we could also get $A_{V,N}$ by rotating **V** towards **N** about the axis **V** × **N** (see Prob. 6.12).

6.6   Find the transformation for mirror reflection with respect to the *xy* plane.

SOLUTION

From Fig. 6-8, it is easy to see that the reflection of $P(x, y, z)$ is $P'(x, y, -z)$. The transformation that performs this reflection is

$$M = \begin{pmatrix} 1 & 0 & 0 \\ 0 & 1 & 0 \\ 0 & 0 & -1 \end{pmatrix}$$

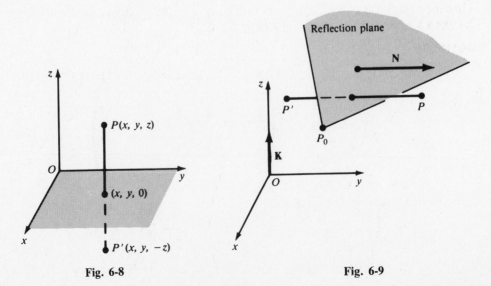

Fig. 6-8   **Fig. 6-9**

6.7   Find the transformation for mirror reflection with respect to a given plane. Refer to Fig. 6-9.

SOLUTION

Let the plane of reflection be specified by a normal vector **N** and a reference point $P_0(x_0, y_0, z_0)$. To reduce the reflection to a mirror reflection with respect to the xy plane:

1. Translate P_0 to the origin.
2. Align the normal vector **N** with the vector **K** normal to the xy plane.
3. Perform the mirror reflection in the xy plane (Prob. 6.6).
4. Reverse steps 1 and 2.

So, with translation vector $\mathbf{V} = -x_0\mathbf{I} - y_0\mathbf{J} - z_0\mathbf{K}$

$$M_{\mathbf{N}, P_0} = T_{\mathbf{V}}^{-1} \cdot A_{\mathbf{N}}^{-1} \cdot M \cdot A_{\mathbf{N}} \cdot T_{\mathbf{V}}$$

Here, $A_{\mathbf{N}}$ is the alignment matrix defined in Prob. 6.2. So if the vector $\mathbf{N} = n_1\mathbf{I} + n_2\mathbf{J} + n_3\mathbf{K}$, then from Prob. 6.2, with $|\mathbf{N}| = \sqrt{n_1^2 + n_2^2 + n_3^2}$ and $\lambda = \sqrt{n_2^2 + n_3^2}$, we find

$$A_{\mathbf{N}} = \begin{pmatrix} \dfrac{\lambda}{|\mathbf{N}|} & \dfrac{-n_1 n_2}{\lambda |\mathbf{N}|} & \dfrac{-n_1 n_3}{\lambda |\mathbf{N}|} & 0 \\[2mm] 0 & \dfrac{n_3}{\lambda} & \dfrac{-n_2}{\lambda} & 0 \\[2mm] \dfrac{n_1}{|\mathbf{N}|} & \dfrac{n_2}{|\mathbf{N}|} & \dfrac{n_3}{|\mathbf{N}|} & 0 \\[2mm] 0 & 0 & 0 & 1 \end{pmatrix} \quad \text{and} \quad A_{\mathbf{N}}^{-1} = \begin{pmatrix} \dfrac{\lambda}{|\mathbf{N}|} & 0 & \dfrac{n_1}{|\mathbf{N}|} & 0 \\[2mm] \dfrac{-n_1 n_2}{\lambda |\mathbf{N}|} & \dfrac{n_3}{\lambda} & \dfrac{n_2}{|\mathbf{N}|} & 0 \\[2mm] \dfrac{-n_1 n_3}{\lambda |\mathbf{N}|} & \dfrac{-n_2}{\lambda} & \dfrac{n_3}{|\mathbf{N}|} & 0 \\[2mm] 0 & 0 & 0 & 1 \end{pmatrix}$$

In addition

$$T_{\mathbf{V}} = \begin{pmatrix} 1 & 0 & 0 & -x_0 \\ 0 & 1 & 0 & -y_0 \\ 0 & 0 & 1 & -z_0 \\ 0 & 0 & 0 & 1 \end{pmatrix} \quad \text{and} \quad T_{\mathbf{V}}^{-1} = \begin{pmatrix} 1 & 0 & 0 & x_0 \\ 0 & 1 & 0 & y_0 \\ 0 & 0 & 1 & z_0 \\ 0 & 0 & 0 & 1 \end{pmatrix}$$

Finally, from Prob. 6.6, the homogeneous form of M is

$$M = \begin{pmatrix} 1 & 0 & 0 & 0 \\ 0 & 1 & 0 & 0 \\ 0 & 0 & -1 & 0 \\ 0 & 0 & 0 & 1 \end{pmatrix}$$

6.8   Find the matrix for mirror reflection with respect to the plane passing through the origin and having a normal vector whose direction is $\mathbf{N} = \mathbf{I} + \mathbf{J} + \mathbf{K}$.

SOLUTION

From Prob. 6.7, with $P_0(0, 0, 0)$ and $\mathbf{N} = \mathbf{I} + \mathbf{J} + \mathbf{K}$, we find $|\mathbf{N}| = \sqrt{3}$ and $\lambda = \sqrt{2}$. Then

$$T_{\mathbf{V}} = \begin{pmatrix} 1 & 0 & 0 & 0 \\ 0 & 1 & 0 & 0 \\ 0 & 0 & 1 & 0 \\ 0 & 0 & 0 & 1 \end{pmatrix} \quad (\mathbf{V} = o\mathbf{I} + o\mathbf{J} + o\mathbf{K}) \quad T_{\mathbf{V}}^{-1} = \begin{pmatrix} 1 & 0 & 0 & 0 \\ 0 & 1 & 0 & 0 \\ 0 & 0 & 1 & 0 \\ 0 & 0 & 0 & 1 \end{pmatrix}$$

$$A_{\mathbf{N}} = \begin{pmatrix} \dfrac{\sqrt{2}}{\sqrt{3}} & \dfrac{-1}{\sqrt{2}\sqrt{3}} & \dfrac{-1}{\sqrt{2}\sqrt{3}} & 0 \\[2mm] 0 & \dfrac{1}{\sqrt{2}} & \dfrac{-1}{\sqrt{2}} & 0 \\[2mm] \dfrac{1}{\sqrt{3}} & \dfrac{1}{\sqrt{3}} & \dfrac{1}{\sqrt{3}} & 0 \\[2mm] 0 & 0 & 0 & 1 \end{pmatrix} \quad A_{\mathbf{N}}^{-1} = \begin{pmatrix} \dfrac{\sqrt{2}}{\sqrt{3}} & 0 & \dfrac{1}{\sqrt{3}} & 0 \\[2mm] \dfrac{-1}{\sqrt{2}\sqrt{3}} & \dfrac{1}{\sqrt{2}} & \dfrac{1}{\sqrt{3}} & 0 \\[2mm] \dfrac{-1}{\sqrt{2}\sqrt{3}} & \dfrac{-1}{\sqrt{2}} & \dfrac{1}{\sqrt{3}} & 0 \\[2mm] 0 & 0 & 0 & 1 \end{pmatrix}$$

and

$$M = \begin{pmatrix} 1 & 0 & 0 & 0 \\ 0 & 1 & 0 & 0 \\ 0 & 0 & -1 & 0 \\ 0 & 0 & 0 & 1 \end{pmatrix}$$

The reflection matrix is

$$M_{N,0} = T_V^{-1} \cdot A_N^{-1} \cdot M \cdot A_N \cdot T_V$$

$$= \begin{pmatrix} \frac{1}{3} & -\frac{2}{3} & -\frac{2}{3} & 0 \\ -\frac{2}{3} & \frac{1}{3} & -\frac{2}{3} & 0 \\ -\frac{2}{3} & -\frac{2}{3} & \frac{1}{3} & 0 \\ 0 & 0 & 0 & 1 \end{pmatrix}$$

Supplementary Problems

6.9   Align the vector $V = I + J + K$ with the vector K.

6.10   Find a transformation which aligns the vector $V = I + J + K$ with the vector $N = 2I - J - K$.

6.11   Show that the alignment transformation satisfies the relation $A_V^{-1} = A_V^T$.

6.12   Show that the alignment transformation $A_{V,N}$ is equivalent to a rotation of $\theta°$ about an axis having the direction of the vector $V \times N$ and passing through the origin (see Fig. 6-10). Here θ is the angle between vectors V and N.

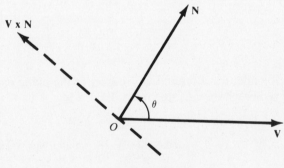

Fig. 6-10

6.13   How can scaling with respect to a point $P_0(x_0, y_0, z_0)$ be defined in terms of scaling with respect to the origin?

Chapter 7

Mathematics of Projection

7.1 INTRODUCTION

For centuries, artists, engineers, designers, drafters, cartographers, and architects have tried to come to terms with the difficulties and constraints imposed by the problem of representing a three-dimensional object or scene in a two-dimensional medium—the problem of *projection*. Volumes have been written describing tools, techniques, and tricks used for this purpose. The implementor of a computerized graphics system faces the same challenge. The media on which the image will be displayed include not only paper but also various forms of illuminated screen (CRT, plasma, LED) or other yet-to-be-invented devices. The ability to plot a computed point enables us to use the screen as a drawing medium. The mathematical description of the projection process allows us to display images of three-dimensional objects and scenes at will.

The two basic methods of projection—*perspective* and *parallel*—were designed to solve the basic but mutually exclusive problems of pictorial representation: showing an object as it appears and preserving its true size and shape.

An important observation (in terms of computer graphics) is that projections preserve lines. That is, the line joining the projected images of the endpoints of the original line is the same as the projection of that line.

7.2 THE VARIOUS KINDS OF PROJECTION

We can construct different projections according to the view that is desired.

Table 7-1 provides a taxonomy of the families of perspective and parallel projections. Some projections have names—cavalier, cabinet, isometric, and so on. Other projections qualify the main type of projection—one principal vanishing-point perspective, and so forth.

7.3 PERSPECTIVE PROJECTION

Basic Principles

The techniques of perspective projection are generalizations of the principles used by artists in preparing perspective drawings of three-dimensional objects and scenes. The eye of the artist is placed at the *center of projection*, and the canvas, or more precisely the plane containing the canvas, becomes the *view plane*. An image point is located at the intersection of a *projector* (a ray drawn from an object point to the center of projection) with the view plane (see Fig. 7-1).

Perspective drawings are characterized by perspective foreshortening and vanishing points. *Perspective foreshortening* is the illusion that objects and lengths appear smaller as their distance from the center of projection increases. The illusion that certain sets of parallel lines appear to meet at a point is another feature of perspective drawings. These points are called *vanishing points*. *Principal vanishing points* are formed by the apparent intersection of lines parallel to one of the three principal x, y, or z axes. The number of principal vanishing points is determined by the number of principal axes intersected by the view plane (Prob. 7.7).

Mathematical Description of a Perspective Projection

A perspective transformation is determined by prescribing a center of projection and a view plane. The view plane is determined by its *view reference point* R_0 and *view plane normal N*. The *object point* P is located in world coordinates at (x, y, z). The problem is to determine the *image point* coordinates $P(x', y', z')$ (see Fig. 7-1).

127

Table 7-1

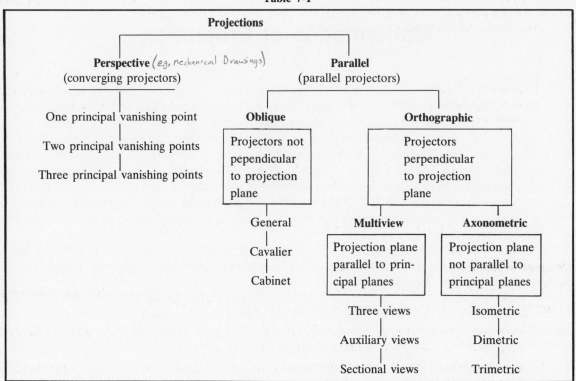

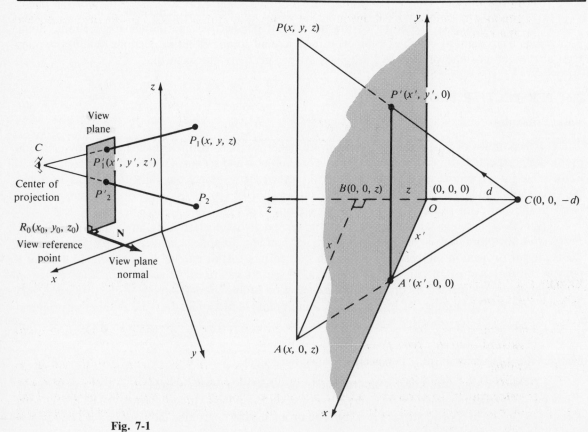

Fig. 7-1

EXAMPLE 1. The standard perspective projection is shown in Fig. 7-2. Here, the view plane is the xy plane, and the center of projection is taken as the point $C(0, 0, -d)$ on the negative z axis.

Using similar triangles ABC and $A'0C$, we find

$$x' = \frac{d \cdot x}{z + d} \qquad y' = \frac{d \cdot y}{z + d} \qquad z' = 0$$

The perspective transformation between object and image point is nonlinear and so cannot be represented as a 3×3 matrix transformation. However, if we use homogeneous coordinates, the perspective transformation can be represented as a 4×4 matrix:

$$\begin{pmatrix} x' \\ y' \\ z' \\ 1 \end{pmatrix} = \begin{pmatrix} d \cdot x \\ d \cdot y \\ 0 \\ z + d \end{pmatrix} = \begin{pmatrix} d & 0 & 0 & 0 \\ 0 & d & 0 & 0 \\ 0 & 0 & 0 & 0 \\ 0 & 0 & 1 & d \end{pmatrix} \begin{pmatrix} x \\ y \\ z \\ 1 \end{pmatrix}$$

The general form of a perspective transformation is developed in Prob. 7.5.

Perspective Anomalies

The process of constructing a perspective view introduces certain anomalies which enhance realism in terms of depth cues but also distort actual sizes and shapes.

1. *Perspective foreshortening.* The farther an object is from the center of projection, the smaller it appears (i.e., its projected size becomes smaller). Refer to Fig. 7-3.

2. *Vanishing points.* Projections of lines that are not parallel to the view plane (i.e., lines that are not perpendicular to the view plane normal) appear to meet at some point on the view plane. A common manifestation of this anomaly is the illusion that railroad tracks meet at a point on the horizon.

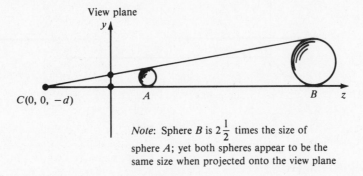

Note: Sphere B is $2\frac{1}{2}$ times the size of sphere A; yet both spheres appear to be the same size when projected onto the view plane

Fig. 7-3

EXAMPLE 2. For the standard perspective projection, the projections L_1' and L_2' of parallel lines L_1 and L_2 having the direction of the vector $\mathbf{K}$ appear to meet at the origin (Prob. 7.8). Refer to Fig. 7-4.

3. *View confusion.* Objects behind the center of projection are projected upside down and backward onto the view plane. Refer to Fig. 7-5.

4. *Topological distortion.* Consider the plane that passes through the center of projection and is parallel to the view plane. The points of this plane are projected to infinity by the perspective transformation. In particular, a finite line segment joining a point which lies in front of the viewer to a point in back of the viewer is actually projected to a broken line of infinite extent (Prob. 7.2) (see Fig. 7-6).

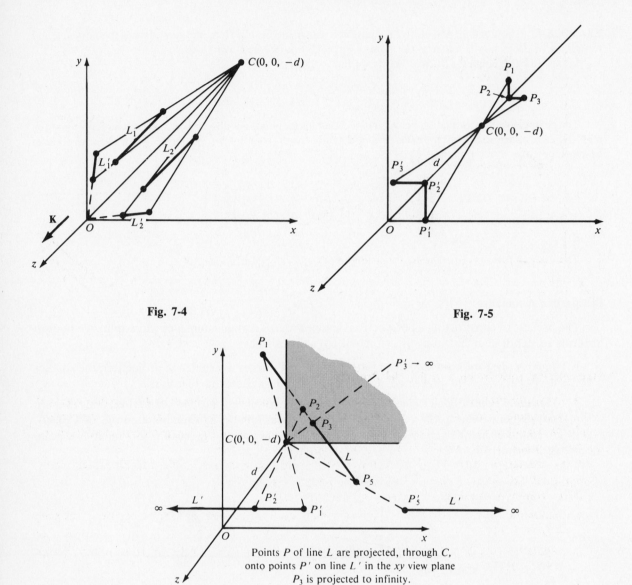

Fig. 7-4   **Fig. 7-5**

Points P of line L are projected, through C,
onto points P' on line L' in the xy view plane
P_3 is projected to infinity.

Fig. 7-6

7.4 PARALLEL PROJECTION

Basic Principles

Parallel projection methods are used by drafters and engineers to create working drawings of an object which preserve its scale and shape. The complete representation of these details often requires two or more views (projections) of the object onto different view planes.

In parallel projection, image points are found as the intersection of the view plane with a projector drawn from the object point and having a fixed direction (see Fig. 7-7). The *direction of projection* is the prescribed direction for all projectors. *Orthographic projections* are characterized by the fact that the direction of projection is perpendicular to the view plane. When the direction of projection is parallel to any of the principal axes, this produces the front, top, and side views of mechanical drawings (also referred to as *multiview drawings*). *Axonometric projections* are orthographic projections in which the direction of projection is not parallel to any of the three principal axes. Nonorthographic parallel projections are called *oblique parallel projections*. Further subcategories of these main types of parallel projection are described in the problems. (See also Fig. 7-8.)

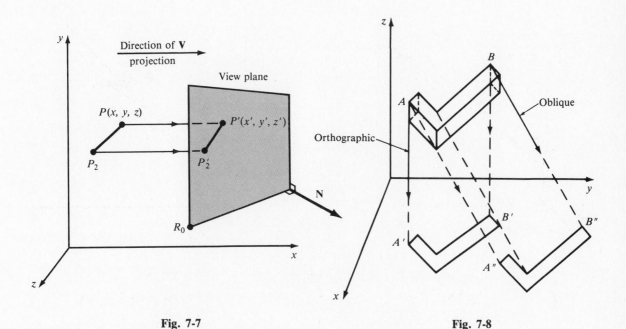

Fig. 7-7   **Fig. 7-8**

Mathematical Description of a Parallel Projection

A *parallel projective transformation* is determined by prescribing a *direction of projection vector* **V** and a view plane. The view plane is specified by its view plane reference point R_0, and view plane normal **N**. The object point P is located at (x, y, z) in world coordinates. The problem is to determine the image point coordinates $P'(x', y', z')$. See Fig. 7-7.

If the projection vector **V** has the direction of the view plane normal **N**, the projection is said to be *orthographic*. Otherwise it is called *oblique* (see Fig. 7-8).

Some common subcategories of orthographic projections are:

1. *Isometric*—the direction of projection makes equal angles with all of the three principal axes (Prob. 7.14).

2. *Dimetric*—the direction of projection makes equal angles with exactly two of the principal axes (Prob. 7.15).

3. *Trimetric*—the direction of projection makes unequal angles with the three principal axes.

Some common subcategories of oblique projections are:

1. *Cavalier*—the direction of projection is chosen so that there is no foreshortening of lines perpendicular to the xy plane (Prob. 7.13).

2. *Cabinet*—the direction of projection is chosen so that lines perpendicular to the xy planes are foreshortened by half their lengths (Prob. 7.13).

EXAMPLE 3. For orthographic projection onto the xy plane, from Fig. 7-9 it is easy to see that

$$Par_K: \begin{cases} x' = x \\ y' = y \\ z' = 0 \end{cases}$$

The matrix form of Par_K is

$$Par_K = \begin{pmatrix} 1 & 0 & 0 & 0 \\ 0 & 1 & 0 & 0 \\ 0 & 0 & 0 & 0 \\ 0 & 0 & 0 & 1 \end{pmatrix}$$

The general parallel projective transformation is derived in Prob. 7.11.

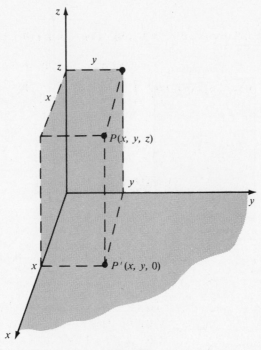

Fig. 7-9

Solved Problems

7.1   The unit cube (Fig. 7-10) is projected onto the *xy* plane. Note the position of the *x*, *y*, and *z* axes. Draw the projected image using the standard perspective transformation with (*a*) *d* = 1 and (*b*) *d* = 10, where *d* is distance from the view plane.

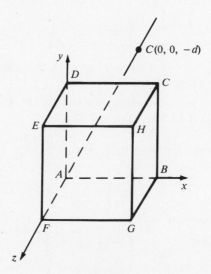

Fig. 7-10

SOLUTION

We represent the unit cube in terms of the homogeneous coordinates of its vertices:

$$\mathbf{V} = (ABCDEFGH) = \begin{pmatrix} 0 & 1 & 1 & 0 & 0 & 0 & 1 & 1 \\ 0 & 0 & 1 & 1 & 1 & 0 & 0 & 1 \\ 0 & 0 & 0 & 0 & 1 & 1 & 1 & 1 \\ 1 & 1 & 1 & 1 & 1 & 1 & 1 & 1 \end{pmatrix}$$

From Example 1 the standard perspective matrix is

$$Per_{\kappa} = \begin{pmatrix} d & 0 & 0 & 0 \\ 0 & d & 0 & 0 \\ 0 & 0 & 0 & 0 \\ 0 & 0 & 1 & d \end{pmatrix}$$

(a) With $d = 1$, the projected coordinates are found by applying the matrix Per_{κ} to the matrix of coordinates $\mathbf{V}$. Then

$$Per_{\kappa} \cdot \mathbf{V} = \begin{pmatrix} 0 & 1 & 1 & 0 & 0 & 0 & 1 & 1 \\ 0 & 0 & 1 & 1 & 1 & 0 & 0 & 1 \\ 0 & 0 & 0 & 0 & 0 & 0 & 0 & 0 \\ 1 & 1 & 1 & 1 & 2 & 2 & 2 & 2 \end{pmatrix}$$

If these homogeneous coordinates are changed to three-dimensional coordinates, the projected image has coordinates:

$$\begin{array}{ll} A' = (0, 0, 0) & E' = (0, \tfrac{1}{2}, 0) \\ B' = (1, 0, 0) & F' = (0, 0, 0) \\ C' = (1, 1, 0) & G' = (\tfrac{1}{2}, 0, 0) \\ D' = (0, 1, 0) & H' = (\tfrac{1}{2}, \tfrac{1}{2}, 0) \end{array}$$

We draw the projected image by preserving the edge connections of the original object (see Fig. 7-11). [Note the vanishing point at $(0, 0, 0)$.]

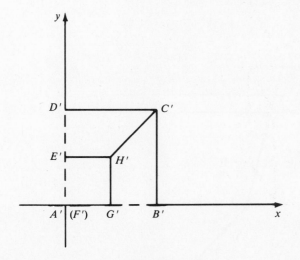

Fig. 7-11

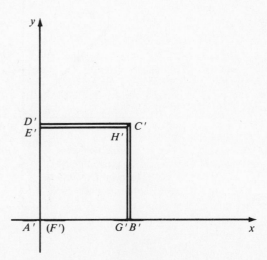

Fig. 7-12

(b) With $d = 10$, the perspective matrix is

$$Per_{\kappa} = \begin{pmatrix} 10 & 0 & 0 & 0 \\ 0 & 10 & 0 & 0 \\ 0 & 0 & 0 & 0 \\ 0 & 0 & 1 & 10 \end{pmatrix}$$

Then

$$Per_{\kappa} \cdot V = \begin{pmatrix} 0 & 10 & 10 & 0 & 0 & 0 & 10 & 10 \\ 0 & 0 & 10 & 10 & 10 & 0 & 0 & 10 \\ 0 & 0 & 0 & 0 & 0 & 0 & 0 & 0 \\ 10 & 10 & 10 & 10 & 11 & 11 & 11 & 11 \end{pmatrix}$$

is the matrix image coordinates in homogeneous form. The projected image coordinates are then

$$A' = (0,0,0) \qquad E' = (0, \tfrac{10}{11}, 0)$$
$$B' = (1,0,0) \qquad F' = (0,0,0)$$
$$C' = (1,1,0) \qquad G' = (\tfrac{10}{11}, 0, 0)$$
$$D' = (0,1,0) \qquad H' = (\tfrac{10}{11}, \tfrac{10}{11}, 0)$$

Note the different perspectives of the face $E'F'G'H'$ in Figs. 7-11 and 7-12. [To a viewer standing at the center of projection $(0, 0, -d)$, this face is the back face of the unit cube.]

7.2 Under the standard perspective transformation Per_{κ}, what is the projected image of (a) a point in the plane $z = -d$ and (b) the line segment joining $P_1(-1, 1, -2d)$ to $P_2(2, -2, 0)$? (See Fig. 7-13.)

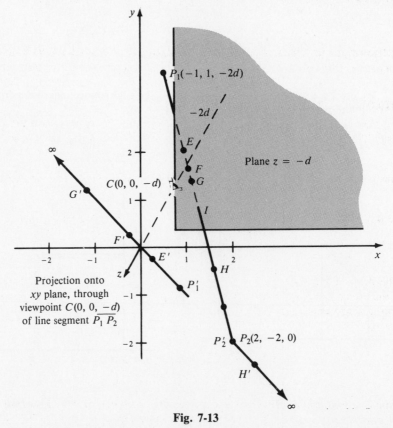

Fig. 7-13

SOLUTION

(a) The plane $z = -d$ is the plane parallel to the xy view plane and located at the center of projection $C(0, 0, -d)$. If $P(x, y, -d)$ is any point in this plane, the line of projection $\overline{CP}$ does not intersect the xy view plane. We then say that P is projected out to infinity (∞).

(b) The line $\overline{P_1 P_2}$ passes through the plane $z = -d$. Writing the equation of the line (App. 2), we have

$$x = -1 + 3t \qquad y = 1 - 3t \qquad z = -2d + 2dt$$

We see that at $t = \frac{1}{2}$: $x = \frac{1}{2}$, $y = -\frac{1}{2}$, and $z = -d$. These are the coordinates of the intersection point I.

We now describe the perspective projection of this line segment.

Applying the standard projection to the equation of the line, we find

$$\begin{pmatrix} d & 0 & 0 & 0 \\ 0 & d & 0 & 0 \\ 0 & 0 & 0 & 0 \\ 0 & 0 & 1 & d \end{pmatrix} \begin{pmatrix} -1 + 3t \\ 1 - 3t \\ -2d + 2dt \\ 1 \end{pmatrix} = \begin{pmatrix} -d + 3dt \\ d - 3dt \\ 0 \\ -d + 2dt \end{pmatrix}$$

Changing from homogeneous to three-dimensional coordinates, the equations of the projected line segment are

$$x = \frac{-d + 3dt}{-d + 2dt} = \frac{-1 + 3t}{-1 + 2t} \qquad y = \frac{d - 3dt}{-d + 2dt} = \frac{1 - 3t}{-1 + 2t} \qquad z = 0$$

(In App. 1, Prob. A1.12, it is shown that this is the equation of a line.) When $t = 0$, then $x = 1$ and $y = -1$. These are the coordinates of the projection P_1' of point P_1. When $t = 1$, it follows that $x = 2$ and $y = -2$ (the coordinates of the projection P_2' of point P_2). However, when $t = \frac{1}{2}$, the denominator is 0. Thus this line segment "passes" through the point at infinity in joining $P_1'(1, -1)$ to $P_2'(2, -2)$. In other words, when a line segment joining endpoints P_1 and P_2 passes through the plane containing the center of projection and which is parallel to the view plane, the projection of this line segment is *not* the simple line segment joining the projected endpoints P_1' and P_2'. (See also Prob. A1.13 in App. 1.)

7.3 Using the origin as the center of projection, derive the perspective transformation onto the plane passing through the point $R_0(x_0, y_0, z_0)$ and having the normal vector $\mathbf{N} = n_1 I + n_2 J + n_3 K$.

SOLUTION

Let $P(x, y, z)$ be projected onto $P'(x', y', z')$. From Fig. 7-14, the vectors $\overline{PO}$ and $\overline{P'O}$ have the same direction. Thus there is a number α so that $\overline{P'O} = \alpha \overline{PO}$. Comparing components, we have

$$x' = \alpha x \qquad y' = \alpha y \qquad z' = \alpha z$$

We now find the value of α. Since any point $P'(x', y', z')$ lying on the plane satisfies the equation (App. 2)

$$n_1 x' + n_2 y' + n_3 z' = d_0$$

(where $d_0 = n_1 x_0 + n_2 y_0 + n_3 z_0$), substitution of $x' = \alpha x$, $y' = \alpha y$, and $z' = \alpha z$ into this equation gives

$$\alpha = \frac{d_0}{n_1 x + n_2 y + n_3 z}$$

This projection transformation cannot be represented as a 3×3 matrix transformation. However, by using the homogeneous coordinate representation for three-dimensional points, we can write the projection transformation as a 4×4 matrix:

$$Per_{N, R_0} = \begin{pmatrix} d_0 & 0 & 0 & 0 \\ 0 & d_0 & 0 & 0 \\ 0 & 0 & d_0 & 0 \\ n_1 & n_2 & n_3 & 0 \end{pmatrix}$$

Application of this matrix to the homogeneous representation $P(x, y, z, 1)$ of point P gives $P'(d_0 x, d_0 y, d_0 z, n_1 x + n_2 y + n_3 z)$, which is the homogeneous representation of $P'(x', y', z')$ found above.

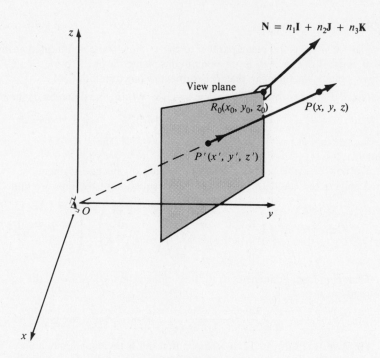

Fig. 7-14

7.4 Find the perspective projection onto the view plane $z = d$ where the center of projection is the origin $(0, 0, 0)$.

SOLUTION

The plane $z = d$ is parallel to the xy plane (and d units away from it). Thus the view plane normal vector $\mathbf{N}$ is the same as the normal vector $\mathbf{K}$ to the xy plane, that is, $\mathbf{N} = \mathbf{K}$. Choosing the view reference point as $R_0(0, 0, d)$, then from Prob. 7.3, we identify the parameters

$$\mathbf{N}(n_1, n_2, n_3) = (0, 0, 1) \qquad R_0(x_0, y_0, z_0) = (0, 0, d)$$

So

$$d_0 = n_1 x_0 + n_2 y_0 + n_3 z_0 = d$$

and then the projection matrix is

$$Per_{\mathbf{K}, R_0} = \begin{pmatrix} d & 0 & 0 & 0 \\ 0 & d & 0 & 0 \\ 0 & 0 & d & 0 \\ 0 & 0 & 1 & 0 \end{pmatrix}$$

7.5 Derive the general perspective transformation onto a plane with reference point $R_0(x_0, y_0, z_0)$, normal vector $\mathbf{N} = n_1 \mathbf{I} = n_2 \mathbf{J} + n_3 \mathbf{K}$, and using $C(a, b, c)$ as the center of projection. Refer to Fig. 7-15.

SOLUTION

As in Prob. 7.3, we can conclude that the vectors $\overline{\mathbf{PC}}$ and $\overline{\mathbf{P'C}}$ satisfy (see Fig. 7-15) $\overline{\mathbf{P'C}} = \alpha \overline{\mathbf{PC}}$. Then

$$x' = \alpha(x - a) + a \qquad y' = \alpha(x - b) + b \qquad z' = \alpha(z - c) + c$$

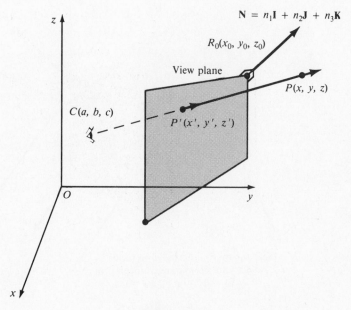

Fig. 7-15

Also, we find (by using the equation of the view plane) that

$$\alpha = \frac{d}{n_1(x - a) + n_2(y - b) + n_3(z - c)}$$

[i.e., $P'(x', y', z')$ is on the view plane and thus satisfies the view plane equation $n_1(x' - x_0) + n_2(y' - y_0) + n_3(z' - z_0) = 0$]. Here, $d = (n_1 x_0 + n_2 y_0 + n_3 z_0) - (n_1 a + n_2 b + n_3 c)$.

From App. 2, Prob. A2.13, d is proportional to the distance D from the view plane to the center of projection, that is, $d = \pm |\mathbf{N}| D$.

To find the homogeneous coordinate matrix representation, it is easiest to proceed as follows:

1. Translate so that the center of projection C lies at the origin. Now $R'_0 = (x_0 - a, y_0 - b, z_0 - c)$ becomes the reference point of the translated plane (the normal vector is unchanged by translation).

2. Project onto the translated plane using the origin as the center of projection by constructing the transformation $Per_{\mathbf{N}, R'_0}$ (Prob. 7.3).

3. Translate back.

Introducing the intermediate quantities

$$d_0 = n_1 x_0 + n_2 y_0 + n_3 z_0 \qquad \text{and} \qquad d_1 = n_1 a + n_2 b + n_3 c$$

we obtain $d = d_0 - d_1$, and so $Per_{\mathbf{N}, R_0, C} = T_C \cdot Per_{\mathbf{N}, R'_0} \cdot T_{-C}$. Then with R'_0 used as the reference point in constructing the projection $P_{\mathbf{N}, R'_0}$,

$$Per_{\mathbf{N}, R_0, C} = \begin{pmatrix} 1 & 0 & 0 & a \\ 0 & 1 & 0 & b \\ 0 & 0 & 1 & c \\ 0 & 0 & 0 & 1 \end{pmatrix} \cdot \begin{pmatrix} d & 0 & 0 & 0 \\ 0 & d & 0 & 0 \\ 0 & 0 & d & 0 \\ n_1 & n_2 & n_3 & 0 \end{pmatrix} \cdot \begin{pmatrix} 1 & 0 & 0 & -a \\ 0 & 1 & 0 & -b \\ 0 & 0 & 1 & -c \\ 0 & 0 & 0 & 1 \end{pmatrix}$$

$$= \begin{pmatrix} d + an_1 & an_2 & an_3 & -ad_0 \\ bn_1 & d + bn_2 & bn_3 & -bd_0 \\ cn_1 & cn_2 & d + cn_3 & -cd_0 \\ n_1 & n_2 & n_3 & -d_1 \end{pmatrix}$$

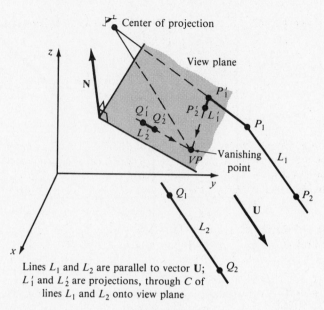

Lines L_1 and L_2 are parallel to vector $\mathbf{U}$;
L_1' and L_2' are projections, through C of
lines L_1 and L_2 onto view plane

Fig. 7-16

7.6   Find the (a) vanishing points for a given perspective transformation in the direction given by a
vector $\mathbf{U}$ and (b) principal vanishing points.

SOLUTION

(a)   The family of (parallel) lines having the direction of $\mathbf{U} = u_1\mathbf{I} + u_2\mathbf{J} + u_3\mathbf{K}$ can be written in
parametric form as

$$x = u_1 t + p \qquad y = u_2 t + q \qquad z = u_3 t + r$$

where $P(p, q, r)$ is any point (see App. 2). Application of the perspective transformation (Prob. 7.5)
to the homogeneous point $(x, y, z, 1)$ produces the result (x', y', z', h), where

$$x' = (d + an_1)(u_1 t + p) + an_2(u_2 t + q) + an_3(u_3 t + r) - ad_0$$
$$y' = bn_1(u_1 t + p) + (d + bn_2)(u_2 t + q) + bn_3(u_3 t + r) - bd_0$$
$$z' = cn_1(u_1 t + p) + cn_2(u_2 t + q) + (d + cn_3)(u_3 t + r) - cd_0$$
$$h = n_1(u_1 t + p) + n_2(u_2 t + q) + n_3(u_3 t + r) - d_1$$

The vanishing point corresponds to the infinite point obtained when $t = \infty$. So after dividing x', y',
and z' by h, we let $t \rightarrow \infty$ to find the coordinates of the vanishing point:

$$x_u = \frac{(d + an_1)u_1 + an_2 u_2 + an_3 u_3}{k} = a + \frac{du_1}{k}$$

(Here, $k = \mathbf{N} \cdot \mathbf{U} = n_1 u_1 + n_2 u_2 + n_3 u_3$.)

$$y_u = \frac{bn_1 u_1 + (d + bn_2)u_2 + bn_3 u_3}{k} = b + \frac{du_2}{k}$$

$$z_u = \frac{cn_1 u_1 + cn_2 u_2 + (d + cn_3)u_3}{k} = c + \frac{du_3}{k}$$

This point lies on the line passing through the center of projection and parallel to the vector $\mathbf{U}$ (see
Fig. 7-16). Note that $k = 0$ only when $\mathbf{U}$ is parallel to the projection plane, in which case there is no
vanishing point.

(b)   The principal vanishing points P_1, P_2, and P_3 correspond to the vector directions $\mathbf{I}$, $\mathbf{J}$, and $\mathbf{K}$. In these cases

$$P_1: \begin{cases} x_1 = a + \dfrac{d}{n_1} \\ y_1 = b \\ z_1 = c \end{cases} \qquad P_2: \begin{cases} x_2 = a \\ y_2 = b + \dfrac{d}{n_2} \\ z_2 = c \end{cases} \qquad P_3: \begin{cases} x_3 = a \\ y_3 = b \\ z_3 = c + \dfrac{d}{n_3} \end{cases}$$

(Recall from Prob. 7.5 that a, b, c are the coordinates of the center of projection. Also, n_1, n_2, n_3 are the components of the view plane normal vector and d is proportional to the distance D from the view plane to the center of projection.) (*Note*: If any of the components of the normal vector are zero, say, $n_1 = 0$, then $k = \mathbf{N} \cdot \mathbf{I} = 0$, and there is no principal vanishing point in the $\mathbf{I}$ direction.)

7.7   Describe the (*a*) one-principal-vanishing-point perspective, (*b*) two-principal-vanishing-point perspective, and (*c*) three-principal-vanishing-point perspective.

SOLUTION

(*a*)   The one-principal-vanishing-point perspective occurs when the projection plane is perpendicular to one of the principal axes (x, y, or z). Assume that it is the z axis. In this case the view plane normal vector $\mathbf{N}$ is the vector $\mathbf{K}$, and from Prob. 7.6, the principal vanishing point is

$$P_3: \begin{cases} x_3 = a \\ y_3 = b \\ z_3 = c + \dfrac{d}{n_3} \end{cases}$$

(*b*)   The two-principal-vanishing-point projection occurs when the projection plane intersects exactly two of the principal axes. Refer to Fig. 7-17, which is a perspective drawing with two principal vanishing

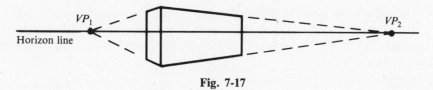

Fig. 7-17

points. In the case where the projection plane intersects the x and y axes, for example, the normal vector satisfies the relationship $\mathbf{N} \cdot \mathbf{K} = 0$ or $n_3 = 0$, and so the principal vanishing points are

$$P_1: \begin{cases} x_1 = a + \dfrac{d}{n_1} \\ y_1 = b \\ z_1 = c \end{cases} \qquad P_2: \begin{cases} x_2 = a \\ y_2 = b + \dfrac{d}{n_2} \\ z_2 = c \end{cases}$$

(*c*)   The three-vanishing-point perspective projection occurs when the projection plane intersects all three of the principal axes—x, y, and z axes. Refer to Fig. 7-18, which is a perspective drawing with three principal vanishing points. In this case, the principal vanishing points are points P_1, P_2, and P_3 from Prob. 7.6(*b*).

7.8   What are the principal vanishing points for the standard perspective transformation?

SOLUTION

In this case, the view plane normal $\mathbf{N}$ is the vector $\mathbf{K}$. From Prob. 7.7, since $k_1 = \mathbf{N} \cdot \mathbf{I} = 0$ and $k_2 = \mathbf{N} \cdot \mathbf{J} = 0$, there are no vanishing points in the directions $\mathbf{I}$ and $\mathbf{J}$. On the other hand, $\mathbf{N} \cdot \mathbf{K} = \mathbf{K} \cdot \mathbf{K} = 1$.

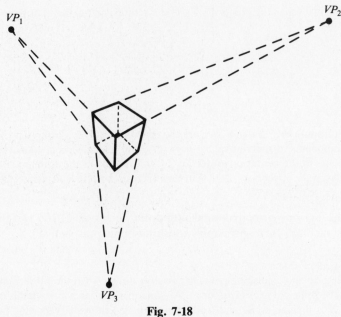

Fig. 7-18

Thus there is only one principal vanishing point, and it is in the $\mathbf{K}$ direction. Also from Prob. 7.7, the coordinates of the principal vanishing point VP in the $\mathbf{K}$ direction are

$$x = a = 0 \qquad y = b = 0 \qquad z = -d + \frac{d}{1} = 0$$

So $VP = (0, 0, 0)$ is the principal vanishing point.

7.9 An artist constructs a two-vanishing-point perspective by locating the vanishing points VP_1 and VP_2 on a given horizon line in the view plane. The horizon line is located by its height h above the ground (Fig. 7-19). Construct the corresponding perspective projection transformation for the cube shown in Fig. 7-19.

SOLUTION

A two-principal-vanishing-point perspective must intersect two axes, say, x and y. We locate the view plane at the point $R_0(1, 1, 0)$ so that it makes angles of 30 and 60° with the corresponding faces of the cube (see Fig. 7-19). In this plane we locate the horizon line a given height h above the "ground" (the xy plane).

The vanishing points VP_1 and VP_2 are located on this horizon line. To construct the perspective transformation, we need to find the normal vector $\mathbf{N} = n_1\mathbf{I} + n_2\mathbf{J} + n_3\mathbf{K}$ of the view plane, the coordinates $C(a, b, c)$ of the center of projection, and the view parameters d_0, d_1, and d (Prob. 7.5). To calculate the coordinates of the vanishing points, we first find the equation of the horizon line. Let I_1 and I_2 be the points of intersection of the view plane and the x and y axes. The horizon line is parallel to line $\overline{I_1 I_2}$ and lies h units above it.

From triangles $I_1 B R_0$ and $I_2 D R_0$, we find

$$I_1 = \left(1 + \frac{1}{\sqrt{3}}, 0, 0\right) = \left(\frac{1+\sqrt{3}}{\sqrt{3}}, 0, 0\right) \qquad \text{and} \qquad I_2 = (0, 1 + \sqrt{3}, 0)$$

The equation of the line through I_1 and I_2 (App. 2) is

$$x = \left(\frac{1+\sqrt{3}}{\sqrt{3}}\right) - \left(\frac{1+\sqrt{3}}{\sqrt{3}}\right)t \qquad y = (1+\sqrt{3})t \qquad z = 0$$

This line lies in the view plane. So if the equation of the horizon line is then taken to be a line parallel to

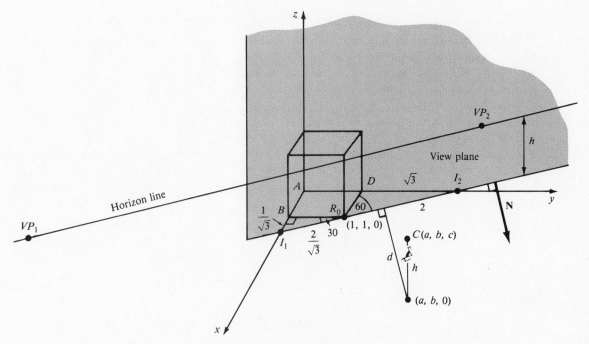

Fig. 7-19

this line and h units above it, the horizon line is guaranteed to be in the view plane. The equation of the horizon line is then

$$x = \left(\frac{1+\sqrt{3}}{\sqrt{3}}\right)(1-t) \qquad y = (1+\sqrt{3})t \qquad z = h$$

The vanishing points VP_1 and VP_2 are chosen to lie on the horizon line. So VP_1 has coordinates of the form

$$VP_1 = \left[\left(\frac{1+\sqrt{3}}{\sqrt{3}}\right)(1-t_1), (1+\sqrt{3})t_1, h\right] \quad \text{and} \quad VP_2 = \left[\left(\frac{1+\sqrt{3}}{\sqrt{3}}\right)(1-t_2), (1+\sqrt{3})t_2, h\right]$$

(Here, t_1 and t_2 are chosen so as to place the vanishing points at the desired locations.)

To find the normal vector $\mathbf{N}$ and the center of projection C, we use the equations in Prob. 7.6, part (b) for locating the vanishing points of a given perspective transformation. So

$$a + \frac{d}{n_1} = \left(\frac{1+\sqrt{3}}{\sqrt{3}}\right)(1-t_1) \quad \text{and} \quad a = \left(\frac{1+\sqrt{3}}{\sqrt{3}}\right)(1-t_2)$$

and

$$b = (1+\sqrt{3})t_1 \quad \text{and} \quad b + \frac{d}{n_2} = (1+\sqrt{3})t_2 \quad \text{and} \quad c = h$$

Using the values

$$a = \left(\frac{1+\sqrt{3}}{\sqrt{3}}\right)(1-t_2) \qquad b = (1+\sqrt{3})t_1 \qquad c = h$$

and then substituting, we find

$$\frac{d}{n_1} = \left(\frac{1+\sqrt{3}}{\sqrt{3}}\right)(t_2 - t_1) \tag{7.1}$$

and

$$\frac{d}{n_2} = (1+\sqrt{3})(t_2 - t_1) \tag{7.2}$$

Since the plane does not intersect the z axis, then $\mathbf{N} \cdot \mathbf{K} = 0$, or using components: $n_3 = 0$. Finally, we choose the normal vector $\mathbf{N}$ to be of unit length

$$|\mathbf{N}| = \sqrt{n_1^2 + n_2^2 + n_3^2} = \sqrt{n_1^2 + n_2^2} = 1$$

From equations (7.1) and (7.2)

$$n_1 = \frac{d\sqrt{3}}{(1+\sqrt{3})(t_2 - t_1)} \qquad n_2 = \frac{d}{(1+\sqrt{3})(t_2 - t_1)}$$

So

$$|\mathbf{N}| = \sqrt{\frac{(d\sqrt{3})^2}{(1+\sqrt{3})^2(t_2 - t_1)^2} + \frac{d^2}{(1+\sqrt{3})^2(t_2 - t_1)^2}} = 1$$

or

$$\frac{2d}{(1+\sqrt{3})(t_2 - t_1)} = 1 \quad \text{and so} \quad d = \frac{1+\sqrt{3}}{2}(t_2 - t_1)$$

Also

$$n_1 = \frac{\sqrt{3} \cdot [(1+\sqrt{3})/2]}{1+\sqrt{3}} = \frac{\sqrt{3}}{2} \quad \text{and} \quad n_2 = \frac{(1+\sqrt{3})/2}{1+\sqrt{3}} = \frac{1}{2}$$

Finally, we have

$$d_1 = n_1 a + n_2 b + n_3 c = \left(\frac{\sqrt{3}}{2} \cdot \frac{1+\sqrt{3}}{\sqrt{3}}\right)(1 - t_2) + \left(\frac{1}{2} \cdot 1 + \sqrt{3}\right)t_1 = \frac{1+\sqrt{3}}{2}[1 - (t_2 - t_1)]$$

and

$$d_0 = d + d_1 = \frac{1+\sqrt{3}}{2}$$

From Prob. 7.5, the perspective transformation matrix is then

$$Per_{\mathbf{N},R_0,C} = \frac{1+\sqrt{3}}{2}\begin{pmatrix} 1 - t_1 & \frac{1}{\sqrt{3}}(1 - t_2) & 0 & -\left(\frac{1+\sqrt{3}}{\sqrt{3}}\right)(1 - t_2) \\ \sqrt{3}t_1 & t_2 & 0 & -(1+\sqrt{3})t_1 \\ \frac{\sqrt{3}h}{1+\sqrt{3}} & \frac{h}{1+\sqrt{3}} & t_2 - t_1 & -h \\ \frac{\sqrt{3}}{1+\sqrt{3}} & \frac{1}{1+\sqrt{3}} & 0 & -[1 - (t_2 - t_1)] \end{pmatrix}$$

In Chap. 8, Prob. 8.2, it is shown how to convert the transformed image of the cube into x, y coordinates for viewing.

7.10 Derive the equations of parallel projection onto the xy plane in the direction of projection $\mathbf{V} = a\mathbf{I} + b\mathbf{J} + c\mathbf{K}$.

SOLUTION

From Fig. 7-20 we see that the vectors $\mathbf{V}$ and $\overline{\mathbf{PP'}}$ have the same direction. This means that $\overline{\mathbf{PP'}} = k\mathbf{V}$. Comparing components, we see that

$$x' - x = ka \qquad y' - y = kb \qquad z' - z = kc$$

So

$$k = -\frac{z}{c} \quad \text{and} \quad x' = x - \frac{a}{c}z \quad \text{and} \quad y' = y - \frac{b}{c}z$$

In 3×3 matrix form, this is

$$Par_{\mathbf{V}} = \begin{pmatrix} 1 & 0 & -\dfrac{a}{c} \\ 0 & 1 & -\dfrac{b}{c} \\ 0 & 0 & 0 \end{pmatrix}$$

and so $P' = Par_{\mathbf{V}} \cdot P$.

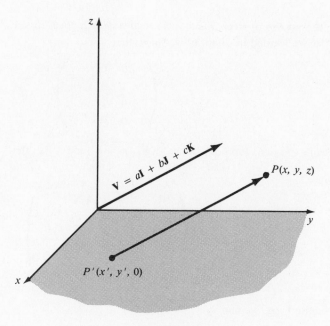

Fig. 7-20

7.11   Derive the general equation of parallel projection onto a given view plane in the direction of a given projector $\mathbf{V}$ (see Fig. 7-21).

SOLUTION

We reduce the problem to parallel projection onto the xy plane in the direction of the projector $\mathbf{V} = a\mathbf{I} + b\mathbf{J} + c\mathbf{K}$ by means of these steps:

1.   Translate the view reference point R_0 of the view plane to the origin using the translation matrix T_{-R_0}.

2.   Perform an alignment transformation $A_{\mathbf{N}}$ so that the view normal vector $\mathbf{N}$ of the view plane points in the direction $\mathbf{K}$ of the normal to the xy plane. The direction of projection vector $\mathbf{V}$ is transformed to a new vector $\mathbf{V}' = A_{\mathbf{N}}\mathbf{V}$.

3.   Project onto the xy plane using $Par_{\mathbf{V}'}$.

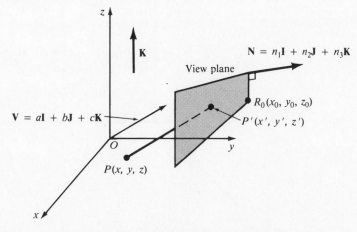

Fig. 7-21

4. Perform the inverse of steps 2 and 1. So finally $Par_{V,N,R_0} = T_{-R_0}^{-1} \cdot A_N^{-1} \cdot Par_V \cdot A_N \cdot T_{-R_0}$. From what we learned in Chap. 6, we know that

$$T_{-R_0} = \begin{pmatrix} 1 & 0 & 0 & -x_0 \\ 0 & 1 & 0 & -y_0 \\ 0 & 0 & 1 & -z_0 \\ 0 & 0 & 0 & 1 \end{pmatrix}$$

and further from Chap. 6, Prob. 6.2, where $\lambda = \sqrt{n_2^2 + n_3^2}$ and $\lambda \neq 0$, that

$$A_N = \begin{pmatrix} \dfrac{\lambda}{|\mathbf{N}|} & \dfrac{-n_1 n_2}{\lambda|\mathbf{N}|} & \dfrac{-n_1 n_3}{\lambda|\mathbf{N}|} & 0 \\ 0 & \dfrac{n_3}{\lambda} & \dfrac{-n_2}{\lambda} & 0 \\ \dfrac{n_1}{|\mathbf{N}|} & \dfrac{n_2}{|\mathbf{N}|} & \dfrac{n_3}{|\mathbf{N}|} & 0 \\ 0 & 0 & 0 & 1 \end{pmatrix}$$

Then, after multiplying, we find

$$Par_{V,N,R_0} = \begin{pmatrix} d_1 - an_1 & -an_2 & -an_3 & ad_0 \\ -bn_1 & d_1 - bn_2 & -bn_3 & bd_0 \\ -cn_1 & -cn_2 & d_1 - cn_3 & cd_0 \\ 0 & 0 & 0 & d_1 \end{pmatrix}$$

Here $d_0 = n_1 x_0 + n_2 y_0 + n_3 z_0$ and $d_1 = n_1 a + n_2 b + n_2 c$. An alternative and much easier method to derive this matrix is by finding the intersection of the projector through P with the equation of the view plane (see Prob. A2.14).

7.12 Find the general form of an oblique projection onto the xy plane.

SOLUTION

Refer to Fig. 7-22. Oblique projections (to the xy plane) can be specified by a number f and an angle θ. The number f prescribes the ratio that any line L perpendicular to the xy plane will be foreshortened after

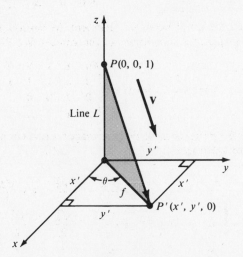

Fig. 7-22

projection. The angle θ is the angle that the projection of any line perpendicular to the xy plane makes with the (positive) x axis.

To determine the projection transformation, we need to find the direction vector **V**. From Fig. 7-22, with line L of length 1, we see that the vector $\overline{P'P}$ has the same direction as **V**. We choose **V** to be this vector.

$$\mathbf{V} = \overline{P'P} = x'\mathbf{I} + y'\mathbf{J} - \mathbf{K} \quad (= a\mathbf{I} + b\mathbf{J} + c\mathbf{K})$$

From Fig. 7-22 we find $a = x' = f\cos\theta$, $b = y' = f\sin\theta$, and $c = -1$.

From Prob. 7.10, the required transformation is

$$Par_\mathbf{V} = \begin{pmatrix} 1 & 0 & f\cos\theta & 0 \\ 0 & 1 & f\sin\theta & 0 \\ 0 & 0 & 0 & 0 \\ 0 & 0 & 0 & 1 \end{pmatrix}$$

7.13 Find the transformation for (*a*) cavalier with $\theta = 45°$ and (*b*) cabinet projections with $\theta = 30°$. (*c*) Draw the projection of the unit cube for each transformation.

SOLUTION

(*a*) A cavalier projection is an oblique projection where there is no foreshortening of lines perpendicular to the xy plane. From Prob. 7.12 we then see that $f = 1$. With $\theta = 45°$, we have

$$Par_{\mathbf{V}_1} = \begin{pmatrix} 1 & 0 & \dfrac{\sqrt{2}}{2} & 0 \\ 0 & 1 & \dfrac{\sqrt{2}}{2} & 0 \\ 0 & 0 & 0 & 0 \\ 0 & 0 & 0 & 1 \end{pmatrix}$$

(*b*) A cabinet projection is an oblique projection with $f = \frac{1}{2}$. With $\theta = 30°$, we have

$$Par_{\mathbf{V}_1} = \begin{pmatrix} 1 & 0 & \dfrac{\sqrt{3}}{4} & 0 \\ 0 & 1 & \dfrac{1}{4} & 0 \\ 0 & 0 & 0 & 0 \\ 0 & 0 & 0 & 1 \end{pmatrix}$$

To construct the projections, we represent the vertices of the unit cube by a matrix whose columns are homogeneous coordinates of the vertices (see Prob. 7.1):

$$V = (ABCDEFGH) = \begin{pmatrix} 0 & 1 & 1 & 0 & 0 & 0 & 1 & 1 \\ 0 & 0 & 1 & 1 & 1 & 0 & 0 & 1 \\ 0 & 0 & 0 & 0 & 1 & 1 & 1 & 1 \\ 1 & 1 & 1 & 1 & 1 & 1 & 1 & 1 \end{pmatrix}$$

(*c*) To draw the cavalier projection, we find the image coordinates by applying the transformation matrix $Par_{\mathbf{V}_1}$ to the coordinate matrix V:

$$Par_{\mathbf{V}_1} \cdot V = \begin{pmatrix} 0 & 1 & 1 & 0 & \dfrac{\sqrt{2}}{2} & \dfrac{\sqrt{2}}{2} & 1+\dfrac{\sqrt{2}}{2} & 1+\dfrac{\sqrt{2}}{2} \\ 0 & 0 & 1 & 1 & 1+\dfrac{\sqrt{2}}{2} & \dfrac{\sqrt{2}}{2} & \dfrac{\sqrt{2}}{2} & 1+\dfrac{\sqrt{2}}{2} \\ 0 & 0 & 0 & 0 & 0 & 0 & 0 & 0 \\ 1 & 1 & 1 & 1 & 1 & 1 & 1 & 1 \end{pmatrix}$$

The image coordinates are then

$$A' = (0, 0, 0) \qquad E' = \left(\frac{\sqrt{2}}{2}, 1 + \frac{\sqrt{2}}{2}, 0 \right)$$

$$B' = (1, 0, 0) \qquad F' = \left(\frac{\sqrt{2}}{2}, \frac{\sqrt{2}}{2}, 0 \right)$$

$$C' = (1, 1, 0) \qquad G' = \left(1 + \frac{\sqrt{2}}{2}, \frac{\sqrt{2}}{2}, 0 \right)$$

$$D' = (0, 1, 0) \qquad H' = \left(1 + \frac{\sqrt{2}}{2}, 1 + \frac{\sqrt{2}}{2}, 0 \right)$$

Refer to Fig. 7-23.

To draw the cabinet projection:

$$Par_{v_2} \cdot V = \begin{pmatrix} 0 & 1 & 1 & 0 & \frac{\sqrt{3}}{4} & \frac{\sqrt{3}}{4} & 1 + \frac{\sqrt{3}}{4} & 1 + \frac{\sqrt{3}}{4} \\ 0 & 0 & 1 & 1 & 1\frac{1}{4} & \frac{1}{4} & \frac{1}{4} & 1\frac{1}{4} \\ 0 & 0 & 0 & 0 & 0 & 0 & 0 & 0 \\ 1 & 1 & 1 & 1 & 1 & 1 & 1 & 1 \end{pmatrix}$$

The image coordinates are then (see Fig. 7-24)

$$A' = (0, 0, 0) \qquad E' = \left(\frac{\sqrt{3}}{4}, 1\frac{1}{4}, 0 \right)$$

$$B' = (1, 0, 0) \qquad F' = \left(\frac{\sqrt{3}}{4}, \frac{1}{4}, 0 \right)$$

$$C' = (1, 1, 0) \qquad G' = \left(1 + \frac{\sqrt{3}}{4}, \frac{1}{4}, 0 \right)$$

$$D' = (0, 1, 0) \qquad H' = \left(1 + \frac{\sqrt{3}}{4}, 1\frac{1}{4}, 0 \right)$$

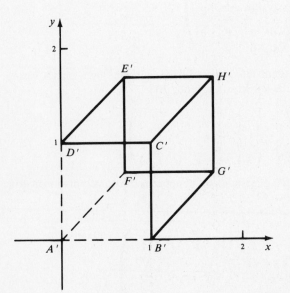

Fig. 7-23

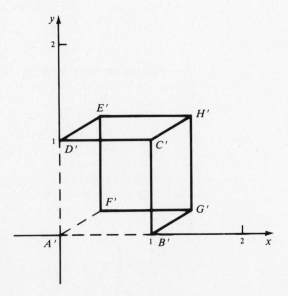

Fig. 7-24

7.14　Construct an isometric projection onto the xy plane. Refer to Fig. 7-25.

SOLUTION

We shall find a "tilting" of the x, y, z axes that transforms the **IJK** vector triad to a new set **I′J′K′** whose orthographic projections onto the xy plane produce vectors of equal lengths.

Denoting the tilting transformation by T and the orthographic projection onto the xy plane by $Par_{\mathbf{K}}$, the final projection can be written as $Par = Par_{\mathbf{K}} \cdot T$, where $Par_{\mathbf{K}}$ is as defined in Example 3 and T is as defined in Prob. 6.1 in Chap. 6. Multiplying, we find

$$Par = \begin{pmatrix} \cos \theta_y & \sin \theta_y \sin \theta_x & \sin \theta_y \cos \theta_x & 0 \\ 0 & \cos \theta_x & -\sin \theta_x & 0 \\ 0 & 0 & 0 & 0 \\ 0 & 0 & 0 & 1 \end{pmatrix}$$

Now

$$Par \cdot \mathbf{I} = (\cos \theta_y, 0, 0) \qquad Par \cdot \mathbf{J} = (\sin \theta_y \sin \theta_x, \cos \theta_x, 0) \qquad Par \cdot \mathbf{K} = (\sin \theta_y \cos \theta_x, -\sin \theta_x, 0)$$

(the projections of the vectors **I**, **J**, and **K**). To complete the specification of the transformation M, we need to find the angles θ_x and θ_y. To do this, we use the requirement that the images $Par \cdot \mathbf{I}$, $Par \cdot \mathbf{J}$, and $Par \cdot \mathbf{K}$ are to all have equal lengths. Now

$$|Par \cdot \mathbf{I}| = \sqrt{\cos^2 \theta_y} \qquad |Par \cdot \mathbf{J}| = \sqrt{\sin^2 \theta_y \sin^2 \theta_x + \cos^2 \theta_x}$$

and

$$|Par \cdot \mathbf{K}| = \sqrt{\sin^2 \theta_y \cos^2 \theta_x + \sin^2 \theta_x}$$

Setting $|Par \cdot \mathbf{J}| = |Par \cdot \mathbf{K}|$ leads to the conclusion that $\sin^2 \theta_x - \cos^2 \theta_x = 0$ and to a solution $\theta_x = 45°$ (and so $\sin \theta_x = \cos \theta_x = \sqrt{2}/2$). Setting $|Par \cdot \mathbf{I}| = |Par \cdot \mathbf{J}|$ leads to $\cos^2 \theta_y = \frac{1}{2}(\sin^2 \theta_y + 1)$. Multiplying both sides by 2 and adding $\cos^2 \theta_y$ to both sides gives $3 \cos^2 \theta_y = 2$ and a solution is $\theta_y = 35.26°$ (and so $\sin \theta_y = \sqrt{1/3}$, $\cos \theta_y = \sqrt{2/3}$). Finally

$$Par = \begin{pmatrix} \sqrt{\dfrac{2}{3}} & \dfrac{1}{2}\sqrt{\dfrac{2}{3}} & \dfrac{1}{2}\sqrt{\dfrac{2}{3}} & 0 \\ 0 & \dfrac{\sqrt{2}}{2} & -\dfrac{\sqrt{2}}{2} & 0 \\ 0 & 0 & 0 & 0 \\ 0 & 0 & 0 & 1 \end{pmatrix}$$

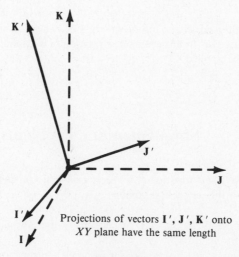

Projections of vectors **I′**, **J′**, **K′** onto
XY plane have the same length

Fig. 7-25

7.15   Construct a dimetric projection onto the xy plane.

SOLUTION

Following the procedures in Prob. 7.14, we shall tilt the x, y, z axes and then project on the xy plane. We then have, as before

$$|Par \cdot \mathbf{I}| = \sqrt{\cos^2 \theta_y} \qquad |Par \cdot \mathbf{J}| = \sqrt{\sin^2 \theta_y \sin^2 \theta_x + \cos^2 \theta_x}$$

and

$$|Par \cdot \mathbf{K}| = \sqrt{\sin^2 \theta_y \cos^2 \theta_x + \sin^2 \theta_x}$$

To define a dimetric projection, we will specify the proportions

$$|Par \cdot \mathbf{I}| : |Par \cdot \mathbf{J}| : |Par \cdot \mathbf{K}| = l : 1 : 1 \qquad (l \neq 1)$$

Setting $|Par \cdot \mathbf{J}| = |Par \cdot \mathbf{K}|$, we find $\sin^2 \theta_x - \cos^2 \theta_x = 0$ and $\theta_x = 45°$, so $\sin \theta_x = \cos \theta_x = \sqrt{2}/2$. Setting $|Par \cdot \mathbf{I}| = l|Par \cdot \mathbf{J}|$ gives

$$\cos^2 \theta_y = \frac{l^2}{2} [\sin^2 \theta_y + 1] \tag{7.3}$$

Multiplying both sides by 2 and adding $l^2 \cos^2 \theta_y$ to both sides gives

$$(2 + l^2) \cos^2 \theta_y = 2l^2$$

So

$$\cos \theta_y = l\sqrt{\frac{2}{2 + l^2}}$$

From equation (7.3) we can also find

$$\sin^2 \theta_y = \frac{2 - l^2}{2 + l^2} \qquad \text{and} \qquad \sin \theta_y = \sqrt{\frac{2 - l^2}{2 + l^2}}$$

(Note the restriction $l \leq \sqrt{2}$). Thus

$$Par = \begin{pmatrix} l\sqrt{\dfrac{2}{2 + l^2}} & \dfrac{\sqrt{2}}{2}\sqrt{\dfrac{2 - l^2}{2 + l^2}} & \dfrac{\sqrt{2}}{2}\sqrt{\dfrac{2 - l^2}{2 + l^2}} & 0 \\ 0 & \dfrac{\sqrt{2}}{2} & \dfrac{-\sqrt{2}}{2} & 0 \\ 0 & 0 & 0 & 0 \\ 0 & 0 & 0 & 1 \end{pmatrix}$$

and $0 \leq l \leq \sqrt{2}$.

Note that any other projection ratio, say, $1:1:l$, can be achieved by performing an appropriate rotation before applying Par. In this example, a rotation of 90° about the y axis aligns the z axis with the x axis so that Par can be applied.

Supplementary Problems

7.16   Construct a perspective transformation given three principal vanishing points and the distance D from the center of projection to the projection plane.

7.17   Draw the (a) isometric and (b) dimetric projections of the unit cube onto the xy plane.

7.18   How many view planes (at the origin) produce isometric projections of an object?

Chapter 8

Three-Dimensional Viewing Transformations and Clipping

8.1 INTRODUCTION

In this chapter we are concerned with the problem of processing the data that represent objects in three-dimensional space in order to produce realistic two-dimensional pictures of different views of these objects.

The complete viewing process consists of the following sequence of transformations:

1. *Object (modeling) transformations*—transformations applied to the object (or, more precisely, the data representing the object in world coordinates) prior to viewing. They include instance transformations, scalings, translations, and rotations. These transformations were discussed in Chaps. 4 and 6.

2. *Image transformations*—two-dimensional transformations applied to the two-dimensional image in normalized device space to produce the final view. These transformations were discussed in Chap. 4.

3. *Viewing transformations*—transformations applied to the desired object to produce a two-dimensional view of the object, described in normalized device coordinates. They include clipping, projection, and various normalization transformations. These transformations are discussed in this chapter.

8.2 THREE-DIMENSIONAL VIEWING

Three-dimensional viewing of an object or picture requires the specification of a projection plane (called the *view plane*), a *center of projection* (or *viewpoint*), and a *view volume* in world coordinates. In addition, a *viewport* on the physical device must be specified (see Chap. 4).

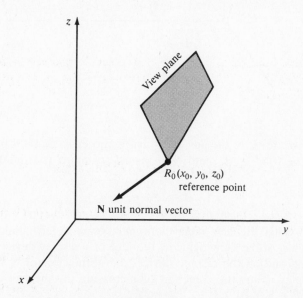

Fig. 8-1

149

Specifying the Projection Plane

We specify the projection plane by prescribing (1) a reference point $R_0(x_0, y_0, z_0)$ in world coordinates and (2) a *unit* normal vector $\mathbf{N} = n_1\mathbf{I} + n_2\mathbf{J} + n_3\mathbf{K}$, $|\mathbf{N}| = 1$, to the projection plane (see Fig. 8-1). From this information, we can construct the projections used in presenting the required view with respect to the given viewpoint (Chap. 7). Also note that other viewing parameters could be used to specify projective views, such as vanishing points or the distance to the projection plane.

View Plane Coordinates

The *view plane coordinate system* can be specified as follows: (1) let the reference point $R_0(x_0, y_0, z_0)$ be the origin of the coordinate system and (2) determine the coordinate axes. To do this, we first choose a reference vector $\mathbf{U}$ called the *up vector*. A *unit* vector $\mathbf{J_q}$ can then be determined by the projection of the vector $\mathbf{U}$ onto the view plane. We let the vector $\mathbf{J_q}$ define the direction of the positive q axis for the view plane coordinate system. To calculate $\mathbf{J_q}$, we proceed as follows: with $\mathbf{N}$ being the view plane unit normal vector, let $\mathbf{U_q} = \mathbf{U} - (\mathbf{N} \cdot \mathbf{U})\mathbf{N}$ (App. 2, Prob. A2.15). Then

$$\mathbf{J_q} = \frac{\mathbf{U_q}}{|\mathbf{U_q}|}$$

is the unit vector that defines the direction of the positive q axis (see Fig. 8-2).

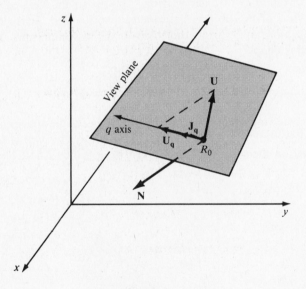

Fig. 8-2

Finally, the direction vector $\mathbf{I_p}$ of the positive p axis is chosen so that it is perpendicular to $\mathbf{J_q}$, and, by convention, so that the triad $\mathbf{I_p}$, $\mathbf{J_q}$, and $\mathbf{N}$ forms a *left-handed* coordinate system. That is:

$$\mathbf{I_p} = \frac{\mathbf{N} \times \mathbf{J_q}}{|\mathbf{N} \times \mathbf{J_q}|}$$

This coordinate system is called the *view plane coordinate system*. A left-handed system is traditionally chosen so that if one thinks of the view plane as the face of a display device, then with the p and q coordinate axes superimposed on the display device, the normal vector $\mathbf{N}$ will point away from an observer facing the display. Thus the direction of increasing distance away from the observer is measured along $\mathbf{N}$ [see Fig. 8-3(a)].

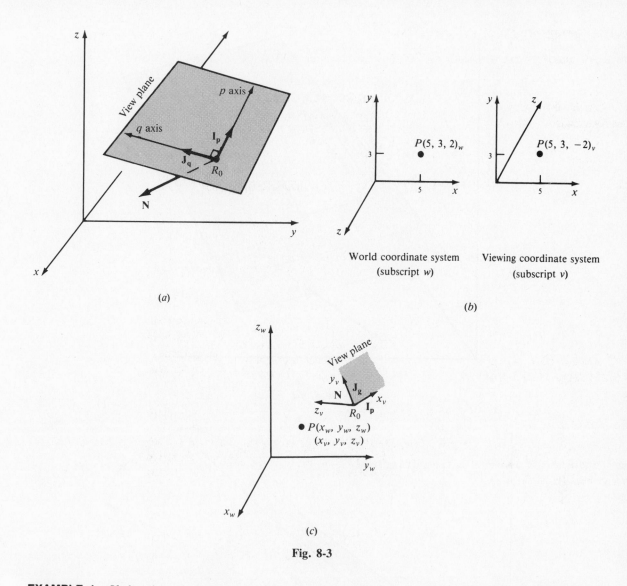

Fig. 8-3

EXAMPLE 1. If the view plane is the xy plane, then $\mathbf{I_p} = \mathbf{I}$, $\mathbf{J_q} = \mathbf{J}$, and the unit normal $\mathbf{N} = -\mathbf{K}$ form a left-handed system. If the center of projection lies along $\mathbf{N}$ (the negative z axis), the z coordinate of a point measures the depth or distance of the point from the view plane. The sign indicates whether the point is in front or in back of the view plane with respect to the center of projection. In this example, we change from right-handed world coordinates (x, y, z) to left-handed view plane coordinates (x', y', z') [see Fig. 8-3(b)] by performing the transformation:

$$T_{RL}: \begin{cases} x' = x \\ y' = y \\ z' = -z \end{cases}$$

In matrix form, for homogeneous coordinates:

$$T_{RL} = \begin{pmatrix} 1 & 0 & 0 & 0 \\ 0 & 1 & 0 & 0 \\ 0 & 0 & -1 & 0 \\ 0 & 0 & 0 & 1 \end{pmatrix}$$

The general transformation for changing from world coordinates to view plane coordinates [see Fig. 8-3(c)] is developed in Prob. 8.3.

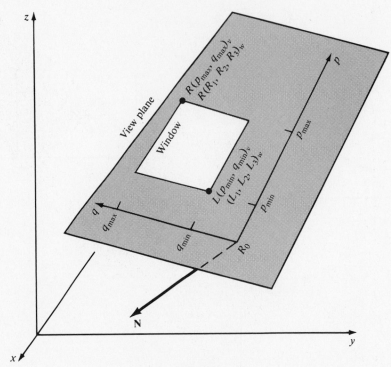

Fig. 8-4

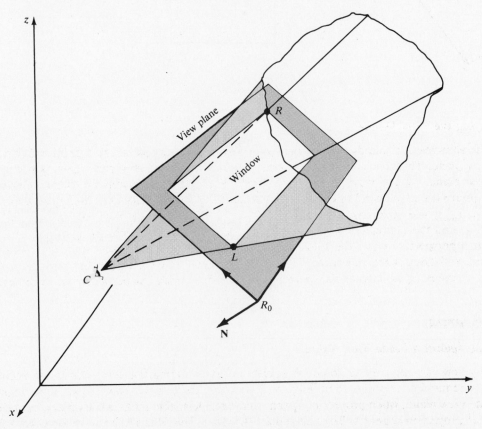

Fig. 8-5

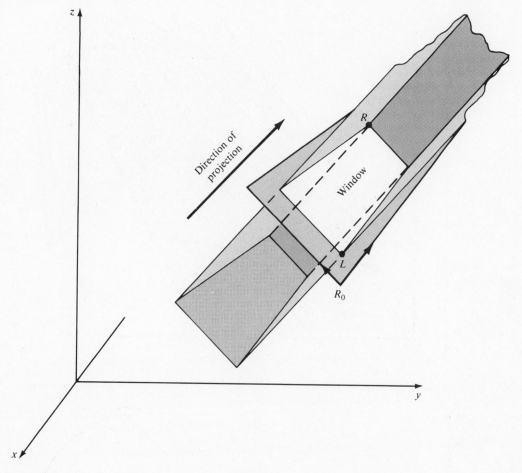

Fig. 8-6

Specifying the View Volume

The view volume bounds a region in world coordinate space that will be clipped and projected onto the view plane. To define a view volume that projects onto a specified rectangular window defined in the view plane, we use view plane coordinates $(p, q)_v$ to locate points on the view plane. Then a rectangular view plane window is defined by prescribing the coordinates of the lower left-hand corner $L(p_{min}, q_{min})_v$ and upper right-hand corner $R(p_{max}, q_{max})_v$ (see Fig. 8-4). We can use the vectors $\mathbf{I_p}$ and $\mathbf{J_q}$ to find the equivalent world coordinates of L and R (see Prob. 8.1).

For a perspective view, the view volume, corresponding to the given window, is a semi-infinite pyramid, with apex at the viewpoint (Fig. 8-5). For views created using parallel projections (Fig. 8-6), the view volume is an infinite parallelepiped with sides parallel to the direction of projection.

8.3   CLIPPING

Clipping against a Finite View Volume

The view volumes created above are infinite in extent. In practice, we prefer to use a finite volume to limit the number of points to be projected. In addition, for perspective views, very distant objects from the view plane, when projected, appear as indistinguishable spots, while objects very close to the center of projection appear to have disjointed structure. This is another reason for using a finite view volume.

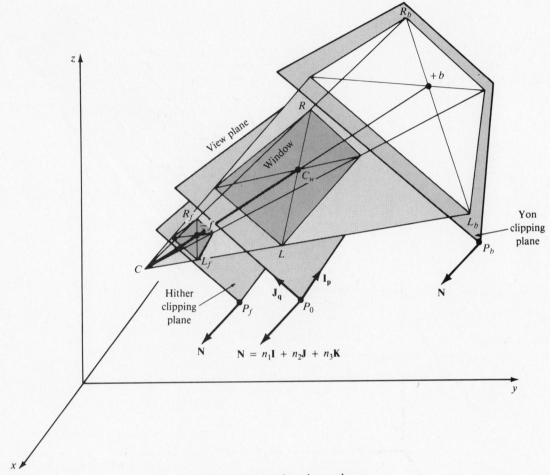

Fig. 8-7 Perspective view volume.

A finite volume is delimited by using *front* (*hither*) and *back* (*yon*) *clipping planes* parallel to the view plane. These planes are specified by giving the front distance f and back distance b relative to the view plane reference point R_0 and measured along the normal vector **N**. The signed distances b and f can be positive or negative (Figs. 8-7 and 8-8).

Clipping Algorithms

Three-dimensional clipping algorithms are direct adaptations of the two-dimensional Cohen-Sutherland, Sutherland-Hodgman, and midpoint subdivision algorithms (Chap. 5). The modifications necessary arise from the fact that we are now clipping lines against the six faces of the view volume, which are planes, as opposed to the four edges of the two-dimensional window, which are lines. The technical differences involve:

1. Finding the intersection of a line and a plane (Prob. 8.11)

2. Assigning outcodes to the endpoints of line segments for the Cohen-Sutherland algorithm (Prob. 8.8)

3. Deciding when a point is to the right (also said to be *outside*) or to the left (*inside*) of a plane for the Sutherland-Hodgman algorithm (Prob. 8.7)

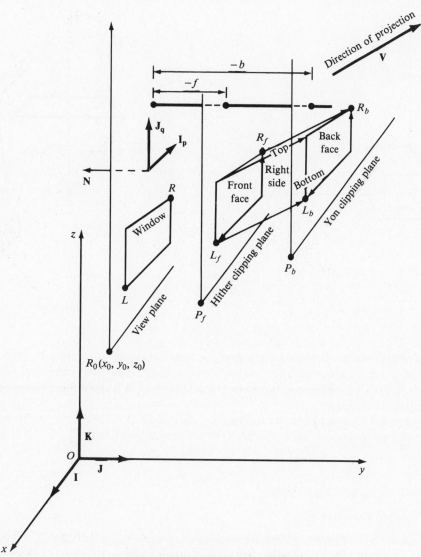

Fig. 8-8 Parallel view volume.

Clipping Strategies

Because of the extraordinary computational effort required for three-dimensional clipping, two differing strategies for reducing this overhead have been devised:

1. *Direct clipping.* In this method, as the name suggests, clipping is done directly against the view volume.

2. *Canonical clipping.* In this method, normalizing transformations are applied which transform the original view volume into a so-called canonical view volume. Clipping is then performed against the canonical view volume.

The canonical view volume for parallel projection is the unit cube whose faces are defined by the planes $x = 0$, $x = 1$, $y = 0$, $y = 1$, $z = 0$, and $z = 1$. The corresponding normalization transformation N_{par} is constructed in Prob. 8.5 (Fig. 8-9).

The canonical view volume for perspective projections is the truncated pyramid whose faces are defined by the planes $x = z$, $x = -z$, $y = z$, $y = -z$, $z = z_f$, and $z = 1$ (where z_f is to be calculated) (Fig. 8-10). The corresponding normalization transformation N_{per} is constructed in Prob. 8.6.

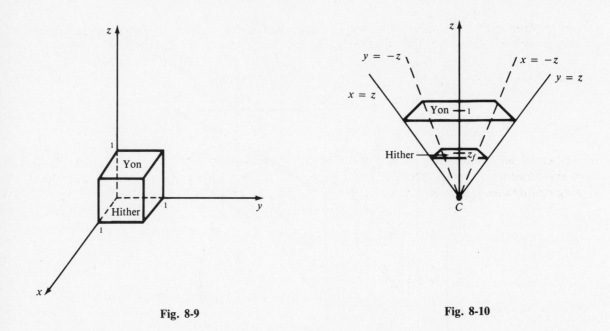

Fig. 8-9   **Fig. 8-10**

The basis of the canonical clipping strategy is the fact that the computations involved in finding the intersections of a line segment with the planes forming the faces of the canonical view volume are minimal (Prob. 8.9). This is balanced by the overhead involved in transforming points, many of which will be subsequently clipped.

For perspective views, additional clipping may be required to avoid the perspective anomalies produced by projecting objects that are behind the viewpoint (see Chap. 7).

8.4   VIEWING TRANSFORMATIONS

Normalized Viewing Coordinates

We can view the normalizing transformations N_{par} and N_{per} from Sec. 8.3, under "Clipping Strategies," as geometric transformations. That is, if Obj is an object defined in the world coordinate system, the transformation

$$Obj' = N_{\mathrm{par}} \cdot Obj \qquad \text{or} \qquad Obj' = N_{\mathrm{per}} \cdot Obj$$

yields an object Obj' defined in the *normalized viewing coordinate system*.

Canonical clipping is now equivalent to clipping in normalized viewing coordinates. That is, the transformed object Obj' is clipped against the canonical view volume. In Chap. 10, where hidden-surface algorithms are discussed, it is assumed that the coordinate description of geometric objects refers to normalized viewing coordinates.

Screen Projection Plane

After clipping in viewing coordinates, we project the resulting image onto the *screen projection plane*. This is the plane that results from applying the transformations N_{par} or N_{per} to the given view plane. In the case of N_{par}, from Prob. 8.5, we find that the screen projection plane is the plane $z = -f/(b - f)$ and that the direction of projection is that of the vector $\mathbf{K}$. Thus the parallel projection is orthographic (Chap. 7) and since the plane $z = -f/(b - f)$ is parallel to the xy plane, we can choose this latter plane as the projection plane. So parallel projection *Par* in normalized viewing coordinates reduces to orthographic projection onto the xy plane. The projection matrix is (Chap. 7, Prob. 7.3)

$$Par = \begin{pmatrix} 1 & 0 & 0 & 0 \\ 0 & 1 & 0 & 0 \\ 0 & 0 & 0 & 0 \\ 0 & 0 & 0 & 1 \end{pmatrix}$$

In the case of perspective projections, the screen projection plane is the plane $z = c_z'/(c_z' + b)$ (Prob. 8.6). The transformed center of projection is the origin. So perspective projection *Per* in normalized viewing coordinates is accomplished by applying the matrix (Chap. 7)

$$Per = \begin{pmatrix} \dfrac{c_z'}{c_z' + b} & 0 & 0 & 0 \\ 0 & \dfrac{c_z'}{c_z' + b} & 0 & 0 \\ 0 & 0 & \dfrac{c_z'}{c_z' + b} & 0 \\ 0 & 0 & 1 & 0 \end{pmatrix}$$

Constructing a Three-Dimensional View

The complete three-dimensional viewing process (without hidden surface removal) is described by the following steps:

1. Transform from world coordinates to normalized viewing coordinates by applying the transformations N_{par} or N_{per}.
2. Clip in normalized viewing coordinates against the canonical clipping volumes.
3. Project onto the screen projection plane using the projections *Par* or *Per*.
4. Apply the appropriate (two-dimensional) viewing transformations (Chap. 5).

In terms of transformations, we can describe the above process in terms of a *viewing transformation* V_T, where

$$V_T = V_2 \cdot Par \cdot CL \cdot N_{par} \qquad \text{or} \qquad V_T = V_2 \cdot Per \cdot CL \cdot N_{per}$$

Here *CL* and V_2 refer to the appropriate clipping operations and two-dimensional viewing transformations.

Solved Problems

8.1 Let $P(p, q)_v$ be the view plane coordinates of a point on the view plane. Find the world coordinates $P(x, y, z)_w$ of the point.

SOLUTION

Refer to Fig. 8-11. Let R_0 be the view plane reference point. Let **R** be the position vector of R_0 and **W**

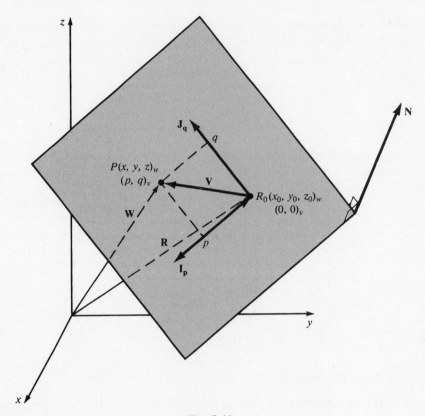

Fig. 8-11

the position vector of P, both with respect to the world coordinate origin (see Fig. 8-11). Let $\mathbf{V}$ be the position vector of P with respect to the view plane origin R_0. Now

$$\mathbf{V} = p\mathbf{I_p} + q\mathbf{J_q} \qquad \text{and} \qquad \mathbf{W} = \mathbf{R} + \mathbf{V}$$

So

$$\mathbf{W} = \mathbf{R} + p\mathbf{I_p} + q\mathbf{J_q}$$

Let the components of $\mathbf{I_p}$ and $\mathbf{J_q}$ be

$$\mathbf{I_p} = a_p\mathbf{I} + b_p\mathbf{J} + c_p\mathbf{K} \qquad \mathbf{J_q} = a_q\mathbf{I} + b_q\mathbf{J} + c_q\mathbf{K}$$

Also

$$\mathbf{R} = x_0\mathbf{I} + y_0\mathbf{J} + z_0\mathbf{K}$$

and so from $\mathbf{W} = \mathbf{R} + p\mathbf{I_p} + q\mathbf{J_q}$ we find

$$\mathbf{W} = (x_0 + pa_p + qa_q)\mathbf{I} + (y_0 + pb_p + qb_q)\mathbf{J} + (z_0 + pc_p + qc_q)\mathbf{K}$$

The required world coordinates of P can be read off from W:

$$P(x_0 + pa_p + qa_q, \; y_0 + pb_p + qb_q, \; z_0 + pc_p + qc_q)_w$$

8.2   Find the projection of the unit cube onto the view plane in Prob. 7.9 in Chap. 7. Find the corresponding view plane coordinates of the projected cube.

SOLUTION

Following Prob. 7.9, we must specify several parameters in order to calculate the corresponding perspective projection matrix $Per_{N, R_0, C}$. Choosing $h = \frac{1}{2}$, $t_1 = 1$, and $t_2 = (1 - \sqrt{3})/(1 + \sqrt{3})$, we obtain

$$
Per_{N, R_0, C} = \frac{1 + \sqrt{3}}{2}
\begin{pmatrix}
0 & \dfrac{2}{1 + \sqrt{3}} & 0 & -2 \\[2mm]
\sqrt{3} & \dfrac{1 - \sqrt{3}}{1 + \sqrt{3}} & 0 & -(1 + \sqrt{3}) \\[2mm]
\dfrac{\sqrt{3}}{2(1 + \sqrt{3})} & \dfrac{1}{2(1 + \sqrt{3})} & \dfrac{-2\sqrt{3}}{1 + \sqrt{3}} & -\dfrac{1}{2} \\[2mm]
\dfrac{\sqrt{3}}{1 + \sqrt{3}} & \dfrac{1}{1 + \sqrt{3}} & 0 & -\left(\dfrac{1 + 3\sqrt{3}}{1 + \sqrt{3}}\right)
\end{pmatrix}
$$

Applying $Per_{N, R_0, C}$ to the matrix V of homogeneous coordinates of the unit cube, we have $Per_{N, R_0, C} \cdot V = V'$, where V' is the matrix $(A'B'C'D'E'F'G'H')$. After matrix multiplication, we have

$$
V' = \frac{1 + \sqrt{3}}{2} \times
$$

$$
\begin{pmatrix}
-2 & -2 & \dfrac{-2\sqrt{3}}{1 + \sqrt{3}} & \dfrac{-2\sqrt{3}}{1 + \sqrt{3}} & \dfrac{-2\sqrt{3}}{1 + \sqrt{3}} & -2 & -2 & \dfrac{-2\sqrt{3}}{1 + \sqrt{3}} \\[2mm]
-(1 + \sqrt{3}) & -1 & \dfrac{-2\sqrt{3}}{1 + \sqrt{3}} & -3 & -3 & -(1 + \sqrt{3}) & -1 & \dfrac{-2\sqrt{3}}{1 + \sqrt{3}} \\[2mm]
-\dfrac{1}{2} & \dfrac{-1}{2(1 + \sqrt{3})} & 0 & \dfrac{-\sqrt{3}}{2(1 + \sqrt{3})} & \dfrac{-5\sqrt{3}}{2(1 + \sqrt{3})} & -\left(\dfrac{1 + 5\sqrt{3}}{2(1 + \sqrt{3})}\right) & -\left(\dfrac{1 + 4\sqrt{3}}{2(1 + \sqrt{3})}\right) & \dfrac{-2\sqrt{3}}{1 + \sqrt{3}} \\[2mm]
-\left(\dfrac{1 + 3\sqrt{3}}{1 + \sqrt{3}}\right) & -\left(\dfrac{1 + 2\sqrt{3}}{1 + \sqrt{3}}\right) & \dfrac{-2\sqrt{3}}{1 + \sqrt{3}} & \dfrac{-3\sqrt{3}}{(1 + \sqrt{3})} & \dfrac{-3\sqrt{3}}{(1 + \sqrt{3})} & -\left(\dfrac{1 + 3\sqrt{3}}{1 + \sqrt{3}}\right) & -\left(\dfrac{1 + 2\sqrt{3}}{1 + \sqrt{3}}\right) & \dfrac{-2\sqrt{3}}{1 + \sqrt{3}}
\end{pmatrix}
$$

Changing from homogeneous coordinates to world coordinates (App. 2), we find the coordinates of the projected cube to be

$$A'\left[2\left(\frac{1 + \sqrt{3}}{1 + 3\sqrt{3}}\right), 2\left(\frac{2 + \sqrt{3}}{1 + 3\sqrt{3}}\right), \frac{1 + \sqrt{3}}{2(1 + 3\sqrt{3})}\right] \qquad E'\left(\frac{2}{3}, \frac{1 + \sqrt{3}}{\sqrt{3}}, \frac{5}{6}\right)$$

$$B'\left[2\left(\frac{1 + \sqrt{3}}{1 + 2\sqrt{3}}\right), \frac{1 + \sqrt{3}}{1 + 2\sqrt{3}}, \frac{1}{2(1 + 2\sqrt{3})}\right] \qquad F'\left[2\left(\frac{1 + \sqrt{3}}{1 + 3\sqrt{3}}\right), \frac{2(2 + \sqrt{3})}{1 + 3\sqrt{3}}, \frac{1 + 5\sqrt{3}}{2(1 + 3\sqrt{3})}\right]$$

$$C'(1, 1, 0) \qquad\qquad\qquad\qquad\qquad\qquad G'\left[2\left(\frac{1 + \sqrt{3}}{1 + 2\sqrt{3}}\right), \frac{1 + \sqrt{3}}{1 + 2\sqrt{3}}, \frac{1 + 4\sqrt{3}}{2(1 + 2\sqrt{3})}\right]$$

$$D'\left(\frac{2}{3}, \frac{1 + \sqrt{3}}{\sqrt{3}}, \frac{1}{6}\right) \qquad\qquad\qquad\quad H'(1, 1, 1)$$

To change from world coordinates to view plane coordinates, we first choose an up vector. Choosing the vector $\mathbf{K}$, the direction of the positive z axis, as the up vector, we next find the view plane coordinate vectors $\mathbf{I_p}$ and $\mathbf{J_q}$.

With our choices t_1 and t_2, we find that the unit normal vector $\mathbf{N}$ (Prob. 7.9) is

$$\mathbf{N} = \frac{\sqrt{3}}{2} \mathbf{I} + \frac{1}{2} \mathbf{J}$$

Choosing $\mathbf{U} = \mathbf{K}$, and using Prob. A2.15 (App. 2), we find that

$$\mathbf{U_q} = \mathbf{U} - (\mathbf{N} \cdot \mathbf{U})\mathbf{N} = \mathbf{U} \quad (\text{since } \mathbf{N} \cdot \mathbf{U} = 0) \quad = \mathbf{K} \quad \text{and} \quad \mathbf{J_q} = \frac{\mathbf{U_q}}{|\mathbf{U_q}|} = \mathbf{K}$$

(Note to student using equation ($A2$-3) of Prob. A2.15: we have used the fact that $|\mathbf{N}| = 1$ and replaced $\mathbf{V_p}$ with $\mathbf{U_q}$ and $\mathbf{V}$ and $\mathbf{U}$.)

Now

$$\mathbf{I_p} = \frac{\mathbf{N} \times \mathbf{J_q}}{|\mathbf{N} \times \mathbf{J_q}|}$$

Calculating (App. 2), we obtain

$$\mathbf{N} \times \mathbf{J_q} = \frac{1}{2} \mathbf{I} - \frac{\sqrt{3}}{2} \mathbf{J} \qquad \text{and} \qquad |\mathbf{N} \times \mathbf{J_q}| = 1$$

So

$$\mathbf{I_p} = \frac{1}{2} \mathbf{I} - \frac{\sqrt{3}}{2} \mathbf{J}$$

To convert a point P with world coordinates $(x, y, z)_w$ to view plane coordinates $(p, q)_v$, we use the equations from Prob. 8.1.

$$x = x_0 + pa_p + qa_q \qquad y = y_0 + pb_p + qb_q \qquad z = z_0 + pc_p + qc_q$$

where (x_0, y_0, z_0) are the coordinates of the view plane reference point R_0. Now

$$\mathbf{I_p} = a_p \mathbf{I} + b_p \mathbf{J} + c_p \mathbf{K} = \frac{1}{2} \mathbf{I} - \frac{\sqrt{3}}{2} \mathbf{J} + 0\mathbf{K} \qquad \mathbf{J_q} = a_q \mathbf{I} + b_p \mathbf{J} + c_q \mathbf{K} = 0\mathbf{I} + 0\mathbf{J} + 1\mathbf{K} .$$

Choosing $R_0(1, 1, 0)$ as the view plane reference point, we find

$$x = \frac{1}{2} p + 1 \qquad y = \frac{-\sqrt{3}}{2} p + 1 \qquad z = q$$

Solving for p and q, we have

$$p = 2(x - 1) \qquad \text{and} \qquad q = z$$

Using these equations, we convert the transformed coordinates to view plane coordinates:

$$A'\left[2\left(\frac{1-\sqrt{3}}{1+3\sqrt{3}}\right), \frac{1+\sqrt{3}}{2(1+3\sqrt{3})}\right] \qquad E'\left(-\frac{2}{3}, \frac{5}{6}\right)$$

$$B'\left[\frac{2}{1+2\sqrt{3}}, \frac{1}{2(1+2\sqrt{3})}\right] \qquad F'\left[2\left(\frac{1-\sqrt{3}}{1+3\sqrt{3}}\right), \frac{1+5\sqrt{3}}{2(1+3\sqrt{3})}\right]$$

$$C'(0,0) \qquad G'\left[\frac{2}{1+2\sqrt{3}}, \frac{1+4\sqrt{3}}{2(1+2\sqrt{3})}\right]$$

$$D'\left(-\frac{2}{3}, \frac{1}{6}\right) \qquad H'(0, 1)$$

Refer to Fig. 8-12. Note also that the coordinates of the view point or center of projection C and the vanishing points VP_1 and VP_2 can be found by using the equations from Prob. 7.9:

$$C(a, b, c) = C\left(2, 1 + \sqrt{3}, \frac{1}{2}\right) \qquad VP_1\left(0, 1 + \sqrt{3}, \frac{1}{2}\right)_w \qquad VP_2\left(2, 1 - \sqrt{3}, \frac{1}{2}\right)_w$$

In view plane coordinates:

$$VP_1\left(-2, \frac{1}{2}\right)_v \qquad \text{and} \qquad VP_2\left(2, \frac{1}{2}\right)_v$$

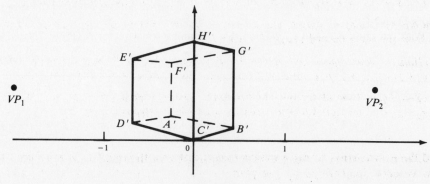

Fig. 8-12

8.3   Find the transformation T_{wv} that relates world coordinates to view plane coordinates.

SOLUTION

The world coordinate axes are determined by the right-handed triad of unit vectors $[\mathbf{I}, \mathbf{J}, \mathbf{K}]$.

The view plane coordinate axes are determined by the left-handed triad of vectors $[\mathbf{I_p}, \mathbf{J_q}, \mathbf{N}]$ and the view reference point $R_0(x_0, y_0, z_0)$.

Referring to Fig. 8-3(a), we construct the transformation T_{wv} through the concatenation of the matrices determined by the following steps:

1.   Translate the view plane reference point $R_0(x_0, y_0, z_0)$ to the world coordinate origin via the translation matrix $T_\mathbf{v}$. Here $\mathbf{V}$ is the vector with components $-x_0\mathbf{I} - y_0\mathbf{J} - z_0\mathbf{K}$.

2.   Align the view plane normal $\mathbf{N}$ with the vector $-\mathbf{K}$ (the direction of the negative z axis) using the transformation $A_{\mathbf{N}, -\mathbf{K}}$ (Chap. 6, Prob. 6.5). Let $\mathbf{I_p'}$ be the new position of the vector $\mathbf{I_p}$ after performing the alignment transformation, i.e.,

$$\mathbf{I_p'} = A_{\mathbf{N}, -\mathbf{K}} \cdot \mathbf{I_p}$$

3.   Rotate $\mathbf{I_p'}$ about the z axis so that it aligns with $\mathbf{I}$, the direction of the x axis. With θ being the angle between $\mathbf{I_p'}$ and $\mathbf{I}$, the rotation is $R_{\theta, \mathbf{K}}$ (Chap. 6).

4.   Change from the right-handed coordinates to left-handed coordinates by applying the transformation T_{RL} from Example 1. Then $T_{wv} = T_{RL} \cdot R_{\theta, \mathbf{K}} \cdot A_{\mathbf{N}, -\mathbf{K}} \cdot T_\mathbf{v}$. If (x_w, y_w, z_w) are the world coordinates of point P, the view plane coordinates (x_v, y_v, z_v) of P can be found by applying the transformation T_{wv}.

8.4   Find the equations of the planes forming the view volume for the general parallel projection.

SOLUTION

The equation of a plane is determined by two vectors that are contained in the plane and a reference point (App. 2, Prob. A2.10). The cross product of the two vectors determines the direction of the normal vector to the plane.

In Fig. 8-8, the sides of the window in the view plane have the directions of the view plane coordinate vectors $\mathbf{I_p}$ and $\mathbf{J_q}$. With $\mathbf{V}$ as the vector determining the direction of projection, we find the following planes:

1.   *Top plane*—determined by the vectors $\mathbf{J_q}$ and $\mathbf{V}$ and reference point R_f the point f units along the unit normal vector $\mathbf{N} = n_1\mathbf{I} + n_2\mathbf{J} + n_3\mathbf{K}$ measured from the upper right corner $R(r_1, r_2, r_3)$ of the window. Reference point R_f has world coordinates $(r_1 + f \cdot n_1, r_2 + f \cdot n_2, r_3 + f \cdot n_3)$.

2.   *Bottom plane*—determined by the vectors $\mathbf{J_q}$ and $\mathbf{V}$ and the reference point L_f, measured from the lower left corner $L(l_1, l_2, l_3)$ of the window. Point L_f has world coordinates $(l_1 + f \cdot n_1, l_2 + f \cdot n_2, l_3 + f \cdot n_3)$.

3.   *Right side plane*—determined by the vectors $\mathbf{I_p}$ and $\mathbf{V}$ and the reference point R_f.

4.   *Left side plane*—determined by the vectors $\mathbf{I_p}$ and $\mathbf{V}$ and the reference point L_f.

Front and back clipping planes, also known as "hither" and "yon", are parallel to the view plane, and thus have the same normal vector $\mathbf{N} = n_1\mathbf{I} + n_2\mathbf{J} + n_3\mathbf{K}$.

5.   (*Hither*) *front plane*—determined by the normal vector $\mathbf{N}$ and reference point $P_f(x_0 + f \cdot n_1, y_0 + f \cdot n_2, z_0 + f \cdot n_3)$, measured from the view reference point $R_0(x_0, y_0, z_0)$.

6.   (*Yon*) *back plane*—determined by the normal vector $\mathbf{N}$ and reference point $P_b(x_0 + b \cdot n_1, y_0 + b \cdot n_2, z_0 + b \cdot n_3)$, measured b units from the view plane reference point R_0.

8.5   Find the normalizing transformation that transforms the parallel view volume to the canonical view volume determined by the planes $x = 0$, $x = 1$, $y = 0$, $y = 1$, $z = 0$, and $z = 1$ (the unit cube).

SOLUTION

Referring to Fig. 8-8, we see that the required transformation N_{par} is built by performing the following series of transformations:

1. Translate so that R_0, the view plane reference point, is at the origin. The required transformation is the translation T_{-R_0}.

2. The vectors $\mathbf{I_p}$, $\mathbf{J_q}$, and $\mathbf{N}$ form the left-handed view plane coordinate system. We next align the view plane normal vector $\mathbf{N}$ with the vector $-\mathbf{K}$ (the direction of the negative z axis). The alignment transformation $A_{\mathbf{N},-\mathbf{K}}$ was developed in Chap. 6, Prob. 6.5. Let $\mathbf{I'_p}$ be the new position of the vector $\mathbf{I_p}$; that is, $\mathbf{I'_p} = A_{\mathbf{N},-\mathbf{K}} \cdot \mathbf{I_p}$.

3. Align the vector $\mathbf{I'_p}$ with the vector $\mathbf{I}$ (the direction of the positive x axis) by rotating $\mathbf{I'_p}$ about the z axis. The required transformation is $R_{\theta,\mathbf{K}}$. Here, θ is the angle between $\mathbf{I'_p}$ and $\mathbf{I}$ (Chap. 6). When $R_{\theta,\mathbf{K}}$ aligns $\mathbf{I'_p}$ with $\mathbf{I}$, the vector $\mathbf{J'_q}$ (where $\mathbf{J'_q} = A_{\mathbf{N},-\mathbf{K}} \cdot \mathbf{J_q}$) is aligned with the vector $\mathbf{J}$ (the direction of the positive y axis).

4. We change from the right-handed world coordinate system to a left-handed coordinate system. The required orientation changing transformation is [see Fig. 8-3(a)] (see also Example 1)

$$T_{RL} = \begin{pmatrix} 1 & 0 & 0 & 0 \\ 0 & 1 & 0 & 0 \\ 0 & 0 & -1 & 0 \\ 0 & 0 & 0 & 1 \end{pmatrix}$$

5. Let $\mathbf{V'}$ be the new position of the direction of projection vector $\mathbf{V}$; that is, $\mathbf{V'} = R_{\theta,\mathbf{K}} \cdot A_{\mathbf{N},-\mathbf{K}} \cdot \mathbf{V}$. The new position of the transformed view volume is illustrated in Fig. 8-13.

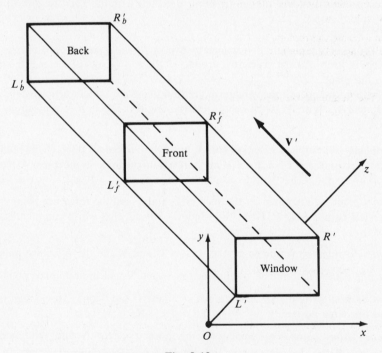

Fig. 8-13

Note how the view volume is skewed along the line having the direction of the vector $\mathbf{V'}$. Suppose that the components of $\mathbf{V'}$ are $\mathbf{V'} = v'_x\mathbf{I} + v'_y\mathbf{J} + v'_z\mathbf{K}$. We now perform a shearing transformation that transforms the newly skewed view volume to a rectangular view volume aligned along the z axis. The required shearing transformation is determined by preserving the new view volume base vectors $\mathbf{I}$ and

J and shearing **V'** to the vector $v'_z\mathbf{K}$ (the **K** component of **V'**); that is, **I** is transformed to **I**, **J** is transformed to **J**, and **V'** is transformed to $v'_z\mathbf{K}$. The required transformation is the matrix

$$Sh = \begin{pmatrix} 1 & 0 & -\dfrac{v'_x}{v'_z} \\ 0 & 1 & -\dfrac{v'_y}{v'_z} \\ 0 & 0 & 1 \end{pmatrix}$$

In order to concatenate the transformations so as to build N_{par}, we use the 4×4 homogeneous form of Sh

$$\begin{pmatrix} & & | & 0 \\ & Sh & | & 0 \\ & & | & 0 \\ \hline 0 & 0 & 0 & 1 \end{pmatrix}$$

6.   We now translate the new view volume so that its lower left corner L'_f will be at the origin. To do this, we note that the first four transformations correspond to the view plane coordinate system transformation in Prob. 8.3. So after performing these transformations $L(p_{min}, q_{min})_v$ (view plane coordinates), we find that the lower left corner of the view plane window transforms to a point L' on the xy plane whose coordinates are $(p_{min}, q_{min}, 0)$. Similarly, the upper right corner R is transformed to $R'(p_{max}, q_{max}, 0)$. After performing the shearing transformation Sh, we see that the view volume is vertical (aligned with the z axis) and the back and front faces are, respectively, b and f units from the xy plane. Thus the lower left corner of the view volume is at $L'_f(p_{min}, q_{min}, f)$, and the bounds of the view volume are $p_{min} \le x \le p_{max}$, $q_{min} \le y \le q_{max}$, $f \le z \le b$. The required translation is $T_{-L'_f}$.

7.   We now scale the rectangular view volume to the unit cube. The base of the present view volume has the dimensions of the base of the original volume, which corresponds to the view plane window; that is

$$l = p_{max} - p_{min} \quad \text{(length)} \qquad w = q_{max} - q_{min} \quad \text{(width)}$$

The height of the new view volume is the distance from the front clipping plane to the back clipping plane: $h = b - f$. The required scaling is the matrix (in 4×4 homogeneous form)

$$S_{1/l,1/w,1/h} = \begin{pmatrix} \dfrac{1}{l} & 0 & 0 & 0 \\ 0 & \dfrac{1}{w} & 0 & 0 \\ 0 & 0 & \dfrac{1}{h} & 0 \\ 0 & 0 & 0 & 1 \end{pmatrix}$$

The required transformation is then

$$N_{par} = S_{1/l,1/w,1/h} \cdot T_{-L'_f} \cdot Sh \cdot T_{RL} \cdot R_{\theta,\mathbf{K}} \cdot A_{\mathbf{N},-\mathbf{K}} \cdot T_{-R_0}$$

Note also that after performing the transformation N_{par}, the view plane transforms to the plane $z = -f/(b - f)$, parallel to the xy plane. Also, the direction of projection vector **V** transforms to a vector parallel to the vector **K** having the direction of the z axis.

8.6   Find the normalizing transformation that transforms the perspective view volume to the canonical view volume determined by the bounding planes $x = z$, $x = -z$, $y = z$, $y = -z$, $z = z_f$, and $z = 1$.

SOLUTION

Referring to Fig. 8-7, we build the normalizing transformation N_{per} through a series of transformations. As in Prob. 8.5:

1. Translate the center of projection C to the origin using the translation T_{-c}.
2. Align the view plane normal $\mathbf{N}$ with the vector $-\mathbf{K}$ using $A_{\mathbf{N},-\mathbf{K}}$.
3. Rotate $\mathbf{I'_p}$ to the vector $\mathbf{I}$ using the rotation $R_{\theta,\mathbf{K}}$. (Recall that $\mathbf{I'_p} = A_{\mathbf{N},-\mathbf{K}} \cdot \mathbf{I_p}$.)
4. We now change from right-handed world coordinates to left-handed coordinates by applying the transformation

$$T_{RL} = \begin{pmatrix} 1 & 0 & 0 & 0 \\ 0 & 1 & 0 & 0 \\ 0 & 0 & -1 & 0 \\ 0 & 0 & 0 & 1 \end{pmatrix}$$

5. The newly transformed view volume is skewed along the centerline joining the origin (the translated center of projection) with the center of the (transformed) view plane window (Fig. 8-14). Let C_w be the coordinates of the center of the original view plane window. Then C_w has view plane coordinates

$$\left(\frac{p_{min} + p_{max}}{2}, \frac{q_{min} + q_{max}}{2} \right)_v$$

These are changed to world coordinates as in Prob. 8.1. Let $\overline{\mathbf{CC}}_w$ be the vector from the center of projection to the center of the window. Let $(\overline{\mathbf{CC}}_w)'$ be the transform of the vector $\overline{\mathbf{CC}}_w$; that is, $(\overline{\mathbf{CC}}_w)' = R_{\theta,\mathbf{K}} \cdot A_{\mathbf{N},-\mathbf{K}} \cdot \overline{\mathbf{CC}}_w$. Then $(\overline{\mathbf{CC}}_w)'$ is the vector that joins the origin to the center of the transformed view plane window (Fig. 8-14). Suppose that $(\overline{\mathbf{CC}}_w)' = c'_x\mathbf{I} + c'_y\mathbf{J} + c'_z\mathbf{K}$. We shear the view volume so that it transforms to a view volume whose center line lies along the z axis. As in Prob.

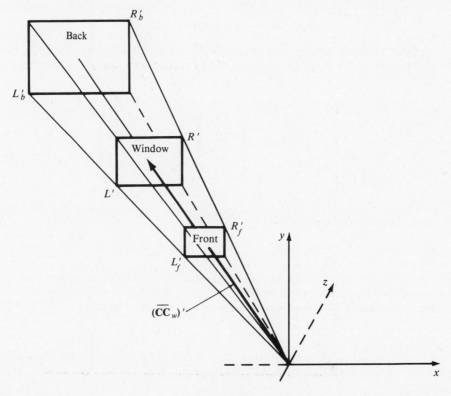

Fig. 8-14

8.5, the required shearing transformation is

$$Sh = \begin{pmatrix} 1 & 0 & -\dfrac{c'_x}{c'_z} & 0 \\ 0 & 1 & -\dfrac{c'_y}{c'_z} & 0 \\ 0 & 0 & 1 & 0 \\ 0 & 0 & 0 & 1 \end{pmatrix}$$

The newly transformed window is, after applying the shearing transformation Sh, located on the z axis at $z = c'_z$.

6. Referring to Fig. 8-15, the transformed window is now centered on the z axis. The dimensions of the window are

$$l = p_{max} - p_{min} \quad \text{(length)} \qquad \text{and} \qquad w = q_{max} - q_{min} \quad \text{(width)}$$

The height of the new view volume is the distance between the front and back clipping planes: $h = b - f$. The transformed window is centered on the z axis at $z = c'_z$ and is bounded by

$$-\frac{l}{2} \leq x \leq \frac{l}{2} \qquad -\frac{w}{2} \leq y \leq \frac{w}{2}$$

The transformed view plane is located at $z = c'_z$. The transformed front clipping plane is located at $z_f = c'_z + f$. The back clipping plane is now located at $z_b = c'_z + b$.

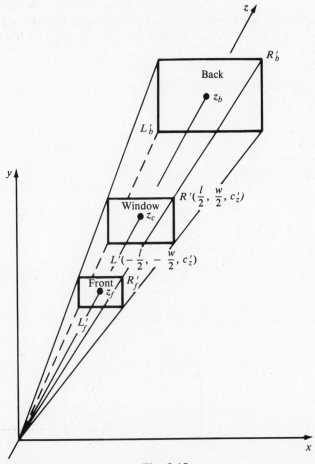

Fig. 8-15

To transform this view volume into the canonical view volume, we first scale in the z direction so that the back-clipping plane is transformed to $z = 1$. The required scale factor is

$$s_z = \frac{1}{c_z' + b}$$

The scaling matrix is

$$S_{1,1,s_z} = \begin{pmatrix} 1 & 0 & 0 & 0 \\ 0 & 1 & 0 & 0 \\ 0 & 0 & \dfrac{1}{c_z' + b} & 0 \\ 0 & 0 & 0 & 1 \end{pmatrix}$$

To find the new window boundaries R'' and L'', we apply this scaling transformation to the present window coordinates

$$R'\left(\frac{l}{2}, -\frac{w}{2}, c_z' \right) \qquad L'\left(-\frac{l}{2}, -\frac{w}{2}, c_z' \right)$$

Then

$$R'' = \left(\frac{l}{2}, \frac{w}{2}, \frac{c_z'}{c_z' + b} \right) \quad \text{and} \quad L'' = \left(-\frac{l}{2}, -\frac{w}{2}, \frac{c_z'}{c_z' + b} \right)$$

Next we scale in the x and y directions so that the window boundaries will be

$$R'''\left(\frac{c_z'}{c_z' + b}, \frac{c_z'}{c_z' + b}, \frac{c_z'}{c_z' + b} \right) \quad \text{and} \quad L'''\left(-\frac{c_z'}{c_z' + b}, -\frac{c_z'}{c_z' + b}, \frac{c_z'}{c_z' + b} \right)$$

That is, the window boundaries will lie on the planes $x = z$, $x = -z$, $y = z$, and $y = -z$. The required scale factors are

$$s_x = \frac{2c_z'}{l(c_z' + b)} \quad \text{and} \quad s_y = \frac{2c_z'}{w(c_z' + b)}$$

The corresponding scaling transformation is

$$S_{s_x,s_y,1} = \begin{pmatrix} \dfrac{2c_z'}{l(c_z' + b)} & 0 & 0 & 0 \\ 0 & \dfrac{2c_z'}{w(c_z' + b)} & 0 & 0 \\ 0 & 0 & 1 & 0 \\ 0 & 0 & 0 & 1 \end{pmatrix}$$

Multiplication of these scaling transformations into one transformation yields

$$S_{s_x,s_y,s_z} = \begin{pmatrix} \dfrac{2c_z'}{l(c_z' + b)} & 0 & 0 & 0 \\ 0 & \dfrac{2c_z'}{w(c_z' + b)} & 0 & 0 \\ 0 & 0 & \dfrac{1}{c_z' + b} & 0 \\ 0 & 0 & 0 & 1 \end{pmatrix}$$

To find the location of the front clipping plane, z_f, we apply the transformation S_{s_x, s_y, s_z} to the present location of the center of the front clipping plane, which is $C_f(0, 0, c_z' + f)$. So

$$S_{s_x, s_y, s_z} \cdot C_f = \left(0, 0, \frac{c_z' + f}{c_z' + b}\right)$$

That is

$$z_f = \frac{c_z' + f}{c_z' + b}$$

The complete transformation can be written as

$$N_{\text{per}} = S_{s_x, s_y, s_z} \cdot Sh \cdot T_{RL} \cdot R_{\theta, \mathbf{K}} \cdot A_{\mathbf{N}, -\mathbf{K}} \cdot T_{-C}$$

Note that after performing the transformation N_{per}, the view plane is transformed to the plane

$$z = \frac{c_z'}{c_z' + b}$$

parallel to the xy plane. Also, the center of projection C is transformed to the origin.

8.7 How do we determine whether a point P is inside or outside the view volume?

SOLUTION

A plane divides space into two sides. The general equation of a plane is (App. 2)

$$n_1(x - x_0) + n_2(y - y_0) + n_3(z - z_0) = 0$$

We define a scalar function, $f(P)$, for any point $P(x, y, z)$ by

$$f(P) \equiv f(x, y, t) = n_1(x - x_0) + n_2(y - y_0) + n_3(z - z_0)$$

We say that a point P is on the same side (with respect to the plane) as point Q if sign $f(P) = $ sign $f(Q)$. Referring to Figs. 8-7 or 8-8, let f_T, f_B, f_R, f_L, f_H, and f_Y be the functions associated with the top, bottom, right, left, hither (front), and yon (back) planes, respectively (Probs. 8.4 and 8.10).

Also, L and R are the lower left and upper right corners of the window and P_b and P_f are the reference points of the back and front clipping planes, respectively.

Then a point P is inside the view volume if all the following hold:

$$P \text{ is on the same side as } L \text{ with respect to } f_T$$

"	R	" f_B
"	L	" f_R
"	R	" f_L
"	P_b	" f_H
"	P_f	" f_Y

Equivalently

$$\text{sign } f_T(P) = \text{sign } f_T(L) \qquad \text{sign } f_L(P) = \text{sign } f_L(R)$$
$$\text{sign } f_B(P) = \text{sign } f_B(R) \qquad \text{sign } f_H(P) = \text{sign } f_H(P_b)$$
$$\text{sign } f_R(P) = \text{sign } f_R(L) \qquad \text{sign } f_Y(P) = \text{sign } f_Y(P_f)$$

8.8 Show how endpoint codes would be assigned to the endpoints of a line segment for the three-dimensional Cohen-Sutherland clipping algorithm for (a) the canonical parallel view volume and (b) the canonical perspective view volume.

SOLUTION

The procedure follows the logic of the two-dimensional algorithm in Chap. 5. For three dimensions, the planes describing the view volume divide three-dimensional space into six regions, plus the interior of the view volume; thus 6-bit codes are used. Let $P(x, y, z)$ be the coordinates of an endpoint.

(a)   For the canonical parallel view volume, each bit is set to true (1) or false (0) according to the scheme

> Bit 1 ≡ endpoint is above view volume = sign $(y - 1)$
> Bit 2 ≡ endpoint is below view volume = sign $(-y)$
> Bit 3 ≡ endpoint is to right of view volume = sign $(x - 1)$
> Bit 4 ≡ endpoint is to left of view volume = sign $(-x)$
> Bit 5 ≡ endpoint is behind view volume = sign $(z - 1)$
> Bit 6 ≡ endpoint is in front of view volume = sign $(-z)$

Recall that sign $a = 1$ if a is positive, 0 otherwise.

(b)   For the canonical perspective view volume:

> Bit 1 ≡ endpoint is above view volume = sign $(y - z)$
> Bit 2 ≡ endpoint is below view volume = sign $(-z - y)$
> Bit 3 ≡ endpoint is to right of view volume = sign $(x - z)$
> Bit 4 ≡ endpoint is to left of view volume = sign $(-z - x)$
> Bit 5 ≡ endpoint is behind view volume = sign $(z - 1)$
> Bit 6 ≡ endpoint is in front of view volume = sign $(z_f - z)$

The category of a line segment (Chap. 5) is (1) visible if both endpoint codes are 000000, (2) not visible if the logical AND of the endpoint codes is *not* 000000, and (3) clipping candidate if the logical AND of the endpoint codes is 000000.

8.9   Find the intersecting points of a line segment with the bounding planes of the canonical view volumes for (a) parallel and (b) perspective projections.

SOLUTION

Let $P_1(x_1, y_1, z_1)$ and $P_2(x_2, y_2, z_2)$ be the endpoints of the line segment. The parametric equations of the line segment are

$$x = x_1 + (x_2 - x_1)t \qquad y = y_1 + (y_2 - y_1)t \qquad z = z_1 + (z_2 - z_1)t$$

From Prob. 8.11, the intersection parameter is

$$t_1 = \frac{-\mathbf{N} \cdot \overline{\mathbf{R}_0 \mathbf{P}_1}}{\mathbf{N} \cdot \overline{\mathbf{P}_2 \mathbf{P}_1}}$$

where $\mathbf{N}$ is the normal vector and R_0 is a reference point on the plane.

(a)   The bounding planes for the parallel canonical view volume are $x = 0$, $x = 1$, $y = 0$, $y = 1$, $z = 0$, and $z = 1$. For the plane $x = 1$, we have $\mathbf{N} = \mathbf{I}$ and R_0 $(1, 0, 0)$. Then

$$t_I = \frac{-(x_1 - 1)}{x_2 - x_1}$$

If $0 \le t_I \le 1$, the line segment intersects the plane. The point of intersection is then

$$x = x_1 + (x_2 - x_1)\left(-\frac{x_1 - 1}{x_2 - x_1}\right) = 1 \qquad y = y_1 + (y_2 - y_1)\left(-\frac{x_1 - 1}{x_2 - x_1}\right)$$

$$z = z_1 + (z_2 - z_1)\left(-\frac{x_1 - 1}{x_2 - x_1}\right)$$

The intersections with the other planes are found in the same way.

(b) The bounding planes for the perspective canonical view volume are $x = z$, $x = -z$, $y = z$, $y = -z$, $z = z_f$, and $z = 1$ (where z_f is calculated as in Prob. 8.6).

   To find the intersection with the plane $x = z$, for example, we write the equation of the plane as $x - z = 0$. From this equation, we read off the normal vector as $\mathbf{N} = \mathbf{I} - \mathbf{K}$ (App. 2, Prob. A2.9), and the reference point is $R_0(0, 0, 0)$. Then

$$t_I = -\frac{x_1 - z_1}{(x_2 - x_1) - (z_2 - z_1)}$$

If $0 \le t_I \le 1$, we substitute t_I into the parametric equations of the line segment to calculate the intersection point.

   The other intersections are found in the same way.

Supplementary Problems

8.10   Find the equations of the planes forming the view volume for the general perspective projection.

8.11   Find the intersection point of a plane and a line segment.

Chapter 9

Geometric Forms and Models

9.1 INTRODUCTION

One of the major concepts in computer graphics is *modeling* of objects and pictures. By this we mean description of the objects and pictures to the computer so as to produce a visual display that simulates the real thing.

One way to do this is to use a set of primitives or geometric forms that are simple enough to be easily implemented on the computer but flexible enough to represent or model a variety of objects. We can build a model of our object by assembling these primitives either through the use of a prepared display file or by interactively constructing the model. Geometric forms that can be used as primitives include, in order of complexity, points, line segments, polylines, polygons, and polyhedra. These are used in the construction of wireframe drawings. More complex geometric forms include curved segments, curved surface patches, and quadric surfaces. Highly realistic representations use color, shading, and texture models to achieve realism.

9.2 SIMPLE GEOMETRIC FORMS

Points and Lines

Points and lines are the basic building blocks of computer graphics. Their implementation in both hardware and software has been described in Chaps. 2 and 3. We specify a point by giving its coordinates in three- (or two-) dimensional space. A *line segment* is specified by giving its endpoints $P_1(x_1, y_1, z_1)$ and $P_2(x_2, y_2, z_2)$.

Polylines

A *polyline* is a chain of connected line segments. It is specified by giving the vertices (nodes) $P_0, \ldots, P_N$ defining the line segments. The first vertex is called the *initial* or *starting point* and the last vertex, the *final* or *terminal point* (see Fig. 9-1).

Polygons

A *polygon* is a closed polyline, that is, one in which the initial and terminal points coincide. A polygon is specified by its *vertex list* $P_0, \ldots, P_N, P_0$. The line segments $\overline{P_0 P_1}, \overline{P_1 P_2}, \ldots, \overline{P_N P_0}$ are called the *edges* of the polygon. (In general, we need not specify P_0 twice, especially when passing the polygon to the Sutherland-Hodgman clipping algorithm.)

A *planar polygon* is a polygon in which all vertices (and thus the entire polygon) lie on the same plane (see Fig. 9-2).

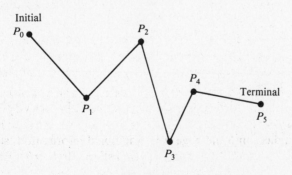

Fig. 9-1

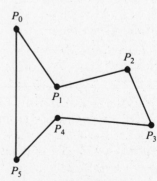

Fig. 9-2

9.3 WIREFRAME MODELS

A *wireframe model* consists of edges, vertices, and polygons. Here vertices are connected by edges, and polygons are sequences of vertices or edges. The edges may be curved or straight line segments. In the latter case, the wireframe model is called a *polygonal net* or *polygonal mesh* (Fig. 9-3).

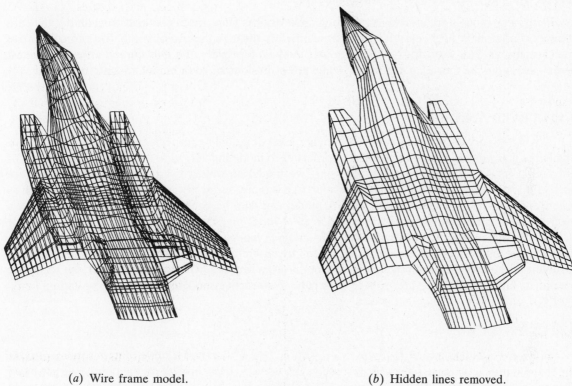

(*a*) Wire frame model.　　　　　　　　(*b*) Hidden lines removed.

Fig. 9-3

Representing a Polygonal Net Model

There are several different ways of representing a polygonal net model.

1. *Explicit vertex list* $V = \{P_0, P_1, P_2, \ldots, P_N\}$. The points $P_i(x_i, y_i, z_i)$ are the vertices of the polygonal net, stored in the order in which they would be encountered by traveling around the model. Although this form of representation is useful for single polygons, it is quite inefficient for a complete polygonal net in that shared vertices are repeated several times (see Prob. 9.1). In addition, when displaying the model by drawing the edges, shared edges are drawn several times.

2. *Polygon listing*. In this form of representation, each vertex is stored exactly once in a vertex list $V = (P_0, \ldots, P_N)$, and each polygon is defined by pointing or indexing into this vertex list (see Prob. 9.2). Again, shared edges are drawn several times in displaying the model.

3. *Explicit edge listing*. In this form of representation, we keep a vertex list in which each vertex is stored exactly once and an edge list in which each edge is stored exactly once. Each edge in the edge list points to the two vertices in the vertex list which define that edge. A polygon is now represented as a list of pointers or indices into the edge list. Additional information, such as those polygons sharing a given edge, can also be stored in the edge list (see Prob. 9.9). Explicit edge listing can be used to represent the more general wireframe model. The wireframe model is displayed by drawing all the edges, and each edge is drawn only once.

Polyhedron

A *polyhedron* is a closed polygonal net (i.e., one which encloses a definite volume) in which each polygon is planar. The polygons are called the *faces* of the polyhedron. In modeling, polyhedrons are quite often treated as solid (i.e., block) objects, as opposed to wireframes or two-dimensional surfaces.

Advantages and Disadvantages of Wireframe Models

Wireframe models are used in engineering applications. They are easy to construct and, if they are composed of straight lines, easy to clip and manipulate through the use of geometric and coordinate transformations. However, for building realistic models, especially of highly curved objects, we must use a very large number of polygons to achieve the illusions of roundness and smoothness.

9.4 CURVED SURFACES

The use of curved surfaces allows for a higher level of modeling, especially for the construction of highly realistic models. There are several approaches to modeling curved surfaces. One is an analog of polyhedral models. Instead of using polygons, we model an object by using small, curved *surface patches* placed next to each other. Another approach is to use surfaces that define solid objects, such as polyhedra, spheres, cylinders, and cones. A model can then be constructed with these solid objects used as building blocks. This process is called *solid modeling*.

There are two ways to construct a model—*additive modeling* and *subtractive modeling*. Additive modeling is the process of building the model by assembling many simpler objects. Subtractive modeling is the process of removing pieces from a given object to create a new object, for example, creating a (cylindrical) hole in a sphere or a cube. Subtractive modeling is akin to sculpting.

9.5 CURVE DESIGN

Given $n + 1$ data points, $P_0(x_0, y_0), \ldots P_n(x_n, y_n)$ we wish to find a curve that, in some sense, fits the shape outlined by these points. If we require the curve to pass through all the points, we are faced with the problem of *interpolation*. If we require only that the curve be near these points, we are faced with the problem of *approximation*. Interpolation arises, for example, in reconstructing the shape of a digitized curved object. Approximation is used in computer graphics to design curves that "look good" or must meet some aesthetic goal. To solve these often quite distinct problems, it is necessary to find ways of building curves out of smaller pieces, or *curve segments*, in order to meet the design criteria. (As discussed in Chap. 3, curves and curve segments can be modeled as polylines, i.e., are drawn with extremely short line segments.) When modeling a curve $f(x)$ by using curve segments, we try to represent the curve as a sum of smaller segments $\Phi_i(x)$ (called *basis* or *blending functions*):

$$f(x) = \sum_{i=0}^{N} a_i \Phi_i(x)$$

We choose these blending functions with an eye toward computation and display. For this reason, polynomials are often the blending functions of choice.

A *polynomial of degree n* is a function that has the form

$$Q(x) = a_n x^n + a_{n-1} x^{n-1} + \cdots + a_1 x + a_0$$

This polynomial is determined by its $n + 1$ *coefficients* $[a_n, \ldots, a_0]$.

A *continuous piecewise polynomial* $Q(x)$ of degree n is a set of k polynomials $q_i(x)$, each of degree n and $k + 1$ *knots* (nodes) $t_0, \ldots, t_k$ so that

$$Q(x) = q_i(x) \quad \text{for} \quad t_i \le x \le t_{i+1} \quad \text{and} \quad i = 0, \ldots, k - 1$$

Note that this definition requires the polynomials to match or piece together at the knots, that is, $q_{i-1}(t_i) = q_i(t_i)$, $i = 1, \ldots, k-1$. This requirement imposes no restrictions on how smoothly the polynomials $q_i(x)$ fit together. For example, there can be corners or sharp contours at the knots (see Fig. 9-4).

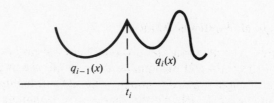

$$q_{i-1}(x) \qquad q_i(x)$$
$$t_i$$

Fig. 9-4

Polynomials of high degree are not very useful for curve designing because of their oscillatory nature.

The most useful piecewise polynomials are those for which the polynomials $q_i(x)$ are cubic (degree 3). There are several reasons for this. One is that the piecewise cubic closely resembles the way a drafter uses a mechanical spline. In addition, 3 is the smallest degree which has the required smoothness properties for describing pleasing shapes. It is also the minimal number needed to represent three-dimensional curves.

9.6 POLYNOMIAL BASIS FUNCTIONS

Let $P_0(x_0, y_0), \ldots, P_n(x_n, y_n)$ represent $n+1$ data points. In addition, let $t_0, t_1, t_2, \ldots,$ be any numbers (called *knots*). The following are common choices for basis or blending functions.

Lagrange Polynomials of Degree n

$$L_i(x) = \prod_{\substack{j=0 \\ j \neq i}}^{n} \frac{x - x_j}{x_i - x_j}, \qquad i = 0, 2, \ldots, n$$

Note that $L_i(x_i) = 1$. (Here Π represents term-by-term multiplication.)

Hermite Cubic Polynomials

Refer to Fig. 9-5.

$$H_i(x) = \begin{cases} -\dfrac{2(x - t_{i-1})^3}{(t_i - t_{i-1})^3} + \dfrac{3(x - t_{i-1})^2}{(t_i - t_{i-1})^2} & t_{i-1} \leq x \leq t_i \\[4mm] -\dfrac{2(t_{i+1} - x)^3}{(t_{i+1} - t_i)^3} + \dfrac{3(t_{i+1} - x)^2}{(t_{i+1} - t_i)^2} & t_i \leq x \leq t_{i+1} \end{cases}$$

$$\bar{H}_i(x) = \begin{cases} \dfrac{(x - t_{i-1})^2(x - t_i)}{(t_i - t_{i-1})^2} & t_{i-1} \leq x \leq t_i \\[4mm] \dfrac{(x - t_i)(t_{i+1} - x)^2}{(t_{i+1} - t_i)^2} & t_i \leq x \leq t_{i+1} \end{cases}$$

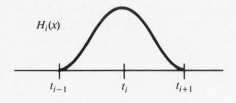

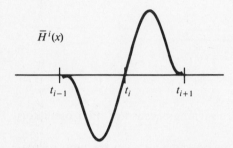

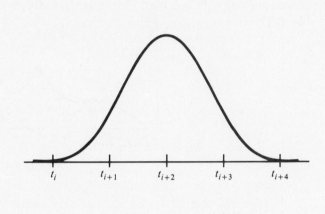

Fig. 9-5 Hermite cubic basis functions.   **Fig. 9-6** Cubic B-spline $B_{i,3}(x)$.

B-Splines

Refer to Fig. 9-6. For the knot set $t_0, t_1, t_2, \ldots,$ the nth-degree B-splines $B_{i,n}$ are defined recursively:

$$B_{i,0}(x) = \begin{cases} 1 & t_i \leq x \leq t_{i+1} \\ 0 & \text{otherwise} \end{cases} \qquad B_{i,n}(x) = \frac{x - t_i}{t_{i+n} - t_i} B_{i,n-1}(x) + \frac{t_{i+n+1} - x}{t_{i+n+1} - t_{i+1}} B_{i+1,n-1}(x)$$

for $t_i \leq x \leq t_{i+n+1}$. Note that $B_{i,n}(x)$ is nonzero only in the interval $[t_i, t_{i+n+1}]$. In particular, the cubic B-spline $B_{i,3}$ is nonzero over the interval $[t_i, t_{i+4}]$ (which spans the knots $t_i, t_{i+1}, t_{i+2}, t_{i+3}, t_{i+4}$). In addition, for nonrepeated knots, the B-spline is zero at the endknots t_i and t_{i+n+1} (from Prob. 9.4), that is,

$$\begin{aligned} B_{i,n}(t_i) &= 0 \\ B_{i,n}(t_{i+n+1}) &= 0 \end{aligned} \qquad (n \geq 1)$$

In using B-splines, we allow for repeated knots, that is, $t_i = t_{i+1} = \cdots$. This means that $B_{i,n}$ can have the form $\frac{0}{0}$ in its definition. By letting $\frac{0}{0} = 0$, we extend the definition of $B_{i,n}$ to incorporate repeated knots.

Bernstein Polynomials

Refer to Fig. 9-7. The Bernstein polynomials of degree n over the interval $[0, 1]$ are defined as

$$BE_{k,n}(x) = \frac{n!}{k!(n-k)!} x^k (1-x)^{n-k}, \qquad 0 \leq x \leq 1$$

The cubic Bernstein polynomials are

$$\begin{aligned} B_{0,3}(x) &= 1 - 3x + 3x^2 - x^3 \\ B_{1,3}(x) &= 3(x - 2x^2 + x^3) \\ B_{2,3}(x) &= 3(x^2 - x^3) \\ B_{3,3}(x) &= x^3 \end{aligned}$$

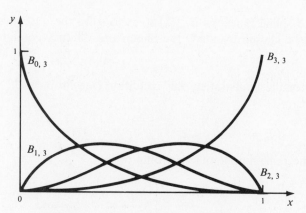

Fig. 9-7 Cubic Bernstein polynomials.

9.7 THE PROBLEM OF INTERPOLATION

Given data points $P_0(x_0, y_0), \ldots, P_n(x_n, y_n)$, we wish to find a curve which passes through these points.

Lagrange Polynomial Interpolation Solution

Here,

$$L(x) = \sum_{i=0}^{n} y_i L_i(x)$$

where $L_i(x)$ are the Lagrange polynomials and $L(x)$ is *the* nth-degree polynomial interpolating the data points.

Hermitian Cubic Interpolation Solution

We wish to find a piecewise polynomial $H(x)$ of degree 3 which passes through the data points and is also continuously differentiable at these points. We also prescribe the values of the derivatives y' (or slope of the tangent line) at the given data points, that is, we prescribe the points $(x_0, y_0'), \ldots, (x_n, y_n')$.

$$H(x) = \sum_{i=0}^{n} [y_i H_i(x) + y_i' \bar{H}_i(x)]$$

where $H_i(x)$ and $\bar{H}_i'(x)$ are the Hermitian cubic basis functions and $t_0 = x_0, t_1 = x_1, t_2 = x_2, \ldots, t_n = x_n$ are the choices for the knot set.

Spline Interpolation

If we require that the interpolating piecewise polynomial be joined as smoothly as possible at the data points, the resulting curve is called a *spline*. Therefore, a spline of degree m has continuous derivatives up to order $m - 1$ at the data points.

It can be shown that any mth-degree spline that passes through $n + 1$ data points can be represented in terms of the B-spline basis functions $B_{i,n}$ as

$$S_m(x) = \sum_{i=0}^{m+n-1} a_i B_{i,m}(x)$$

In order to define the *B*-spline functions $B_{i,m}(x)$ so as to solve the interpolation problem, the knots $t_0, t_1, \ldots, t_{m+n+1}$ must be chosen to satisfy the Shoenberg-Whitney condition:

$$t_i < x_i < t_{i+m+1}, \qquad i = 0, \ldots, n$$

The following choices for the knots satisfy this condition (see Prob. 9.4):

Step 1.   Choose

$$t_0 = \cdots = t_m < x_0 \qquad t_{n+1} = \cdots = t_{m+n+1} > x_n$$

Step 2.   Choose the remaining knots according to

$$t_{i+m+1} = \frac{x_{i+1} + \cdots + x_{i+m}}{m}, \qquad i = 0, \ldots, n - m - 1$$

For cubic splines ($m = 3$), an alternative to step 2, requiring less computation, is step 2'. Choose

$$t_{i+4} = x_{i+2}, \qquad i = 0, \ldots, n - 4$$

The splines $S_2(x)$ and $S_3(x)$ are called *quadratic* and *cubic splines*, respectively.

$$S_2(x) = \sum_{i=0}^{n+1} a_i B_{i,2}(x) \quad \text{and} \quad S_3(x) = \sum_{i=0}^{n+2} a_i B_{i,3}(x)$$

Confining our attention to the cubic spline, we see that there are $n + 3$ coefficients a_i to evaluate, requiring $n + 3$ equations.

The interpolation criterion $S_3(x_j) = y_j$, $j = 0, \ldots, n$ provides $n + 1$ equations:

$$y_j = S_3(x_j) = \sum_{i=0}^{n+2} a_i B_{i,3}(x_j)$$

The remaining two equations are usually specified as boundary conditions at the endpoints x_0 and x_n. Some choices for boundary conditions are

1.   *Natural spline condition*

$$S_3''(x_0) = 0 \qquad S_3''(x_n) = 0$$

2.   *Clamped spline condition*

$$S_3'(x_0) = y_0' \qquad S_3'(x_n) = y_n'$$

where y_0' and y_n' are prescribed derivative values.

3.   *Cyclic spline condition*

$$S_3'(x_0) = S_3'(x_n) \qquad S_3''(x_0) = S_3''(x_n)$$

This is useful for producing closed curves.

4.   *Anticyclic spline condition*

$$S_3'(x_0) = -S_3'(x_n) \qquad S_3''(x_0) = -S_3''(x_n)$$

This is useful in producing splines with parallel endings whose tangent vectors are equal in magnitude but opposite in direction.

For technical reasons, boundary condition 1, the so-called natural boundary condition, is the least preferred choice.

9.8 THE PROBLEM OF APPROXIMATION

The problem is to provide a smooth representation of a three-dimensional curve which approximates given data so as to yield a given shape. Usually the data is given interactively in the form of a guiding polyline determined by *control points* $P_0(x_0, y_0, z_0)$, $P_1(x_1, y_1, z_1), \ldots, P_n(x_n, y_n, z_n)$. We would like to find a curve which approximates the shape of this guiding polyline (see Fig. 9-8).

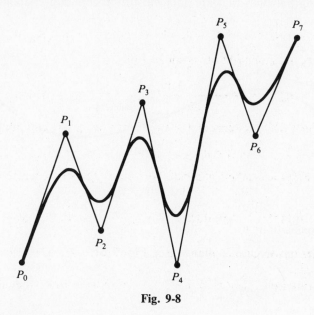

Fig. 9-8

Bézier-Bernstein Approximation

Using the Bernstein polynomials, we form the parametric curves:

$$P(t): \begin{cases} x(t) = \displaystyle\sum_{i=0}^{n} x_i BE_{i,n}(t) \\[2mm] y(t) = \displaystyle\sum_{i=0}^{n} y_i BE_{i,n}(t) \qquad 0 \le t \le 1 \\[2mm] z(t) = \displaystyle\sum_{i=0}^{n} z_i BE_{i,n}(t) \end{cases}$$

where $P(t)$ is called the *Bézier curve*.

Properties of the Bézier-Bernstein Approximation

There are four basic properties:

1. The Bézier curve has the same endpoints as the guiding polyline, that is:

    $$P_0 = P(0) = [x(0), y(0), z(0)] \qquad P_n = P(1) = [x(1), y(1), z(1)]$$

2. The direction of the tangent vector at the endpoints P_0, P_n is the same as that of the vector determined by the first and last segments $\overline{P_0 P_1}$, $\overline{P_{n-1} P_n}$ of the guiding polyline. In particular $P'(0) = n \cdot (P_1 - P_0)$ [i.e., $x'(0) = n(x_1 - x_0)$, $y'(0) = n(y_1 - y_0)$, $z'(0) = n(z_1 - z_0)$] and $P'(1) = n \cdot (P_n - P_{n-1})$.

3. The Bézier curve lies entirely within the convex hull of the guiding polyline. In two dimensions, the *convex hull* is the polygon formed by placing a "rubber band" about the collection of points $P_0, \ldots, P_n$.

4. Bézier curves are suited to interactive design. In fact, Bézier curves can be pieced together so as to ensure continuous differentiability at their juncture by letting the edges of the two different guiding polylines that are adjacent to the common endpoint be collinear (see Fig. 9-9).

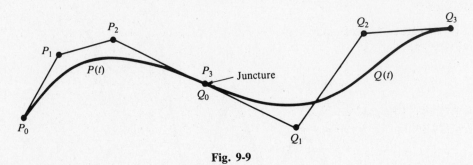

Fig. 9-9

Bézier–B-Spline Approximation

For this approximation, we use B-splines (see Fig. 9-10)

$$P(t): \begin{cases} x(t) = \displaystyle\sum_{i=0}^{n} x_i B_{i,m}(t) \\[2mm] y(t) = \displaystyle\sum_{i=0}^{n} y_i B_{i,m}(t) \qquad 0 \le t \le n - m + 1 \\[2mm] z(t) = \displaystyle\sum_{i=0}^{n} z_i B_{i,m}(t) \end{cases}$$

The mth-degree B-splines $B_{i,m}(t)$, $i = 0, \ldots, n$, are defined for t in the parameter range

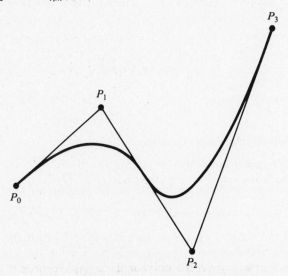

Fig. 9-10 Cubic Bézier B-spline.

$[0, \; n - m + 1]$. The knot set $t_0, \ldots, t_{n+m+1}$ is chosen to be the set $\underbrace{0, \ldots, 0}_{m+1}, 1, 2, \ldots, n - m,$ $\underbrace{n - m + 1, \ldots, n - m + 1}_{m+1}$. This use of repeated knots ensures that the endpoints of the spline coincide with the endpoints of the guiding polyline (Prob. 9.6).

Since the knot spacing is uniform, we can also use an explicit form for calculating the B-splines (Prob. 9.10).

Closed Curves

To construct a closed B-spline curve which approximates a given closed guiding polygon, we need only choose the knots $t_0, \ldots, t_{n+m+1}$ to be cyclic, i.e., $[0, 1, \ldots, n, 0, 1, \ldots]$. So

$$t_{m+1} = t_0 = 0 \qquad t_{m+2} = t_1 = 1 \qquad t_{m+1+i} = t_i$$

In practice, the quadratic and cubic B-splines $B_{i,2}$ and $B_{i,3}$ are the easiest to work with and provide enough flexibility for use in a wide range of curve design problems.

Properties of Bézier–B-Spline Approximation

There are five basic properties:

1. The Bézier–B-spline approximation has the same properties as the Bézier-Bernstein approximation; in fact, they are the same piecewise polynomial if $m = n$. This includes the properties of agreement with the guiding polygon and the tangent vectors at the endpoints and the convex hull property.

2. If the guiding polyline has $m + 1$ consecutive vertices (control points) which are collinear, the resulting span of the Bézier–B-spline will be linear. So this approximation allows for linear sections to be embedded within the curve.

3. The Bézier–B-spline approximation provides for the local control of curve shape. If a single control point is changed, portions of the curve that lie far away are not disturbed. In fact, only $m + 1$ of the spans are affected. This is due to the local nature of the B-spline basis functions.

4. Bézier–B-splines produce a closer fit to the guiding polygon than do the Bézier-Bernstein approximation.

5. The Bézier–B-spline approximation allows the use of control points P_i counted with *multiplicities* of 2 or more. That is, $P_i = P_{i+1} = \cdots = P_{i+k}$ for $k \geq 1$. This results in an approximation which is pulled closer toward this control point. In fact, if the point has multiplicity $m + 1$, the curve will pass through it.

9.9   CURVED-SURFACE DESIGN

The modeling and approximation of curved surfaces is difficult and involves many complex issues. We will look at two methods for representing a surface: *guiding nets* and *interpolating surface patches*.

Guiding Nets

This technique is a direct generalization of the Bézier-Bernstein and Bézier–B-spline approximation methods for curves. A *guiding net* is a polygonal net with vertices $P_{ij}(x_{ij}, y_{ij}, z_{ij})$, $i = 0, \ldots, m$, and $j = 0, \ldots, n$ (see Fig. 9-11).

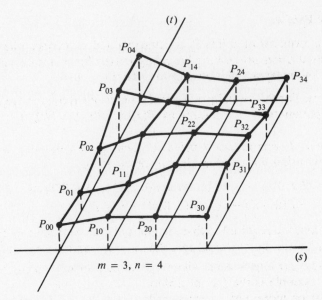

Fig. 9-11

1. *Bézier-Bernstein surface*. This is the surface with parametric equations:

$$Q(s, t): \begin{cases} x(s, t) = \displaystyle\sum_{i=0}^{m} \sum_{j=0}^{n} x_{ij} BE_{i,m}(s) BE_{j,n}(t) \\[2mm] y(s, t) = \displaystyle\sum_{i=0}^{m} \sum_{j=0}^{n} y_{ij} BE_{i,m}(s) BE_{j,n}(t) \\[2mm] z(s, t) = \displaystyle\sum_{i=0}^{m} \sum_{j=0}^{n} z_{ij}, \ BE_{i,m}(s) BE_{j,n}(t) \end{cases}$$

Here $0 \le s, t \le 1$ and BE are the Bernstein polynomials. This approximation has properties analogous to the one-dimensional case with respect to the corner points P_{00}, P_{m0}, P_{0n}, and P_{mn}. The convex hull property is also satisfied.

2. *Bézier–B-spline approximation*. In parametric form this is expressed as

$$Q(s, t): \begin{cases} x(s, t) = \displaystyle\sum_{i=0}^{m} \sum_{j=0}^{n} x_{ij} B_{i,\alpha}(s) B_{j,\beta}(t) \\[2mm] y(s, t) = \displaystyle\sum_{i=0}^{m} \sum_{j=0}^{n} y_{ij} B_{i,\alpha}(s) B_{j,\beta}(t) \\[2mm] z(s, t) = \displaystyle\sum_{i=0}^{m} \sum_{j=0}^{n} z_{ij} B_{i,\alpha}(s) B_{j,\beta}(t) \end{cases}$$

where $0 \le s \le m - \alpha + 1$ and $0 \le s \le n - \beta + 1$. The knot sets for s and t used to define the B-splines $B_{i,\alpha}(s)$ and $B_{j,\beta}(t)$ are determined as in the one-dimensional case.

Quadratic approximation occurs when $\alpha = \beta = 2$. Cubic approximation occurs when $\alpha = \beta = 3$. In general, quadratic or cubic B-splines are most often used. For both these methods, the construction of the guiding net (by locating the control points P_{ij}) is left to the user.

Interpolating Surface Patches

Instead of using a given set of points P_{ij} to construct a given surface, the process of interpolating surface patches is based upon prescribing boundary curves for a surface patch and "filling in" the interior of the patch by interpolating between the boundary curves.

1. *Coons surfaces*. For this technique, a patch is determined by specifying four bounding curves, denoted in parametric vector form as $P(s, 0)$, $P(s, 1)$, $P(0, t)$, and $P(1, t)$, $0 \le s$, $t \le 1$ Fig. 9-12).

   The (linear) *Coons surface patch* interpolating the boundary curves can be written in vector form by using linear interpolation (or blending):

   $$Q(s, t) = P(s, 0)(1 - t) + P(s, 1)t + P(0, t)(1 - s) + P(1, t)s - P(0, 0)(1 - s)(1 - t)$$
   $$- P(0, 1)(1 - s)t - P(1, 0)s(1 - t) - P(1, 1)st$$

   (The subtractions are required so that the interpolators between corner points are not counted twice.) This idea can be extended to define more general surface patches.

2. *Lofted surfaces*. *Lofting* is used where the surface to be constructed stretches in a given direction; an example is the hull of a ship.

   Given two or more space curves, called *cross-section curves*, *lofting* is the process of blending the cross sections together using longitudinal blending curves. The simplest example is *linear blending* between cross-section curves $P_1(s)$ and $P_2(s)$. The lofted surface is $Q(s, t) = (1 - t)P_1(s) + tP_2(s)$ (see Fig. 9-13).

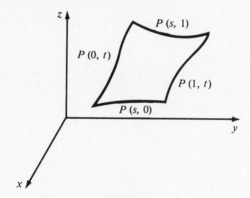

Fig. 9-12

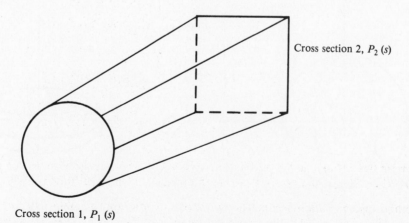

Fig. 9-13

9.10 TRANSFORMING CURVES AND SURFACES

All the curve and surface models that we have constructed have the general form

$$x = \Sigma x_i \Phi_i \qquad \text{and} \qquad y = \Sigma y_i \Phi_i$$

(Add a z component for three dimensions.)

If M is a 2×2 transformation matrix

$$M = \begin{pmatrix} a & b \\ c & d \end{pmatrix}$$

we can apply M to the functions x and y:

$$\begin{pmatrix} a & b \\ c & d \end{pmatrix}\begin{pmatrix} \Sigma x_i \Phi_i \\ \Sigma y_i \Phi_i \end{pmatrix} = \begin{pmatrix} a(\Sigma x_i \Phi_i) + b(\Sigma y_i \Phi_i) \\ c(\Sigma x_i \Phi_i) + d(\Sigma y_i \Phi_i) \end{pmatrix} = \begin{pmatrix} \Sigma(ax_i + by_i)\Phi_i \\ \Sigma(cx_i + dy_i)\Phi_i \end{pmatrix}$$

The transformed functions are then

$$\bar{x} = \Sigma(ax_i + by_i)\Phi_i \qquad \bar{y} = \Sigma(cx_i + dy_i)\Phi_i$$

In other words, to transform these curves and surfaces, it is necessary only to transform the coefficients (x_i, y_i). In most cases these coefficients represent data or control points. So the transformation of the approximation of a curve or surface is found by first transforming the control points and then forming the approximation based on the transformed points.

9.11 QUADRIC SURFACES

Spheres, cylinders, and cones are part of the family of surfaces called *quadric surfaces*. A quadric surface is defined by an equation which is of the second degree (in x, y, or z).

The canonical quadric surfaces are as follows:

Sphere

From Fig. 9-14:

$$x^2 + y^2 + z^2 = R^2$$

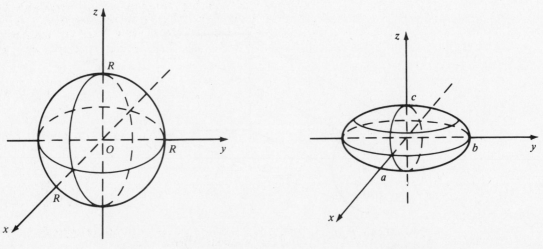

Fig. 9-14   Fig. 9-15

Ellipsoid

From Fig. 9-15:

$$\frac{x^2}{a^2} + \frac{y^2}{b^2} + \frac{z^2}{c^2} = 1$$

One-Sheeted Hyperboloid

From Fig. 9-16:

$$\frac{x^2}{a^2} + \frac{y^2}{b^2} - \frac{z^2}{c^2} = 1$$

Two-Sheeted Hyperboloid

From Fig. 9-17:

$$\frac{z^2}{c^2} - \frac{x^2}{a^2} - \frac{y^2}{b^2} = 1$$

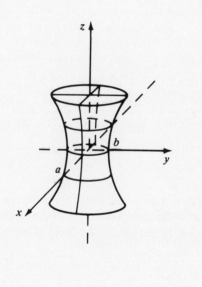

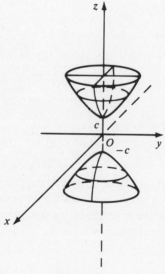

Fig. 9-16   Fig. 9-17

Elliptic Cylinder

From Fig. 9-18:

$$\frac{x^2}{a^2} + \frac{y^2}{b^2} = 1$$

When $a = b = R$, the cylinder is a circular cylinder of radius R.

Elliptic Paraboloid

From Fig. 9-19:

$$\frac{x^2}{a^2} + \frac{y^2}{b^2} = cz$$

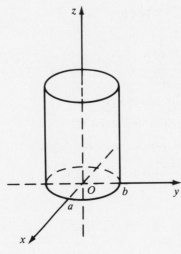

Fig. 9-18   Fig. 9-19

Hyperbolic Paraboloid

From Fig. 9-20:

$$\frac{x^2}{a^2} - \frac{y^2}{b^2} = cz$$

Elliptic Cone

From Fig. 9-21:

$$\frac{x^2}{a^2} + \frac{y^2}{b^2} = z^2$$

When $a = b = R$, we have a right circular cone. If we restrict z so that $z > 0$, we have the upper cone.

Note that for cones and cylinders, the mathematical definition produces a figure of infinite extent. To use it for computer graphics, we must enter bounds for the surface in the form of bounding clipping planes having the form $z = h$.

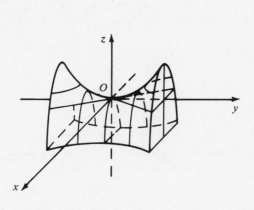

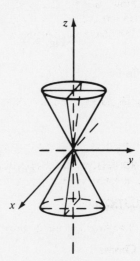

Fig. 9-20   Fig. 9-21

Solved Problems

9.1   Represent a cube by using an explicit vertex list.

SOLUTION

Using the notation in Fig. 7-10, one possible representation is

$$V = \{ABCDAFEDCHEFGHGB\}$$

Note the vertex repetitions in the list V and the repetition of edge FE as EF.

9.2   Represent a cube by using polygon listing.

SOLUTION

Referring to Fig. 7-10, we form the vertex list

$$V = \{ABCDEFGH\}$$

The faces of the cube are polygons (which, in this case, are squares) $P_1, \ldots, P_6$, where

$$P_1 = \{ABCD\} \qquad P_4 = \{ABGF\}$$
$$P_2 = \{CDEH\} \qquad P_5 = \{BCHG\}$$
$$P_3 = \{ADEF\} \qquad P_6 = \{EFGH\}$$

Note the edge repetitions encountered in drawing the polygons. For example, polygons P_2 and P_3 share the edge DE.

9.3   Show that the nth-degree B-spline basis functions $B_{i,n}(x)$ satisfy

$$B_{i,n}(x) = 0 \quad \text{if} \quad x < t_i \quad \text{or} \quad x > t_{i+n+1}$$

SOLUTION

Since the B-spline basis functions $B_{i,n}(x)$ are defined recursively in terms of the lower-order B-splines $B_{i,n-1}(x)$ and $B_{i+1,n-1}(x)$ of degree $n-1$, we shall indicate only the first step of a general induction argument. Therefore, we illustrate what happens for the first-degree B-spline $B_{i,1}(x)$.

Now suppose that $x < t_i$. Then also $x < t_{i+1}$, so at x the zero-degree B-splines have the values $B_{i,0}(x) = 0$ and $B_{i+1,0}(x) = 0$. From these values we find, in turn, that $B_{i,1}(x) = 0$.

Now suppose that the knot set is nonrepeating. Let $x = t_i$. Then $B_{i,0}(t_i) = 1$, but $B_{i+1,0}(t_i) = 0$. So

$$B_{i,0}(t_i) = \frac{t_i - t_i}{t_{i+1} - t_i}\,(1) + \frac{t_{i+2} - t_i}{t_{i+2} - t_{i+1}}\,(0) = 0$$

Thus $B_{i,1}(x) = 0$ if $x \le t_i$. Similar arguments show that $B_{i,1}(x) = 0$ if $x \ge t_{i+1}$.

9.4   Let $P_0(0,0)$, $P_1(1,2)$, $P_2(2,1)$, $P_3(3,-1)$, $P_4(4,10)$, and $P_5(5,5)$ be given data points. If interpolation based on cubic B-splines is used to find a curve interpolating these data points, find a knot set $t_0, \ldots, t_9$ that can be used to define the cubic B-splines.

SOLUTION

The knot set can be chosen according to one of two schemes. With $m = 3$ and $n = 5$:

1. Choose

$$t_0 = t_1 = t_2 = t_3 = -1 \ (<x_0) \qquad \text{and} \qquad t_6 = t_7 = t_8 = t_9 = 6 \ (>x_n)$$

The remaining knots are chosen according to

$$t_{i+m+1} = \frac{x_{i+1} + \cdots + x_{i+m}}{m}, \qquad i = 0, \ldots, n-m-1$$

So

$$t_4 = \frac{1+2+3}{3} = 2 \qquad t_5 = \frac{2+3+4}{3} = 3$$

2. An alternative scheme for cubic splines is

$$t_0 = t_1 = t_2 = t_3 = -1 \qquad\qquad t_6 = t_7 = t_8 = t_9 = 6$$

and the remaining knots are chosen according to

$$t_{i+4} = x_{i+2}, \qquad i = 0, \ldots, n-4$$

So

$$t_4 = 2 \qquad t_5 = 3$$

The agreement between knot sets chosen according to these two schemes is a result of the uniform spacing of the data points along the x axis.

9.5   Write the equations that can be used to find an interpolating cubic spline curve to fit the data in Prob. 9.4 using cubic B-spline basis functions.

SOLUTION

With $m = 3$ and $n = 5$, the interpolating cubic spline can be written in terms of cubic B-splines as

$$S_3(x) = \sum_{i=0}^{7} a_i B_{i,3}(x)$$

The interpolation equations for the data points (x_j, y_j), $j = 0, \ldots, 5$ are

$$y_j = S_3(x_j), \qquad j = 0, \ldots, 5$$

With the knot set chosen in Prob. 9.4, the intervals $[t_j, t_{j+4}]$ defined by the knots t_j, $j = 0, \ldots, 9$ are

j	t_j	t_{j+4}
0	−1	2
1	−1	3
2	−1	6
3	−1	6
4	2	6
5	3	6

Because $B_{i,3}(x)$ is nonzero only for $t_i < x < t_{i+4}$, the interpolation equations become

$$y_j = S_3(x_j)$$
$$0 = a_0 B_{0,3}(0) + a_1 B_{1,3}(0) + a_2 B_{2,3}(0) + a_3 B_{3,3}(0)$$
$$2 = a_0 B_{0,3}(1) + a_1 B_{1,3}(1) + a_2 B_{2,3}(1) + a_3 B_{3,3}(1)$$
$$1 = a_1 B_{1,3}(2) + a_2 B_{2,3}(2) + a_3 B_{3,3}(2)$$
$$-1 = a_2 B_{2,3}(3) + a_3 B_{3,3}(3) + a_4 B_{4,3}(3)$$
$$10 = a_2 B_{2,3}(4) + a_3 B_{3,3}(4) + a_4 B_{4,3}(4) + a_5 B_{5,3}(4)$$
$$5 = a_2 B_{2,3}(5) + a_3 B_{3,3}(5) + a_4 B_{4,3}(5) + a_5 B_{5,3}(5)$$

The remaining two equations can be chosen to satisfy prescribed boundary conditions at $x_0 = 0$ and $x_5 = 5$.

9.6 Show that the knot set used in constructing the Bézier–B-spline approximation to a guiding polyline guarantees that the endpoints of the spline coincide with the endpoints of the guiding polyline.

SOLUTION

For an m-degree Bézier–B-spline approximation, the knot set used is

$$\underbrace{0,\ldots,0}_{m+1}, 1, 2, \ldots, n-m, n-m-1, \underbrace{n-m-1,\ldots,n-m-1}_{m+1}$$

Let $P_0(x_0, y_0, z_0)$ be the first control point of the guiding polyline and $P_n(x_n, y_n, z_n)$ the last. Now $x(t) = \sum_{i=0}^n x_i B_{i,m}(t)$ with similar expressions for $y(t)$ and $z(t)$. We wish to show that

$$x(0) = x_0, \; y(0) = y_0, \; z(0) = z_0 \quad \text{and} \quad x(n-1) = x_n, y(n-1) = y_n, z(n-1) = z_n$$

Let us restrict ourselves to $m = 2$ (quadratic) B-splines. Then the knot set is

$$0, 0, 0, 1, 2, 3, \ldots, n-2, n-1, n-1, n-1$$
$$t_0, t_1, t_2, t_3, t_4, t_5, \ldots, t_{n+1}, t_{n+2}, t_{n+3}, t_{n+4}$$

Since $B_{i,2}(x)$ is nonzero only over the interval $t_i \le x \le t_{i+3}$, it follows that $B_{i,2}(0)$ is nonzero only if $i = 0, 1,$ and 2. So then

$$x(0) = \sum_{i=0}^n x_i B_{i,2}(0) = x_0 B_{0,2}(0) + x_1 B_{1,2}(0) + x_2 B_{2,2}(0)$$

To calculate $B_{0,2}$, using the definition and the convention that $\frac{0}{0} = 0$, we obtain

$$B_{0,2}(0) = B_{1,1}(0) \quad \text{and} \quad B_{1,1}(0) = B_{2,0}(0) \quad \text{and} \quad B_{2,0}(0) = 1$$

So $B_{0,2}(0) = 1$ (compare with Prob. 9.3).

To calculate $B_{1,2}(0)$, using the definition

$$B_{1,2}(0) = \frac{2}{2} B_{2,1}(0) \quad \text{and} \quad B_{2,1}(0) = \frac{2}{2-1} B_{3,0}(0) \quad \text{and} \quad B_{3,0}(0) = 0 \quad \text{since} \quad 0 \le t_3 = 1$$

So we have $B_{1,2}(0) = 0$. In a similar manner, we find $B_{2,2}(0) = 0$. Thus, $x(0) = x_0$ and the same for the y and z coordinates.

Similar calculations show that $x(n-1) = x_n$, $y(n-1) = y_n$, and $z(n-1) = z_n$.

9.7 Find the linear Coons surface patch that interpolates the curves of Fig. 9-22.

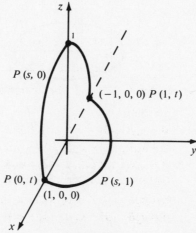

Fig. 9-22

SOLUTION

The four bounding curves can be described parametrically as follows (see Fig. 9-22):

1. $P(s, 0) = (\cos \pi s, 0, \sin \pi s)\ 0 \le s \le 1$
2. $P(1, t) = (-1, 0, 0)\ 0 \le t \le 1$
3. $P(s, 1) = (\cos \pi s, \sin \pi s, 0)\ 0 \le s \le 1$
4. $P(0, t) = (1, 0, 0)\ 0 \le t \le 1$

Note that curves 2 and 4 are constant curves, that is, points.

The linear Coons surface interpolating these curves can be written as

$$Q(s, t) = P(s, 0)(1 - t) + P(s, 1)t + P(0, t)(1 - s) + P(1, t)s - P(0, 0)(1 - s)(1 - t)$$
$$- P(0, 1)(1 - s)t - P(1, 0)s(1 - t) - P(1, 1)st$$

In terms of coordinates:

$$x(s, t) = (\cos \pi s)(1 - t) + (\cos \pi s)t + (1)(1 - s) + (-1)s$$
$$- (1)(1 - s)(1 - t) - (1)(1 - s)t - (-1)s(1 - t) - (-1)st$$

or

$$x(s, t) = \cos \pi s$$

Now

$$y(s, t) = (0)(1 - t) + (\sin \pi s)t + (0)(1 - s) + (0)s - (0)(1 - s)(1 - t) - (0)(1 - s)t - (0)s(1 - t) - (0)st$$

or

$$y(s, t) = t \sin \pi s$$

Finally

$$z(s, t) = (\sin \pi s)(1 - t) + (0)t + (0)(1 - s) + (0)s - (0)(1 - s)(1 - t) - (0)(1 - s)t - (0)s(1 - t) - (0)st$$

or

$$z(s, t) = (1 - t) \sin \pi s$$

The linear Coons surface is

$$Q(s, t) = [\cos \pi s, t \sin \pi s, (1 - t) \sin \pi s] \qquad 0 \le s, t \le 1$$

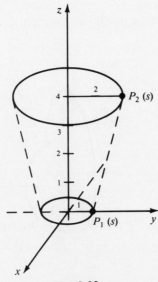

Fig. 9-23

9.8   Find the lofting surface defined by linear blending between the cross-section curves in Fig. 9-23.

SOLUTION

The curves in Fig. 9-23 are circles whose equations can be defined parametrically as

$$P_1(s) = (\cos 2\pi s, \sin 2\pi s, 0)\ 0 \le s \le 1$$

and

$$P_2(s) = (2 \cos 2\pi s, 2 \sin 2\pi s, 4)\ 0 \le s \le 1$$

The lofting surface is then

$$Q(s, t) = (1 - t)P_1(s) + tP_2(s)$$

In terms of coordinates, we find that

$$x(s, t) = (1 - t)(\cos 2\pi s) + t(2 \cos 2\pi s) = (1 + t) \cos 2\pi s$$
$$y(s, t) = (1 - t)(\sin 2\pi s) + t(2 \sin 2\pi s) = (1 + t) \sin 2\pi s$$
$$z(s, t) = (1 - t)(0) + t(4) = 4t$$

Thus

$$Q(s, t) = (1 + t) \cos 2\pi s, (1 + t) \sin 2\pi s, 4t$$

Supplementary Problems

9.9   Represent a cube using an explicit edge listing.

9.10 Find an explicit representation for linear (degree 1) B-splines in the case of uniformly spaced knots, i.e., $t_{i+1} - t_i = L$.

9.11 For the knot set $t_1 = 1$, $t_2 = 2, \ldots, t_i = 1$, calculate $B_{i,3}$ (5.5).

Chapter 10

Hidden Surfaces

10.1 INTRODUCTION

Whenever a picture contains opaque objects and surfaces, those that are closer to the eye and in the line of sight of other objects will block those objects from view. The blocked or hidden surfaces must be removed in order to render a realistic screen image. The identification and removal of these surfaces is called the *hidden-surface problem*. The solution involves the determination of depth and visibility for all the surfaces in the picture.

There are many different hidden-surface algorithms, no one of which is best. Different algorithms stem from different, sometimes specialized requirements. The algorithms described here represent the main approaches used. All can be extended and combined to produce new algorithms tailored for different applications.

10.2 DEPTH COMPARISONS

We assume that all coordinates (x, y, z) are described in the normalized viewing coordinate system (Chap. 8).

Any hidden-surface algorithm must determine which edges and surfaces are visible either from the center of projection for perspective projections or along the direction of projection for parallel projections.

The question of visibility reduces to this: given two points $P_1(x_1, y_1, z_1)$ and $P_2(x_2, y_2, z_2)$, does either point obscure the other? This is answered in two steps:

1. Are P_1 and P_2 on the same projection line?
2. If not, neither point obscures the other. If so, a depth comparison tells us which point is in front of the other.

For an orthographic parallel projection onto the xy plane, P_1 and P_2 are on the same projector if $x_1 = x_2$ and $y_1 = y_2$. In this case, depth comparison reduces to comparing z_1 and z_2. If $z_1 < z_2$, then P_1 obscures P_2 [see Fig. 10-1(a)].

For a perspective projection [see Fig. 10-1(b)], the calculations are more complex (Prob. 10.1). However, this complication can be avoided by transforming all three-dimensional objects so that parallel projection of the transformed object is equivalent to a perspective projection of the original object (see Fig. 10-2). This is done with the use of the *perspective to parallel transform* T_p (Prob. 10.2).

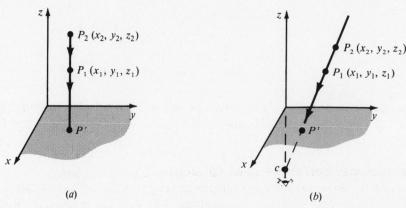

(a)　　　　　　　　(b)

Fig. 10-1

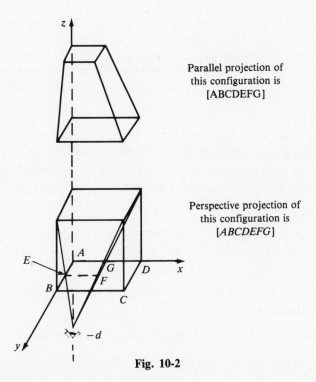

Parallel projection of
this configuration is
[ABCDEFG]

Perspective projection of
this configuration is
[ABCDEFG]

Fig. 10-2

If the original object lies in the normalized perspective view volume (Chap. 8), the *normalized perspective to parallel transform*

$$NT_p = \begin{pmatrix} \frac{1}{2} & 0 & \frac{1}{2} & 0 \\ 0 & \frac{1}{2} & \frac{1}{2} & 0 \\ 0 & 0 & \frac{1}{1-z_f} & \frac{-z_f}{1-z_f} \\ 0 & 0 & 1 & 0 \end{pmatrix}$$

(where z_f is the location of the front clipping plane of the normalized perspective view volume) transforms the normalized perspective view volume into the unit cube bounded by $0 \le x \le 1$, $0 \le y \le 1$, $0 \le z \le 1$ (Prob. 10.3). We call this cube the *normalized display space*. A critical fact is that the normalized perspective to parallel transform preserves lines, planes, and depth relationships.

If our display device has display coordinates $H \times V$, application of the scaling matrix

$$S_{H,V,1} = \begin{pmatrix} H & 0 & 0 & 0 \\ 0 & V & 0 & 0 \\ 0 & 0 & 1 & 0 \\ 0 & 0 & 0 & 1 \end{pmatrix}$$

transforms the normalized display space $0 \le x \le 1$, $0 \le y \le 1$, $0 \le z \le 1$ onto the region $0 \le x \le H$, $0 \le y \le V$, $0 \le z \le 1$. We call this region the *display space*. The *display transform* DT_p

$$DT_p = S_{H,V,1} \cdot NT_p$$

transforms the normalized perspective view volume onto the display space.

Clipping must be done against the normalized perspective view volume prior to applying the transform NT_p. An alternative to this is to combine NT_p with the normalizing transformation N_{per}

(Chap. 8), forming the single transformation $NT'_p = NT_p \cdot N_{per}$. Then clipping is done in homogeneous coordinate space. This method for performing clipping is not covered in this book.

We now describe several algorithms for removing hidden surfaces from pictures containing objects defined with planar (i.e., flat), polygonal faces. We assume that the display transform DT_p has been applied (if a perspective projection is being used), so that we always deal with parallel projections in display space.

10.3 Z-BUFFER ALGORITHM (DEPTH BUFFER ALGORITHM)

We say that a point in display space is "seen" from pixel (x, y) if the projection of the point is scan-converted to this pixel (Chap. 3). The Z-buffer algorithm essentially keeps track of the smallest z coordinate (also called the *depth value*) of those points which are seen from pixel (x, y). These Z values are stored in what is called the Z buffer.

Let $Z_{buf}(x, y)$ denote the current depth value that is stored in the Z buffer at pixel (x, y). We work with the (already) projected polygons P of the scene to be rendered.

The Z-buffer algorithm consists of the following steps:

1. Initialize the screen to a background color. Initialize the Z buffer to the depth of the yon clipping plane. That is, set

    $$Z_{buf}(x, y) = Z_{yon}, \quad \text{for every pixel } (x, y)$$

2. Scan-convert each (projected) polygon P in the scene (Chap. 3) and during this scan-conversion process, for each pixel (x, y) that lies inside the polygon:

    (a) Calculate $Z(x, y)$, the depth of the polygon at pixel (x, y).

    (b) If $Z(x, y) < Z_{buf}(x, y)$, set $Z_{buf}(x, y) = Z(x, y)$ and set the pixel value at (x, y) to the color of the polygon P at (x, y) see Fig. 10-3. There, points P_1 and P_2 are both scan-converted to pixel (x, y), however, since $z_1 < z_2$, P_1 will obscure P_2 and the P_1 z value, z_1, will be stored in the Z buffer.

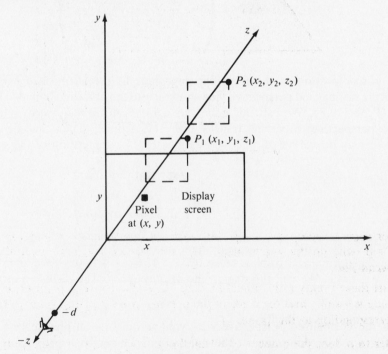

Fig. 10-3

Although the Z-buffer algorithm requires Z-buffer memory storage proportional to the number of pixels on the screen, it does not require additional memory for storing all the objects comprising the picture. In fact, since the algorithm processes objects one at a time, the total number of polygons in a picture can be arbitrarily large.

10.4 SCAN-LINE ALGORITHMS

A scan-line algorithm consists essentially of two nested loops, an x-scan loop nested within a y-scan loop.

y Scan

For each y value, say, $y = \alpha$, intersect the polygons to be rendered with the scan plane $y = \alpha$. This scan plane is parallel to the xz plane, and the resulting intersections are line segments in this plane (see Fig. 10-4).

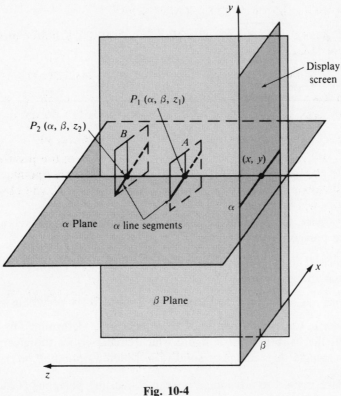

Fig. 10-4

x Scan

1. For each x value, say, $x = \beta$, intersect the line segments found above with the x-scan line $x = \beta$ lying on the y-scan plane. This intersection results in a set of points that lies on the x-scan line.

2. Sort these points with respect to their z coordinates. The point (x, y, z) with the smallest z value is visible, and the color of the polygon containing this point is the color set at the pixel corresponding to this point.

In order to reduce the amount of calculation in each scan-line loop, we try to take advantage of relationships and dependencies, called *coherences*, between different elements that comprise a scene.

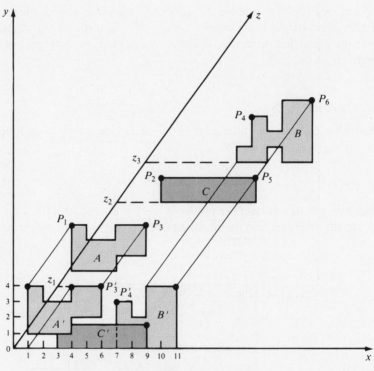

Fig. 10-5

Types of Coherence

1. *Scan-line coherence.* If a pixel on a scan line lies within a polygon, pixels near it will most likely lie within the polygon.

2. *Edge coherence.* If an edge of a polygon intersects a given scan line, it will most likely intersect scan lines near the given one.

3. *Area coherence.* A small area of an image will most likely lie within a single polygon.

4. *Spatial coherence.* Certain properties of an object can be determined by examining the *extent* of the object, that is, a geometric figure which circumscribes the given object. Usually the extent is a rectangle or rectangular solid (also called a *bounding box*).

Scan-line coherence is used to advantage in scan-converting polygons (Chap. 3).

Spatial coherence is often used as a preprocessing step. For example, when determining whether polygons intersect, we can eliminate those polygons that don't intersect by finding the rectangular extent of each polygon and checking whether the extents intersect—a much simpler problem (see Fig. 10-5). [*Note*: In Fig. 10-5 objects A and B do not intersect; however, objects A and C and B and C do intersect. In preprocessing, corner points would be compared to determine whether there is an intersection. For example, the edge of object A is at coordinate $P_3 = (6, 4)$ and the edge of object B is at coordinate $P_4 = (7, 3)$.] The intersection points are determined in Probs. 10.12 and 10.13. Of course, even if the extents intersect, this does not guarantee that the polygons intersect. See Fig. 10-6 and note that the extents of A' and B' overlap even though the polygons do not.

Coherences also simplify calculations by making them incremental, as opposed to absolute. This is illustrated in Prob. 10.13.

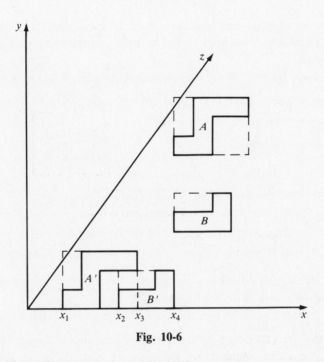

Fig. 10-6

A Scan-Line Algorithm

In the following algorithm, scan line and edge coherence are used to enhance the processing done in the y-scan loop as follows. Since the y-scan loop constructs a list of potentially visible line segments, instead of reconstructing this list each time the y-scan line changes (absolute calculation), we keep the list and update it according to how it has changed (incremental calculation). This processing is facilitated by the use of what is called the *active edge list* (AEL), and its efficient construction and maintenance is at the heart of the algorithm (see Chap. 3, sec. 3.8, under "Polygon Scan Conversion").

The following data structures are created:

1. *The edge list*—contains all nonhorizontal edges (horizontal edges are automatically displayed) for all the polygons in the picture. The edges are sorted by the edge's smaller y coordinate (y_{min}) into cells, each cell corresponding to a pixel row of a y-scan line. Within those cells, the edges are further sorted based on the x coordinate of the corresponding y_{min} value. Any ties are broken by using the smaller value of $1/m$, the inverse of the edge slope. Each edge entry in the edge list contains

    (*a*)   The x coordinate x_A of the end of the edge with the smaller y coordinate (y_{min}).

    (*b*)   The y coordinate of the edge's other end (y_{max}).

    (*c*)   The increment $\Delta x = 1/m$.

    (*d*)   A pointer indicating the polygon(s) to which the edge belongs.

2. *The polygon list*—for each polygon, contains

    (*a*)   The equation of the plane within which the polygon lies—used for depth determination, i.e., to find the z value at pixel (x, y) (if the polygon is a line, we use the equation of the line).

    (*b*)   An IN/OUT flag, initialized to OUT (this flag is set depending on whether a given scan line is in or out of the polygon).

    (*c*)   Color information for the polygon.

3.   *The active edge list* (AEL)—contains at each y-scan value, the set of edges intersected by the y-scan plane. These edges are kept sorted in order of increasing x_A values, where x_A is the x coordinate of y_{min}.

4.   *The active polygon list* (APL)—at each x-scan value, this table contains

   (*a*)   All polygons whose IN/OUT flag is currently set to IN.

   (*b*)   The number of polygons in this list.

The algorithm proceeds as follows:

   I.   *Initialization.*

   (*a*)   Initialize the AEL to empty.

   (*b*)   Initialize each screen pixel to a background color.

   (*c*)   Set y to the first nonempty cell value in the edge list.

   Repeat steps II and III (below) until no further processing can be performed on the AEL.

   II.   *y-scan loop.* Update the AEL by merging into it the information contained in the cell y of the edge list. Sort the AEL in order of increasing x_A.

   III.   *x-scan loop.* Process, from left to right, each edge of the AEL as follows:

   (*a*)   Invert the IN/OUT flag of the polygon(s) in the polygon list which contains the edge. Count the number of polygons in the APL. If this number is 1, the polygon containing the edge is visible unless the polygon is a line, in which case a depth comparison at the pixel is performed to determine its color. In the former case all pixel values from this edge and up to and including the next edge are set to the color of the polygon. If this number is greater than 1, determine the visible polygon by the smallest z value of each polygon at the pixel under consideration. These z values are found from the equation of the plane containing the polygon. The pixels from this edge and up to and including the next edge are set to the color of this polygon, unless the polygon is a line, in which case these pixels are unchanged. If this number is 0, pixels from this edge and up to and including the next one are left unchanged.

   (*b*)   Set the IN/OUT flag of any lines in the polygon list that were just processed to OUT.

   (*c*)   When the last edge in the AEL is processed, we then process the AEL as follows:

   1.   Remove those edges for which the scan-converted value of y_{max} equals the present scan-line value y. If no edges remain, the algorithm has finished.

   2.   For each remaining edge, in order, replace x_A by $x_A + 1/m$. This is the edge intersection with the next scan line $y + 1$ (see Prob. 10.13).

   3.   Sort the AEL (on x_A).

   4.   Increment y to $y + 1$, the next scan line, and repeat step II.

Scan-line algorithms have two advantages: they can be implemented in hardware and can be generalized to handle nonlinear (i.e., nonpolygonal) patches.

10.5   THE PAINTER'S ALGORITHM

Also called the *depth sort* or *priority algorithm*, the painter's algorithm processes polygons as if they were being painted onto the screen in the order of their distance from the viewer. More distant polygons are painted first. Nearer polygons are painted on or over more distant polygons, partially or totally obscuring them from view. The key to implementing this concept is to find a priority ordering of the polygons in order to determine which polygons are to be painted (i.e., scan-converted) first.

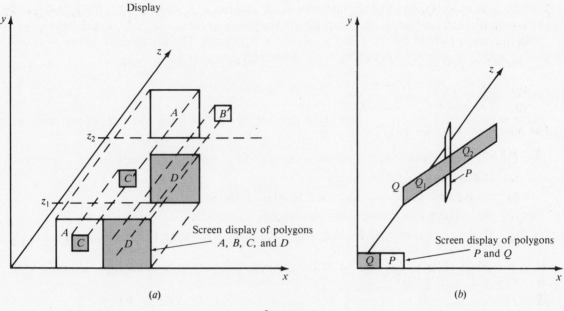

Fig. 10-7

Any attempt at a priority ordering based on depth sorting alone results in ambiguities that must be resolved in order to correctly assign priorities. For example, when two polygons overlap, how do we decide which one obscures the other? (See Fig. 10-7.)

Assigning Priorities

We assign priorities to polygons based on depth by determining which polygons obscure a given polygon P. The first step is a preprocessing step to determine whether a polygon Q does *not* obscure P.

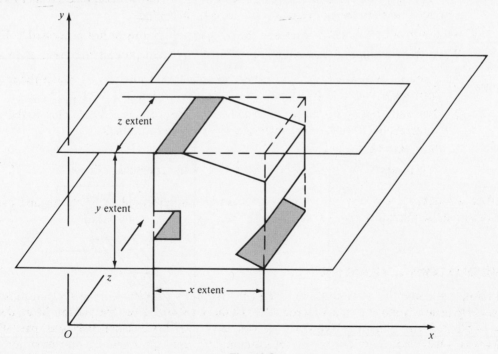

Fig. 10-8

The z extent of a polygon is the region between the planes $z = z_{min}$ and $z = z_{max}$ (Fig. 10-8). Here, z_{min} is the smallest of the z coordinates of all the polygon's vertices, and z_{max} is the largest.

Similar definitions hold for the x and y extents of a polygon. The intersection of the x, y, and z extents is called the *extent*, or bounding box, of the polygon.

Testing Whether P Obscures Q

Polygon P does not obscure polygon Q if any one of the following tests, applied in sequential order, is true:

Test 0:   the z extents of P and Q do not overlap and $z_{Q_{max}}$ of Q is smaller than $z_{P_{min}}$ of P. Refer to Fig. 10-9.

Test 1:   the y extents of P and Q do not overlap. Refer to Fig. 10-10.

Test 2:   the x extents of P and Q do not overlap.

Test 3:   all the vertices of P lie on that side of the plane containing Q which is farthest from the viewpoint. Refer to Fig. 10-11.

Test 4:   all the vertices of Q lie on that side of the plane containing P which is closest to the viewpoint. Refer to Fig. 10-12.

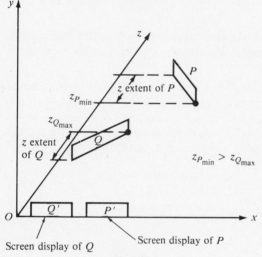

Fig. 10-9

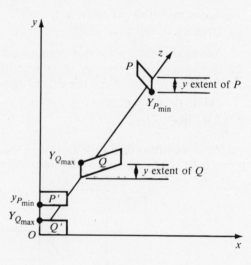

Fig. 10-10

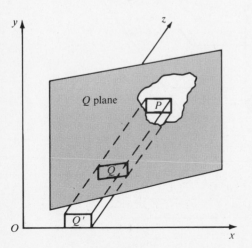

Fig. 10-11

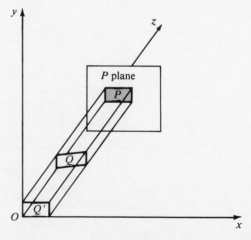

Fig. 10-12

Test 5:   the projections of the polygons P and Q onto the xy screen do not overlap. This is checked by comparing each edge of one polygon against each edge of the other polygon to search for intersections.

The Algorithm

1.   Sort all polygons into a polygon list according to z_{max} (the largest z coordinate of each polygon's vertices). Starting from the end of the list, assign priorities for each polygon P, in order, as described in steps 2 and 3 (below).

2.   Find all polygons Q (preceding P) in the polygon list whose z extents overlap that of P (test 0).

3.   For each Q, perform tests 1 through 5 until true.

   (a)   If every Q passes, scan-convert polygon P.

   (b)   If false for some Q, swap P and Q on the list. Tag Q as swapped. If Q has already been tagged, use the plane containing polygon P to divide polygon Q into two polygons, Q_1 and Q_2 [see Fig. 10-7(b)]. The polygon-clipping techniques described in Chap. 5 can be used to perform the division. Remove Q from the list and place Q_1 and Q_2 on the list, in sorted order.

Sometimes the polygons are subdivided into triangles before processing, thus reducing the computational effort for polygon subdivision in step 3.

10.6   SUBDIVISION ALGORITHMS

Subdivision algorithms are recursive procedures based on a two-step strategy that first decides which projected polygons overlap a given area A on the screen and are therefore potentially visible in that area. Second, in each area these polygons are further tested to determine which ones will be visible within this area and should therefore be displayed. If a visibility decision cannot be made, this

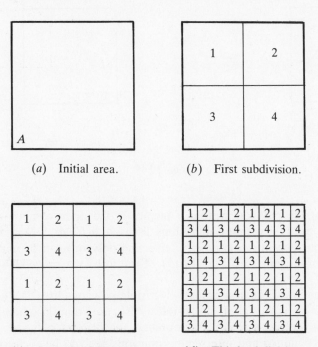

(a)   Initial area.   (b)   First subdivision.

(c)   Second subdivision.   (d)   Third subdivision.

Fig. 10-13

screen area, usually a rectangular window, is further subdivided either until a visibility decision can be made, or until the screen area is a single pixel.

Starting with the full screen as the initial area, the algorithm divides an area at each stage into four smaller areas, thereby generating a quad tree (see Fig. 10-13).

The processing exploits area coherence by classifying polygons P with respect to a given screen area A into the following categories: (1) *surrounding polygon*—polygon that completely contains the area [Fig. 10-14(a)], (2) *intersecting polygon*—polygon that intersects the area [Fig. 10-14(b)], (3) *contained polygon*—polygon that is completely contained within the area [Fig. 10-14(c)], and (4) *disjoint polygon*—polygon that is disjoint from the area [Fig. 10-14(d)].

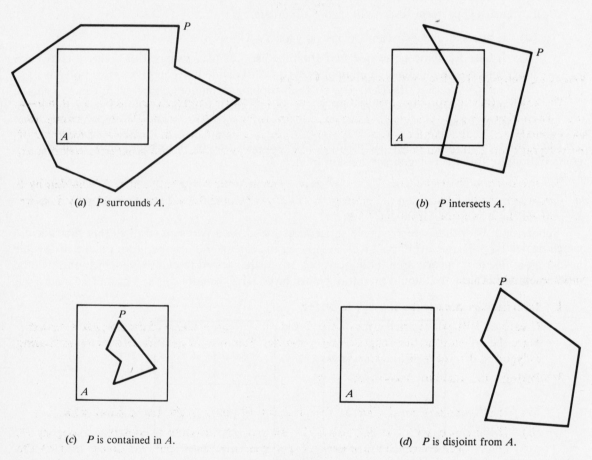

(a) P surrounds A.

(b) P intersects A.

(c) P is contained in A.

(d) P is disjoint from A.

Fig. 10-14

The classification of the polygons within a picture is the main computational expense of the algorithm and is analogous to the clipping algorithms discussed in Chap. 5. With the use of one of these clipping algorithms, a polygon in category 2 (intersecting polygon) can be clipped into a contained polygon and a disjoint polygon (see Fig. 10-15). Therefore, we proceed as if category 2 were eliminated.

For a given screen area, we keep a potentially visible polygons list (PVPL), those in categories 1, 2, and 3. (Disjoint polygons are clearly not visible.) Also, note that on subdivision of a screen area, surrounding and disjoint polygons remain surrounding and disjoint polygons of the newly formed areas. Therefore, only contained and intersecting polygons need to be reclassified.

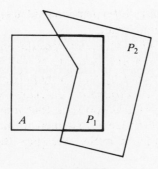

Fig. 10-15

Removing Polygons Hidden by a Surrounding Polygon

The key to efficient visibility computation lies in the fact that a polygon is not visible if it is in back of a surrounding polygon. Therefore, it can be removed from the PVPL. To facilitate processing, this list is sorted by $z_{\min}$, the depth of the vertex closest to the viewpoint (i.e., the smallest z coordinate of the polygon's vertices). In addition, for each surrounding polygon S, we record its largest z coordinate, $z_{S_{\max}}$.

If, for a polygon P on the list, $z_{P_{\min}} > z_{S_{\max}}$ (for a surrounding polygon S), then P is hidden by S and thus is not visible. In addition, all other polygons after P on the list will also be hidden by S, so we can remove these polygons from the PVPL.

Subdivision Algorithm

1. Initialize the area to be the whole screen.

2. Create a PVPL with respect to an area, sorted on $z_{\min}$ (the smallest of the polygon's vertices). Place the polygons in their appropriate categories. Remove polygons hidden by a surrounding polygon and remove disjoint polygons.

3. Perform the visibility decision tests:

   (a) If all polygons are disjoint to the area, set all pixels to the background color.

   (b) If there is exactly one polygon in the list and it is classified as contained (category 3), color (scan-convert) the contained polygon, and color the remaining area to the background color.

   (c) If there is exactly one polygon on the list and it is a surrounding one, color the area the color of the surrounding polygon.

   (d) If a surrounding polygon is closer to the viewpoint than all other polygons, so that all the polygons are hidden by it, color the area the color of this polygon.

   (e) If the area is the pixel (x, y), and neither 1, 2, 3, nor 4 applies, compute the z coordinate $z(x, y)$ at pixel (x, y) of all polygons on the PVPL. The pixel is then set to the color of the polygon with the smallest z coordinate.

4. If none of the above cases has occurred, subdivide the screen area into fourths. For each area, go to step 2.

10.7   HIDDEN-LINE ELIMINATION

Although there are special-purpose hidden-line algorithms, each of the above algorithms can be modified to eliminate hidden lines or edges. This is especially useful for wireframe polygonal models where the polygons are unfilled. The idea is to use a color rule which fills all the polygons with the background color—say, black—and the edges and lines a different color—say, white. The use of a hidden-surface algorithm now becomes a hidden-line algorithm.

10.8   RAY TRACING

The design of hidden-surface algorithms to deal with nonpolygonal, nonplanar surface patches is an area of active research. One algorithm in particular, called the *ray-tracing algorithm*, provides the flexibility to handle both flat and curved surfaces and can be easily modified to provide realistic shading if needed. It is based on the principles of light and optics. We shall consider only its use in solving the hidden-surface problem and thus disregard its use for shading surfaces. We shall assume opaque surfaces of given colors and deal directly with the perspective projection transformation without applying the perspective to parallel transform T_p from Prob. 10.2.

The fundamental idea is to trace light rays and determine which ones arrive back at the eye or viewpoint. Since this involves an infinite number of light rays, we work backward. That is, we trace a ray from the viewpoint through a pixel until it reaches a surface. Since this represents the first surface seen at the given pixel, we set the pixel to the color of the surface at the point where the light ray strikes it (see Fig. 10-16). If the resolution of the screen is $N \times M$, there are NM pixels, and so NM light rays are traced.

Each ray is tested for intersections with each object in the picture, including the yon clipping plane. Since each ray can intersect several objects, we find the intersection point I which is closest to the viewpoint (Prob. 10.26). We set the pixel belonging to the given ray to the color of the surface on which this point I lies. This represents the first surface intersected by the ray. We repeat this process for each pixel.

The computational expense can be reduced by the use of the extent or bounding box of an object or surface. If a ray does not intersect a bounding box, there is no need to check for intersections with the enclosed surface.

The main reason for using the ray-tracing method is to create extremely realistic renderings of pictures by incorporating the laws of optics for reflecting and transmitting light rays.

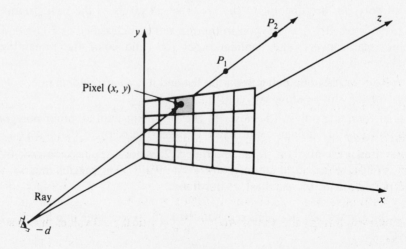

Fig. 10-16

10.9   THE RENDERING OF MATHEMATICAL SURFACES

In plotting a mathematical surface described by an equation $z = F(x, y)$, where $x_{min} \le x \le x_{max}$ and $y_{min} \le y \le y_{max}$, we could use any of the hidden-surface algorithms so far described. However, these general algorithms are inefficient when compared to specialized algorithms that take advantage of the structure of this type of surface.

The mathematical surface is rendered as a wireframe model by drawing both the *x-constant curves* $z = F(\text{const}, y)$ and the *y-constant curves* $z = F(x, \text{const})$ (see Fig. 10-17). Each such curve is rendered as a polyline, where the illusion of smoothness is achieved by using a fine resolution (i.e., short line segments) in drawing the polyline (Chap. 3).

Choose an $M \times N$ plotting resolution

$$x_{min} \le x_1 < x_2 < \cdots < x_M \le x_{max} \qquad \text{and} \qquad y_{min} \le y_1 < y_2 < \cdots < y_N \le y_{max}$$

The corresponding z values are $z_{ij} = F(x_i, y_j)$. An x-constant polyline, say, $x = x_j$, has vertices

$$P_1(x_j, y_1), \ldots, P_N(x_j, y_N)$$

Similarly, the $y = y_k$ polyline has vertices

$$Q_1(x_1, y_k), \ldots, Q_M(x_M, y_k)$$

Choosing a view plane and a center of projection or viewpoint $C(a, b, c)$, we create a perspective view of the surface onto this view plane by using the transformations developed in Chap. 7. So a point $[x, y, F(x, y)]$ on the surface projects to a point (p, q) in view plane coordinates. By applying an appropriate viewport transformation (Chap. 5), we can suppose that p and q lie within the horizontal and vertical plotting dimensions of the plotting device, say, $H \times V$ pixels.

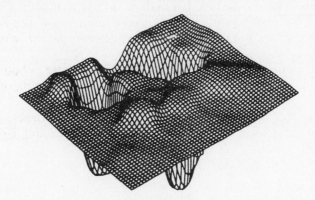

Fig. 10-17

The Perimeter Method for Rendering the Surface

Each plotted x and y constant polyline outlines a polygonal region on the plotting screen (Fig. 10-18).

The algorithm is based on the following observations: (1) *ordering*—the x- and y-constant curves (i.e., polylines) are drawn in order starting with the one closest to the viewpoint and (2) *visibility*—we draw only that part of the polyline that is outside the perimeter of all previously drawn regions (Fig. 10-19). One implementation of the visibility condition uses a min-max array A, of length H (that of the plotting device), which contains, at each horizontal pixel position i, the maximum (and/or minimum) vertical pixel value drawn thus far at i; that is $A(i) = \frac{max}{min}$ (vertical pixel values drawn so far at i) (Fig. 10-20). Selection of the max results in a drawing of the top of the surface. The min is used to render the bottom of the surface, and the max and min yields both top and bottom.

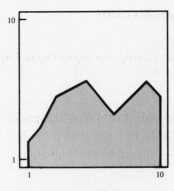

Fig. 10-18

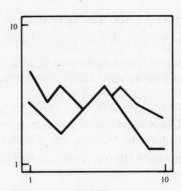

Fig. 10-19

(0)   (1)   (2)

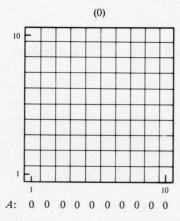

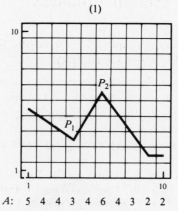

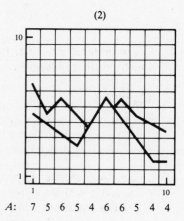

A: 0 0 0 0 0 0 0 0 0 0   A: 5 4 4 3 4 6 4 3 2 2   A: 7 5 6 5 4 6 6 5 4 4

Fig. 10-20   Updating min-max array A (using maximum values only).

The Visibility Test

Suppose that (p', q') is the pixel that corresponds to the point (p, q). Then this pixel is *visible* if either

$$q' > A(p') \qquad \text{or} \qquad q' < A(p')$$

where A is the min-max array.

The visibility criteria for a line segment are: (1) the line segment is visible if both its endpoints are visible; (2) the line segment is invisible if both its endpoints are not visible; and (3) if only one endpoint is visible, the min-max array is tested to find the visible part of the line.

Drawing the x- or y-constant polylines thus consists of testing for the visibility of each line segment and updating the min-max array as necessary. Since a line segment will, in general, span several horizontal pixel positions (see segment $\overline{P_1 P_2}$ in Fig. 10-20), the computation of $A(i)$ for these intermediate pixels is found by using the slope of the line segment or by using Bresenham's method described in Chap. 3.

The Wright Algorithm for Rendering Mathematical Surfaces

The drawing of the surface $z = F(x, y)$ proceeds as follows:

1. To perform initialization, determine whether the viewpoint is closer to the x or the y axis. Suppose that it is closer to the x axis. We next locate the x-constant curve that is closest to the viewpoint at $x = 1$.

(a) Initialize the min-max array to some base value, say, zero.

(b) Start with the x-constant curve found above.

2. Repeat the following steps using the visibility test for drawing line segments and updating the min-max array each time a line segment is drawn:

(a) Draw the x-constant polyline.

(b) Draw those parts of each y-constant polyline that lie between the previously drawn x-constant polyline and the next one to be drawn.

(c) Proceed, in the direction of increasing x, to the next x-constant polyline.

Solved Problems

10.1 Given points $P_1(1, 2, 0)$, $P_2(3, 6, 20)$, and $P_3(2, 4, 6)$ and a viewpoint $C(0, 0, -10)$, determine which points obscure the others when viewed from C.

SOLUTION

The line joining the viewpoint $C(0, 0, -10)$ and point $P_1(1, 2, 0)$ is (App. 2)

$$x = t \qquad y = 2t \qquad z = -10 + 10t$$

To determine whether $P_2(3, 6, 20)$ lies on this line, we see that $x = 3$ when $t = 3$, and then at $t = 3$, $x = 3$, $y = 6$, and $z = 20$. So P_2 lies on the projection line through C and P_1.

Next we determine which point is in front with respect to C. Now C occurs on the line at $t = 0$, P_1 occurs at $t = 1$, and P_2 occurs at $t = 3$. Thus comparing t values, P_1 is in front of P_2 with respect to C; that is, P_1 obscures P_2.

We now determine whether $P_3(2, 4, 6)$ is on the line. Now $x = 2$ when $t = 2$ and then $y = 4$, and $z = 10$. Thus $P_3(2, 4, 6)$ is not on this projection line and so it neither obscures nor is obscured by P_1 and P_2.

10.2 Construct the perspective to parallel transform T_p which produces an object whose parallel projection onto the xy plane yields the same image as the perspective projection of the original object onto the normalized view plane $z = c_z'/(c_z' + b)$ (Chap. 8, Prob. 8.6) with respect to the origin as the center of projection.

SOLUTION

The perspective projection onto the plane $z = c_z'/(c_z' + b)$ with respect to the origin is (Chap. 7, Prob. 7.4):

$$Per = \begin{pmatrix} z_v & 0 & 0 & 0 \\ 0 & z_v & 0 & 0 \\ 0 & 0 & z_v & 0 \\ 0 & 0 & 1 & 0 \end{pmatrix}$$

where $z_v = c_z'/(c_z' + b)$. The perspective projection onto the view plane of a point $P(x, y, z)$ is the point

$$P'\left(\frac{z_v \cdot x}{z}, \frac{z_v \cdot y}{z}, z_v\right)$$

Define the perspective to parallel transform T_p to be

$$T_p = \begin{pmatrix} z_v & 0 & 0 & 0 \\ 0 & z_v & 0 & 0 \\ 0 & 0 & \dfrac{1}{1-z_f} & \dfrac{-z_f}{1-z_f} \\ 0 & 0 & 1 & 0 \end{pmatrix}$$

(where $z = z_f$ is the location of the normalized front clipping plane; see Chap. 8, Prob. 8.6).

Now, applying the perspective to parallel transform T_p to the point $P(x, y, z)$, we produce the point

$$Q'\left(\frac{z_v \cdot x}{z}, \frac{z_v \cdot y}{z}, \frac{z - z_f}{z(1 - z_f)}\right)$$

The parallel projection of Q' onto the xy plane produces the point

$$Q'\left(\frac{z_v \cdot x}{z}, \frac{z_v \cdot y}{z}, 0\right)$$

So Q' and P' produce the same projective image. Furthermore, T_p transforms the normalized perspective view volume bounded by $x = z$, $x = -z$, $y = z$, $y = -z$, $z = z_f$, and $z = 1$ to the rectangular volume bounded by $x = z_v$, $x = -z_v$, $y = z_v$, $y = -z_v$, $z = 0$, and $z = 1$.

10.3 Show that the normalized perspective to parallel transform NT_p preserves the relationships of the original perspective transformation while transforming the normalized perspective view volume into the unit cube.

SOLUTION

From Prob. 10.2, the perspective to parallel transform T_p transforms a point $P(x, y, z)$ to a point

$$Q\left(\frac{z_v \cdot x}{z}, \frac{z_v \cdot y}{z}, \frac{z - z_f}{z(1 - z_f)}\right)$$

The image under parallel projection of this point onto the xy plane is

$$Q'\left(\frac{z_v \cdot x}{z}, \frac{z_v \cdot y}{z}, 0\right)$$

The factor z_v can be set equal to 1 without changing the relation between points Q and Q'.

The matrix that transforms $P(x, y, z)$ to the point $Q\left(\dfrac{x}{z}, \dfrac{y}{z}, \dfrac{z - z_f}{z(1 - z_f)}\right)$ is then

$$\bar{T}_p = \begin{pmatrix} 1 & 0 & 0 & 0 \\ 0 & 1 & 0 & 0 \\ 0 & 0 & \dfrac{1}{1-z_f} & \dfrac{-z_f}{1-z_f} \\ 0 & 0 & 1 & 0 \end{pmatrix}$$

In addition, this matrix transforms the normalized perspective view volume to the rectangular view volume bounded by $x = 1$, $x = -1$, $y = 1$, $y = -1$, $z = 0$, and $z = 1$.

We next translate this view volume so that the corner point $(-1, -1, 0)$ translates to the origin. The translation matrix that does this is

$$T_{(1,1,0)} = \begin{pmatrix} 1 & 0 & 0 & 1 \\ 0 & 1 & 0 & 1 \\ 0 & 0 & 1 & 0 \\ 0 & 0 & 0 & 1 \end{pmatrix}$$

The new region is a volume bounded by $x = 0$, $x = 2$, $y = 0$, $y = 2$, $z = 0$, and $t = 1$.

Finally, we scale in the x and y direction by a factor $\frac{1}{2}$ so that the final view volume is the unit cube: $x = 0$, $x = 1$, $y = 0$, $y = 1$, $z = 0$, and $z = 1$. The scaling matrix is

$$
S_{1/2,1/2,1} = \begin{pmatrix} \frac{1}{2} & 0 & 0 & 0 \\ 0 & \frac{1}{2} & 0 & 0 \\ 0 & 0 & 1 & 0 \\ 0 & 0 & 0 & 1 \end{pmatrix}
$$

The final normalized perspective to parallel transform is

$$
NT_p = S_{1/2,1/2,1} \cdot T_{(1,1,0)} \cdot \bar{T}_p = \begin{pmatrix} \frac{1}{2} & 0 & \frac{1}{2} & 0 \\ 0 & \frac{1}{2} & \frac{1}{2} & 0 \\ 0 & 0 & \dfrac{1}{1-z_f} & \dfrac{-z_f}{1-z_f} \\ 0 & 0 & 1 & 0 \end{pmatrix}
$$

10.4   Why are hidden-surface algorithms needed?

SOLUTION

Hidden-surface algorithms are needed to determine which objects and surfaces will obscure those objects and surfaces that are in back of them, thus rendering a more realistic image.

10.5   What two steps are required to determine whether any given point $P_1(x_1, y_1, z_1)$ obscures another point $P_2(x_2, y_2, z_2)$? (See Fig. 10-1.)

SOLUTION

It must be determined (1) whether the two points lie on the same projection line and (2) if they do, which point is in front of the other.

10.6   Why is it easier to locate hidden surfaces when parallel projection is used?

SOLUTION

There are no vanishing points in parallel projection. As a result, any point $P(a, b, z)$ will lie on the same projector as any other point having the same x and y coordinates (a, b). Thus only the z component must be compared to determine which point is closest to the viewer.

10.7   How does the Z-buffer algorithm determine which surfaces are hidden?

SOLUTION

The Z-buffer algorithm sets up a two-dimensional array which is like the frame buffer; however, the Z buffer stores the depth value at each pixel rather than the color, which is stored in the frame buffer. By setting the initial values of the Z buffer to some large number, usually the distance of the yon clipping plane, the problem of determining which surfaces are closer is reduced to simply comparing the present depth value stored in the Z buffer at pixel (x, y) with the newly calculated depth value at pixel (x, y). If this new value is less than the present Z-buffer value (i.e., closer along the line of sight), this value replaces the present value and the pixel color is changed to the color of the new surface.

10.8   Using a 2×2 pixel display, show how the Z-buffer algorithm would determine the color of each
pixel for the given objects A and B in Fig. 10-21.

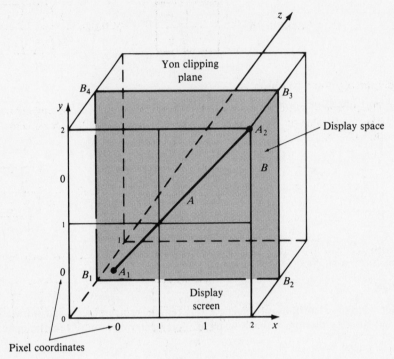

Fig. 10-21

SOLUTION

The display space for the 2×2 pixel display is the region $0 \le x \le 2$, $0 \le y \le 2$, and $0 \le z \le 1$. In Fig.
10-21, A is the line with display space coordinates $A_1(\frac{1}{2}, \frac{1}{2}, 0)$ and $A_2(2, 2, 0)$; line A is on the display
screen in front of square B. B is the square with display space coordinates $B_1(0, 0, \frac{1}{2})$, $B_2(2, 0, \frac{1}{2})$,
$B_3(2, 2, \frac{1}{2})$, and $B_4(0, 2, \frac{1}{2})$. The displayed image of A (after projection and scan conversion) would
appear on a 2×2 pixel display as

1	y	a
0	a	y
	0	1

where a is the color of A and y is the background color. We have used the fact (Chap. 3, Sec. 3.2) that a
point (x, y) scan converts to the pixel $[\text{INT}(x), \text{INT}(y)]$. (We assume for consistency that $2 \equiv 1.99 \ldots$.)
The displayed image of B is

1	b	b
0	b	b
	0	1

where b is the color of B. We apply the Z-buffer algorithm to the picture composed of objects A and B as
follows:

1. Perform initialization. The Z buffer is set equal to the depth of the yon clipping plane $z = 1$, and the frame buffer is initialized to a background color y.

Frame buffer =
$$
\begin{array}{c|c|c|}
1 & y & y \\
\hline
0 & y & y \\
\hline
 & 0 & 1 \\
\end{array}
$$
$\qquad$ Z buffer =
$$
\begin{array}{c|c|c|}
1 & 1 & 1 \\
\hline
0 & 1 & 1 \\
\hline
 & 0 & 1 \\
\end{array}
$$

2. Apply the algorithm to object A.

    (a) The present Z-buffer value at pixel $(0,0)$ is that of the yon clipping plane, i.e., $Z_{buf}(0,0) = 1$. The depth value of A at pixel $(0,0)$ is $z = 0$. Then $Z_{buf}(0,0)$ is changed to 0 and pixel $(0,0)$ has the color of A.

Frame buffer =
$$
\begin{array}{c|c|c|}
1 & y & y \\
\hline
0 & a & y \\
\hline
 & 0 & 1 \\
\end{array}
$$
$\qquad$ Z buffer =
$$
\begin{array}{c|c|c|}
1 & 1 & 1 \\
\hline
0 & 0 & 1 \\
\hline
 & 0 & 1 \\
\end{array}
$$

    (b) Object A is not seen from pixel $(1,0)$, so the Z-buffer value is unchanged.

Frame =
$$
\begin{array}{c|c|c|}
1 & y & y \\
\hline
0 & a & y \\
\hline
 & 0 & 1 \\
\end{array}
$$
$\qquad$ $Z_{buf} =$
$$
\begin{array}{c|c|c|}
1 & 1 & 1 \\
\hline
0 & 0 & 1 \\
\hline
 & 0 & 1 \\
\end{array}
$$

    (c) Object A is not seen from pixel $(0,1)$, so the Z-buffer value is unchanged.

Frame =
$$
\begin{array}{c|c|c|}
1 & y & y \\
\hline
0 & a & y \\
\hline
 & 0 & 1 \\
\end{array}
$$
$\qquad$ $Z_{buf} =$
$$
\begin{array}{c|c|c|}
1 & 1 & 1 \\
\hline
0 & 0 & 1 \\
\hline
 & 0 & 1 \\
\end{array}
$$

    (d) The depth value of A at pixel $(1,1)$ is 0. Since this is less than the present Z-buffer value of 1, pixel $(1,1)$ takes the color of A.

Frame =
$$
\begin{array}{c|c|c|}
1 & y & a \\
\hline
0 & a & y \\
\hline
 & 0 & 1 \\
\end{array}
$$
$\qquad$ $Z_{buf} =$
$$
\begin{array}{c|c|c|}
1 & 1 & 0 \\
\hline
0 & 0 & 1 \\
\hline
 & 0 & 1 \\
\end{array}
$$

3. Apply the algorithm to B.

    (a) The depth value for B at pixel $(0,0)$ is 0, and $Z_{buf}(0,0) = 1$. So the color of pixel $(0,0)$ is unchanged.

Frame =
$$
\begin{array}{c|c|c|}
1 & y & a \\
\hline
0 & a & y \\
\hline
 & 0 & 1 \\
\end{array}
$$
$\qquad$ $Z_{buf} =$
$$
\begin{array}{c|c|c|}
1 & 1 & 0 \\
\hline
0 & 0 & 1 \\
\hline
 & 0 & 1 \\
\end{array}
$$

(b) The depth value of B at pixel $(1, 0)$ is $\frac{1}{2}$. The present Z-buffer value is 1. So the Z-buffer value is set to $\frac{1}{2}$ and pixel $(1, 0)$ takes the color of B.

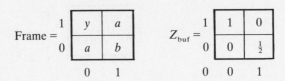

$$\text{Frame} = \begin{array}{c} 1 \\ 0 \end{array} \begin{array}{|c|c|} \hline y & a \\ \hline a & b \\ \hline \end{array} \qquad Z_{\text{buf}} = \begin{array}{c} 1 \\ 0 \end{array} \begin{array}{|c|c|} \hline 1 & 0 \\ \hline 0 & \frac{1}{2} \\ \hline \end{array}$$

(c) The depth value of B at pixel $(0, 1)$ is $\frac{1}{2}$. The present Z-buffer value is 1, so the color at pixel $(0, 1)$ is set to that of B, and the Z buffer is updated.

$$\text{Frame} = \begin{array}{c} 1 \\ 0 \end{array} \begin{array}{|c|c|} \hline b & a \\ \hline a & b \\ \hline \end{array} \qquad Z_{\text{buf}} = \begin{array}{c} 1 \\ 0 \end{array} \begin{array}{|c|c|} \hline \frac{1}{2} & 0 \\ \hline 0 & \frac{1}{2} \\ \hline \end{array}$$

(d) The depth value of B at pixel $(1, 1)$ is $\frac{1}{2}$. The present Z-buffer value is 0. So the color at pixel $(1, 1)$ remains unchanged.

$$\text{Frame} = \begin{array}{c} 1 \\ 0 \end{array} \begin{array}{|c|c|} \hline b & a \\ \hline a & b \\ \hline \end{array} \qquad Z_{\text{buf}} = \begin{array}{c} 1 \\ 0 \end{array} \begin{array}{|c|c|} \hline \frac{1}{2} & 0 \\ \hline 0 & \frac{1}{2} \\ \hline \end{array}$$

The final form of the Z buffer indicates that line A lies in front of B.

10.9 What is the maximum number of objects that can be presented by using the Z-buffer algorithm?

SOLUTION

The total number of objects that can be handled by the Z-buffer algorithm is arbitrary because each object is processed one at a time. As a result, the maximum number of objects is limited only by either the computer's capacity to store objects or the user's patience with the required processing time.

10.10 How does the scan-line method determine which surfaces are hidden?

SOLUTION

The scan-line method looks one at a time at each of the horizontal lines of pixels on the display. On a 640×200 display, this involves looking at each of the 200 lines in turn. For example, at the horizontal pixel line $y = \alpha$, the graphics data structure (consisting of all scan-converted polygons) is searched to find all polygons with any horizontal (y) pixel values equal to α.

Next, the algorithm looks at each individual pixel in the α row. At pixel (α, β), the depth values (z values) of each polygon found above are compared to find the polygon having the smallest z value at this pixel. The color of pixel (α, β) is then set to the color of the corresponding polygon at this pixel.

10.11 Using the four pixel display and the graphics objects A and B from Prob. 10.8, show how the scan-line method would display these objects.

SOLUTION

First we initialize the display to the color y of the yon clipping plane (located at $z = 1$).

$$\text{Frame buffer} = \begin{array}{c} 1 \\ 0 \end{array} \begin{array}{|c|c|} \hline y & y \\ \hline y & y \\ \hline \end{array}$$
$$\qquad\qquad 0 \quad 1$$

1. Set $y = 0$. The scan-converted representations of A and B certain pixels on the $y = 0$ scan line.

    (a) Set $x = 0$. Comparing the z values of A and B at pixel $(0, 0)$, we find that the smaller z value is 0, which belongs to A. Thus A is seen from pixel $(0, 0)$; that is, pixel $(0, 0)$ is set to the color of A.

$$\begin{array}{c} 1 \\ 0 \end{array} \begin{array}{|c|c|} \hline y & y \\ \hline a & y \\ \hline \end{array}$$
$$0 \quad 1$$

    (b) Set $x = 1$. Since A is not seen from pixel $(1, 0)$ while B is seen, the color of pixel $(1, 0)$ is set to that of B.

$$\begin{array}{c} 1 \\ 0 \end{array} \begin{array}{|c|c|} \hline y & y \\ \hline a & b \\ \hline \end{array}$$
$$0 \quad 1$$

2. Set $y = 1$. The scan-converted representations of A and B contain pixels on the $y = 1$ scan line.

    (a) Set $x = 0$. Because A is not seen at pixel $(0, 1)$ while B is seen, pixel $(0, 1)$ is set to the color of B.

$$\begin{array}{c} 1 \\ 0 \end{array} \begin{array}{|c|c|} \hline b & y \\ \hline a & b \\ \hline \end{array}$$
$$0 \quad 1$$

    (b) Set $x = 1$. Both A and B are "seen" from pixel $(1, 1)$. The depth of A at pixel $(1, 1)$ is 0, that of B is $\frac{1}{2}$. Thus A is visible at pixel $(1, 1)$.

$$\begin{array}{c} 1 \\ 0 \end{array} \begin{array}{|c|c|} \hline b & a \\ \hline a & b \\ \hline \end{array}$$
$$0 \quad 1$$

This represents the final image displayed.

10.12 How does edge coherence help to reduce computational effort?

SOLUTION

It is based on the assumption that if an edge or line intersects a given scan line, it will most likely intersect those scan lines next to it. Thus if those pixels that intersect the edge are to be found, instead of intersecting each scan line with the edge, it is necessary to locate only one intersection pixel and then find the others using the slope m of the edge (see Prob. 10.13).

10.13 Show how the calculation of the intersection of an edge with a scan line can be made incremental as opposed to absolute.

SOLUTION

The absolute calculation requires that we find the x intersection value of the edge (e.g., with equation $y = mx + b$) with the scan line $y = \alpha$ for each α.

The incremental solution to the problem is based on the following observations. Suppose that x_α is the x intersection of the edge with the scan line α. Then the intersection $x_{\alpha+1}$ of the edge with the next scan line $y = \alpha + 1$ can be found as illustrated in Fig. 10-22. From Fig. 10-22. where m is the slope of the edge,

$$\frac{\Delta y}{\Delta x} = \frac{(\alpha + 1) - \alpha}{x_{\alpha+1} - x_\alpha} = m$$

Solving for $x_{\alpha+1}$, we obtain

$$x_{\alpha+1} = x_\alpha + \frac{1}{m}$$

Thus the calculation of the next intersection point is incremental; that is, it is found from the previous intersection point by adding $1/m$ to it.

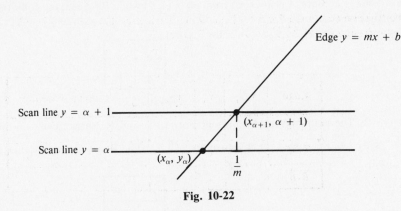

Fig. 10-22

10.14 How does area coherence reduce computational effort?

SOLUTION

Area coherence is based on the assumption that a small enough region of pixels will most likely lie within a single polygon. This reduces computational effort in searching for those polygons which contain a given screen area (region of pixels) as in the subdivision algorithms.

10.15 How is spatial coherence determined?

SOLUTION

Spatial coherence is determined by examining the extent of an object. The rectangular extent (bounding box) of an object is determined by finding the minimum and maximum x, y, and z coordinate values of the points that belong to the object. The extent is the rectangular region bounded by the planes $z = z_{min}$, $z = z_{max}$, $y = y_{min}$, $y = y_{max}$, $x = x_{min}$, and $x = x_{max}$.

10.16 Draw two polygons such that their extents intersect but the polygons themselves don't intersect.

SOLUTION

Figure 10-23 shows one possible solution.

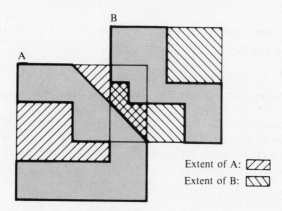

Fig. 10-23

10.17 Apply the scan-line algorithm from sec. 10.4, under "A Scan-Line Algorithm," to the display of objects A and B in Prob. 10.8.

SOLUTION

We first construct the edge list (EL) and the polygon list (PL). From Fig. 10-21, the edge entries for the nonhorizontal edges $\overline{A_1A_2}$, $\overline{B_1B_4}$, and $\overline{B_2B_3}$ are

Edge	y_{min}	x_A	y_{max}	$\dfrac{1}{m}$	Polygon pointer
$\overline{A_1A_2}$	$\frac{1}{2}$	$\frac{1}{2}$	2	1	A
$\overline{B_1B_4}$	0	0	2	0	B
$\overline{B_2B_3}$	0	2	2	0	B

Here, y_{min} is the edge's smaller y coordinate and x_A the corresponding x coordinate; y_{max} is the larger y coordinate, and m is the slope of the edge. From this information, we construct the (sorted) edge list by finding the pixel row (scan line) corresponding to the y_{min} values and then sorting on the value of x_A (ties are broken by the smaller of $1/m$).

$$EL = \begin{array}{|c|c|c|c|} \hline \multirow{1}{*}{y Scan line} & \multicolumn{3}{c|}{\text{(Sorted) edges}} \\ \hline \text{Cell 1} & \overline{B_1B_4} & \overline{A_1A_2} & \overline{B_2B_3} \\ \hline \text{Cell 0} & \multicolumn{3}{c|}{—} \\ \hline \end{array}$$

Form the PL:

$$PL = \begin{array}{|c|c|c|c|} \hline \text{Polygon} & \text{Equation} & \text{IN/OUT flag} & \text{Color} \\ \hline \begin{array}{c} A \\ \text{(line)} \end{array} & \begin{array}{c} x = y \\ z = 0 \end{array} & \text{OUT} & a \\ \hline B & z = 1 & \text{OUT} & b \\ \hline \end{array}$$

The algorithm proceeds as follows:

I. *Initialization*.

    (*a*) Set the active edge list (AEL) to empty.

    (*b*) We initialize the screen display to the color y of the yon clipping plane (located at $z = 1$).

$$\text{Frame buffer} = \begin{array}{c c} 1 \\ 0 \end{array} \begin{array}{|c|c|} \hline y & y \\ \hline y & y \\ \hline \end{array}$$
$$\qquad\qquad 0 \quad\ 1$$

    (*c*) Set the scan line to $y = 0$.

II. *y-scan loop*. Update the AEL at $y = 0$ and sort on x_A:

$$\text{AEL} = $$

Edges	x_A
$\overline{B_1 B_4}$	0
$\overline{A_1 A_2}$	$\frac{1}{2}$
$\overline{B_2 B_3}$	2

III. *x-scan loop*.

    (*a*) Process edge $\overline{B_1 B_4}$. First invert the appropriate IN/OUT flags in the PL:

$$\text{PL} = $$

Polygon	Equation	IN/OUT flag	Color
A	$x = y$ $z = 0$	OUT	a
B	$z = 1$	IN	b

Next, we form the active polygon list (APL):

$$\text{APL} = $$

Polygons with IN/OUT flag = IN
B

The number of polygons in the APL is one. Thus B is visible at pixel $(0, 0)$ and all pixels on scan line $y = 0$ between edges $\overline{B_1 B_4}$ and $\overline{A_1 A_2}$ are set to the color of B. In our case, this is just the pixel $(0, 0)$.

$$\begin{array}{c c} 1 \\ 0 \end{array} \begin{array}{|c|c|} \hline y & y \\ \hline b & y \\ \hline \end{array}$$
$$\qquad 0 \quad\ 1$$

    (*b*) Since polygon B is not a line, its IN/OUT flag is unchanged.

    (*a*) Now we repeat step (*a*), processing edge $\overline{A_1 A_2}$. We update the PL:

$$\text{PL} = $$

Polygon	Equation	IN/OUT flag	Color
A	$x = y$ $z = 0$	IN	a
B	$z = 1$	IN	b

Next, we form the APL:

$$APL = \boxed{\begin{array}{c} \text{Polygons with IN/OUT flag} = \text{IN} \\ \hline A, B \end{array}}$$

The number of polygons in the APL is 2. At pixel $(0,0)$ the depth value (z value) of polygon A is 0 and of polygon B is $\frac{1}{2}$. Thus polygon A is visible at pixel $(0,0)$, so the color is set to a. The color of all pixels between edges $\overline{A_1A_2}$ and $\overline{B_3B_4}$ are unchanged since A is a line.

1	y	y
0	a	y
	0	1

(b)　Since A is a line, set the IN/OUT flag of line A to OUT.

Polygon	. . .	IN/OUT flag	. . .
A	—	OUT	—
B	—	IN	—

PL = (table above)

(a)　Again, we repeat step (a), processing edge $\overline{B_2B_3}$. We update the PL:

Polygon	. . .	IN/OUT flag	. . .
A	—	OUT	—
B	—	OUT	—

PL = (table above)

The number of polygons in the APL is 0. We set pixel $(1,0)$ to the color of polygon B, which contains edge $\overline{B_2B_3}$.

1	y	y
0	a	b
	0	1

(b)　B is a polygon so its IN/OUT flag is unchanged.

(c)　Having processed $\overline{B_2B_3}$, the last edge in the AEL, we process the AEL:

(1)　All the $y_{\max}$ values are equal to 2. These values scan-convert (see Prob. 10.8) to 1. The present y scan line value is 0. So no edges are removed from the AEL.

(2)–(3)　Incrementing x_A by $1/m$ and sorting,

$\overline{B_1B_4}$	0
$\overline{A_1A_2}$	$\frac{3}{2}$
$\overline{B_2B_3}$	2

AEL = (table above)

(4)　Set $y = 1$.

Now we repeat steps II and III.

II.   *y-scan loop*. With $y = 1$, we update that AEL by merging into it the information contained in the cell $y = 1$ of the edge list. Since in our example this cell is empty, the AEL is not changed and remains as above.

III. *x-scan loop*.

(a)   Process edge $\overline{B_1B_4}$. We update the PL:

PL =

Polygon	...	IN/OUT flag	...
A	—	OUT	—
B	—	IN	—

We form the APL:

APL =

Polygons with IN/OUT flag = IN
B

The number of polygons in the APL is 1. Thus B is visible at pixel $(0, 1)$ and all pixels between edge $\overline{B_1B_4}$ and $\overline{A_1A_2}$ on scan line $y = 1$ are set to the color of B.

1	b	b
0	a	b
	0	1

(b) B is a polygon, so its IN/OUT flag is unchanged.

(a)   Now we repeat step (a), processing edge $\overline{A_1A_2}$. We update the PL:

PL =

Polygon	...	IN/OUT flag	...
A	—	IN	—
B	—	IN	—

There are two polygons in the APL. A depth comparison at pixel $(1, 1)$ shows that it is set to the color of line $\overline{A_1A_2}$.

1	b	a
0	a	b
	0	1

(b)   Since A is a line, we set the IN/OUT flag of A to OUT.

(a)   Again we repeat step (a), processing edge $\overline{B_2B_3}$. We update the PL:

PL =

Polygon	Equation	IN/OUT flag	Color
A	$x = y$ $z = 0$	OUT	a
B	$z = 1$	OUT	b

The number of polygons in the APL is 0. The color at pixel $(1, 1)$ is left unchanged.

1	b	a
0	a	b
	0	1

(b)   Since B is a polygon its IN/OUT flag is unchanged.

(c)   Having processed the last edge $\overline{B_2B_3}$ in the AEL, we remove those edges for which y_{max} equals the y scan value of 1. Since this includes all the edges, i.e., $y_{max} = 2$, the algorithm stops.

10.18   What is the underlying concept of the painter's or the priority algorithm?

SOLUTION

The painter's algorithm sorts polygons by depth and then paints (scan-converts) each polygon onto the screen starting with the most distant polygon.

10.19   What difficulties are encountered in implementing the painter's algorithm?

SOLUTION

First, there is the question of what the "depth" of a polygon is, especially if the polygon is tilted out of the xy plane. Second, if two polygons have the same depth, which one should be painted first?

10.20   If polygon Q has the same depth value as polygon P, which polygon has priority, that is, which is painted first?

SOLUTION

We perform tests 0, 1, 2, 3, 4, 5 (from Sec. 10.5, under "Testing Whether P Obscures Q") in order. If any one of the tests is true, we say that polygon P does not obscure polygon Q, and so polygon P is painted first.

If none of the tests is true, we have an ambiguity that must be resolved.

We resolve the ambiguity by switching the roles of P and Q and then reapply tests 0, 1, 2, 3, 4, and 5. If any one of these tests is true, Q does not obscure polygon P and so polygon Q is painted first.

If again none of the tests is true, polygon Q must be subdivided into two polygons Q_1 and Q_2, using the plane containing polygon P as the dividing plane [Fig. 10-7(b)].

10.21   Apply the painter's algorithm to display objects A and B in Prob. 10.8.

SOLUTION

We first find the depth values z_{max} for A and B. Since z_{max} is the largest z value from all the polygon's vertices, then for A, $z_{A_{max}} = 0$, and for B, $z_{B_{max}} = \frac{1}{2}$. Then sorting on z_{max}, we see that polygon B has a higher depth value than polygon A.

Next, we assign priorities by applying tests 0 through 5 in order (see page 198). In test 0, the z extent of B is $z_{min} = \frac{1}{2}$, $z_{max} = \frac{1}{2}$. The z extent of A is $z_{min} = 0$, $z_{max} = 0$.

Thus the z extents of A and B do not overlap and $z_{A_{max}}$ is smaller than $z_{B_{min}}$. Thus test 0 is true, and so we scan-convert polygon B first:

Frame buffer =	1	b	b
	0	b	b
		0	1

Next, we scan-convert polygon A (i.e., we "paint" over polygon B):

1	b	a
0	a	b
	0	1

This is the final image displayed in the frame buffer.

10.22 What are the basic concepts underlying the subdivision algorithm?

SOLUTION

First, is that a polygon is seen from within a given area of the display screen if the projection of that polygon overlaps the given area. Second, of all polygons that overlap a given screen area, the one that is visible in this area is the one in front of all the others. Third, if we cannot decide which polygon is visible (in front of the others) from a given region, we subdivide the region into smaller regions until visibility decisions can be made (even if we must subdivide down to the pixel level).

10.23 Apply the subdivision algorithm to the display of objects A and B from Prob. 10.8.

SOLUTION

1. *Initialization.* We initialize the area to the whole screen. We create the PVPL, sorted on z_{min}, the smallest of the z values of the polygon's vertices.

2. *Forming the potentially visible polygon list.*

PVPL =

Polygon	z_{min}	Category
A	0	Contained
B	$\frac{1}{2}$	Surrounding

3. *Visibility decision.* We apply criteria (a) through (e) in Sec. 10.6, under "Visibility Decision." Since the polygons are classified as contained and surrounding, we pass to step 4 and subdivide the area into four subregions.

After subdivision, the four newly formed regions are, in our example, the individual pixels. We apply the algorithm to each pixel in turn.
    Region 1: pixel $(0, 0)$.

2. *Forming the PVPL.*

PVPL =

Polygon	z_{min}	Category
A	0	Surrounding
B	$\frac{1}{2}$	Surrounding

3. *Visibility decision.* Applying tests (a) through (d), we now apply test (e) since the region is pixel size. The z coordinate of A at pixel $(0, 0)$ is 0, and that of B is $\frac{1}{2}$. Thus A is visible at pixel $(0, 0)$:

$$\text{Frame buffer} = \begin{array}{c} 1 \\ 0 \end{array} \begin{array}{|c|c|} \hline & \\ \hline a & \\ \hline \end{array}$$
$$\hspace{3.5cm} 0 \quad 1$$

Region 2: pixel $(0, 1)$.

2. *Forming the PVPL.* Note that A is disjoint from this region:

PVPL =

Polygon	z_{min}	Category
B	$\frac{1}{2}$	Surrounding

3. *Visibility decision.* From test (c), there is only one polygon and it is surrounding, so we color pixel $(0, 1)$ that of B:

$$\begin{array}{c} 1 \\ 0 \end{array} \begin{array}{|c|c|} \hline & \\ \hline a & b \\ \hline \end{array}$$
$$\hspace{1cm} 0 \quad 1$$

Region 3: pixel $(0, 1)$.

2. *Forming the PVPL.* Since A is disjoint from this region, we have

PVPL =

Polygon	z_{min}	Category
B	$\frac{1}{2}$	Surrounding

3. *Visibility decision.* From test (c), there is only one polygon B and it is surrounding. So region 3 is colored b:

$$\begin{array}{c} 1 \\ 0 \end{array} \begin{array}{|c|c|} \hline b & \\ \hline a & b \\ \hline \end{array}$$
$$\hspace{1cm} 0 \quad 1$$

Region 4: pixel $(1, 1)$.

2. *Forming the PVPL.*

PVPL =

Polygon	z_{min}	Category
A	0	Surrounding
B	$\frac{1}{2}$	Surrounding

3. *Visibility decision.* Having applied tests (*a*) through (*d*), we now apply test (*e*). The z coordinate of A at pixel $(1, 1)$ is less than that of B. Thus pixel $(1, 1)$ is set to the color of A:

This is the final image in the frame buffer.

10.24 What property of raster displays makes the technique of ray tracing possible?

SOLUTION

Ray tracing projects a ray from the viewpoint or center of projection C, through a pixel P, for each pixel in the display. Since two points determine a line, we can use C and P to find the equation of the ray. This equation is then used to find the z coordinate of the intersection of the ray with the objects in the picture. These z coordinates are sorted to find the smallest z value. The color of pixel P is then set to the color of the object belonging to this z value.

If there is no intersection of the ray with any object in the picture, the color at pixel P is set to the background color.

10.25 What are some of the advantages of the ray-tracing method?

SOLUTION

It is independent of the projection technique. For parallel projection, the equation of the ray through the center of pixel (h, k) is

$$x = h + \tfrac{1}{2} \qquad y = k + \tfrac{1}{2}$$

[The center of pixel (h, k) is the point $(h + \tfrac{1}{2}, k + \tfrac{1}{2})$]. For perspective projection, the parametric equation of the ray through the viewpoint $C(a, b, c)$ and the center of pixel (h, k) is (App. 2)

$$x = a + ([h + \tfrac{1}{2}] - a)t \qquad y = b + ([h + \tfrac{1}{2}] - a)t \qquad z = c(1 - t)$$

Another advantage is that the ray-tracing method can be used without modification to remove hidden curved surfaces since it is essentially based on solving the intersection equations of a line and a surface.

10.26 Use ray tracing to display the objects in Prob. 10.8. Take $C(0, 0, -10)$ as the center of projection.

SOLUTION

The equation of line A is $x = y$, $z = 0$. The equation of the plane containing B is $z = \tfrac{1}{2}$. Pixels $(0, 0)$ and $(1, 0)$ should be treated as follows:

1. *Pixel $(0, 0)$.* The parametric equation of the ray through C and the center of pixel $(0, 0)$ is, from Prob. 10.25,

$$x = \tfrac{1}{2}t \qquad y = \tfrac{1}{2}t \qquad z = -10(1 - t)$$

   (*a*) *Intersection with A.* Since $z = 0$, intersection should occur when $t = 1$, and so $x = \tfrac{1}{2}$ and $y = \tfrac{1}{2}$. Since $x = y$, this point is also on line A.

   (*b*) *Intersection with B.* Since $z = \tfrac{1}{2}$, we find $t = \tfrac{21}{20}$, and so $x = \tfrac{21}{40}$, $y = \tfrac{21}{40}$. The point $(\tfrac{21}{40}, \tfrac{21}{40}, \tfrac{1}{2})$ lies in B.

The intersection z values are 0 and $\tfrac{1}{2}$. Choosing the smaller value, 0, which belongs to A, we find that A is visible from C at pixel $(0, 0)$ and we set the color of pixel $(0, 0)$ to a

$$\text{Frame buffer} = \begin{array}{c|c|c|} & & \\ 1 & - & - \\ \hline 0 & a & - \\ \hline & 0 & 1 \end{array}$$

2. *Pixel* $(1, 0)$. The equation of the ray through C and the center of pixel $(1, 0)$ is, from Prob. 10.25,

$$x = 1\tfrac{1}{2}t \qquad y = \tfrac{1}{2}t \qquad z = -10(1 - t)$$

(a) *Intersection with A.* Since $z = 0$, it follows that $t = 1$ and $x = 1\tfrac{1}{2}$, $y = \tfrac{1}{2}$. However, the point $(1\tfrac{1}{2}, \tfrac{1}{2}, 0)$ does not lie on line A, and so the ray does not intersect line A.

(b) *Intersection with B.* Since $z = \tfrac{1}{2}$, the $t = \tfrac{21}{20}$ and $x = \tfrac{63}{40}$, $y = \tfrac{21}{40}$. The intersection point is $\left(\tfrac{63}{40}, \tfrac{21}{40}, \tfrac{1}{2}\right)$.

This point is within polygon B, and so the color of pixel $(1, 0)$ is set to the color of B:

The remaining pixels are treated in the same manner. We should point out that, in general, ray tracing does not handle lines properly because of the coarseness of the pixel resolution. That is, the intersection of a ray through the center of a pixel will not necessarily intersect a given line even when the scan-converted display of the line contains this pixel. So lines must be processed differently from polygons. Our example is artificial in the sense that ray tracing will process line A correctly.

10.27 How can we use the special structure of a convex polyhedron to identify its hidden faces?

SOLUTION

Suppose that on each face of the polyhedron there is an outward-pointing normal vector **N**, attached at a point P of the face (Fig. 10-24). For each face of the polyhedron, let the *line-of-sight vector* **L** be the vector pointing from the face to the viewer. For a parallel projection, this is the direction of projection from the object to the projection plane. For a perspective projection, it is the vector $\overline{PC}$ from the normal vector attached at point P to the viewpoint at point C (Fig. 10-24).

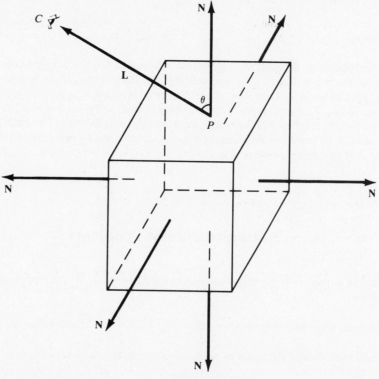

Fig. 10-24

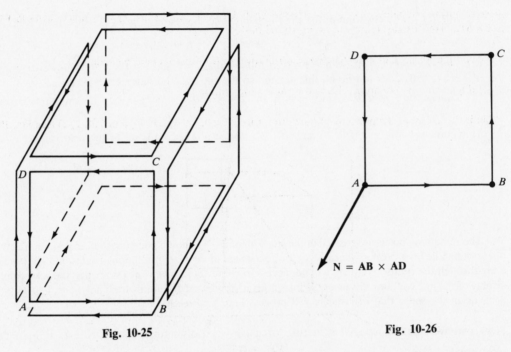

Fig. 10-25   Fig. 10-26

A face is *visible* if the angle θ made by the line-of-sight vector **L** and the normal vector **N** is less than or equal to 90°. It is *hidden* if this angle is larger than 90°. If $0° \le \theta \le 90°$, then $0 \le \cos\theta \le 1$; if $90° < \theta \le 180°$, then $-1 \le \cos\theta < 0$. Since (from App. 2)

$$\cos\theta = \frac{\mathbf{L}\cdot\mathbf{N}}{|\mathbf{L}|\,|\mathbf{N}|}$$

the face is visible if

$$0 \le \frac{\mathbf{L}\cdot\mathbf{N}}{|\mathbf{L}|\,|\mathbf{N}|} \le 1$$

and hidden otherwise. To use this visibility test, we need to find the outward-pointing normal vectors for the faces of the polyhedron. To do this, we label the faces of the polyhedron so that the polyhedron is *oriented*. That is, any edge shared by adjacent faces is traversed in opposite directions with respect to the faces (Fig. 10-25). This guarantees that the normal vectors will point outward. To construct the outward normal vectors, we label each polygon with a counterclockwise labeling (Fig. 10-26). Then a normal vector can be found by taking the cross product of vectors determined by two adjacent sides of the polygon and attaching it at one of the vertices (Fig. 10-26).

Supplementary Problems

10.28 How may the properties of parallel projection be used to simplify hidden-surface calculations for any form of projection?

10.29 What happens when two polygons have the same z value and the Z-buffer algorithm is used?

10.30 How would the Z-buffer algorithm be altered to allow figures to be superimposed on a surface (see Prob. 10.29)?

10.31   Assuming that one allows 256 depth value levels to be used, approximately how much memory would a 512×512 pixel display require to store the Z buffer?

10.32   How can the amount of computation required by the scan-line method be reduced?

10.33   How does scan-line coherence help to reduce computation?

10.34   What is the extent of the polygon whose vertices are $A(0, 0, 1)$, $B(2, 0, 1)$, and $C(1, 2, 2)$ (see Fig. 10-27)?

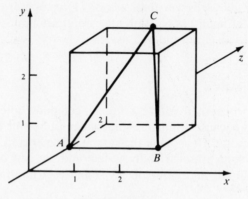

Fig. 10-27

10.35   Why are only nonhorizontal lines stored in the edge list of the scan-line algorithm?

10.36   How is the depth of a polygon determined by the painter's algorithm?

10.37   How does the subdivision algorithm exploit area coherence?

10.38   How can hidden-surface algorithms be used to eliminate hidden lines as applied to polygonal mesh models (Chap. 9)?

10.39   How can the computational effort involved in using the ray-tracing method be reduced?

Chapter 11

Computer Graphics Applications

11.1 INTRODUCTION

Beyond a basic knowledge of computer graphics concepts, the design of an effective computer graphics application requires knowledge in three areas: (1) computer ergonomics, (2) information structures, and (3) the field of application. Without careful attention to all three areas, the most sophisticated graphics routines may be rendered useless.

11.2 COMPUTER ERGONOMICS

Computer ergonomics is concerned with the human-computer interface (often called the *user interface*). It is very important because ultimately someone must be able to use the graphics system to produce useful, meaningful results. The goal of the system designer is to strike a balance between the cost of time related to developing a user-friendly system and the cost of user errors. Generally, six areas are considered in developing an ergonomically sound user interface:

    (1)   compatibility

    (2)   brevity

    (3)   flexibility

    (4)   response time

    (5)   consistency

    (6)   operator workload

Compatibility

The term "compatibility" means that expected user input and computer output will be consistent with the user's model of the world. For example, STOP written in red would be user-compatible, while STOP written in green would cause user confusion. A compatible system reduces the amount of *information recoding* required of the user. High compatibility can be attained when the user is presented with nonconflicting information and by reinforcing standard expectations, matching output with expected user input, and presenting output in a directly usable form. Graphic symbols called *icons* can be used to represent menu selections. These are common examples of the application of the concept of compatibility.

Brevity

Both psychological theory and common experience suggest that there is an upper limit on the amount of information that a human mind can process in a given period of time. The amount of information the average person can hold in short-term memory is limited to about 7 or 8 *bits*. (Here, a bit represents a basic chunk of information.) For example, with difficulty a seven-digit number (e.g., 1735824) can be held in short-term memory.

In this case, each digit is considered to be a bit. The human mind always attempts to group items together and thus reduce the number of bits of information that must be remembered. For example, the number 217-582-1894 can be readily remembered by most persons because a process called *chunking* takes place. Chunking is the automatic collecting of information into groups by the brain.

Brevity is important because messages containing more than 8 bits of information even after chunking generally cannot be remembered and acted on. In addition, information should be presented in a fashion that is conducive to chunking. This is accomplished by placing similar information in the same general display location.

Flexibility

A good system can adapt to the skill level of the user. For example, naive users generally tend to be most comfortable with menu-driven systems. However, after the user becomes more proficient with the system, a direct command language is better because users find the menu system slow and awkward. A good system will allow for a smooth transition from one type of dialogue to another.

Response Time

A computer graphics system is usually installed in a location where users will be engaged in activities that require a high degree of concentration and creativity. In such a setting, even seasoned computer professionals tend to quickly forget the complexity of the tasks that the computer is performing and become impatient after only a few seconds. Current research indicates that the system should respond immediately to any user input and thus acknowledge the user's action. Furthermore, after the system acknowledges the user's action, no more than 3 to 6 s should pass before the system "updates" the user as to the status of the action that was requested. For example, if the computer is requested to compute the volume or area of an object on the display, a message such as "computing" should not be allowed to "hang" on the display for 10 s. A better interface would let the user know how the task was progressing.

Response time should also be consistent, particularly where data input from the keyboard is required. For example, some systems buffer keyboard entries and then, at random intervals, write the typed characters to the screen as time becomes available in bursts. The user, unaware of the processing that is taking place, often becomes confused as characters appear on the display at what appear to be random time intervals.

Consistency

All aspects of the user interface should be as consistent as possible. Similar information should always be presented in the same display area. The results of user actions should also have consistent results. For example, one popular system requires the user to enter either "E," "1," "7," "←," or "8" to exit the system at various stages of the dialogue. Because of this inconsistency, the user is forced to make note of which stage of the system is currently active, read the menu options, and then respond every time exiting is desired.

Operator Workload

All the concepts discussed so far—compatibility, brevity, flexibility, response time, and consistency—will serve to reduce operator workload. However, the system designer must also step back and examine the specific types of tasks the user will expect to perform. In general, graphics tasks tend to be rather complex. The designer should attempt to reduce workload by (1) using redundancy, (2) limiting the amount of information on the display at any time, and (3) shifting as much of the workload as possible off the user and onto the computer.

Many of the ergonomic concepts discussed so far have been incorporated into the user interfaces of popular systems. For example, most quality graphics systems now make use of icons (pictorial representations of concepts) and consistent display layout. While development of a good interface is often time-consuming and expensive, the long-term saving will usually justify the effort.

11.3 INFORMATION STRUCTURES

A well-designed computer graphics system requires a fast *dynamic information structure*. A dynamic information structure, as compared to a static information structure, changes with computation. For example an array, which is static, contains a fixed number and type of elements while a dynamic information structure such as a data base system changes. Prior to designing the information structure, the system designer must carefully examine the typical behavior of a user performing the types of tasks that will be expected. For example, the information structure that will be used for sketching will differ greatly from that of a system that will be used for computer-aided design (CAD) or business graphics. It is important to remember that, while the information structure need not follow the user's thinking patterns, the interface must. In meeting this requirement, the designer has available two basic methods of structuring information:

1. All graphics information can be in display memory, or
2. Graphics information may be stored as a command-data list (also called the *display file*).

Display Memory Only Information Structures

When all graphics information is stored in display memory, the system will typically be easier to develop and will react more rapidly because it does not have to store and convert commands and data to alter display memory. However, editing will be limited under certain conditions. For example, assume that the display shown in Fig. 11-1 is stored in display memory only. To move, rotate, or

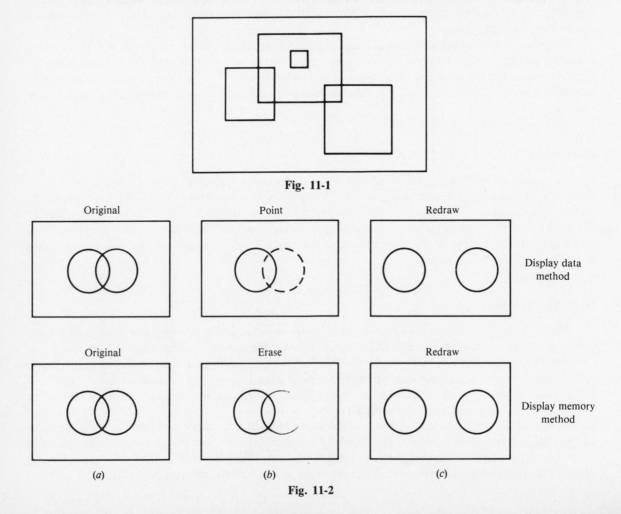

Fig. 11-1

Fig. 11-2

perform any other operation on one of the squares, the user would have to selectively erase lines and then redraw the object. By contrast, a dynamic information structure, representing the image as a command-data object, would allow the user to "point" to the square to be edited, then perform an editing operation. The differences between the tasks that would be required of the user are demonstrated in Figs. 11-2(*a*) through 11-2(*c*). Notice that, ultimately, the user is required to perform two tasks regardless of the type of information structure on which the system is based. However, the task of erasure is far more time-consuming and difficult than the task of pointing.

Command-Data Information Structures

For reasons suggested in the section on ergonomics, the dynamic command-data information structure will usually be more compatible with the needs of the user.

The command-data list (display file) and its associated display are shown in Figs. 11-3(*a*) through 11-3(*c*). The entire display is given the name "View." The user has developed the dynamic structure "House" and placed it at three locations. Each house is composed of the primitives "Triangle" and "Square." To provide the user with the full degree of flexibility that will be expected, editing must be allowed on several levels:

1. The user should be able to edit the basic definition of house, thus causing a global change to every instance of House.

2. The user should be able to edit each House individually.

3. The user should be able to form a nested structure called, in this case, "View."

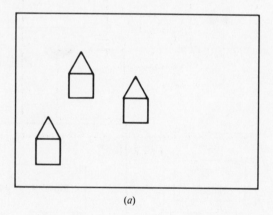

(*a*)

Frame Name: View

    House (*x, y, ...*)

    House (*x, y, ...*)

    House (*x, y, ...*)

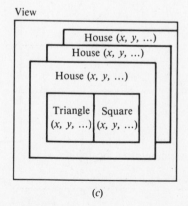

(*b*)   (*c*)

Fig. 11-3

The original information structure may be represented as shown in Fig. 11-4(*a*). Note that each occurrence of House is dynamically linked to the definition of "House." When the user makes a global change, the structure would be altered as shown in Fig. 11-4(*b*). In Fig. 11-4(*c*), an instance of House is locally edited. Notice that a new label must be assigned, "House 1." House 1 now becomes the entry node of a new structure that is only loosely bound to the original structure House, in the sense that they are both displayed in the same frame, View.

In the final example [Fig. 11-4(*d*)] the entire image is declared a single, nested structure, as indicated by the surrounding box, thus allowing the three houses to be treated as a single object.

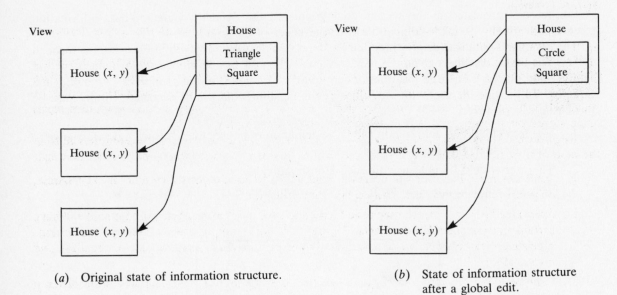

(*a*) Original state of information structure.

(*b*) State of information structure after a global edit.

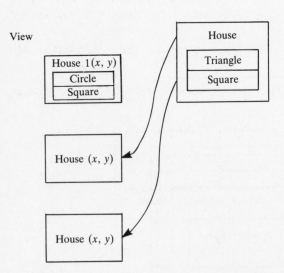

(*c*) State of information after local edit.

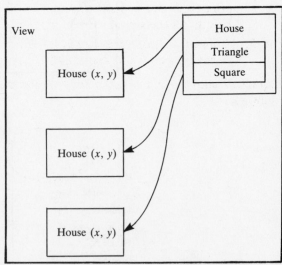

(*d*) State of information structure after declaring "View" a nested structure.

Fig. 11-4

11.4 FIELDS OF APPLICATION

Computer graphics is generally used for artistic creation, charting, drafting and design, or combination of the three. The tools developed in the previous chapters provide all the components required to build any combination of the three application types. However, before an application can be developed, the system designer must be able to communicate with the eventual end users of the system. It would be impossible to cover in one section all the terminology used in artistic creation, charting, and drafting and designing. The purpose of this section, therefore, is to introduce some of the terminology used by each of the various application user groups.

Artistic Creation

Actually, all types of application involve some degree of artistic creation. In this section, however, we will limit our discussion to typography and the development of presentations.

Often a user will wish to enhance a presentation with pictures, typically wanting to develop a professional-looking viewgraph, slide, or hard-copy chart. *Viewgraphs* are simply oversized slides designed for presentation on an overhead projector. A *slide show* designed by computer can either be converted to be shown on actual slides (created by exposing film to the output of the graphics system) or be stored on a magnetic disk and shown on a computer display.

Regardless of the type of output device used, the user will want to develop presentations without the help of a trained artist. Typically the user will ask for the following functions to meet that end.

1. *Basic objects.*   The user will normally want access to basic objects shown in Fig. 11-5 (circle, ellipse, square frame, line, dashed line, and triangle).

2. *Specialized objects.*   Each specialized field and each institution practicing that field will have certain unique specialized objects. Figure 11-6, for example, shows some of the various specialized symbols that would be required by electrical, mechanical, industrial, chemical, and civil engineers.

3. *User-definable objects.*   As discussed in the previous section, the user will often develop structures. These structures represent new symbols the user will use repeatedly at a given installation; an example of this is a company logo.

4. *Basic editing.*   The user creating a graphic will also expect to be able to erase lines, fill, or print (with and without patterns), move, delete, rotate, zoom, skew, elasticize, and mirror objects on the screen.

5. *Drawing.*   The ability to draw freehand lines should exist. In addition, the user should be able to change pen width and slant.

Equipped with these tools, the user should be able to create reasonably professional computer drawings.

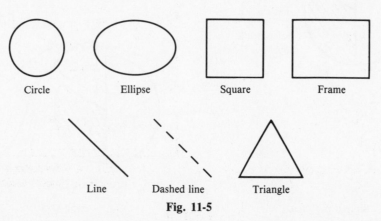

Fig. 11-5

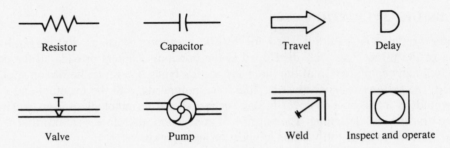

Resistor   Capacitor   Travel   Delay

Valve   Pump   Weld   Inspect and operate

Fig. 11-6

The user will often want to include labels, titles, and other types of graphics that require text. Many systems offer computer typography abilities which will allow the user to construct virtually any font, with full control over point size, pen slant, ascenders, descenders, and other typographic characteristics. While such systems are highly specialized, all graphics systems should give the user access to several font types and allow some degree of font modification.

Charting

The types of graphics which the user will want to enhance artistically are usually charts. The basic types of graphs and charts are as follows:

1. *Pie chart.* This is a graphic representation used to compare relative percentages (see Fig. 11-7). The graphics programmer can approach the development of a pie chart by building the chart (*a*) from a series of sectors or (*b*) by drawing a circle and then dividing it.

2. *Exploded pie chart.* To focus attention on a specific sector of a pie chart, the user usually breaks one sector of the pie slightly away from the others by offsetting its center [Fig. 11-8(*a*)].

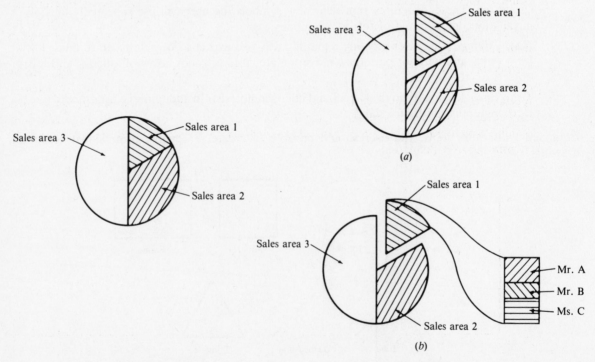

(*a*)

(*b*)

Fig. 11-7 Simple pie chart.   **Fig. 11-8**

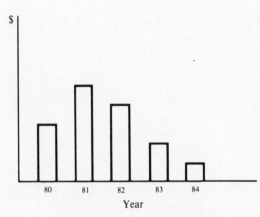

Fig. 11-9   Simple bar chart.

A more detailed graphic can be developed by breaking the exploded sector into several subpieces [Fig. 11-8(b)]. This type of graphic is constructed by drawing an exploded pie chart and then connecting it with lines or arcs to a rectangle divided by percentage into subpieces.

3. *Bar chart.*   This is used to represent comparative quantities, as are pie charts. However, bar charts allow another dimension to be compared [Fig. 11-9]. A bar chart is composed of two basic graphics components, axis and rectangles. The *axis* function is built from the line command as follows: (a) a horizontal line and a vertical line are drawn [Fig. 11-10(a)]; and (b) then a series of short lines, called *tick marks*, are drawn at regular intervals [Fig. 11-10(b)]. The spacing of tick marks is usually based on one of four basic graph types: normal-normal [Fig. 11-11(a)], log-normal [Fig. 11-11(b)], normal-log [Fig. 11-11(c)], and log-log [Fig. 11-11(d)]. The *rectangle* component is used to represent the quantities the user wishes to compare by varying rectangle height. The rectangles can be organized in three ways to develop three basic types of bar chart: the *simple bar chart* [Fig. 11-12(a)], the *clustered bar chart* [Fig. 11-12(b)], and the *stacked bar chart* [Fig. 11-12(c)]. Bar charts are commonly represented in both *vertical* [Fig. 11-13(a)] and *horizontal* [Fig. 11-13(b)] format.

4. *Pictogram.*   This is similar to the simple bar chart in which pictures and symbols are used to represent quantities [Fig. 11-14]. When the user develops a pictogram, typically a basic, specialized, or user-defined symbol will be used. Generally, axes are not used in pictograms. Instead, a key is given to show the value of each full symbol. In one of the easiest methods of building a pictogram, BITBLT graphics are used, allowing the user to build a pictogram simply by printing user-defined characters.

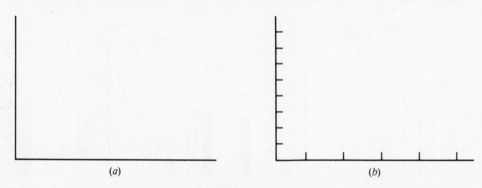

Fig. 11-10

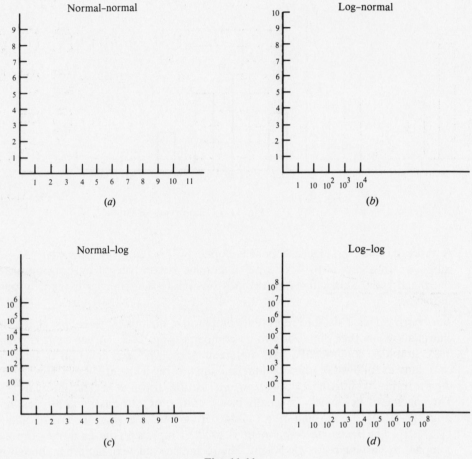

Fig. 11-11

5. *Line chart.*   This is used to represent continuous data. Three-dimensional line charts allow up to three variables to be expressed. Generally, the *x* axis represents time, the *y* axis the quantity being measured, and the lines themselves the quantities being compared. A line chart is constructed from either one or two basic components, depending on the characteristics of data being represented. If the data are linear, the line chart may be built from the line command only [Fig. 11-15(*a*)]. However, if the data are curvilinear, both the line and point plot commands will be needed [Fig. 11-15(*b*)]. The line chart is built by first drawing the axis and then plotting the quantities to be represented. As with the bar chart, the axis can have the tick marks placed in normal-normal, log-normal, normal-log, or log-log fashion.

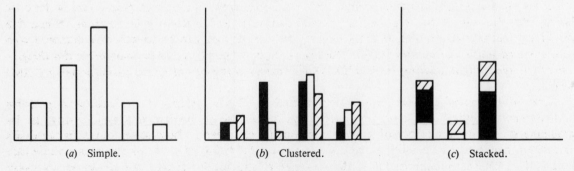

Fig. 11-12   Types of bar charts.

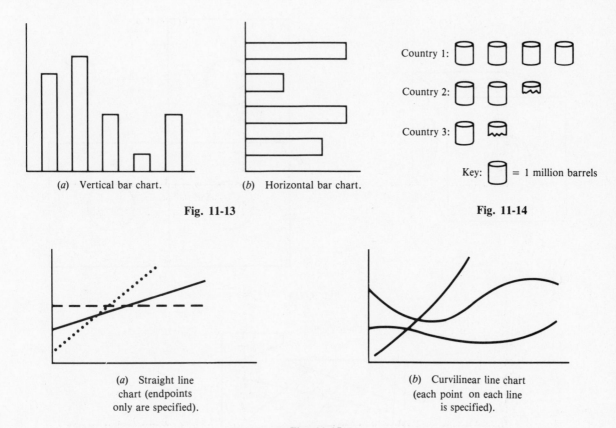

(a)   Vertical bar chart.   (b)   Horizontal bar chart.

Fig. 11-13

Country 1:
Country 2:
Country 3:

Key: = 1 million barrels

Fig. 11-14

(a)   Straight line
chart (endpoints
only are specified).

(b)   Curvilinear line chart
(each point on each line
is specified).

Fig. 11-15

Drafting and Designing

Engineers will generally need, in addition to charting and artistic creation capabilities, specific drafting, part description, and analysis functions. Engineers require a system that can show a part in many projections. While the computer system can easily transform three-dimensional objects, it is difficult to design an interface with which the user will be comfortable.

The interface the draftsperson will generally be most comfortable with will be based on the *glass* or *projection box* technique generally used in design [see Figs. 11-16(*a*) and 11-16(*b*)]. With this technique, the user will typically work within a three-coordinate–three-cursor system. As the user moves the input stylus, the movement is simultaneously projected in three planes.

Modern engineering graphics systems also allow the engineer or drafter to define rather than simply draw a part. When a part is defined, it allows the engineer to actually design the part with the system. Such systems, called *computer-aided design* (CAD) systems, tie together the "bill of materials" (a listing of component parts) and simulation with computer graphics. This is done by linking the drawing of the part to its physical attributes and machining instructions. When full machining instructions are linked to the object, the part defined can be directly manufactured with *computerized numerical control* (CNC) machinery. Such systems are called *computer-aided design–computer-aided manufacturing* (CAD/CAM) systems or *computer-integrated manufacturing* (CIM) systems.

One of the most popular capabilities offered by CAD systems is the ability to perform *finite-element analysis*. This allows the designer to simulate the mechanical behavior of a structure by modeling it as a finite number of simpler components (elements) whose states can be more easily calculated than would be possible by directly simulating the behavior of the structure as a whole (see Fig. 11-17). These simulations allow the designer to graphically display the results in an easily understandable graphic form.

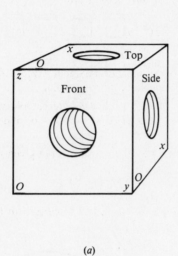

(a)

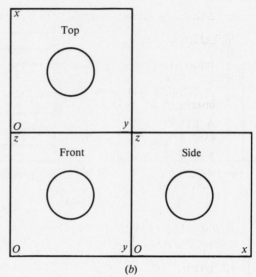

(b)

Fig. 11-16

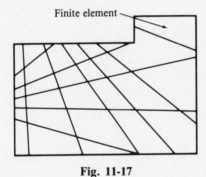

Fig. 11-17

Solved Problems

11.1 Development of a computer graphics system that meets the user's needs requires the systems designer to have knowledge in three areas besides computer graphics. What are they?

SOLUTION

These three areas are computer ergonomics, data structures, and the specific application field.

11.2 What five areas are generally considered when developing a user interface?

SOLUTION

The five areas considered when developing a user interface are brevity, operator workload, compatibility, flexibility, and response time.

11.3 Define the term "compatible" as it applies to computer graphics ergonomics.

SOLUTION

A compatible system is one which does not require the user to recode information.

11.4   Give three examples of an interface which would require information recoding.

SOLUTION

Information recoding would be required in the following types of interface:

1.   In a drafting application, if the user were required to enter data in terms of decimal feet (e.g., 12.5 ft) instead of the standard units (12 ft 6 in), the user would be forced to perform recoding.

2.   A STOP message printed in green on a color display would be contrary to stereotypic user expectations and require recoding because the user is conditioned to associate green with "go" and red with "stop."

3.   An error message such as "Fatal Error #3" requires recoding because the message is not given in a directly usable form.

11.5   Memory theory suggests that there is an upper limit to the number of bits of information the human brain can hold in short-term memory. What is that upper limit?

SOLUTION

The upper limit of human memory is approximately 7 or 8 bits of information.

11.6   Give an example of chunking.

SOLUTION

When presented with a number such as 5823714, the brain will generally attempt to group items together (chunking) in an effort to enhance short-term memory. In the example given above, most people will attempt to group the number as either 582-3714, 5823-714, or 58-23-714 in an effort to enhance short-term memory.

11.7   Give an example of how the concepts of brevity and chunking can be used to develop a better user interface.

SOLUTION

Like items should be grouped together in similar display areas. For example, all information concerning data input could be grouped in one area and all information concerning system status grouped in another. In addition, all information not required by the user at that moment should be removed from the display.

11.8   Why should the user interface be flexible?

SOLUTION

Flexibility of the user interface is necessary for two reasons. First, the intended user group may exhibit widely varied skills and expectations when first introduced to the graphics system. Users should be presented with an interface suited to those varied skills and expectations. Second, flexibility is required because users will learn as they spend time using the system. After a period of time, the users will become impatient with a system designed for naive users only.

11.9   Poor response times cause two major adverse effects. What are they?

SOLUTION

The user often becomes annoyed when the system provides no feedback for periods over 3 to 6 s and as a result may reject use of the system. Users also tend to have a higher error rate when the system does not react immediately and consistently to their actions.

11.10 What are the attributes of a good user interface? How may they be attained?

SOLUTION

A good user interface provides the user with the functionality required to complete tasks in a format that minimizes workload, exhibits flexibility, responds regularly and rapidly, and is consistent and compatible. These goals may be attained by designing the system so that the user's typical behavior will result in the correct system responses.

11.11 Compare static information structures with dynamic information structures.

SOLUTION

A static information structure is fixed. For example, an array is usually declared with a fixed number of elements of a specific data type. By contrast, a dynamic information structure will change with computation.

11.12 Why should the user's requirements be considered prior to designing a graphics system information structure?

SOLUTION

The user's requirements should be considered prior to designing the graphics system information structure because the type of information structure developed will greatly affect the user interface. Since the designer ultimately desires to build a usable system, the interface must reflect the user's typical behavior, which, in turn, will be reflected in the information structure design.

11.13 What two methods of structuring and storing information are available to the graphics system designer?

SOLUTION

Graphics information is typically structured and stored in one of two ways: (1) directly in display memory or (2) in the form of a command-data list (display file).

11.14 What is the major disadvantage of storing information structures in display memory only?

SOLUTION

It is difficult to edit because the system no longer recognizes discrete objects. Therefore, if a user tries to delete one of two overlapping squares, for example, each pixel must be individually erased.

11.15 Why is the command-data list generally better suited for engineering tasks?

SOLUTION

Engineers often have to move standard symbols when designing a system. For example, an electrical engineer will make frequent use of the following symbols:

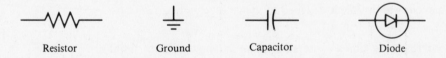

Resistor   Ground   Capacitor   Diode

The command-data list information structure would allow these symbols to be defined and then used repeatedly. The display-memory-only type of structure would require the engineer to redraw each symbol every time it was needed.

11.16 Describe how complex objects are built using command-data list information structures.

SOLUTION

Complex objects are built by dynamically linking together and naming simple graphics objects, such as lines, circles, squares, and triangles.

11.17 Describe the three levels of editing which a command-data list information structure should allow, and give an example of each.

SOLUTION

A command-data list information structure should allow global editing. For example, if a user has defined a complex object such as that shown in Fig. 11-18, it should be possible to change the object definition and as a result change all instances of that object.

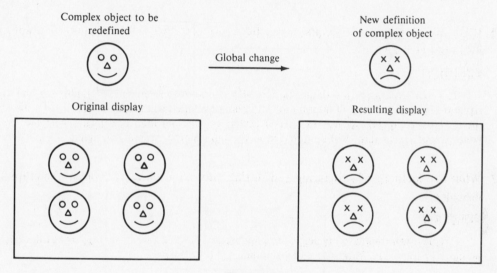

Fig. 11-18

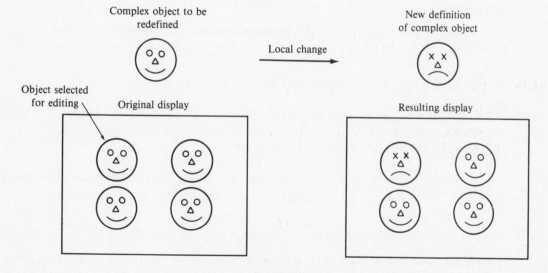

Fig. 11-19

The user should also be able to change a single instance of a complex object, thereby making a local change. For example, it should be possible to change the object definition of a single complex object (see Fig. 11-19) without affecting the other instances of that object.

Finally, the user should be able to construct new complex objects built from other complex objects. For example, it should be possible to link all the objects shown in Fig. 11-20 and define them as a single complex object.

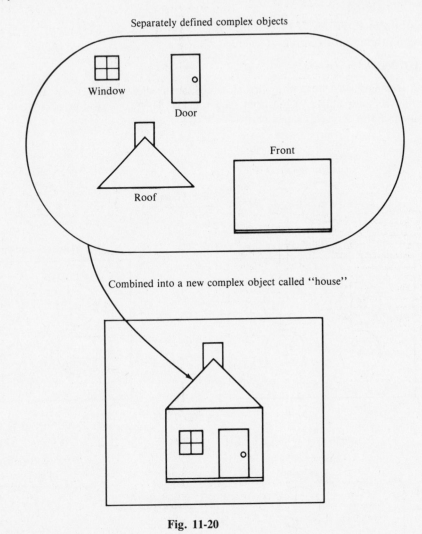

Fig. 11-20

11.18 Draw a diagram showing how the three levels of editing affect the information structure described in Prob. 11.17.

SOLUTION

Global edit is shown in Fig. 11-21(*a*), local edit in Fig. 11-21(*b*), and nested structure formation in Fig. 11-21(*c*).

11.19 What three basic application types are computer graphics used for?

SOLUTION

Computer graphics is used primarily for artistic creation, charting, and drafting and designing.

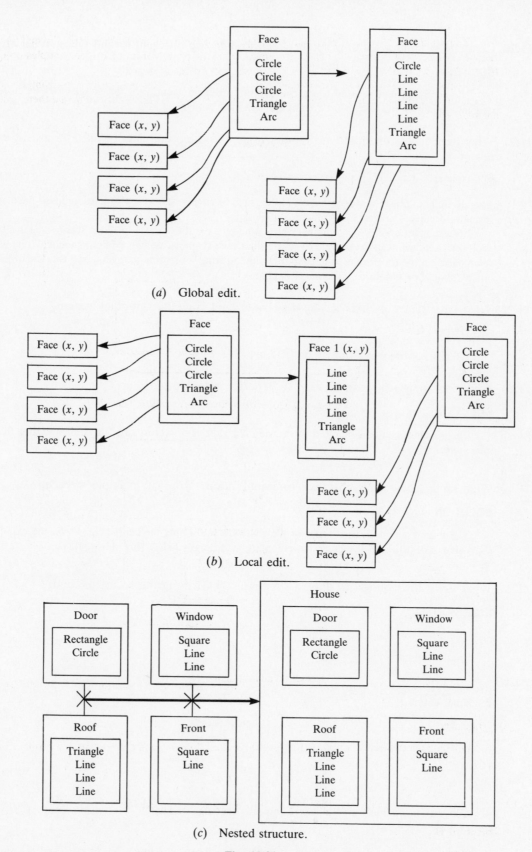

(a) Global edit.

(b) Local edit.

(c) Nested structure.

Fig. 11-21

11.20 Computers can be used to generate slide shows in two different format types. What are they?

SOLUTION

The computer can be used to expose film and print on acetate, or the images may be stored on a magnetic medium and shown on a computer graphics system.

11.21 What basic functions should a computer graphics system that is to be used for artistic creation possess?

SOLUTION

Users should have access to basic objects, such as circles, squares, and lines and also have access to specialized objects unique to a trade.

For example, an electrical engineer may want to have the symbol for a resistor (-⋁⋁⋁-) available. In addition, users will want to be able to create their own symbols, such as company logos. Users will need some basic editing tools, such as erasing, deleting, moving, mirroring, copying, and rotating objects and, finally, should be able to draw objects freehand.

11.22 What basic types of chart can be developed on a computer graphics system?

SOLUTION

Pie charts, bar charts, pictograms, and line charts.

11.23 What two approaches can be used to generate a simple pie chart?

SOLUTION

The pie chart can be generated by drawing (1) a series of sectors or (2) a circle and then dividing it into sectors with lines.

11.24 What three types of pie chart are commonly used? Draw an example of each.

SOLUTION

The three commonly used types of pie chart are the simple pie chart (Fig. 11-7), the exploded pie chart [Fig. 11-8(a)], and the exploded pie chart with detailed slice [Fig. 11-8(b)].

11.25 What steps are required to draw a simple pie chart using the sector method?

SOLUTION

There are five basic steps:

1. Print headings:

$$\text{Let } d_i = \text{value assigned to each data class}$$

2. Total data:

$$T = \Sigma d_i$$

3. Divide each data class value by the total:

$$P_i = \frac{d_i}{T}$$

4. Convert each value found in step 3 into a percentage of a circle:

$$P'_i = P_i 2\pi$$

5. Plot a sector for each data class, using the angle P'_i from step 4.

11.26 How would the solution to Prob. 11.25 have to be changed to create an exploded pie chart?

SOLUTION

The center point of the sector that is to be exploded would have to be moved away from the center point used for the other sectors.

11.27 What are the three basic types of bar chart? Draw an example of each.

SOLUTION

A simple bar chart is shown in Fig. 11-12(a), a clustered bar chart in Fig. 11-12(b), and a stacked bar chart in Fig. 11-12(c).

11.28 What steps are required to draw the positive x and y axes with a normal-normal scale?

SOLUTION

Let x be the desired length of the x axis and y the desired length of the y axis. The required steps are:

1. Select location of origin.
2. Draw a horizontal line from the origin to $(x, 0)$.
3. Draw a vertical line from the origin to $(0, y)$.
4. At the required interval I draw tick marks as follows.

x tick marks (let XI be a counter):

(a) Check to see whether last tick mark is drawn.
(b) Draw a line from (XI, Y_1) to (XI, Y_2). (This draws a tick mark at XI of length $Y_2 - Y_1$.)
(c) Increment XI.
(d) Go to step a.

y tick marks (let YI be a counter):

(a) Check to see whether last tick mark is drawn.
(b) Draw a line from (X_1, YI) to (X_2, YI).
(c) Increment YI.
(d) Go to step a.

11.29 What steps are required to generate a simple bar chart?

SOLUTION

1. Draw an axis with one tick for each data class to be represented.
2. At each tick mark, draw a rectangle with a fixed base and whose height is proportional to the data values.

11.30 How is a pictogram generated?

SOLUTION

There are two basic steps:

1. The number of full symbols to be drawn is found by dividing the value of a data class by the value assigned to each picture.
2. Any remainder from step 1 is used to determine what portion of a partial picture should be drawn.

11.31 What steps are required to plot a linear line chart?

SOLUTION

There are essentially two steps: (1) draw axis; and (2) for each pair of data points, draw a line from endpoint to endpoint.

11.32 If the data is curvilinear and represented by a function, what changes would be made to the solution to Prob. 11.31?

SOLUTION

Step 2 of Prob. 11-31 is replaced with the following: each point is found by evaluating the equation over the desired range of x values.

11.33 What are the special graphics needs of engineers and drafters?

SOLUTION

Generally engineers and drafters will require a system that can generate many views of an item. When using a CAD system, the engineer expects to be able to input part specifications, cutting speeds, and so on, along with a simple drawing of the part. Engineers and drafters also need a system that allows them to enter pictures in standard views and then perform simulations.

Supplementary Problems

11.34 It is estimated that the addition of a specific routine to a graphics system will decrease user errors by 10 percent. Currently there are 100 users, who are paid on the average $35,000/year, using the system. Analysis shows that each error takes approximately 10 s to correct and that there are approximately 250 errors made per day per user. The cost of developing the routine is estimated at $50,000.

    (*a*)   What is the current annual cost of errors?

    (*b*)   How long will it take for the additional routine to pay for itself?

11.35 What are two common mistakes made by system designers in an attempt to achieve brevity by eliminating information from the display that is not needed at the moment by the user?

11.36 What is wrong with a system that presents both of the following screens during a dialogue?

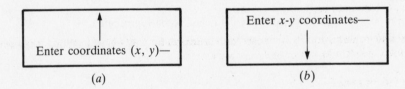

                        (*a*)   (*b*)

11.37 A particular system makes use of redundancy by printing STOP in a red octagon and sounding a tone every time the user is about to make a serious error. How much redundancy is used? What are the specific signals that warn the user to stop?

11.38 How can display density be reduced without reducing information density?

11.39 How can user workload be reduced by shifting activities from the user to the computer?

11.40 Does a computer graphics system information structure have to mimic the user's thought process? Why or why not?

11.41 Why is coding relatively simple when all graphics information is stored directly in display memory?

11.42 Why do graphics systems that store graphics information in display memory generally react more rapidly than those that do not?

11.43 What steps would be required to move a square defined by the command-data list method?

11.44 List some examples of computer graphics artistic creation applications.

11.45 What is a viewgraph?

11.46 Why are freehand drawings discouraged in applications using the command-data list information structure?

11.47 Define character font.

11.48 What is point size?

11.49 Show the steps that would be taken to generate a simple pie chart using the following data: $A = 100$, $B = 50$, and $C = 50$.

11.50 What steps would have to be added to the solution to Prob. 11.49 to generate an exploded pie chart with a detailed slice?

11.51 What modifications would be made to the solution to Prob. 11.28 in order to generate log-log axis?

11.52 How would the solution to Prob. 11.29 be modified to generate a stacked bar chart?

11.53 How would the solution to Prob. 11.29 be modified to generate a clustered bar chart?

11.54 How would Prob. 11.29 be modified to generate a horizontal bar chart?

11.55 Assuming that ⚲ is used as the picture in a pictogram, what steps would be taken to generate a pictogram for the following data? (Let each full picture = 100 people.) Number of people in city A is 1000; number of people in city B is 850.

11.56 What does CAD stand for?

11.57 What does CAM stand for?

11.58 What term and its acronym are often used as a synonym for CAD/CAM? Why is the use of this term as a synonym for CAD/CAM not entirely accurate?

11.59 What is a bill of materials?

11.60 What is finite-element analysis?

Chapter 12

Introduction to
Graphics Kernel System

12.1 INTRODUCTION

The graphics kernel system (GKS) was developed in response to the need for a standardized method of developing graphics programs. It represents a standard graphics interface with consistent syntax. Furthermore, GKS was designed so that it may be bound by means of subroutines to most common programming languages such as C, FORTRAN 77, PASCAL, and BASIC.

GKS represents a programming language in the sense that it presents the programmer with a consistent set of reserved words with specific language bindings used within a specific syntactical structure. For example, the GKS reserved word for plotting points is "POLYMARKER." (The reserved word POLYMARKER is followed by its corresponding parameters, n, X, Y, where n is the number of points, X is the array of the x coordinates and Y is the array of the y coordinates.) Thus the GKS statements

$$X(1) = 3 \quad Y(1) = 2$$
$$\text{POLYMARKER } (1, X, Y)$$

represent a language-independent command-data list that would plot the point (3, 2). In actual implementation with a programming language, in this case FORTRAN, the command-data structure would appear in this form:

$$\text{DIMENSION } X(1), Y(1)$$
$$X(1) = 3$$
$$Y(1) = 2$$
$$\text{CALL GPM } (n, X, Y)$$

(*Note*: In the BASIC implementation, an ampersand interpreter is used.)

It is important to remember that GKS presents a standardized body of consistent commands, procedures, and language bindings and syntax. This allows a GKS-based system to be portable and take advantage of improved algorithms. For example, a system using the slope method of line plotting (Chap. 3) could easily be upgraded to make use of Bresenham's line algorithm (Chap. 3).

To avoid confusion, from this point on only the GKS names of commands will be shown. For example, the FORTRAN implementation CALL GPM (n, X, Y), will be shown only as POLY-MARKER (n, X, Y).

12.2 GKS PRIMITIVES

The graphics kernel system is based on four basic primitives: POLYLINE, POLYMARKER, FILL AREA, and TEXT. The syntax of each of the primitives is as follows:

$$\text{POLYLINE } (n, X, Y)$$
$$\text{POLYMARKER } (n, X, Y)$$
$$\text{FILL AREA } (n, X, Y)$$

where n = number of data points
   X = X array
   Y = Y array

$$\text{TEXT } (x, y, \text{"string"})$$

where (x, y) = the starting coordinates for the string and "string" = the text that is to be output.

244

12.3 GKS PRIMITIVE ATTRIBUTES

Each GKS primitive can have many attributes, which are set with an index number and the SET command. For example, the default value for POLYLINE INDEX is 1. A POLYLINE INDEX of 1 generates a solid line. Therefore, if the X array $= (1, 4)$ and the Y array $= (2, 8)$, the following would generate a solid line from point $(1, 2)$ to point $(4, 8)$ (see Fig. 12-1).

SET POLYLINE INDEX (1)
POLYLINE (2, X, Y)

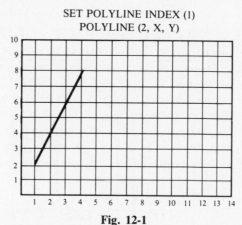

Fig. 12-1

The GKS POLYLINE INDEX of 2 creates a dashed line. Thus, using the same data, X array $= (1, 4)$ and Y array $= (2, 8)$, the following code would generate a dashed line from $(1, 2)$ to $(4, 8)$ (see Fig. 12-2).

SET POLYLINE INDEX (2)
POLYLINE (2, X, Y)

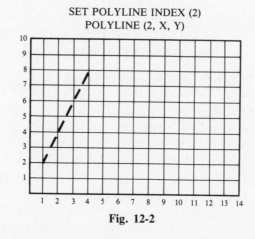

Fig. 12-2

In addition to the POLYLINE INDEX, there are also index settings for POLYMARKER, FILL AREA, and TEXT. In each case, the SET function INDEX is used to set the attributes of the command prior to its use. For example, using the data X array $= (2, 6, 6, 2)$ and Y array $= (2, 2, 6, 6)$ with the commands

SET POLYLINE INDEX (1)
POLYLINE (4, X, Y)

would appear as shown in Fig. 12-3(a),

SET POLYMARKER INDEX (3)
POLYMARKER (4, X, Y)

would appear as shown in Fig. 12-3(b), and

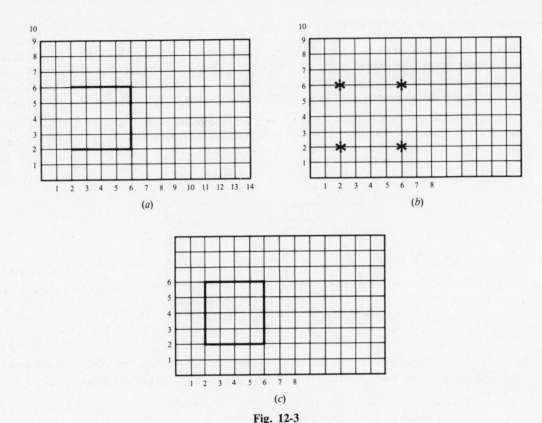

Fig. 12-3

SET FILL AREA INDEX (0)
FILL AREA (4, X, Y)

would appear as shown in Fig. 10-3(*c*). Note that FILL AREA always connects the first and last points in the array [Fig. 12-3(*c*)].

Other attributes supported by GKS allow the programmer to set the width of lines, change, color, select the style of marker used by POLYMARKER, and change the style and pattern used by FILL AREA. For example, the attribute value 3 for POLYMARKER gives an asterisk [see Fig. 12-3(*b*)].

Text font is selected with the SET TEXT INDEX (n) command. However, text has several other attributes which can be changed with other set commands. These set commands allow the programmer to select character height, slant, color, spacing, and angle. Unique to text are the SET CHARACTER UP VECTOR (X, Y) and the SET TEXT PATH (path) commands. CHARACTER UP VECTOR (X, Y) sets the slope at which text will be printed. Here, X represents the change in x, and Y, the change in y. For example

SET CHARACTER UP VECTOR (1, 1)
TEXT (2, 2, "HELLO")

would appear as in Fig. 12-4(*a*), while

SET CHARACTER UP VECTOR (1, 0)
TEXT (2, 2, "HELLO")

would appear as in Fig. 12-4(*b*).

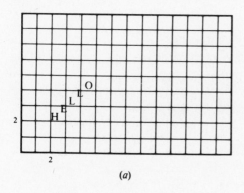

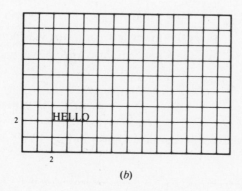

Fig. 12-4

SET CHARACTER PATH (UP)
TEXT (2, 2, "HELLO")

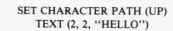

SET CHARACTER PATH (DOWN)
TEXT (8, 8, "HELLO")

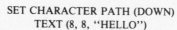

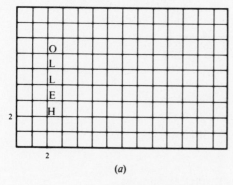

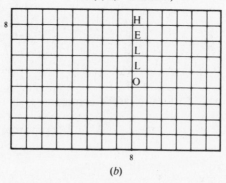

SET CHARACTER PATH (LEFT)
TEXT (8, 2, "HELLO")

SET CHARACTER PATH (RIGHT)
TEXT (2, 2, "HELLO")

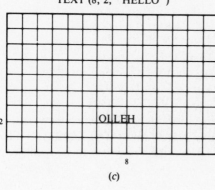

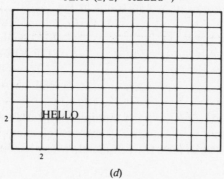

Fig. 12-5

The character path attribute sets the direction in which the characters will be printed. The programmer can set character path UP, DOWN, LEFT, or RIGHT [see Figs. 12-5(a) through 12-5(d)].

12.4 GKS WINDOW AND VIEWPORT

The format of the GKS VIEWPORT command is as follows:

$$\text{SET VIEWPORT } (n, x_1, x_2, y_1, y_2)$$

where   n = nth viewport

(x_1, y_1) = lower left corner of viewport in display coordinates

(x_2, y_2) = upper right corner of viewport in display coordinates

For example,

$$\text{SET VIEWPORT (n, 10, 100, 10, 100)}$$

would define the area shown in Fig. 12-6.

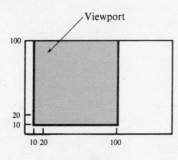

Fig. 12-6

The GKS WINDOW command is as follows:

$$\text{SET WINDOW (n, } x_1, x_2, y_1, y_2)$$

where   n = nth window

(x_1, y_1) = value of lower left corner of window in world coordinates

(x_2, y_2) = value of upper right corner of window in world coordinates

The WINDOW command thus specifies how data will be mapped onto the display. For example, the following would result in Fig. 12-7:

$$X(1) = 10, \ Y(1) = 10$$
$$\text{SET VIEWPORT } (1, 0, 20, 0, 10)$$
$$\text{SET WINDOW } (1, 10, 100, 10, 100)$$
$$\text{POLYMARKER } (1, X, Y)$$

As GKS supports multiple viewports and windows, a provision to indicate which viewport is to be written to is required. Viewport selection is done with the SELECT NORMALIZATION TRANS-FORMATION (n) command, where n represents the number of the viewport to be selected.

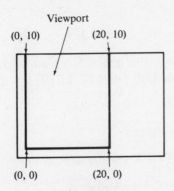

Fig. 12-7

12.5 GKS CLIPPING

The clipping function can be set to either of two states, CLIP or NOCLIP, and takes the following form: SET CLIPPING INDICATOR (ind), where "ind" equals either CLIP or NOCLIP.

Finally, viewports may be assigned priorities with the SET VIEWPORT INPUT PRIORITY (T1, T2, HIGHER) command. Note that viewports are assigned priorities relative to one another. This is done to prevent viewports from overlapping.

12.6 GKS PROGRAMMER PRIMITIVE CONSTRUCTION

While the four basic primitives supported by GKS—POLYLINE, POLYMARKER, FILL AREA, and TEXT—along with their attributes allow the programmer to construct a wide range of images, most developers would like to have access to some other commonly used primitives. For example, in a charting application, use of an axis command would be valuable.

When constructing commands, it is important to allow for future flexibility. For example, an axis command should allow control over tick mark intervals, length of tick marks, style of tick marks, length of axes, and axes intersection point. For the simplest case, no tick marks are used; the axes run the length of the current window and intersect at the origin. The resulting code for simple axes might appear as follows:

```
SUBROUTINE AXIS (X, Y)
DIMENSION XA(2) YA(2)
XA(1) = X(1)
YA(1) = 0
XA(2) = X(2)
YA(2) = 0
CALL GPL (2, XA, YA)
XA(1) = 0
YA(1) = Y(1)
XA(2) = 0
YA(2) = Y(2)
CALL GPL (2, XA, YA)
```

where X(1) = X MIN

X(2) = X MAX

Y(1) = Y MIN

Y(2) = Y MAX

GPL is the subroutine to draw a POLYLINE

12.7 GKS SEGMENTS

Any group of valid GKS code can be clustered together into a segment through the use of the CREATE SEGMENT (n) command. A segment listing is terminated with the CLOSE SEGMENT command.

The segment command is the GKS method of developing complex objects (see Chap. 11). For example, if a square were described with the coordinates arrays

$$X = (1, 2, 2, 1, 1) \qquad Y = (1, 1, 2, 2, 1)$$

the following sequence of commands would generate a segment for drawing a square:

```
CREATE SEGMENT (1)
POLYLINE (5, X, Y)
CLOSE SEGMENT
```

Finally, a segment is deleted with the DELETE SEGMENT (n) command, where n is the segment number.

12.8 GKS SEGMENT TRANSFORMATIONS

The graphics kernel system allows the user to rotate, scale, and translate segments through the use of the SET SEGMENT TRANSFORMATION (segment number, transformation matrix) command, where *segment number* is the number of the segment as defined in the CREATE SEGMENT routine, and *transformation matrix* is the 2×3 transformation matrix formed as follows:

EVALUATE TRANSFORMATION MATRIX (fx, fy, tx, ty, r, sx, sy, switch, MATRIX)

where   (fx, fy) = fixed point (center of operation)

       (tx, ty) = the x and y translation vector

           r = angle of rotation in rads

     (sx, sy) = *x* and *y* scaling factors

      switch = a parameter that tells the procedure to use either WC (world coordinates) or NDC (normalized device coordinates)

   MATRIX = 2×3 transformation matrix returned by the subroutine

Note: GKS was originally designed for two-dimensional renderings. Thus the 3×3 homogeneous form of the transformation matrix can be truncated to a 2×3 matrix because the third row provides no needed information in two dimensions.

12.9 GKS INPUT

The graphics kernel system allows many types of input devices to be used in conjunction with GKS-based software. The graphics kernel system sees all input devices as fitting into one of the following logical input device categories: Choice, Locator, Pick, String, Stroke, and Valuator.

Choice allows the user to select from a menu with a light pen, trackball, or similar device.

Locator is used for locating objects on the display.

Pick indicates when an object on the display has been located.

String allows keyboard input.

Stroke allows for continuous drawing with a device such as a tablet (magnetic or acoustical), light pen, or mouse.

Valuator allows world coordinate values to be entered from either a potentiometer or the keyboard.

12.10 MULTIUSERS

The graphics kernel system allows multiple users to work on a single application. Each user is allowed to see different portions of the entire picture by setting terminal windows. Each user is also allowed to share or make private alterations on a single terminal. Local experiments on workstations can thus be performed. This feature can be of great value on large engineering projects involving the simultaneous work of many drafters and engineers.

Finally, the GKS system allows each remote user's terminal and peripherals to be uniquely defined as a *workstation*. Therefore, one user could work with 1024×1024 pixel storage tube device, while another works on the same drawing with a 640×200 pixel raster device. Thus, GKS provides functionality needed to manage workstations and control the state of the graphics environment. As such, GKS represents more than just a subroutine library.

12.11 IMPLEMENTATION

All standards should be used in their most up-to-date version whenever a new application is developed. The latest version of GKS may be obtained through the American National Standards Institute (ANSI).

Solved Problems

12.1 What does GKS stand for?

SOLUTION

It is the acronym for graphics kernel system.

12.2 Why was GKS developed?

SOLUTION

It was developed because no widely accepted standards for graphics languages had evolved; only regional, de facto graphics standards were available. This made graphics code expensive to develop, because (*a*) only a few programmers were competent in any given language, and (*b*) new code had to be developed for every new piece of hardware to enter the market because language features often were dependent on specific hardware.

12.3 What does the GKS standard represent?

SOLUTION

The GKS standard represents a series of consistently defined graphics procedures and a syntax for passing information to and from these procedures. In addition, it provides the functionality for managing the graphics environment.

12.4 What are the four basic GKS output primitives?

SOLUTION

POLYLINE, POLYMARKER, FILL AREA, and TEXT.

12.5 By GKS convention, POLYLINE requires three parameters. What are they? What do they represent?

SOLUTION

POLYLINE requires the parameters n, X, and Y, where n represents the length of arrays X and Y, X represents the array of x coordinates and Y represents the array of y coordinates.

12.6 What would be the value of n in a POLYLINE statement using the data given in Prob. 12.7?

SOLUTION

The X and Y arrays both contain five elements. Therefore, n would equal 5.

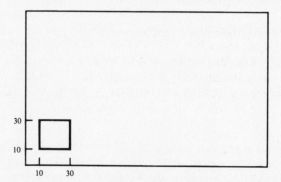

Fig. 12-8

12.7 (*a*)   What would be the GKS command to plot the square shown in Fig. 12-8?

(*b*)   What values would each of the elements in the *x* and *y* arrays have?

SOLUTION

(*a*)   POLYLINE (5, X, Y).

(*b*) $X = (10, 30, 30, 10, 10)$; $Y = (10, 10, 30, 30, 10)$.

12.8   Why were five coordinates necessary to describe the square drawn in Fig. 12-8?

SOLUTION

The graphics kernel system draws from coordinates (x_i, y_i) to coordinates (x_{i+1}, y_{i+1}); thus a line is drawn from $(10, 10)$ to $(30, 10)$ to $(30, 30)$ to $(10, 30)$ to $(10, 10)$. If the last coordinate were eliminated, the last line would not be drawn, and Fig. 12-8 would appear as shown in Fig. 12-9.

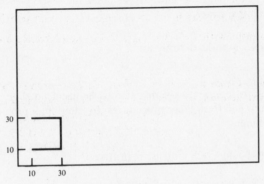

Fig. 12-9

12.9   By GKS convention, POLYMARKER requires three parameters. What are they? What do they represent?

SOLUTION

POLYMARKER requires the parameters n, X, and Y, where n represents the length of arrays X and Y, X represents the array of *x* coordinates, and Y represents the array of *y* coordinates.

12.10   By GKS convention, what three parameters are passed to the FILL AREA routine? What does each parameter represent?

SOLUTION

FILL AREA is passed n, X, and Y, where n represents the length (number of elements) of the X and Y arrays, X represents the *x* array, and Y represents the *y* array.

12.11   Are the following commands syntactically correct? Why or why not?

POLYLINE (M, XAR, YAR)
POLYMARKER (I, AR1 AR2)
FILL AREA (NUMBER, X ARRAY, Y ARRAY)

SOLUTION

All three statements are correct because the GKS standard only describes the definitions of specific commands and the order in which parameters are passed. Therefore, in the POLYLINE, POLYMARKER, and FILL AREA commands, the first variable always represents the number of elements in the *x* and *y* arrays, the second variable represents the *x* array, and the third variable represents the *y* array.

12.12 By GKS convention, the TEXT command is passed three parameters. What are they? What do they represent?

SOLUTION

The graphics kernel system is passed (x, y) and "string." Coordinates x and y represent the starting coordinates of a string that is to be printed. The term "string" represents the string of characters desired. For example TEXT (5, 29 "This is a test") would print "This is a test" starting at coordinate (5, 29).

12.13 What are GKS primitive attributes used for?

SOLUTION

Attributes are used to define exactly how a specific GKS output primitive will appear. For example, the attribute of POLYLINE can be changed to create a solid or dashed line.

12.14 (*a*)   What is the GKS format used to change GKS output primitive attributes?

(*b*)   Give an example with POLYLINE, POLYMARKER, and FILL AREA.

SOLUTION

(*a*)   The GKS format for changing attributes is, "SET command INDEX (n)," where command is the name of the primitive whose attributes are to be changed and n = the attribute number.

(*b*)   SET POLYLINE INDEX (2)
                             SET POLYMARKER INDEX (1)
                             SET AREA FILL INDEX (3)

12.15 What are the GKS commands required to generate the display shown in Fig. 12-10?

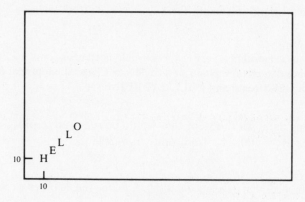

Fig. 12-10

SOLUTION

                SET CHARACTER UP VECTOR (1, 1)
                TEXT (10, 10, "HELLO")

12.16 What four values can the variable "path" take on in the command SET TEXT PATH (path)?

SOLUTION

"Path" can be set equal to UP, DOWN, LEFT, or RIGHT.

12.17 How would the display appear after the following commands were executed?

SET TEXT PATH (LEFT)

TEXT (8, 2 "HELLO")

SOLUTION

See Fig. 12-5(*c*).

12.18 Write a GKS subroutine to generate a rectangle segment.

SOLUTION

Since all GKS plot procedures must receive parameters as arrays, and rectangles are usually specified with two values, your procedure, say Rectangle (X, Y), must generate a five-element array. We will assume that the two arrays X and Y contain the coordinates of the diagonal corners of a rectangle. Thus

CREATE SEGMENT (1)

Rectangle (X, Y)

XA(1) = X(1)

YA(1) = Y(1)

XA(2) = X(2)

YA(2) = Y(1)

YA(3) = X(2)

YA(3) = Y(2)

XA(4) = X(1)

XA(4) = Y(2)

XA(5) = X(1)

YA(5) = Y(1)

POLYLINE (5, XA, YA)

CLOSE SEGMENT

12.19 How could a circle be plotted using GKS?

SOLUTION

Since Bresenham's algorithm is very fast, one would need to use only the POLYMARKER routine or the POLYLINE routine to plot the points of a circle (see Chap. 3). Note that the command "plot" would be replaced with the GKS command POLYMARKER.

12.20 Using the following data, list the steps that would be required to plot a simple pie chart without labels using GKS: $A_1 = 100$, $A_2 = 200$, and $A_3 = 300$.

SOLUTION

Using the sector algorithm developed in Prob. 3.26, the simple pie chart segment would be generated as follows:

1. Find the total of the data class values:

$$\text{Total} = A_1 + A_2 + A_3 \qquad 600 = 100 + 200 + 300$$

2. Calculate the percent of the circle in radians that each slice makes up by dividing each element by the total and multiplying by 2π:

$$\text{Slice } 1 = \frac{A_1}{\text{total}} * 2\pi = \frac{100}{600} * 2\pi = (1/3)\pi$$

$$\text{Slice } 2 = \frac{A_2}{\text{total}} * 2\pi = \frac{200}{600} * 2\pi = (2/3)\pi$$

$$\text{Slice } 3 = \frac{A_3}{\text{total}} * 2\pi = \frac{300}{600} * 2\pi = \pi$$

3. Set $\theta_1 = 0$. Starting at $\theta_1 = 0$ rad, $\theta_2 =$ slice 1.

4. Plot each sector for each slice based on the values found in step 2: $\theta_2 =$ slice $1 + \theta_1$; sector $(x, y,$ radius, $\theta_1, \theta_2)$ where x, $y =$ center of pie.

5. Reset the starting point for the next sector: $\theta_1 = \theta_2$.

6. Advance counter i: $i = i + 1$.

7. Check to determine whether the last slice was plotted. If not, go to step 4. Note that this routine will be repeated three times.

8. Close the segment.

Notice that the use of GKS does not affect the algorithm. Instead it provides a method for creating a pie chart primitive routine.

12.21 (*a*) What data would be required by a GKS axis routine?

(*b*) What might the procedure cell look like?

SOLUTION

(*a*) The axis routine will require the following data: x tick mark interval; y tick mark interval; and (x, y) location of the axis origin in screen coordinates. (*Note*: This should default to the lower left corner of the window.)

(*b*) Axis (x tick, y tick, x, y).

12.22 What steps would be required to develop a GKS axis segment?

SOLUTION

Open the segment; then

1. Draw x axis:

$$X(1) = \text{left side of window}$$
$$X(2) = \text{right side of window}$$
$$Y(1) = \text{vertical location of the } x \text{ axis}$$
$$Y(2) = Y(1)$$
$$\text{POLYLINE } (X, Y)$$

2. Draw y axis:

$$X(1) = \text{horizontal location of the } y \text{ axis}$$
$$X(2) = X(1)$$
$$Y(1) = \text{top of window}$$
$$Y(2) = \text{bottom of window}$$
$$\text{POLYLINE } (X, Y)$$

3. Draw x tick marks.

4. Draw y tick marks.

5. Close the segment.

12.23 What steps would be required to generate a simple bar chart using GKS?

SOLUTION

The two basic steps are:

1. Generate axes as developed in Prob. 12.22:

$$\text{Axis (X TIC, Y TIC, X, Y)}$$

2. For each data class, plot a rectangle where the height of each rectangle is equal to the data class value to be represented:

$$\text{Rectangle (X, Y)}$$

Refer to Prob. 12.18.

12.24 How could a line chart be generated using GKS?

SOLUTION

By two steps:

1. Generate axes:

$$\text{Axis (X TIC, Y TIC, X, Y)}$$

2. Plot line:

$$\text{POLYLINE (X, Y)}$$

where X and Y are arrays containing the data coordinates.

12.25 How could you set up the three viewports shown in Fig. 12-11 using GKS?

SOLUTION

These could be set up as follows:

$$\text{SET VIEWPORT } (1, 20, 170, 33, 166)$$
$$\text{SET VIEWPORT } (2, 200, 400, 100, 166)$$
$$\text{SET VIEWPORT } (3, 180, 275, 10, 66)$$

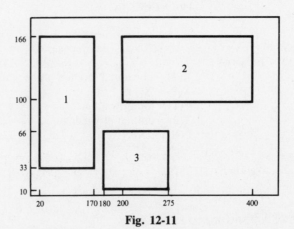

Fig. 12-11

12.26 How could the window corresponding to all the viewports created in Prob. 12.25 be set such that the lower left corner is at $(0, 0)$ and the upper right is at $(100, 100)$?

SOLUTION

These viewport windows could be set as follows:

$$\text{SET WINDOW } (1, 0, 100, 0, 100)$$

12.27 How is GKS clipping initialized?

SOLUTION

Clipping is initialized by using the SET CLIPPING INDICATOR (CLIP) command.

12.28 Which viewport in Fig. 12-12 has highest priority? Why? (Assume that clipping is on.)

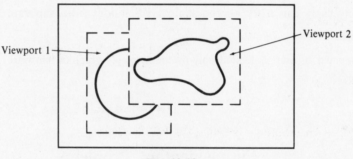

Fig. 12-12

SOLUTION

Viewport 2 probably has highest priority. This is indicated by the fact that the circle in viewport 1 is clipped by viewport 2 and because the closed figure in viewport 2 overlaps viewport 1.

12.29 How are new primitives built?

SOLUTION

Each new primitive is written as a command-data list comprised of some or all of the four basic GKS output primitives. An example is the rectangle primitive described in Prob. 12.18.

12.30 What is a segment?

SOLUTION

A segment is any object described by GKS commands and data that starts with the CREATE SEGMENT (n) command and terminates with the CLOSE SEGMENT command.

12.31 How are segments transformed in GKS?

SOLUTION

First, a transformation matrix is set up with the EVALUATE TRANSFORMATION MATRIX (fx, fy, tx, ty, r, sx, sy, switch, MATRIX) command. Next, the segment is transformed with the SET SEGMENT TRANSFORMATION (segment #, MATRIX) command.

12.32 What six classes of logical input device does GKS recognize? Describe each.

SOLUTION

The graphics kernel system recognizes input from

1. Choice—allows menu selections
2. Locator—locates objects on display
3. Pick—indicates which object or display has been located
4. String—allows keyboard entry
5. Stroke—allows continuous drawing
6. Valuator—allows world coordinate values to be entered.

12.33 How many users can work on the same GKS model from separate terminals at one time?

SOLUTION

The number of users is limited only by the available graphics hardware.

Supplementary Problems

12.34 What common programming language is GKS based on?

12.35 What do the elements in the POLYLINE X and Y arrays represent?

12.36 What do the elements in the X and Y arrays represent in the POLYMARKER command?

12.37 Assuming that $X = (10, 20, 20, 10)$ and $Y = (10, 10, 20, 20)$, the commands

SET FILL AREA INDEX (0)
FILL AREA (4, X, Y)

will generate a square with only four instead of five elements in the X and Y arrays. Why?

12.38 What are some of the types of attributes that can be changed for (*a*) FILL AREA, (*b*) POLYMARKER, and (*c*) POLYLINE?

12.39 What are some of the types of attributes that can be changed for TEXT?

12.40 What would a display look like after the following commands?

SET CHARACTER UP VECTOR (1, −1)
TEXT (10, 30, "HELLO")

12.41 How would the display appear after the following commands were executed?

SET TEXT PATH (LEFT)
SET CHARACTER UP VECTOR (1, 0)
TEXT (8, 2, "HELLO")

12.42 How would the display appear after the following commands were executed?

SET TEXT PATH (UP)
TEXT (2, 2, "HELLO")

12.43 How would the display appear after the following commands were executed?

SET TEXT PATH (DOWN)
TEXT (8, 8, "HELLO")

12.44 What effect would changing the algorithm that draws lines used in POLYLINE have on the solution to Prob. 12.18?

12.45 How could a sector be plotted using GKS?

12.46 How could Prob. 12.20 be modified to create an exploded pie chart?

12.47 How must Prob. 12.20 be modified to print labels for each slice?

12.48 What steps would be required to generate a simple bar chart using the following data?

Year	Sales
1980	100
1981	200
1982	300

12.49 What steps would have to be added to Prob. 12.48 in order to generate a clustered bar chart?

12.50 What steps would have to be added to Prob. 12.48 in order to generate a stacked bar chart?

12.51 Roughly sketch how a circle and a square mapped to each of the viewports generated in Prob. 12.25 would appear.

12.52 Explain why the circles and squares in Prob. 12.51 would be distorted.

12.53 What function do segments perform?

12.54 How are segments removed in GKS?

12.55 A 10×10 square is centered at coordinates $(50, 50)$ in world coordinates. Assuming that the square has been defined as segment 1: (a) translate the center to $(20, 20)$; (b) rotate the square $\frac{1}{2}\pi$ about its center; and (c) double the size of the square with respect to its center.

12.56 Do multiple GKS users interfere with each other?

12.57 Before implementation of GKS, what should the head designer do?

Appendix 1

Mathematics for Two-Dimensional Graphics

A1.1 INTRODUCTION

The key to understanding how geometric objects can be described and manipulated within a computer graphics system lies in understanding the interplay between geometry and numbers. While we have an innate geometric intuition which enables us to understand verbal descriptions such as *line*, *angle*, and *shape* and descriptions of the manipulation of objects (*rotating*, *shifting*, *distorting*, etc.), we also have the computer's ability to manipulate numbers. The problem then is to express our geometric ideas in numeric form so that the computer can do our bidding.

A *coordinate system* provides a framework for translating geometric ideas into numerical expressions. We start with our intuitive understanding of the concept of a two-dimensional plane.

A1.2 THE TWO-DIMENSIONAL CARTESIAN COORDINATE SYSTEM

In a two-dimensional plane, we can pick any point and single it out as a reference point called the *origin*. Through the origin we construct two perpendicular number lines called *axes*. These are traditionally labeled the x axis and the y axis. An orientation or sense of the plane is determined by the positions of the positive sides of the x and y axes. If a counterclockwise rotation of 90° about the origin aligns the positive x axis with the positive y axis, the coordinate system is said to have a *right-handed* orientation [see Fig. A1-1(a)]; otherwise, the coordinate system is called *left-handed* [see Fig. A1-1(b)].

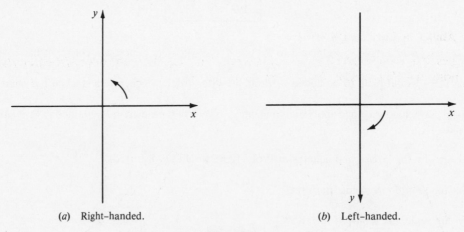

(a) Right–handed.   (b) Left–handed.

Fig. A1-1

The system of lines perpendicular to the x axis and perpendicular to the y axis forms a rectangular grid over the two-dimensional plane. Every point P in the plane lies at the intersection of exactly one line perpendicular to the x axis and one line perpendicular to the y axis. The number pair (x, y) associated with the point P is called the *Cartesian coordinates* of P. In this way every point in the plane is assigned a pair of coordinates (see Fig. A1-2).

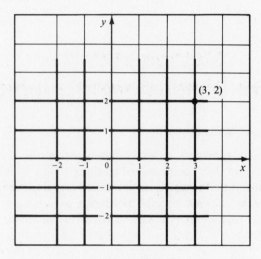

Fig. A1-2

Measuring Distances in Cartesian System

The distance between any two points P_1 and P_2 with coordinates (x_1, y_1) and (x_2, y_2) can be found with the formula

$$D = \sqrt{(x_2 - x_1)^2 + (y_2 - y_1)^2}$$

The length of a line segment can be measured by finding the distance between the endpoints of the segment using the formula given in Example 1.

EXAMPLE 1. The length of the line segment joining points $P_0(-1, 2)$ and $P_1(3, 5)$ can be found by

$$D = \sqrt{(5 - 2)^2 + [3 - (-1)]^2} = \sqrt{3^2 + 4^2} = 5$$

Measuring Angles in Cartesian System

The angles of a triangle can be measured in terms of the lengths of the sides of the triangle (see Fig. A1-3), by using the Law of Cosines, which is stated as

$$c^2 = a^2 + b^2 - 2ab (\cos \theta)$$

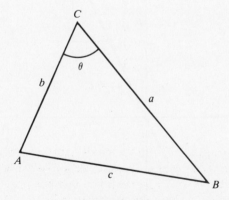

Fig. A1-3

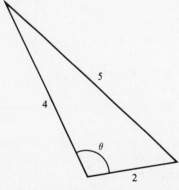

Fig. A1-4

EXAMPLE 2. Refer to Fig. A1-4. To find the angle θ, we use the Law of Cosines:

$$5^2 = 4^2 + 2^2 - 2(4)(2)\cos\theta \quad \text{or} \quad \cos\theta = \frac{-5}{16} \quad \text{so} \quad \theta = 108.21°$$

The angle formed by two intersecting lines can be measured by forming a triangle and applying the Law of Cosines.

Describing a Line in Cartesian System

The line is a basic concept of geometry. In a coordinate system, the description of a line involves an equation which enables us to find the coordinates of all those points which make up the line. The fact that a line is straight is incorporated in the quantity called the *slope m* of the line. Here $m = \tan\theta$, where θ is the angle formed by the line and the positive x axis.

From Fig. A1-5 we see that $\tan\theta = \Delta y/\Delta x$. This gives an alternate formula for the slope: $m = \Delta y/\Delta x$.

EXAMPLE 3. The slope of the line passing through the points $P_0(-1, 2)$ and $P_1(3, 5)$ is found by

$$\Delta y = 5 - 2 = 3 \qquad \Delta x = 3 - (-1) = 4$$

so $m = \Delta y/\Delta x = \frac{3}{4}$. Angle θ is found by $\tan\theta = m = \frac{3}{4}$ or $\theta = 36.87°$.

The straightness of a line is expressed by the fact that the slope of the line is the same regardless of which two points are used to calculate it. This enables us to find the equation of a line.

EXAMPLE 4. To find the equation of the line whose slope is 2 and passes through the point $P_0(1, 2)$, let $P(x, y)$ be any point on the line. The slope is the same regardless of which two points are used in calculating it. Using P and P_0, we obtain

$$\Delta y = y - 2 \qquad \Delta x = x - 1$$

so

$$m = \frac{\Delta y}{\Delta x} \quad \text{or} \quad 2 = \frac{y-2}{x-1}$$

Solving, we have $y = 2x$ (see Fig. A1-6).

Every line has an equation which can be put in the form $y = mx + b$, where m is the slope of the line and the point $(0, b)$ is the y intercept of the line (the point where the line intercepts the y axis).

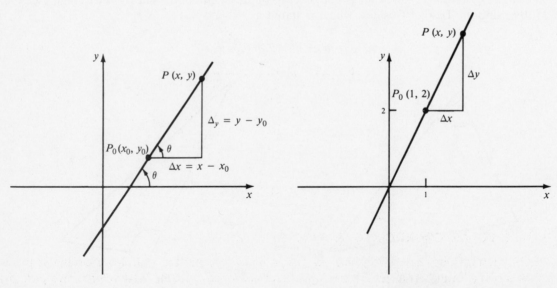

Fig. A1-5   Fig. A1-6

Curves and Parametric Equations

The equation of a curve is a mathematical expression which enables us to determine the coordinates of the points that make up the curve.

EXAMPLE 5. The parametric equation of a circle of radius r and center at the origin $(0, 0)$ can be written as $x = r \cos t$ and $y = r \sin t$, where t lies in the interval $0 \le t \le 2\pi$.

The equation of a circle of radius r whose center lies at the point (h, k) is

$$(x - h)^2 + (y - k)^2 = r^2$$

It is often more convenient to write the equation of a curve in parametric form; that is

$$x = f(t) \qquad y = g(t)$$

The parametric equations of a line can be written in the form (Probs. A1.21 and A1.23)

$$x = at + x_0 \qquad y = bt + y_0$$

A parameter t might be regarded as representing the "moment" at which the curve arrives at the point (x, y).

A geometric curve consists of an infinite number of points. Thus any plot of such a curve can only approximate its real shape. Plotting a curve requires the calculation of the x and y coordinates of a certain number of the points of the curve and the placing of these points on the coordinate system. The more points plotted, the better the approximation to the actual shape. This process of calculating coordinates and plotting the subsequent points is best done by computer.

EXAMPLE 6. Plot five points of the equations $x = t$, $y = t^2$ for t in the interval $[-1, 1]$.

t	-1	$-\frac{1}{2}$	0	$\frac{1}{2}$	1
x	-1	$-\frac{1}{2}$	0	$\frac{1}{2}$	1
y	1	$\frac{1}{4}$	0	$\frac{1}{4}$	1

Plotting (x, y) gives Fig. A1-7. We can approximate the actual curve by joining the plotted points by line segments.

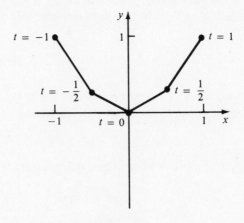

Fig. A1-7

A1.3 THE POLAR COORDINATE SYSTEM

The Cartesian coordinate system is only one of many schemes for attaching coordinates to the points of a plane. Another useful system is the *polar coordinate system*. To develop it, we pick any point in the plane and call it the origin. Through the origin we choose any *ray* (half-line) as the *polar*

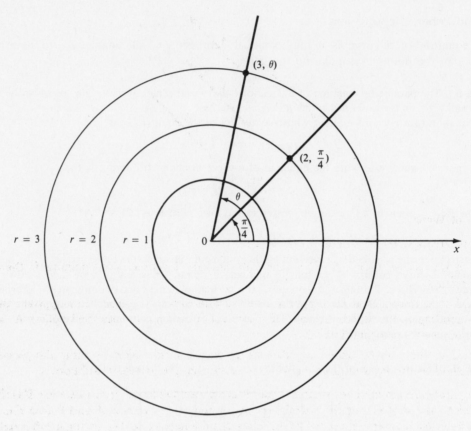

Fig. A1-8

axis. Any point in the plane can be located at the intersection of a circle of radius r and a ray from the origin making an angle θ with the polar axis (see Fig. A1-8).

The polar coordinates of a point are given by the pair (r, θ). The polar coordinates of a point are *not* unique. This is because the addition or subtraction of any multiple of 2π (360°) to θ describes the same ray as that described by θ.

Changing Coordinate Systems

How are the Cartesian coordinates of a point related to the polar coordinates of that point? If (r, θ) are the polar coordinates of point P, the Cartesian coordinates (x, y) are given by

$$x = r \cos \theta \qquad y = r \sin \theta$$

Conversely, the polar coordinates of a point whose Cartesian coordinates are known can be found by

$$r^2 = x^2 + y^2 \qquad \theta = \arctan \frac{y}{x}$$

A1.4 VECTORS

Vectors provide a link between geometric reasoning and arithmetic calculation. A vector is represented by a family of directed line segments that all have the same length or magnitude. That is, any two line segments pointing in the same direction and having the same lengths are considered to be the same vector, regardless of their location (see Fig. A1-9).

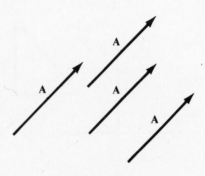

Fig. A1-9

Properties of Vectors

Vectors have special arithmetic properties:

1. If **A** is a vector, then $-$**A** is a vector with the same length as **A** but pointing in the opposite direction.

2. If **A** is a vector, then k**A** is a vector whose direction is the same as or opposite that of **A**, depending on the sign of the number k, and whose length is k times the length of **A**. This is an example of scalar multiplication.

3. Two vectors can be added together to produce a third vector by using the *parallelogram method* or the *head-to-tail method*. This is an example of vector addition.

In the parallelogram method, vectors **A** and **B** are placed tail to tail. Their sum **A** + **B** is the vector determined by the diagonal of the parallelogram formed by the vectors **A** and **B** (see Fig. A1-10).

In the head-to-tail method, the tail of **B** is placed at the head of **A**. The vector **A** + **B** is determined by the line segment pointing from the tail of **A** to the head of **B** (see Fig. A1-11).

Both methods of addition are equivalent, but the head-to-tail is easier to use when adding several vectors.

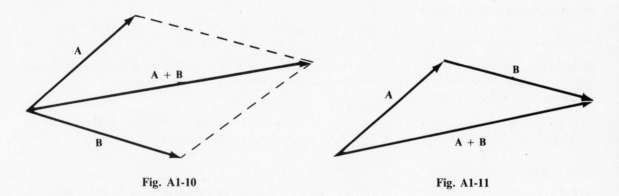

Fig. A1-10   Fig. A1-11

Coordinate Vectors and Components

In a Cartesian coordinate system, vectors having lengths equal to 1 and pointing in the positive direction along the x and y coordinate axes are called the *natural coordinate vectors* and are designated as **I** and **J** (see Fig. A1-12).

By use of scalar multiplication and vector addition, any vector **V** can be written as a linear combination of the natural coordinate vectors. That is, we can find numbers a and b so that **V** = a**I** + b**J**. The numbers $[a, b]$ are called the *components* of **V**. The components of a vector can be determined from the coordinates of the head and the coordinates of the tail of the vector. If (h_x, h_y)

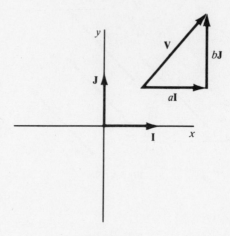

Fig. A1-12

and (t_x, t_y) are the coordinates of the head and the tail, respectively, the components of **V** are given by

$$a = h_x - t_x \qquad b = h_y - t_y$$

Notice that if the tail of **V** is placed at the origin, the components of the vector are the coordinates of the head of **V**.

The introduction of components allows us to translate the geometric properties of vectors into computational properties. If the vector **A** has components $[x_1, y_1]$ and the vector **B** has components $[x_2, y_2]$, the length of **A**, denoted as $|\mathbf{A}|$, can be computed by

$$|\mathbf{A}| = \sqrt{x_1^2 + y_1^2}$$

To perform scalar multiplication by a number c, we have

$$c\mathbf{A} = cx_1\mathbf{I} + cy_1\mathbf{J}$$

and to perform vector addition

$$\mathbf{A} + \mathbf{B} = (x_1 + x_2)\mathbf{I} + (y_1 + y_2)\mathbf{J}$$

EXAMPLE 7. Find the components of the vector **A** whose tail is at $P_1(1, 2)$ and whose head is at $P_2(3, 5)$ (see Fig. A1-13). To find the components, we shift the tail of **A** to the origin. The head is at

$$x = 3 - 1 = 2 \qquad y = 5 - 2 = 3$$

Thus $\mathbf{A} = 2\mathbf{I} + 3\mathbf{J}$. The length of **A** is

$$|\mathbf{A}| = \sqrt{2^2 + 3^2} = \sqrt{13}$$

If $\mathbf{B} = -3\mathbf{I} + 2\mathbf{J}$, then $\mathbf{A} + \mathbf{B} = (2 - 3)\mathbf{I} + (3 + 2)\mathbf{J} = -\mathbf{I} + 5\mathbf{J}$.

The Dot Product

The dot product $\mathbf{A} \cdot \mathbf{B}$ is the translation of the Law of Cosines into the language of vectors. It is defined as

$$\mathbf{A} \cdot \mathbf{B} = |\mathbf{A}|\,|\mathbf{B}|\cos\theta$$

where θ is the smaller angle between the vectors **A** and **B** (see Fig. A1-14). If **A** has components $[x_1, y_1]$ and **B** has components $[x_2, y_2]$, then $\mathbf{A} \cdot \mathbf{B} = x_1x_2 + y_1y_2$ (componentswise multiplication). (*Note*: since $\cos 90° = 0$, two nonzero vectors **A** and **B** are perpendicular if and only if $\mathbf{A} \cdot \mathbf{B} = 0$.)

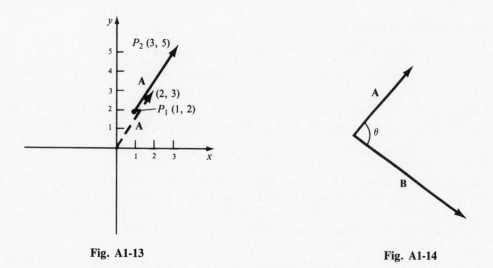

Fig. A1-13   Fig. A1-14

EXAMPLE 8. To find the angle θ between the vectors $\mathbf{A} = 2\mathbf{I} + 3\mathbf{J}$ and $\mathbf{B} = \mathbf{J}$, we use the definition of the dot product to find

$$\cos \theta = \frac{\mathbf{A} \cdot \mathbf{B}}{|\mathbf{A}||\mathbf{B}|}$$

$$\mathbf{A} \cdot \mathbf{B} = (2\mathbf{I} + 3\mathbf{J}) \cdot (0\mathbf{I} + \mathbf{J}) = 2 \cdot 0 + 3 \cdot 1 = 3$$

$$|\mathbf{A}| = \sqrt{2^2 + 3^2} = \sqrt{13} \qquad |\mathbf{B}| = \sqrt{0^2 + 1^2} = 1$$

So

$$\cos \theta = \frac{3}{\sqrt{13}} \qquad \text{and} \qquad \theta = 33.69°$$

A1.5   MATRICES

A *matrix* is a rectangular array or table of numbers, arranged in rows and columns. The notation a_{ij} is used to designate the matrix entry at the intersection of row i with column j (see Fig. A1-15).

The *size* or *dimension* of a matrix is indicated by the notation $m \times n$, where m is the number of rows in the matrix and n is the number of columns.

A matrix can be used as an organizational tool to represent the information content of data in tabular form. For example, a polygonal figure can be represented as an ordered array of the coordinates of its vertices. The geometric transformations used in computer graphics can also be represented by matrices.

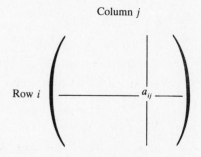

Fig. A1-15

Arithmetic Properties of Matrices

Examples of these properties are as follows:

1. *Scalar multiplication.* The matrix $k\mathbf{A}$ is the matrix obtained by multiplying every entry of $\mathbf{A}$ by the number k.

2. *Matrix addition.* Two $m \times n$ matrices $\mathbf{A}$ and $\mathbf{B}$ can be added together to form a new $m \times n$ matrix $\mathbf{C}$ whose entries are the sum of the corresponding entries of $\mathbf{A}$ and $\mathbf{B}$. That is,

$$c_{ij} = a_{ij} + b_{ij}$$

3. *Matrix multiplication.* An $m \times p$ matrix $\mathbf{A}$ can be multiplied by a $p \times n$ matrix $\mathbf{B}$ to form an $m \times n$ matrix $\mathbf{C}$. The entry c_{ij} is found by taking the dot product of the i row of $\mathbf{A}$ with the j column of $\mathbf{B}$ (see Fig. A1-16). So $c_{ij} = (\text{row } i) \cdot (\text{column } j) = a_{i1}b_{1j} + a_{i2}b_{2j} + \cdots + a_{im}b_{mj}$. Matrix multiplication is not commutative in general. So $\mathbf{AB} \neq \mathbf{BA}$. Matrix multiplication is also called *matrix concatenation*.

4. *Matrix transpose.* The transpose of a matrix $\mathbf{A}$ is a matrix, denoted as $\mathbf{A}^T$, formed by exchanging the rows and columns of $\mathbf{A}$. If $\mathbf{A}$ is an $m \times n$ matrix, then $\mathbf{A}^T$ is an $n \times m$ matrix. A matrix is said to be symmetrical if $\mathbf{A} = \mathbf{A}^T$.

Two basic properties of the transpose operation are (1) $(\mathbf{A} + \mathbf{B})^T = \mathbf{A}^T + \mathbf{B}^T$ and (2) $(\mathbf{AB})^T = \mathbf{B}^T\mathbf{A}^T$.

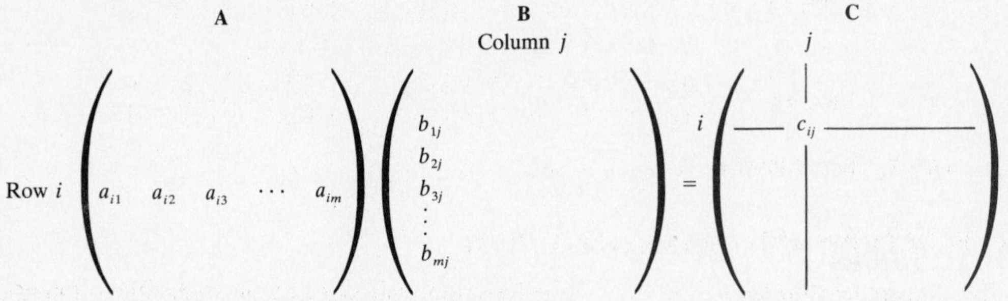

Fig. A1-16

EXAMPLE 9.

$$\mathbf{A} = \begin{pmatrix} 3 & 2 & 5 \\ 1 & -1 & 2 \end{pmatrix} \quad \text{and} \quad \mathbf{B} = \begin{pmatrix} -1 & 0 \\ 2 & 3 \\ 1 & 2 \end{pmatrix}$$

$$-2\mathbf{A} = -2\begin{pmatrix} 3 & 2 & 5 \\ 1 & -1 & 2 \end{pmatrix} = \begin{pmatrix} -6 & -4 & -10 \\ -2 & 2 & -4 \end{pmatrix}$$

$$\mathbf{AB} = \begin{pmatrix} 3 & 2 & 5 \\ 1 & -1 & 2 \end{pmatrix}\begin{pmatrix} -1 & 0 \\ 2 & 3 \\ 1 & 2 \end{pmatrix} = \begin{pmatrix} [3 \cdot (-1)] + (2 \cdot 2) + (5 \cdot 1) & (3 \cdot 0) + (2 \cdot 3) + (5 \cdot 2) \\ [1 \cdot (-1)] + [(-1) \cdot 2] + (2 \cdot 1) & (1 \cdot 0) + [(-1) \cdot 3] + (2 \cdot 2) \end{pmatrix}$$

$$= \begin{pmatrix} 6 & 16 \\ -1 & 1 \end{pmatrix}$$

$$\mathbf{A}^T = \begin{pmatrix} 3 & 1 \\ 2 & -1 \\ 5 & 2 \end{pmatrix}$$

Matrix Inversion and the Identity Matrix

The $n \times n$ matrix whose entries along the main diagonal are all equal to 1 and all other entries are 0 is called the *identity matrix* and is denoted by $\mathbf{I}$ (Fig. A1-17).

If $\mathbf{A}$ is also an $n \times n$ matrix, then $\mathbf{AI} = \mathbf{IA} = \mathbf{A}$. That is, multiplication by the identity matrix $\mathbf{I}$ leaves the matrix $\mathbf{A}$ unchanged. Therefore, multiplication by the identity matrix is analogous to multiplication of a real number by 1.

An $n \times n$ matrix $\mathbf{A}$ is said to be *invertible* or to have an *inverse* if there can be found an $n \times n$ matrix, denoted as $\mathbf{A}^{-1}$, such that $\mathbf{A}^{-1}\mathbf{A} = \mathbf{AA}^{-1} = \mathbf{I}$. The inverse matrix, if there is one, will be unique.

$$\mathbf{I} = \begin{pmatrix} 1 & 0 & 0 & \cdots & 0 \\ 0 & 1 & 0 & \cdots & 0 \\ 0 & 0 & 1 & \cdots & 0 \\ \vdots & & & & \vdots \\ 0 & 0 & 0 & \cdots & 1 \end{pmatrix}$$

Fig. A1-17

EXAMPLE 10.

$$\mathbf{A} = \begin{pmatrix} 1 & 0 \\ 2 & 1 \end{pmatrix} \quad \text{and} \quad \mathbf{B} = \begin{pmatrix} 1 & 0 \\ -2 & 1 \end{pmatrix}$$

Then

$$\mathbf{AB} = \begin{pmatrix} 1 & 0 \\ 2 & 1 \end{pmatrix} \cdot \begin{pmatrix} 1 & 0 \\ -2 & 1 \end{pmatrix} = \begin{pmatrix} 1 \cdot 1 + 0 \cdot (-2) & 1 \cdot 0 + 0 \cdot 1 \\ 2 \cdot 1 + 1 \cdot (-2) & 2 \cdot 0 + 1 \cdot 1 \end{pmatrix} = \begin{pmatrix} 1 & 0 \\ 0 & 1 \end{pmatrix}$$

and

$$\mathbf{BA} = \begin{pmatrix} 1 & 0 \\ -2 & 1 \end{pmatrix} \cdot \begin{pmatrix} 1 & 0 \\ 2 & 1 \end{pmatrix} = \begin{pmatrix} 1 \cdot 1 + 0 \cdot 2 & 1 \cdot 0 + 0 \cdot 1 \\ -2 \cdot 1 + 1 \cdot 2 & -2 \cdot 0 + 1 \cdot 1 \end{pmatrix} = \begin{pmatrix} 1 & 0 \\ 0 & 1 \end{pmatrix}$$

So $\mathbf{BA} = \mathbf{AB} = \mathbf{I}$. Thus $\mathbf{B}$ must be $\mathbf{A}^{-1}$.

A1.6 FUNCTIONS AND TRANSFORMATIONS

The concept of a *function* is at the very heart of mathematics and the application of mathematics as a tool for modeling the real world. Stated simply, a function is any process or program which accepts an input and produces a unique output according to a definite rule. Although a function is most often regarded in mathematical terms, this need not be the case. The concept can be usefully extended to include processes described in nonmathematical ways, such as a chemical formula, a recipe or a prescription, and such related concepts as a computer subroutine or a program module. All convey the idea of changing an input to an output. Some synonyms for the word function are *operator*, *mapping*, and *transformation*.

The quantities used as input to the function are collectively called the *domain* of the function. The outputs are called the *range* of the function. Various notations are used to denote functions.

EXAMPLE 11.   Some examples of functions are:

1. The equation $f(x) = x^2 + 2x + 1$ is a numerical function whose domain consists of all real numbers and whose range consists of all real numbers greater than or equal to -1.

2. The relationship $T(\mathbf{V}) = 2\mathbf{V}$ is a transformation between vectors. The domain of T is all real vectors, as is the range. This function transforms each vector into a new vector which is twice the original one.

3. The expression $H(x, y) = (x, -y)$ represents a mapping between points of the plane. The domain consists of all points of the plane, as does the range. Each individual point is mapped to that point which is the reflection of the original point about the x axis.

4. If $\mathbf{A}$ is a matrix and $\mathbf{X}$ is a column matrix, the row matrix $\mathbf{Y}$ found by multiplying $\mathbf{A}$ and $\mathbf{X}$ can be regarded as a function $\mathbf{Y} = \mathbf{AX}$.

Graphs of Functions

If x and y are real numbers (scalars), the graph of a function $y = f(x)$ consists of all points in the plane whose coordinates have the form $[x, f(x)]$, where x lies in the domain of f. The graph of a function is the curve associated with the function, and it consists of an infinite number of points. In practice, plotting the graph of a function is done by computing a table of values and plotting the results. This gives an approximation to the actual graph of f.

EXAMPLE 12. Plot five points for the function $y = x^2$ over the interval $[-1, 1]$.

x	-1	$-\frac{1}{2}$	0	$\frac{1}{2}$	1
x^2	1	$\frac{1}{4}$	0	$\frac{1}{4}$	1

Plotting the points (x, x^2) calculated in the table and joining these points with line segments gives an approximation to the actual graph of $y = x^2$. See Fig. A1-7 for the plot of the graph.

The *plotting resolution* is determined by the number of x values used in plotting the graph. The higher the plotting resolution, the better the approximation. The process of calculating the values to be plotted and the actual plotting of the results is a chore eminently suited for the computer and plays an important part in scientific and business applications.

Composing Functions

If the process performed by a function H can be described by the successive steps of first applying a function G and then applying a function F to the results of G, we say that H is the *composition* of F and G. We write $H = F \circ G$. If the input to the function is denoted by x, the output $H(x)$ is evaluated by

$$H(x) = F[G(x)]$$

That is, first G operates on x; then the result $G(x)$ is passed to F as input.

Composition of functions is not commutative in general; that is, $F \circ G \neq G \circ F$.

The concept of composition is not restricted to only two functions but extends to any number of functions. For functions that are represented by matrices, composition of functions is equivalent to matrix multiplication; that is, $A \circ B = AB$.

EXAMPLE 13.

1.   If $f(x) = x^2 + 2$ and $g(x) = 2x + 1$, then $f[g(x)] = [g(x)]^2 + 2 = (2x + 1)^2 + 2 = 4x^2 + 4x + 3$.
2.   If

$$A = \begin{pmatrix} 1 & 3 \\ 0 & 2 \end{pmatrix} \quad \text{and} \quad B = \begin{pmatrix} -5 & 4 \\ 2 & 2 \end{pmatrix}$$

then

$$A \circ B = AB = \begin{pmatrix} 1 & 3 \\ 0 & 2 \end{pmatrix} \begin{pmatrix} -5 & 4 \\ 2 & 2 \end{pmatrix} = \begin{pmatrix} 1 & 10 \\ 4 & 4 \end{pmatrix}$$

The Inverse Function

The inverse of a function f (with respect to composition) is a function, denoted by f^{-1}, that satisfies the relationships $f^{-1} \circ f = i$ and $f \circ f^{-1} = i$, where i is the identity function $i(x) = x$. Applying the above compositions to an element x, we obtain the equivalent statements:

$$f^{-1}[f(x)] = x \qquad f[f^{-1}(x)] = x$$

The inverse operator thus "undoes" the work that f has performed.

Not every function has an inverse, and it is often very difficult to tell whether a given function has an inverse. One must often rely on geometric intuition to establish the inverse of an operator.

EXAMPLE 14. Let R be the transformation which rotates every point in the plane by an angle of 30° (in the positive or counterclockwise direction). Then it is clear that R^{-1} is the transformation that rotates every point by an angle of $-30°$ (a rotation of 30° in the clockwise direction).

A1.7 NUMBER SYSTEMS

Before discussing how the computer converts information stored in its random-access memory (RAM) to an image on a CRT, we must understand the three number systems involved and how they are related to each other.

The three number systems involved are (1) decimal or base 10 number system, (2) binary or base 2 number system, and (3) hexadecimal or base 16 number system.

The *decimal number system* is the most commonly used number system. It is used in routine arithmetic and uses the symbols 0, 1, 2, 3, 4, 5, 6, 7, 8, 9.

The *binary system* is the number system used by computers. The binary system uses the binary units 0, 1 as its symbols. Actually the computer internally represents 0 with a low voltage and 1 with a higher voltage. Each storage position in the computer's memory is known as a *bit*.

The *hexadecimal system* is a number system used to assist the programmer in understanding what is in the computer's memory. The hexadecimal number system assists the programmer by presenting an intermediate step between binary and decimal representation of a computer's memory (see Table A1-1).

A computer typically stores numbers in groups of 8 bits. Each 8-bit group is called a *byte*. As can be seen in Table A1-1, any 8 bits in a computer's memory can be represented by two hexadecimal digits.

Table A1-1

Binary	Hexadecimal	Decimal
0000	0	1
0001	1	1
0010	2	2
0011	3	3
0100	4	4
0101	5	5
0110	6	6
0111	7	7
1000	8	8
1001	9	9
1010	A	10
1011	B	11
1100	C	12
1101	D	13
1110	E	14
1111	F	15

Each byte can be broken down into equal sections consisting of 4 bits. Each 4-bit section is sometimes called a *nibble*. A nibble can take on 16 different values from 0 to 15 in decimal notation (see Table A1-1).

Base Conversion

Decimal

The value of a digit in the base 10 or decimal system increases by one power of 10 for each place we move to the left of the decimal point.

EXAMPLE 15. The number $1345 = 1 * 10^3 + 3 * 10^2 + 4 * 10^1 + 5 * 10^0$.

$$
\begin{array}{rcr}
5 * 10^0 &=& 5 \\
4 * 10^1 &=& 40 \\
3 * 10^2 &=& 300 \\
1 * 10^3 &=& \underline{1000} \\
& & 1345
\end{array}
$$

Binary

Each unit we move to the left of the decimal place when using the binary system increases the value of the digit by a power of 2.

EXAMPLE 16. Convert the binary number 10011011 to base 10. Since each place we move to the left of the decimal place we increase by a power of 2, it follows that

$$
\begin{array}{rcr}
1 * 2^0 &=& 1 \\
1 * 2^1 &=& 2 \\
0 * 2^2 &=& 0 \\
1 * 2^3 &=& 8 \\
1 * 2^4 &=& 16 \\
0 * 2^5 &=& 0 \\
0 * 2^6 &=& 0 \\
1 * 2^7 &=& \underline{128} \\
& & 155
\end{array}
$$

Hexadecimal

The hexadecimal system converts to base 10 in the same manner as the decimal and binary systems, except that each place we move to the left of the decimal place represents an increase by a power of 16.

EXAMPLE 17. Convert FA 09 (see Table A1-1) to base 10. Since each place we move to the left of the decimal place represents an increase by a power of 16, it follows that

$$
\begin{array}{rclcr}
9 * 10^0 &=& 9 * & 1 &=& 9 \\
0 * 16^1 &=& 0 * & 16 &=& 0 \\
A * 16^2 &=& 10 * & 256 &=& 2560 \\
F * 16^4 &=& 15 * & 4096 &=& \underline{61440} \\
& & & & & 64009
\end{array}
$$

Solved Problems

A1.1 Find the distance between the points whose coordinates are (*a*) $(5, 2)$ and $(7, 3)$, (*b*) $(-3, 1)$ and $(5, 2)$, (*c*) $(-3, -1)$ and $(-5, -2)$, and (*d*) $(0, 1)$ and $(2, 0)$.

SOLUTION

(*a*) $$D = \sqrt{(7-5)^2 + (3-2)^2} = \sqrt{2^2 + 1^2} = \sqrt{5}$$

(*b*) $$D = \sqrt{[5-(-3)]^2 + (2-1)^2} = \sqrt{(8)^2 + (1)^2} = \sqrt{65}$$

(*c*) $$D = \sqrt{[-5-(-3)]^2 + [-2-(-1)]^2} = \sqrt{(-2)^2 + (-1)^2} = \sqrt{5}$$

(*d*) $$D = \sqrt{(2-0)^2 + (0-1)^2} = \sqrt{2^2 + (-1)^2} = \sqrt{5}$$

A1.2 Derive the equation for a straight line (see Fig. A1-5).

SOLUTION

A straight line never changes direction. We determine the direction of a line by the angle θ the line makes with the positive x axis. Then at any point P_0 on the line, the angle formed by the line and a segment through P parallel to the x axis is also equal to θ. Let $P_0(x_0, y_0)$ be a point on the line. Then if $P(x, y)$ represents any point on the line, drawing the right triangle with hypotenuse $\overline{P_0 P}$, we find

$$\tan \theta = \frac{y - y_0}{x - x_0}$$

The quantity $\tan \theta$ is called the slope of the line and is traditionally denoted by m.

We rewrite the equation as

$$m = \frac{y - y_0}{x - x_0} \quad \text{or} \quad m = \frac{\Delta y}{\Delta x}$$

(The term Δy is often called the "rise" and Δx, the "run.") This can be solved for y in terms of x.

A1.3 Write the equation of the line whose slope is 2 and which passes through the point $(-1, 2)$.

SOLUTION

Let $P(x, y)$ represent any point on the line. Then

$$\Delta y = y - 2 \qquad \Delta x = x - (-1) = x + 1$$

and $m = 2$. Using $\Delta y / \Delta x = m$, we find

$$\frac{y - 2}{x + 1} = 2 \quad \text{or} \quad y - 2 = 2(x + 1) = 2x + 2$$

thus $y = 2x + 4$

A1.4 Write the equation of the line passing through $P_1(1, 2)$ and $P_2(3, -2)$.

SOLUTION

Let $P(x, y)$ represent any point on the line. Then using P_1, we compute

$$\Delta y = y - 2 \qquad \Delta x = x - 1$$

To find the slope m, we use P_1 and P_2 to find

$$\Delta y = -2 - 1 = -3 \qquad \Delta x = 3 - 1 = 2$$

Then

$$m = \frac{\Delta y}{\Delta x} = \frac{-3}{2} \qquad \text{so} \qquad \frac{y-2}{x-1} = \frac{-3}{2}$$

Then

$$y - 2 = \frac{-3}{2}x + \frac{3}{2} \qquad \text{and} \qquad y = \frac{-3}{2}x + \frac{7}{2}$$

A1.5   Show that lines are parallel if and only if their slopes are equal.

SOLUTION

Refer to Fig. A1-18. Suppose that lines l_1 and l_2 are parallel. Then the alternate interior angles θ_1 and θ_2 are equal, and so are the slopes $\tan \theta_1$ and $\tan \theta_2$.

Conversely, if the slopes $\tan \theta_1$ and $\tan \theta_2$ are equal, so are the alternate interior angles θ_1 and θ_2. Consequently lines l_1 and l_2 are parallel.

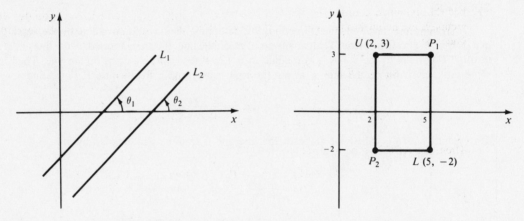

Fig. A1-18   Fig. A1-19

A1.6   Let $U(2, 3)$ and $L(5, -2)$ be the upper left and lower right corners, respectively, of a rectangle whose sides are parallel to the x and y axes. Find the coordinates of the remaining two vertices.

SOLUTION

Referring to Fig. A1-19, we see that the x coordinate of P_1 is the same as that of L, namely 5, and the y coordinate that of U, namely 3. So $P_1 = (5, 3)$. Similarly, $P_2 = (2, -2)$.

A1.7   Plot the points $A(1, 1)$, $B(-1, 1)$, and $C(-4, 2)$. Then (a) show that ABC is a right triangle and (b) find a fourth point D such that $ABCD$ is a rectangle (see Fig. A1-20).

SOLUTION

(a)   Show that the Pythagorean theorem is satisfied:

$$\overline{AC}^2 = \overline{AB}^2 + \overline{BC}^2$$

Use the distance formula to compute the lengths of the sides of ABC:

$$\overline{AB} = \sqrt{[1 - (-1)]^2 + [1 - (-1)]^2} = \sqrt{2^2 + 2^2} = \sqrt{8}$$
$$\overline{BC} = \sqrt{[-1 - (-4)]^2 + (-1 - 2)^2} = \sqrt{(3)^2 + (-3)^2} = \sqrt{18}$$
$$\overline{AC} = \sqrt{[1 - (-4)]^2 + (1 - 2)^2} = \sqrt{5^2 + (-1)^2} = \sqrt{26}$$

So

$$\overline{AC}^2 = 26 = \overline{AB}^2 + \overline{BC}^2 = 8 + 18$$

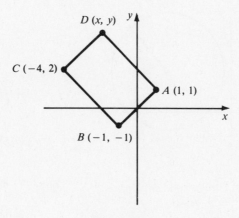

Fig. A1-20

(b) Let the unknown coordinates of D be denoted by (x, y). Use the fact that opposite sides of a rectangle are parallel to find x and y. Since parallel lines have equal slopes, compute the slopes of all four sides:

$$\text{Slope } \overline{AB} = \frac{-1-1}{-1-1} = \frac{-2}{-2} = 1 \qquad \text{Slope } \overline{CD} = \frac{y-2}{x-(-4)} = \frac{y-2}{x+4}$$

$$\text{Slope } \overline{BC} = \frac{-1-(2)}{-1-(-4)} = \frac{-3}{3} = -1 \qquad \text{Slope } \overline{DA} = \frac{y-1}{x-1}$$

Then, for $ABCD$ to be a rectangle

$$\text{Slope } \overline{CD} = \text{slope } \overline{AB} \qquad \text{Slope } \overline{DA} = \text{slope } \overline{BC}$$

or

$$\frac{y-2}{x+4} = 1 \qquad \text{and} \qquad \frac{y-1}{x-1} = -1$$

This leads to the equations

$$y - 2 = x + 4 \qquad \text{and} \qquad y - 1 = -x + 1$$

or

$$-x + y = 6 \qquad \text{and} \qquad x + y = 2$$

Solving, $x = -2$ and $y = 4$.

A1.8 Find the equation of a circle that has radius r and its center at the point (h, k).

SOLUTION

Refer to Fig. A1-21. If $P(x, y)$ is any point lying on the circle, its distance from the center of the circle must be equal to r. Using the distance formula to express this mathematically, we have

$$D = \sqrt{(x-h)^2 + (y-k)^2} = r$$

So $(x-h)^2 + (y-k)^2 = r^2$, which is the equation of the circle.

A1.9 Given any three points, not all lying on a line, find the equation of the circle determined by them.

SOLUTION

Refer to Fig. A1-22. Let $P_1(a_1, b_1)$, $P_2(a_2, b_2)$, and $P_3(a_3, b_3)$ be the coordinates of the points. Let r

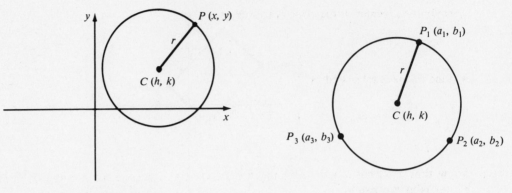

Fig. A1-21   Fig. A1-22

be the radius of the circle and (h, k) the center. Since each point is distance r from the center, then

$$(a_1 - h)^2 + (b_1 - k)^2 = r^2$$
$$(a_2 - h)^2 + (b_2 - k)^2 = r^2$$
$$(a_3 - h)^2 + (b_3 - k)^2 = r^2$$

This yields, after multiplying and collecting like terms:

$$(a_2 - a_1)h + (b_2 - b_1)k = \frac{a_2^2 - a_1^2}{2} + \frac{b_2^2 - b_1^2}{2}$$

$$(a_3 - a_2)h + (b_3 - b_2)k = \frac{a_3^2 - a_2^2}{2} + \frac{b_3^2 - b_2^2}{2}$$

These equations can be solved for h and k to yield

$$h = \frac{1}{2} \frac{[d_1^2(b_2 - b_3) + d_2^2(b_3 - b_1) + d_3^2(b_1 - b_2)]}{d}$$

$$k = \frac{-1}{2} \frac{[d_1^2(a_2 - a_3) + d_2^2(a_3 - a_1) + d_3^2(a_1 - a_2)]}{d}$$

Here, $d_1^2 = a_1^2 + b_1^2$, $d_2^2 = a_2^2 + b_2^2$, $d_3^2 = a_3^2 + b_3^2$, and $d = a_1(b_2 - b_3) + a_2(b_3 - b_1) + a_3(b_1 - b_2)$. Finally, r can be found:

$$r = \sqrt{(a_1 - h)^2 + (b_1 - k)^2}$$

A1.10 Find the equation of the circle passing through the three points $P_1(1, 2)$, $P_2(3, 0)$, and $P_3(0, -4)$.

SOLUTION

As in Prob. A1.9, we find

$$
\begin{array}{lll}
d_1^2 = a_1^2 + b_1^2 = 5 & a_2 - a_3 = 3 & b_2 - b_3 = 4 \\
d_2^2 = a_2^2 + b_2^2 = 9 & a_3 - a_1 = -1 & b_2 - b_1 = -6 \\
d_3^2 = a_3^2 + b_3^2 = 16 & a_1 - a_2 = -2 & b_1 - b_2 = 2
\end{array}
$$

So

$$d = 1(4) + 3(-6) + 0(2) = -14$$

and

$$h = \frac{-1[5(4) + 9(-6) + 16(2)]}{28} = \frac{2}{28} = \frac{1}{14}$$

$$k = \frac{1[5(3) + 9(-1) + 16(-2)]}{28} = \frac{-26}{28} = \frac{-13}{14}$$

Therefore, the center of the circle is located at

$$\left(\frac{1}{14}, \frac{-13}{14}\right)$$

and the radius is calculated by

$$r = \sqrt{\left(1 - \frac{1}{14}\right)^2 + \left(2 + \frac{13}{14}\right)^2} = \frac{5}{14}\sqrt{74}$$

A1.11 Show that $x = r\cos t$, $y = r\sin t$ are the parametric equations of a circle of radius r whose center is at the origin.

SOLUTION

By Prob. A1.8 we must show that $x^2 + y^2 = r^2$. Using the trigonometric identity $\cos^2 t + \sin^2 t = 1$, we obtain

$$x^2 + y^2 = (r\cos t)^2 + (r\sin t)^2 = r^2\cos^2 t + r^2\sin^2 t = r^2(\cos^2 t + \sin^2 t) = r^2$$

A1.12 Show that the parametric equations

$$x = \frac{a + bt}{e + ft} \qquad y = \frac{c + dt}{e + ft}$$

are the equations of a line in the plane.

SOLUTION

We show that the slope

$$\frac{\Delta y}{\Delta x} = \frac{y_2 - y_1}{x_2 - x_1}$$

is a constant, independent of the parameter t. So

$$\frac{y_2 - y_1}{x_2 - x_1} = \frac{(c + dt_2)/(e + ft_2) - (c + dt_1)/(e + ft_1)}{(a + bt_2)/(e + ft_2) - (a + bt_1)/(e + ft_1)}$$

$$= \frac{ce + det_2 + dft_1 + dft_2 t_1 - ce - cft_2 - det_1 - dft_2 t_1}{ae + aft_1 + let_2 + bft_2 t_1 - ae - aft_2 - ebt_1 - bft_2 t_1}$$

$$= \frac{de(t_2 - t_1) - cf(t_2 - t_1)}{be(t_2 - t_1) - af(t_2 - t_1)} = \frac{de - cf}{be - af}$$

So if $be - af \neq 0$, the slope $\Delta y/\Delta x$ is constant, and so this is the equation of a line.

A1.13 Let the equations of a line be given by (Prob. A1.12)

$$x = \frac{1 + t}{1 - t} \qquad y = \frac{2 + t}{1 - t}$$

Then (*a*) plot the line for all values of t, (*b*) plot the line segment over the interval $[0, 2]$, and (*c*) find the slope of the line.

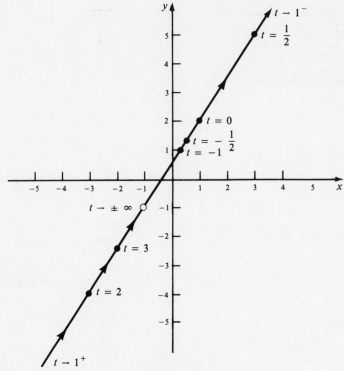

Fig. A1-23

SOLUTION

Making a table of values, we have

t	$-\frac{1}{2}$	-1	0	$\frac{1}{2}$	2	3
x	$\frac{1}{3}$	0	1	3	-3	-2
y	1	$\frac{1}{2}$	2	5	-4	$-\frac{5}{2}$

The resulting line is shown in Fig. A1-23.

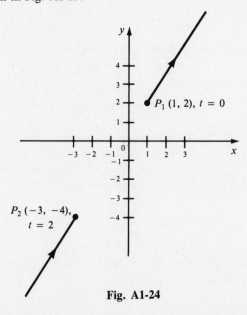

Fig. A1-24

(a) We observe the following: (1) the line is undefined at $t = 1$, (2) $(x, y) \to (\infty, \infty)$ as $t \to 1^-$, (3) $(x, y) \to (-\infty, -\infty)$ as $t \to 1^+$, and (4) $(x, y) \to (-1, -1)$ as $t \to \pm\infty$ (see Fig. A1-23).

(b) The interval $[0, 2]$ includes the infinite point at $t = 1$. The corresponding region is the exterior line segment between points $P_1(1, 2)$ at $t = 0$ and $P_2(-3, -4)$ at $t = 2$ (see Fig. A1-24).

(c) From Prob. A1.12, the slope of the line is, with $a = 1$, $b = 1$, $c = 2$, $d = 1$, $e = 1$, and $f = -1$

$$\frac{\Delta y}{\Delta x} = \frac{(1)(1) - (2)(-1)}{(1)(1) - (1)(-1)} = \frac{3}{2}$$

A1.14 Let $\mathbf{A} = 2\mathbf{I} + 7\mathbf{J}$, $\mathbf{B} = -3\mathbf{I} + \mathbf{J}$, and $\mathbf{C} = \mathbf{I} - 2\mathbf{J}$. Find (a) $2\mathbf{A} - \mathbf{B}$ and (b) $-3\mathbf{A} + 5\mathbf{B} - 2\mathbf{C}$.

SOLUTION

Perform the scalar multiplication and then the addition.

(a)
$$2\mathbf{A} - \mathbf{B} = 2(2\mathbf{I} + 7\mathbf{J}) - (-3\mathbf{I} + \mathbf{J}) = (4\mathbf{I} + 14\mathbf{J}) + (3\mathbf{I} - \mathbf{J})$$
$$= (4 + 3)\mathbf{I} + (14 - 1)\mathbf{J} = 7\mathbf{I} + 13\mathbf{J}$$

(b)
$$-3\mathbf{A} - 5\mathbf{B} - 2\mathbf{C} = -3(2\mathbf{I} + 7\mathbf{J}) - 5(-3\mathbf{I} + \mathbf{J}) - 2(\mathbf{I} - 2\mathbf{J})$$
$$= (-6\mathbf{I} - 21\mathbf{J}) + (15\mathbf{I} - 5\mathbf{J}) + (-2\mathbf{I} + 4\mathbf{J})$$
$$= (-6 + 15 - 2)\mathbf{I} + (-21 - 5 + 4)\mathbf{J} = 7\mathbf{I} - 22\mathbf{J}$$

A1.15 Find x and y such that $2x\mathbf{I} + (y - 1)\mathbf{J} = y\mathbf{I} + (3x + 1)\mathbf{J}$.

SOLUTION

Since vectors are equal only if their corresponding components are equal, we solve the equations (1) $2x = y$ and (2) $y - 1 = 3x + 1$. Substituting into equation 2, we have $(2x) - 1 = 3x + 1$ and $-2 = x$ and finally $y = 2x = 2(-2) = -4$, so $x = -2$ and $y = -4$.

A1.16 The tail of vector $\mathbf{A}$ is located at $P(-1, 2)$, and the head is at $Q(5, -3)$. Find the components of $\mathbf{A}$.

SOLUTION

Translate vector $\mathbf{A}$ so that its tail is at the origin. In this position, the coordinates of the head will be the components of $\mathbf{A}$.

Translating P to the origin is the same as subtracting 1 from the x component and 2 from the y component. Thus the new head of $\mathbf{A}$ will be located at point Q_1, whose coordinates (x_1, y_1) can be found by

$$x_1 = 5 - (-1) = 6 \qquad y_1 = -3 - 2 = -5$$

Thus $\mathbf{A} = 6\mathbf{I} - 5\mathbf{J}$.

A1.17 Given the vectors $\mathbf{A} = \mathbf{I} + 2\mathbf{J}$ and $\mathbf{B} = 2\mathbf{I} - 3\mathbf{J}$, find (a) the length, (b) the dot product, and (c) the angle θ between the vectors.

SOLUTION

(a)
$$|A| = \sqrt{1^2 + 2^2} = \sqrt{5} \qquad |\mathbf{B}| = \sqrt{2^2 + (-3)^2} = \sqrt{13}$$

(b)
$$\mathbf{A} \cdot \mathbf{B} = (\mathbf{I} + 2\mathbf{J}) \cdot (2\mathbf{I} - 3\mathbf{J}) = (1 \cdot 2) + [2 \cdot (-3)] = 2 - 6 = -4$$

(c) From the definition of the dot product, we can solve for $\cos \theta$:

$$\cos \theta = \frac{\mathbf{A} \cdot \mathbf{B}}{|\mathbf{A}||\mathbf{B}|} = \frac{-4}{\sqrt{5}\sqrt{13}}$$

So $\theta = 119.74°$.

A1.18 Find the unit vector $\mathbf{U_A}$ having the direction of $\mathbf{A} = 2\mathbf{I} - 3\mathbf{J}$.

SOLUTION

Since $\mathbf{U_A} = \dfrac{\mathbf{A}}{|\mathbf{A}|}$, it follows that

$$|\mathbf{A}| = \sqrt{2^2 + (-3)^2} = \sqrt{13} \quad \text{or} \quad \mathbf{U_A} = \frac{\mathbf{A}}{|\mathbf{A}|} = \frac{2\mathbf{I} - 3\mathbf{J}}{\sqrt{13}} = \frac{2}{\sqrt{13}}\mathbf{I} - \frac{3}{\sqrt{13}}\mathbf{J}$$

A1.19 Show that the distributive law for the dot product

$$(\mathbf{A} + \mathbf{B}) \cdot \mathbf{C} = \mathbf{A} \cdot \mathbf{C} + \mathbf{B} \cdot \mathbf{C}$$

holds for any vectors $\mathbf{A}$, $\mathbf{B}$, and $\mathbf{C}$.

SOLUTION

Let

$$\mathbf{A} = a_1\mathbf{I} + a_2\mathbf{J} \qquad \mathbf{B} = b_1\mathbf{I} + b_2\mathbf{J} \qquad \mathbf{C} = c_1\mathbf{I} + c_2\mathbf{J}$$

So

$$\mathbf{A} + \mathbf{B} = (a_1 + b_1)\mathbf{I} + (a_2 + b_2)\mathbf{J}$$

and

$$(\mathbf{A} + \mathbf{B}) \cdot \mathbf{C} = (a_1 + b_1)c_1 + (a_2 + b_2)c_2 = a_1c_1 + b_1c_1 + a_2c_2 + b_2c_2$$

On the other hand,

$$\mathbf{A} \cdot \mathbf{C} = a_1b_1 + a_1c_2 \qquad \mathbf{B} \cdot \mathbf{C} = b_1c_1 + b_2c_2$$

so

$$\mathbf{A} \cdot \mathbf{C} + \mathbf{B} \cdot \mathbf{C} = a_1c_1 + a_2c_2 + b_1c_1 + b_2c_2$$

Comparing both expressions, we see that they are equal.

A1.20 Find the number c such that the vector $\mathbf{A} = \mathbf{I} + c\mathbf{J}$ is orthogonal to $\mathbf{B} = 2\mathbf{I} - \mathbf{J}$.

SOLUTION

Two nonzero vectors are orthogonal (perpendicular) if and only if their dot product is zero. So

$$\mathbf{A} \cdot \mathbf{B} = (\mathbf{I} + c\mathbf{J}) \cdot (2\mathbf{I} - \mathbf{J}) = (1 \cdot 2) + [c(-1)] = 2 - c$$

So $\mathbf{A}$ and $\mathbf{B}$ are orthogonal if $2 - c = 0$ or $c = 2$.

A1.21 Show that the equation of a line can be determined by specifying a vector $\mathbf{V}$ having the direction of the line and by a point on the line.

SOLUTION

Suppose that $\mathbf{V}$ has components $[a, b]$ and the point $P_0(x_0, y_0)$ is on the line (see Fig. A1-25). If $P(x, y)$ is any point on the line, the vector $\overline{P_0P}$ has the same direction as $\mathbf{V}$, and so, by the definition of a vector, it must be a (scalar) multiple of $\mathbf{V}$, that is $\overline{P_0P} = t\mathbf{V}$. The components of $\overline{P_0P}$ are $[x - x_0, y - y_0]$ and those of $t\mathbf{V}$ are $[a, b]$. Equating components, we obtain the parametric equations of the line:

$$x - x_0 = ta \qquad y - y_0 = tb \quad \text{or} \quad x = at + x_0 \qquad y = bt + y_0$$

The nonparametric form of the equation can be determined by eliminating the parameter t from both equations. So

$$\frac{x - x_0}{a} = t = \frac{y - y_0}{b}$$

Solving for y, we have

$$y = \frac{b}{a}x + \left(y_0 - \frac{b}{a}x_0\right)$$

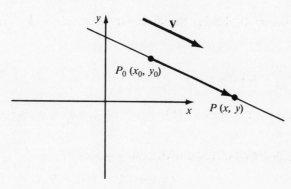

Fig. A1-25

A1.22 Find the (*a*) parametric and (*b*) nonparametric equation of the line passing through the point $P_0(1, 2)$ and parallel to the vector $\mathbf{V} = 2\mathbf{I} + \mathbf{J}$.

SOLUTION

As in Prob. A1.21, we find, with $a = 2$, $b = 1$, $x_0 = 1$, and $y_0 = 2$, that (*a*) $x = 2t + 1$, $y = t + 2$ and (*b*) with $b/a = \frac{1}{2}$, $y = \frac{1}{2}x + (2 - \frac{1}{2}) = \frac{1}{2}x + \frac{3}{2}$.

A1.23 Find the parametric equation of the line passing through points $P_1(1, 2)$ and $P_2(4, 1)$. What is the general form of the parametric equation of a line joining points $P_1(x_1, y_1)$ and $P_2(x_2, y_2)$?

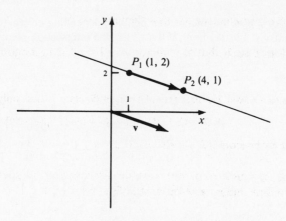

Fig. A1-26

SOLUTION

Refer to Fig. A1-26. Choosing $\mathbf{V} = \overline{P_1 P_2} = (4 - 1)\mathbf{I} + (1 - 2)\mathbf{J} = 3\mathbf{I} - 1\mathbf{J}$. Then as in Prob. A1.21, $x = 3t - 1$ and $y = -t - 2$. In the general case, the direction vector $\mathbf{V}$ is chosen, as above, to be $\overline{P_1 P_2} = (x_2 - x_1)\mathbf{I} + (y_2 - y_1)\mathbf{J}$. The equation of the line is then

$$x = x_1 + (x_2 - x_1)t \qquad y = y_1 + (y_2 - y_1)t$$

A1.24 Find the intersection of a line segment determined by endpoints $P_1(x_1, y_1)$ and $P_2(x_2, y_2)$ with the circle $(x - h)^2 + (y - k)^2 = r^2$.

SOLUTION

As in Prob. A1.23, the equation of the line segment is

$$x = x_1 + (x_2 - x_1)t \qquad y = y_1 + (y_2 - y_1)t$$

Substituting into the equation of the circle, we have

$$[(x_1 - h) + (x_2 - x_1)t]^2 + [(y_1 - k) + (y_2 - y_1)t]^2 = r^2$$

and squaring

$$(x_1 - h)^2 + 2(x_1 - h)(x_2 - x_1)t + (x_2 - x_1)^2t^2 + (y_1 - k)^2 + 2(y_1 - k)(y_2 - y_1)t + (y_2 - y_1)^2t^2 = r^2$$

or

$$[(x_2 - x_1)^2 + (y_2 - y_1)^2]t^2 + 2[(x_1 - h)(x_2 - x_1) + (y_1 - k)(y_2 - y_1)]t + (x_1 - h)^2 + (y_1 - k)^2 - r^2 = 0$$

with

$$L^2 = (x_2 - x_1)^2 + (y_2 - y_1)^2 \qquad \text{and} \qquad S = (x_1 - h)(x_2 - x_1) + (y_1 - k)(y_2 - y_1)$$

and

$$C = (x_1 - h)^2 + (y_1 - k)^2 - r^2$$

The equation then becomes

$$L^2t^2 + 2St + C = 0$$

Using the quadratic formula, we obtain

$$t_I = \frac{-2S \pm \sqrt{4S^2 - 4L^2C}}{2L^2} \qquad \text{or} \qquad \frac{-S \pm \sqrt{S^2 - L^2C}}{L^2}$$

There are 0, 1, or 2 possible intersection points t_I depending on whether $S^2 - L^2C$ is negative, zero, or positive, respectively. Furthermore, if $0 \le t_I \le 1$, the intersection points are on the line segment between P_1 and P_2, and they are

$$x_I = x_1 + (x_2 - x_1)t_I \qquad y_I = y_1 + (y_2 - y_1)t_I$$

A1.25 Compute:

(a)
$$\begin{pmatrix} 5 & 4 & 1 \\ 0 & -1 & 7 \end{pmatrix} + \begin{pmatrix} 2 & -1 & 3 \\ 2 & 0 & 1 \end{pmatrix}$$

(b)
$$\begin{pmatrix} 5 & 3 & 1 \\ 1 & 2 & 3 \end{pmatrix} + \begin{pmatrix} 4 & 1 \\ 1 & 5 \end{pmatrix}$$

(c)
$$3\begin{pmatrix} 5 & 4 & 1 \\ 0 & -1 & 7 \end{pmatrix}$$

SOLUTION

(a) Adding corresponding entries, we obtain

$$\begin{pmatrix} 5 & 4 & 1 \\ 0 & -1 & 7 \end{pmatrix} + \begin{pmatrix} 2 & -1 & 3 \\ 2 & 0 & 1 \end{pmatrix} = \begin{pmatrix} 5+2 & 4-1 & 1+3 \\ 0+2 & -1+0 & 7+1 \end{pmatrix} = \begin{pmatrix} 7 & 3 & 4 \\ 2 & -1 & 8 \end{pmatrix}$$

(b) Since the matrices are of different sizes, we cannot add them.

(c) Multiplying each entry by 3, we have

$$3\begin{pmatrix} 5 & 4 & 1 \\ 0 & -1 & 7 \end{pmatrix} = \begin{pmatrix} 15 & 12 & 3 \\ 0 & -3 & 21 \end{pmatrix}$$

A1.26 Let

$$\mathbf{A} = \begin{pmatrix} 3 & 2 \\ 0 & 1 \end{pmatrix} \qquad \mathbf{B} = \begin{pmatrix} 5 & -7 \\ 3 & -2 \end{pmatrix}$$

Find $2\mathbf{A} - 3\mathbf{B}$.

SOLUTION

First multiply, and then add:

$$2\mathbf{A} - 3\mathbf{B} = 2\begin{pmatrix} 3 & 2 \\ 0 & 1 \end{pmatrix} - 3\begin{pmatrix} 5 & -7 \\ 3 & -2 \end{pmatrix} = \begin{pmatrix} 6 & 4 \\ 0 & 2 \end{pmatrix} + \begin{pmatrix} -15 & 21 \\ -9 & 6 \end{pmatrix} = \begin{pmatrix} 6-15 & 4+21 \\ 0-9 & 2+6 \end{pmatrix} = \begin{pmatrix} -9 & 25 \\ -9 & 8 \end{pmatrix}$$

A1.27 Determine the size of the following matrix multiplications $\mathbf{A} \cdot \mathbf{B}$, where the sizes of $\mathbf{A}$ and $\mathbf{B}$ are given as (a) (3×5), (5×2); (b) (1×2), (3×1); (c) (2×2), (2×1); and (d) (2×2), (2×2).

SOLUTION

(a) (3×2); (b) undefined, since the column size of $\mathbf{A}$ (2) and the row size of $\mathbf{B}$ (3) are not equal; (c) (2×1); (d) (2×2).

A1.28 Find the sizes of $\mathbf{A}$ and $\mathbf{B}$ so that $\mathbf{AB}$ and $\mathbf{BA}$ can both be computed. Show that if both $\mathbf{A}$ and $\mathbf{B}$ are square matrices of the same size, both $\mathbf{AB}$ and $\mathbf{BA}$ are defined.

SOLUTION

Let the size of $\mathbf{A}$ be $(m \times n)$ and the size of $\mathbf{B}$ be $(r \times s)$. Then $\mathbf{AB}$ is defined only if $r = n$. Also, $\mathbf{BA}$ is defined only if $s = m$. Thus, if $\mathbf{A}$ is $(m \times n)$, then $\mathbf{B}$ must be $(n \times m)$. If $\mathbf{A}$ is square, say, $(n \times n)$, and $\mathbf{B}$ is also $(n \times n)$, then both $\mathbf{AB}$ and $\mathbf{BA}$ are defined.

A1.29 Given

$$\mathbf{A} = \begin{pmatrix} 1 & 2 \\ 5 & 1 \\ 6 & 3 \end{pmatrix}$$

find $\mathbf{A}^T$.

SOLUTION

Exchanging the rows and columns of $\mathbf{A}$, we obtain

$$\mathbf{A}^T = \begin{pmatrix} 1 & 5 & 6 \\ 2 & 1 & 3 \end{pmatrix}$$

A1.30 Compute $\mathbf{AB}$ for

(a) $$\mathbf{A} = \begin{pmatrix} 2 & 3 \\ 1 & 2 \end{pmatrix} \qquad \text{and} \qquad \mathbf{B} = \begin{pmatrix} -4 \\ 7 \end{pmatrix}$$

(b) $$\mathbf{A} = \begin{pmatrix} 2 & 3 \\ 1 & 2 \end{pmatrix} \qquad \text{and} \qquad \mathbf{B} = \begin{pmatrix} -4 & 5 \\ 7 & 6 \end{pmatrix}$$

(c) $$\mathbf{A} = \begin{pmatrix} 2 & 3 \\ 1 & 2 \end{pmatrix} \qquad \text{and} \qquad \mathbf{B} = \begin{pmatrix} -4 & 5 & 9 \\ 7 & 6 & 10 \end{pmatrix}$$

SOLUTION

(a) Since **A** is (2×2) and **B** is (2×1), then **AB** is (2×1)

$$\mathbf{AB} = \begin{pmatrix} 2 & 3 \\ 1 & 2 \end{pmatrix}\begin{pmatrix} -4 \\ 7 \end{pmatrix} = \begin{pmatrix} 2 \cdot (-4) + 3 \cdot 7 \\ 1 \cdot (-4) + 2 \cdot 7 \end{pmatrix} = \begin{pmatrix} 13 \\ 10 \end{pmatrix}$$

(b) $$\mathbf{AB} = \begin{pmatrix} 2 & 3 \\ 1 & 2 \end{pmatrix}\begin{pmatrix} -4 & 5 \\ 7 & 6 \end{pmatrix} = \begin{pmatrix} 2 \cdot (-4) + 3 \cdot 7 & 2 \cdot 5 + 3 \cdot 6 \\ 1 \cdot (-4) + 2 \cdot 7 & 1 \cdot 5 + 2 \cdot 6 \end{pmatrix} = \begin{pmatrix} 13 & 28 \\ 10 & 17 \end{pmatrix}$$

(c) $$\mathbf{A} \cdot \mathbf{B} = \begin{pmatrix} 2 & 3 \\ 1 & 2 \end{pmatrix}\begin{pmatrix} -4 & 5 & 9 \\ 7 & 6 & 10 \end{pmatrix} = \begin{pmatrix} 2 \cdot (-4) + 3 \cdot 7 & 2 \cdot 5 + 3 \cdot 6 & 2 \cdot 9 + 3 \cdot 10 \\ 1 \cdot (-4) + 2 \cdot 7 & 1 \cdot 5 + 2 \cdot 6 & 1 \cdot 9 + 2 \cdot 10 \end{pmatrix} = \begin{pmatrix} 13 & 28 & 48 \\ 10 & 17 & 29 \end{pmatrix}$$

A1.31 Let $$\mathbf{A} = \begin{pmatrix} 3 & 2 \\ 5 & 6 \\ 2 & 1 \end{pmatrix} \quad \text{and} \quad \mathbf{B} = \begin{pmatrix} 6 & 2 & 1 \\ 3 & 5 & 8 \end{pmatrix}$$

Find (a) **AB** and (b) **BA**.

SOLUTION

(a) $$\mathbf{AB} = \begin{pmatrix} 3 & 2 \\ 5 & 6 \\ 2 & 1 \end{pmatrix}\begin{pmatrix} 6 & 2 & 1 \\ 3 & 5 & 8 \end{pmatrix} = \begin{pmatrix} 3 \cdot 6 + 2 \cdot 3 & 3 \cdot 2 + 2 \cdot 5 & 3 \cdot 1 + 2 \cdot 8 \\ 5 \cdot 6 + 6 \cdot 3 & 5 \cdot 2 + 6 \cdot 5 & 5 \cdot 1 + 6 \cdot 8 \\ 2 \cdot 6 + 1 \cdot 3 & 2 \cdot 2 + 1 \cdot 5 & 2 \cdot 1 + 1 \cdot 8 \end{pmatrix} = \begin{pmatrix} 24 & 16 & 19 \\ 48 & 40 & 53 \\ 15 & 9 & 10 \end{pmatrix}$$

(b) $$\mathbf{BA} = \begin{pmatrix} 6 & 2 & 1 \\ 3 & 5 & 8 \end{pmatrix}\begin{pmatrix} 3 & 2 \\ 5 & 6 \\ 2 & 1 \end{pmatrix} = \begin{pmatrix} 6 \cdot 3 + 2 \cdot 5 + 1 \cdot 2 & 6 \cdot 2 + 2 \cdot 6 + 1 \cdot 1 \\ 3 \cdot 3 + 5 \cdot 5 + 8 \cdot 2 & 3 \cdot 2 + 5 \cdot 6 + 8 \cdot 1 \end{pmatrix} = \begin{pmatrix} 30 & 25 \\ 50 & 44 \end{pmatrix}$$

A1.32 Find the inverse of $\mathbf{A} = \begin{pmatrix} 1 & 2 \\ 3 & 4 \end{pmatrix}$

SOLUTION

We wish to find a matrix $\begin{pmatrix} p & q \\ r & s \end{pmatrix}$ so that

$$\begin{pmatrix} 1 & 2 \\ 3 & 4 \end{pmatrix}\begin{pmatrix} p & q \\ r & s \end{pmatrix} = \begin{pmatrix} 1 & 0 \\ 0 & 1 \end{pmatrix}$$

Multiplying, we have

$$\begin{pmatrix} p + 2r & q + 2s \\ 3p + 4r & 3q + 4s \end{pmatrix} = \begin{pmatrix} 1 & 0 \\ 0 & 1 \end{pmatrix}$$

So $p + 2r = 1$, $q + 2s = 0$, $3p + 4r = 0$, and $3q + 4s = 1$. Solving the first and third equations we find $p = -2$, $r = \frac{3}{2}$. Solving the second and fourth equations gives $q = 1$ and $s = -\frac{1}{2}$. So

$$\mathbf{A}^{-1} = \begin{pmatrix} -2 & 1 \\ \frac{3}{2} & -\frac{1}{2} \end{pmatrix}$$

A1.33 Let G be the function which multiplies a given vector by 2 and F be the function that adds the vector **b** to a given vector. Find (a) $F + G$, (b) $F \circ G$, (c) $G \circ F$, (d) F^{-1}, and (e) G^{-1}.

SOLUTION

If **v** is any vector, the functions F and G operate on **v** as $F(\mathbf{v}) = 2\mathbf{v}$ and $G(\mathbf{v}) = \mathbf{v} + \mathbf{b}$.

1. $(F + G)(\mathbf{v}) = F(\mathbf{v}) + G(\mathbf{v}) = (2\mathbf{v}) + (\mathbf{v} + \mathbf{b}) = 3\mathbf{v} + \mathbf{b}$.

2. $(F \circ G)(\mathbf{v}) = F[G(\mathbf{v})] = 2[G(\mathbf{v})] = 2[\mathbf{v} + \mathbf{b}] = 2\mathbf{v} + 2\mathbf{b}$.

3. $(G \circ F)(\mathbf{v}) = G[F(\mathbf{v})] = [F(\mathbf{v})] + \mathbf{b} = 2\mathbf{v} + \mathbf{b}$.

4. We can guess that $F^{-1}(\mathbf{v}) = \frac{1}{2}\mathbf{v}$. To check this, we set $F^{-1}[F(\mathbf{v})] = \frac{1}{2}[F(\mathbf{v})] = \frac{1}{2}[2\mathbf{v}] = \mathbf{v}$ and $F[F^{-1}(\mathbf{v})] = 2[F^{-1}(\mathbf{v})] = 2[(\frac{1}{2})\mathbf{v}] = \mathbf{v}$.

5. We can verify that $G^{-1}(\mathbf{v}) = \mathbf{v} - \mathbf{b}$: $G^{-1}[G(\mathbf{v})] = G^{-1}(\mathbf{v} + \mathbf{b}) = (\mathbf{v} + \mathbf{b}) - \mathbf{b} = \mathbf{v}$ and $G[G^{-1}(\mathbf{v})] = G^{-1}(\mathbf{v}) + \mathbf{b} = (\mathbf{v} - \mathbf{b}) + \mathbf{b} = \mathbf{v}$.

A1.34 Show that $\mathbf{A} \circ \mathbf{B} = \mathbf{AB}$ for any two matrices (that can be multiplied together).

SOLUTION

The terms $\mathbf{A} \circ \mathbf{B}$ and $\mathbf{AB}$ produce the same effect on any column matrix $\mathbf{X}$, i.e., $(\mathbf{A} \circ \mathbf{B})(\mathbf{X}) = \mathbf{ABX}$. Recall that any matrix function $\mathbf{A}(\mathbf{X})$ is defined by $\mathbf{A}(\mathbf{X}) = \mathbf{AX}$. So

$$(\mathbf{A} \circ \mathbf{B})(\mathbf{X}) = \mathbf{A}[\mathbf{B}(\mathbf{X})] = \mathbf{A}(\mathbf{BX}) = \mathbf{ABX}$$

A1.35 Given that $\mathbf{A}$ is a 2×2 matrix and $\mathbf{b}$ is a vector, show that the function $F(\mathbf{X}) = \mathbf{AX} + \mathbf{b}$, called an affine transformation, can be considered as either a transformation between vectors or as a mapping between points of the plane.

SOLUTION

Suppose that

$$\mathbf{A} = \begin{pmatrix} a_{11} & a_{12} \\ a_{21} & a_{22} \end{pmatrix}$$

and $\mathbf{b}$ has components $[b_1, b_2]$. If $\mathbf{X}$ is a vector with components $[x_1, x_2]$, then

$$\mathbf{AX} = \begin{pmatrix} a_{11} & a_{12} \\ a_{21} & a_{22} \end{pmatrix}\begin{pmatrix} x_1 \\ x_2 \end{pmatrix}$$

can be identified with the vector having components $[a_{11}x_1 + a_{12}x_2, a_{21}x_1 + a_{22}x_2]$. And so $\mathbf{AX} + \mathbf{b}$ is a vector.

If $X = (x_1, x_2)$ is a point of the plane, then as a point mapping, $F(X) = [f_1(X), f_2(X)]$, where the coordinate functions f_1 and f_2 are

$$f_1(X) = a_{11}x_1 + a_{12}x_2 + b_1 \qquad \text{and} \qquad f_2(X) = a_{21}x_1 + a_{22}x_2 + b_2$$

A1.36 Show that for any 2×2 matrix $\mathbf{A}$ and any vector $\mathbf{b}$ the transformation $F(\mathbf{X}) = \mathbf{AX} + \mathbf{b}$ transforms lines into lines.

SOLUTION

Let $x = at + x_0$ and $y = bt + y_0$ be the parametric equations of a line. With $\mathbf{X} = (x, y)$ then

$$\mathbf{AX} = \begin{pmatrix} a_{11} & a_{12} \\ a_{21} & a_{22} \end{pmatrix}\begin{pmatrix} at + x_0 \\ bt + y_0 \end{pmatrix} = \begin{pmatrix} a_{11}at + a_{11}x_0 + a_{12}bt + a_{12}y_0 \\ a_{21}at + a_{21}x_0 + a_{22}bt + a_{22}y_0 \end{pmatrix}$$

So

$$F(\mathbf{X}) = \mathbf{AX} + \mathbf{b} = \begin{pmatrix} t(a_{11}a + a_{12}b) + (a_{11}x_0 + a_{12}y_0 + b_1) \\ t(a_{21}a + a_{22}b) + (a_{21}x_0 + a_{22}y_0 + b_2) \end{pmatrix}$$

This can be recognized as the parametric equation of a line (Prob. A1.21) passing through the point with coordinates $(a_{11}x_0 + a_{12}y_0 + b_1, a_{21}x_0 + a_{22}y_0 + b_2)$ and having the direction of the vector $\mathbf{v}$ with components $[a_{11}a + a_{12}b, a_{21}a + a_{22}b]$.

A1.37 Show that the transformation $F(\mathbf{X}) = \mathbf{AX} + \mathbf{b}$ transforms a line passing through points P_1 and P_2 into a line passing through $F(P_1)$ and $F(P_2)$.

SOLUTION

As in Prob. A1.23, the parametric equation of the line passing through P_1 and P_2 can be written as

$$x = x_1 + (x_2 - x_1)t \qquad y = y_1 + (y_2 - y_1)t$$

As in Prob. A1.36 with $a = x_2 - x_1$ and $b = y_2 - y_1$, we find that F transforms this line into another line. Now when $t = 0$, this line passes through the point

$$(a_{11}x_1 + a_{12}y_1 + b_1, \ a_{21}x_1 + a_{22}y_1 + b_2) = F(P_1)$$

and when $t = 1$, it passes through the point

$$(a_{11}a + a_{12}b + a_{11}x_1 + a_{12}y_1 + b_1, \ a_{21}a + a_{22}b + a_{21}x_1 + a_{22}y_1 + b_2) = F(P_2)$$

A1.38 What two values can a bit symbolically represent?

SOLUTION

A bit symbolically represents either a zero or a one.

A1.39 What are a series of 8 bits grouped together called?

SOLUTION

A series of 8 bits are collectively called a byte.

A1.40 What is a series of 4 bits grouped together called?

SOLUTION

A series of 4 bits are collectively called a nibble.

A1.41 How does a bit symbolically represent values?

SOLUTION

By convention, a bit in the high-voltage state is considered to have a binary value of one and a low voltage has the binary value of zero.

A1.42 How many different values can be represented by a nibble? A byte?

SOLUTION

A nibble can represent 2^4 or 16 different values. A byte can represent 2^8 or 256 different values.

A1.43 What three number systems are typically used in work with a computer?

SOLUTION

Binary, decimal, and hexadecimal are often used in work with a computer.

A1.44 What two symbols are used to represent all values in the binary number system?

SOLUTION

The binary number system uses the symbols "0" and "1" to represent all values.

A1.45 What 10 symbols are used to represent all values in the decimal number system?

SOLUTION

The decimal number system uses the symbols "0" through "9" to represent all values.

A1.46 What 16 symbols are used to represent all values in the hexadecimal number system?

SOLUTION

The hexadecimal number system uses the symbols "0" through "9" and "A" through "F" to represent all values.

A1.47 Convert the following numbers from base 10 to hexadecimal: (*a*) 123, (*b*) 74, (*c*) 14,193, and (*d*) 64,000.

SOLUTION

(*a*) To convert to base 16, we must find how many times each power of 16 can be divided into the decimal number. In this case the largest power of 16 that will divide 123 is 16^1: $7*16^1 = 112$. This leaves a remainder of 11 from 123. The power of 16 that will divide 11 is 16^0. So $123 = 7 + 16^1 + 11 + 16^0$. The hexadecimal symbol that represents the number 7 is 7, and the hexadecimal symbol that represents the number 11 is B. The solution is then 7B.

(*b*) To convert 78 base 10 to hexadecimal, we find the largest power of 16 that can be divided into 78: $4*16^1 = 64$. We must now find the remainder: $78 - 64 = 14$. The largest power of 16 that will divide into 14 is 16^0. So $78 = 4*16 + 14*16^0$. The hexadecimal symbol that represents the number 4 is 4, and the hexadecimal symbol that represents the decimal value 14 is E. Therefore, the solution is 4E.

(*c*) To convert 14,193 base 10 to hexadecimal, we find the largest power of 16 that can be divided into 14,193: $3*16^3 = 12,288$. We must now find the remainder: $14,193 - 12,288 = 1905$. The largest power of 16 that will divide into 1905 is 16^2: $7*16^2 = 1792$. We must now find the remainder: $1905 - 1792 = 113$. The largest power of 16 that will divide into 113 is 16^1: $7*16^1 = 112$. We now find the remainder: $113 - 112 = 1$. So $14,193 = 3*16^3 + 7*16^2 + 7*16^1 + 1 + 16^0$. In hexadecimal notation, this is 3771.

(*d*) To convert 64,000 base 10 to hexadecimal, we find the largest power of 16 that can be divided into 64,000: $15*16^3 = 61,440$. We must now find the remainder: $64,000 - 61,440 = 2560$. The largest power of 16 that will divide 2560 is 16^2: $10*16^2 = 2560$. We must now find the remainder: $2560 - 2560 = 0$. Since there is no remainder, the division stops. So $64,000 = 15*16^3 + 10*16^2 + 0*16^1 + 0*16^0$. The hexadecimal symbols for the numbers 15 and 10 are F and A, respectively. Therefore, the solution is FA00.

A1.48 Convert the following numbers from base 16 to base 2: (*a*) FF3A, (*b*) ABCD, (*c*) 1234, and (*d*) 1000.

SOLUTION

(*a*) The easiest method of converting from hexadecimal to binary is to memorize the nibble that represents each hexadecimal character. For now, refer to Table A1-1.

	F	F	3	A —hexadecimal value
	1111	1111	0011	1010—binary value from Table A1-1
(*b*)	A	B	C	D —hexadecimal value
	1010	1011	1100	1101—binary value from Table A1-1
(*c*)	1	2	3	4 —hexadecimal value
	0001	0010	0011	0100—binary value from Table A1-1
(*d*)	1	0	0	0 —hexadecimal value
	0001	0000	0000	0000—binary value from Table A1-1

A1.49 Convert the following numbers from hexadecimal to decimal: (*a*) FA, (*b*) 09, (*c*) 10, and (*d*) F1AA.

SOLUTION

The conversion from hexadecimal to decimal is done in three steps: (1) change the hexadecimal symbol to the equivalent decimal symbol. (The conversion may be obtained from Table A1-1), (2) multiply the decimal symbol found in step 1 by 16^n (where n = the number of places to the left of the first symbol), and (3) add the results from step 2.

(*a*) Step 1: F   A—hexadecimal value
         15   10—decimal value from Table A1-1
      Step 2: $10*(16^0) = 10$
              $15*(16^1) = 240$
      Step 3: $240 + 10 = 250$

(*b*) Step 1: 0   9—hexadecimal value
          9   9—decimal value from Table A1-1
      Step 2: $9*(16^0) = 9$
              $0*(16^1) = 0$
      Step 3: $0 + 9 = 9$

(*c*) Step 1: 1   0—hexadecimal value
          1   0—decimal value from Table A1-1
      Step 2: $0*(16^0) = 0$
              $1*(16^1) = 16$
      Step 3: $16 + 0 = 16$

(*d*) Step 1: F   1   A   A—hexadecimal value
         16   1   10   10—decimal value from Table A1-1
      Step 2: $10*(16^0) = 10$
              $10*(16^1) = 160$
              $1*(16^2) = 256$
              $16*(16^3) = 61,440$
      Step 3: $61,440 + 256 + 160 + 10 = 61,866$

A1.50 Convert the following numbers from decimal to binary: (*a*) 138, (*b*) 6502, (*c*) 1, and (*d*) 10.

SOLUTION

Conversion from decimal to binary is most easily done in two steps: (1) convert the decimal value to its hexadecimal equivalent and (2) convert the hexadecimal to its binary equivalent (use Table A1-1).

(*a*) Step 1: $8*(16^1) = 128$; the remainder is 10, $10*(16^0) = 10$; the hexadecimal characters that represent the numbers 8 and 10 are 8 and A, respectively, so $138_{10} = 8A_{16}$
      Step 2: 8   A   —hexadecimal value from step 1
              1000   1010—binary value from Table A1-1

(*b*) Step 1: Remainder
              $1*(16^3) = 4096$
              2406: $9*(16^2) = 2304$
              102:   $6*(16^1) = 96$
              6:   $6*(16^0) = 6$
      The hexadecimal characters that represent the numbers 1, 9, and 6 are 1, 9, and 6, respectively, so $6502_0 = 1966_H$
      Step 2: 1   9   6   6   —hexadecimal value from step 1
              0001   1001   0110   0110—binary symbol from Table A1-1.

(*c*) Step 1: $1*(16^0) = 1$; the hexadecimal character that represents one is 1, so $1_{10} = 1_{16}$
      Step 2: 1—hexadecimal value from step 1
              0001—binary symbol from Table A1-1

(*d*) Step 1: $10*(16^0) = 10$; the hexadecimal character that represents the number 10 is A, so $10_{10} = A_{16}$
      A—hexadecimal value from step 1
      1010—binary symbol from Table A1-1

A1.51 Convert the following numbers from binary to hexadecimal: (*a*) 11100110, (*b*) 00010001, (*c*) 11111101, and (*d*) 10101010.

SOLUTION

The easiest way to convert from binary to hexadecimal is to use Table A1-1.

(*a*) 11100110—binary symbol
     E   6—hexadecimal symbol from Table A1-1

(*b*) 00010001—binary symbol
     1   1—hexadecimal symbol from Table A1-1

(*c*) 11111101—binary symbol
     F   D—hexadecimal symbol from Table A1-1

(*d*) 10101010—binary symbol
     A   A—hexadecimal symbol from Table A1-1

Appendix 2

Mathematics for
Three-Dimensional Computer Graphics

A2.1 THREE-DIMENSIONAL CARTESIAN COORDINATES

The three-dimensional Cartesian (rectangular) coordinates system consists of a reference point, called the *origin*, and three mutually perpendicular lines passing through the origin. These mutually perpendicular lines are taken to be number lines and are labeled the x, y, and z coordinate axes. The labels are placed on the positive ends of the axes (see Fig. A2-1).

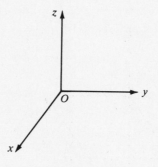

Fig. A2-1

Orientation

The labeling of the x, y, and z axes is arbitrary. However, any labeling falls into one of two classifications, called *right-* and *left-handed orientation*. The orientation is determined by the *right-hand rule*.

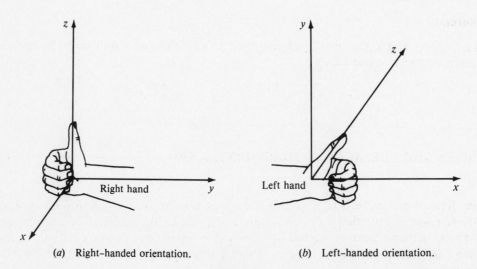

    (*a*) Right–handed orientation.   (*b*) Left–handed orientation.

Fig. A2-2

The Right-Hand Rule

A labeling of the axes is a *right-handed orientation* if whenever the fingers of the right hand are aligned with the positive x axis and are then rotated (through the smaller angle) toward the positive y axis, then the thumb of the right-hand points in the direction of the positive z axis. Otherwise, the orientation is a *left-handed orientation* (see Fig. A2-2).

Cartesian Coordinates of Points in Three-Dimensional Space

Any point P in three-dimensional space can have coordinates (x, y, z) associated with it as follows:

1. Let the x coordinate be the directed distance that P is above or below the yz plane.
2. Let the y coordinate be the directed distance that P is above or below the xz plane.
3. Let the z coordinate be the directed distance that P is above or below the xy plane.

See Figure A2-3.

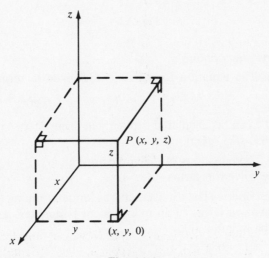

Fig. A2-3

Distance Formula

If $P_0(x_0, y_0, z_0)$ and $P_1(x_1, y_1, z_1)$ are any two points in space, the distance D between these points is given by the distance formula:

$$D = \sqrt{(x_1 - x_0)^2 + (y_1 - y_0)^2 + (z_1 - z_0)^2}$$

A2.2   CURVES AND SURFACES IN THREE DIMENSIONS

Curves

A three-dimensional curve is an object in space that has direction only, much like a thread (see Fig. A2-4). A curve is specified by an equation (or group of equations) that has only one free (independent) variable or parameter, and the x, y, and z coordinates of any point on the curve are determined by this free variable or parameter. There are two types of curve description, nonparametric and parametric.

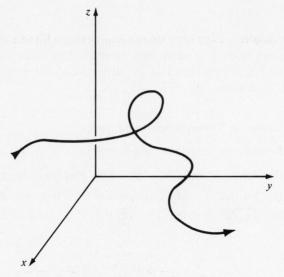

Fig. A2-4

1. *Nonparametric curve description.*

   (*a*) *Explicit form.* The equation for curve C are given in terms of a variable, say, x, as

   $$C: \quad y = f(x) \qquad z = g(x)$$

   That is, y and z can be calculated explicitly in terms of x. Any point P on the curve has coordinates $P[x, f(x), g(x)]$.

   (*b*) *Implicit form.* The equations of the curve are $F(x, y, z) = 0$ and $G(x, y, z) = 0$. Here, y and z must be solved in terms of x.

2. *Parametric curve description.* The three equations for determining the coordinates of any point on the curve are given in terms of an independent parameter, say, t, in a parameter range $[a, b]$, which may be infinite:

   $$C: \quad \begin{aligned} x &= f(t) \\ y &= g(t), \qquad a \le t \le b \\ z &= h(t) \end{aligned}$$

   Any point P on the curve has coordinates $[f(t), g(t), h(t)]$.

3. *Equations of a straight line.* The equations of a line L determined by two points $P_0(x_0, y_0, z_0)$ and $P_1(x_1, y_1, z_1)$ are given by:

   (*a*) *Nonparametric form*

   $$L: \quad \begin{aligned} y &= m_1 x + b_1 = \left(\frac{y_1 - y_0}{x_1 - x_0}\right) x + \left(\frac{y_0 x_1 - y_1 x_0}{x_1 - x_0}\right) \\[2mm] z &= m_2 x + b_2 = \left(\frac{z_1 - z_0}{x_1 - x_0}\right) x + \left(\frac{z_0 x_1 - z_1 x_0}{x_1 - x_0}\right) \end{aligned}$$

   (*b*) *Parametric form*

   $$x = x_0 + (x_1 - x_0)t \qquad y = y_0 + (y_1 - y_0)t \qquad z = z_0 + (z_1 - z_0)t$$

   Note that when $t = 0$, then $x = x_0$, $y = y_0$, and $z = z_0$. When $t = 1$, then $x = x_1$, $y = y_1$, and $z = z_1$. Thus, when the parameter t is restricted to the range $0 \le t \le 1$, the parametric equations describe the line segment $\overline{P_0 P_1}$.

Surfaces

A surface in three-dimensional space is an object that has breadth and width, much like a piece of cloth (see Fig. A2-5).

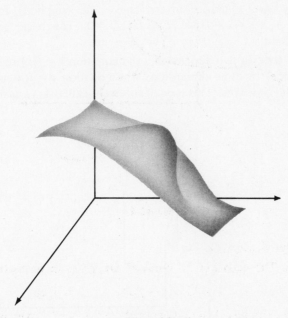

Fig. A2-5

A surface is specified by an equation (or group of equations) that has two free (or independent) variables or parameters. There are two types of surface description, nonparametric and parametric:

1. *Nonparametric surface description*

    (*a*) *Explicit form.* The z coordinate of any point on the surface S is given in terms of two free variables x and y, that is, $z = f(x, y)$. Any point P on the surface has coordinates $[x, y, f(x, y)]$.

    (*b*) *Implicit form.* The equation of the surface is given in the form $F(x, y, z) = 0$. Here, z is to be solved in terms of x and y. There is no restriction as to which variables are free. The convention is to represent z in terms of x and y, but nothing disallows a representation of x in terms of y and z or y in terms of x and z.

2. *Parametric description.* The three equations for determining the coordinates of any point on the surface S are described in terms of parameters, say, s and t, and in parameter ranges $[a, b]$ and $[c, d]$, which may be infinite:

$$S: \quad \begin{aligned} x &= f(s, t), & a \leq s \leq b \\ y &= g(s, t), & c \leq t \leq d \\ z &= h(s, t) \end{aligned}$$

The coordinates of any point P on the surface have the form $[F(s, t), G(s, t), H(s, t)]$.

    (*a*) *Equations of a plane.* The equation of a plane can be written in explicit form as $z = ax + by + c$ or in implicit form as $Ax + By + Cz + D = 0$ (see Prob. A2.8). The equation of a plane is linear in the variables x, y, and z. A plane divides three-dimensional space into two separate regions. The implicit form of the equation of a plane can be used to determine whether two points are on the same or opposite sides of the plane. Given the implicit equation of the plane $Ax + By + Cz + D = 0$, let $f(x, y, z) = Ax + By + Cz + D$. The two sides of the plane R^+, R^- are determined by the sign of $f(x, y, z)$; that is, point $P(x_0, y_0, z_0)$ lies in region R^+ if $f(x_0, y_0, z_0) > 0$ and in region R^- if $f(x_0, y_0, z_0) < 0$. If $f(x_0, y_0, z_0) = 0$, the point lies on the plane.

(b) *Quadric surfaces.* Quadric surfaces have the (implicit) form $Ax^2 + By^2 + Cz^2 + Dxy + Exz + Fyz + Gx + Hy + Hy + Iz + J = 0$. The basic quadric surfaces are described in Chap. 9.

(c) *Cylinder surfaces.* In two dimensions, the equation $y = f(x)$ represents a (planar) curve in the xy plane. In three dimensions, the equation $y = f(x)$ is a surface. That is, the variables x and z are free. This type of surface is called a *cylinder surface* (see Fig. A2-6).

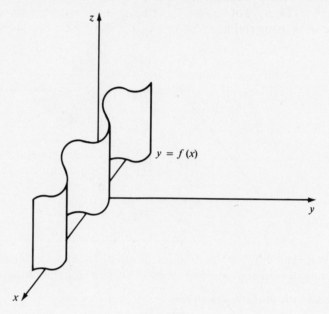

Fig. A2-6

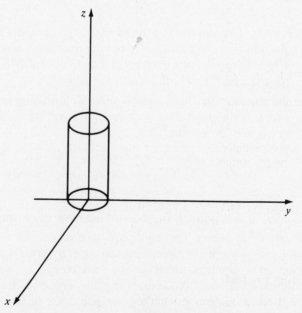

Fig. A2-7

EXAMPLE 1. The equation $x^2 + y^2 = 1$ is a circle in the xy plane. However, in three dimensions, it represents a cylinder (see Fig. A2-7).

The equations $x = 0$, $y = 0$, and $z = 0$ represent the yz, xz, and xy planes, respectively.

A2.3 VECTORS IN THREE DIMENSIONS

The definition of a vector and the concepts of magnitude, scalar multiplication, and vector addition are completely analogous to the two-dimensional case in App. 1.

In three dimensions, there are three natural coordinate vectors **I**, **J**, and **K**. These vectors are unit vectors (magnitude 1) having the direction of the positive x, y, and z axes, respectively. Any vector **V** can be resolved into components in terms of **I**, **J**, and **K**: $\mathbf{V} = a\mathbf{I} + b\mathbf{J} + c\mathbf{K}$.

The components $[a, b, c]$ of vectors **V** are also the Cartesian coordinates of the head of the vector **V** when the tail of **V** is placed at the origin of the Cartesian coordinate system (see Fig. A2-8).

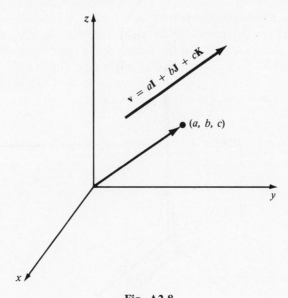

Fig. A2-8

EXAMPLE 2. Let $P_0(x_0, y_0, z_0)$ and $P_1(x_1, y_1, z_1)$ be two points in space. The directed line segment $\overline{P_0P_1}$ defines a vector whose tail is at P_0 and head is at P_1.

To find the components of $\overline{P_0P_1}$, we must translate so that the tail P_0 is placed at the origin. The head of the vector will then be at the point $(x_1 - x_0, y_1 - y_0, z_1 - z_0)$. The components of $\overline{P_0P_1}$ are then

$$\overline{P_0P_1} = (x_1 - x_0)\mathbf{I} + (y_1 - y_0)\mathbf{J} + (z_1 - z_0)\mathbf{K}$$

Vector addition and scalar multiplication can be performed componentwise, as in App. 1. The magnitude of a vector **V**, $|\mathbf{V}|$, is given by the formula

$$|\mathbf{V}| = \sqrt{a^2 + b^2 + c^2}$$

For any vector **V**, a *unit vector* (magnitude 1) $\mathbf{U_V}$ having the direction of **V** can be written as

$$\mathbf{U_V} = \frac{\mathbf{V}}{|\mathbf{V}|}$$

The Dot and the Cross Product

Let $\mathbf{V}_1 = a_1\mathbf{I} + b_1\mathbf{J} + c_1\mathbf{K}$ and $\mathbf{V}_2 = a_2\mathbf{I} + b_2\mathbf{J} + c_2\mathbf{K}$ be two vectors.

The *dot* or *scalar product* of two vectors is defined geometrically as $\mathbf{V}_1 \cdot \mathbf{V}_2 = |\mathbf{V}_1||\mathbf{V}_2| \cos \theta$, where θ

is the smaller angle between $\mathbf{V}_1$ and $\mathbf{V}_2$ (when the vectors are placed tail to tail). The component form of the dot product can be shown to be

$$\mathbf{V}_1 \cdot \mathbf{V}_2 = a_1 a_2 + b_1 b_2 + c_1 c_2$$

Note that the dot product of two vectors is a number and the order of the dot product is immaterial: $\mathbf{V}_1 \cdot \mathbf{V}_2 = \mathbf{V}_2 \cdot \mathbf{V}_1$. This formula enables us to calculate the angle θ between two vectors from the formula

$$\cos \theta = \frac{\mathbf{V}_1 \cdot \mathbf{V}_2}{|\mathbf{V}_1||\mathbf{V}_2|} = \frac{a_1 a_2 + b_1 b_2 + c_1 c_2}{\sqrt{a_1^2 + b_1^2 + c_1^2}\sqrt{a_2^2 + b_2^2 + c_2^2}}$$

Note that two vectors are *perpendicular* (*orthogonal*) (i.e., $\theta = 90°$) if and only if their dot product $\mathbf{V}_1 \cdot \mathbf{V}_2 = 0$. This provides a rapid test for determining whether two vectors are perpendicular. (Equivalently, we say that two vectors are *parallel* if they are scalar multiples of each other, i.e., $\mathbf{V}_1 = k\mathbf{V}_2$ for some number k.)

The *cross product* of two vectors, denoted $\mathbf{V}_1 \times \mathbf{V}_2$, produces a new vector defined geometrically as follows: $\mathbf{V}_1 \times \mathbf{V}_2$ is a vector whose magnitude is $|\mathbf{V}_1 \times \mathbf{V}_2| = |\mathbf{V}_1||\mathbf{V}_2| \sin \theta$, where θ is the angle between $\mathbf{V}_1$ and $\mathbf{V}_2$ and whose direction is determined by the right-hand rule: $\mathbf{V}_1 \times \mathbf{V}_2$ is a vector perpendicular to both $\mathbf{V}_1$ and $\mathbf{V}_2$ and whose direction is that of the thumb of the right hand when the fingers are aligned with $\mathbf{V}_1$ and rotated toward $\mathbf{V}_2$ through the smaller angle (see Fig. A2-9).

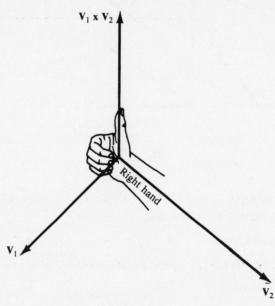

Fig. A2-9

From this definition, we see that the order in which the cross product is performed is relevant. In fact:

$$\mathbf{V}_1 \times \mathbf{V}_2 = -(\mathbf{V}_2 \times \mathbf{V}_1)$$

Note also that $\mathbf{V} \times \mathbf{V} = \mathbf{0}$ for any vector $\mathbf{V}$, since $\theta = 0°$. The component form for the cross product can be calculated as a determinant as follows:

$$\mathbf{V}_1 \times \mathbf{V}_2 = \begin{vmatrix} \mathbf{I} & \mathbf{J} & \mathbf{K} \\ a_1 & b_1 & c_1 \\ a_2 & b_2 & c_2 \end{vmatrix} = \begin{vmatrix} b_1 & c_1 \\ b_2 & c_2 \end{vmatrix}\mathbf{I} - \begin{vmatrix} a_1 & c_1 \\ a_2 & c_2 \end{vmatrix}\mathbf{J} + \begin{vmatrix} a_1 & b_1 \\ a_2 & b_2 \end{vmatrix}\mathbf{K}$$

$$= (b_1 c_2 - b_2 c_1)\mathbf{I} + (c_1 a_2 - c_2 a_1)\mathbf{J} + (a_1 b_2 - a_2 b_1)\mathbf{K}$$

EXAMPLE 3. For a right-handed Cartesian coordinate system, we have $\mathbf{I} \times \mathbf{J} = \mathbf{K}$, $\mathbf{J} \times \mathbf{K} = \mathbf{I}$, $\mathbf{I} \times \mathbf{K} = -\mathbf{J}$.

The Vector Equation of a Line

A line L in space is determined by its direction and a point $P_0(x_0, y_0, z_0)$ that the line passes through. If the direction is specified by a vector $\mathbf{V} = a\mathbf{I} + b\mathbf{J} + c\mathbf{K}$ and if $P(x, y, z)$ is any point on the line, the direction of the vector $\overline{P_0 P}$ determined by the points P_0, and P is parallel to the vector $\mathbf{V}$ (see Fig. A2-10). Thus, $\overline{P_0 P} = t\mathbf{V}$ for some number t.

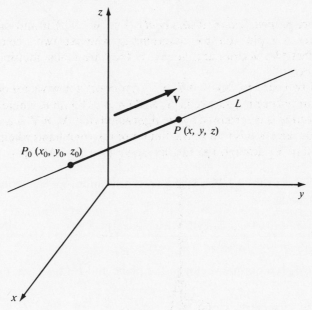

Fig. A2-10

In component form, we find that $(x - x_0)\mathbf{I} + (y - y_0)\mathbf{J} + (z - z_0)\mathbf{K} = ta\mathbf{I} + tb\mathbf{J} + tc\mathbf{K}$. Comparison of components leads to the parametric equations:

$$x = x_0 + at \qquad y = y_0 + bt \qquad z = z_0 + ct$$

In Probs. A2.5 and A2.6 it is shown how the equations of a line are determined when given two points on the line.

The Vector Equation of a Plane

A vector $\mathbf{N}$ is said to be a *normal vector* to a given plane if $\mathbf{N}$ is perpendicular to any vector $\mathbf{V}$ which lies on the plane; that is, $\mathbf{N} \cdot \mathbf{V} = 0$ for any $\mathbf{V}$ in the plane (see Fig. A2-11). A plane is uniquely determined by specifying a point $P_0(x_0, y_0, z_0)$ that is on the plane and a normal vector $\mathbf{N} = n_1\mathbf{I} + n_2\mathbf{J} + n_3\mathbf{K}$. Let $P(x, y, z)$ be any point on the plane. Then the vector $\overline{P_0 P}$ lies on the plane. Therefore, $\mathbf{N}$ is perpendicular to it. So $\mathbf{N} \cdot \overline{P_0 P} = 0$.

In component form, we obtain

$$[n_1\mathbf{I} + n_2\mathbf{J} + n_3\mathbf{K}] \cdot [(x - x_0)\mathbf{I} + (y - y_0)\mathbf{J} + (z - z_0)\mathbf{K}] = 0$$

or

$$n_1(x - x_0) + n_2(y - y_0) + n_3(z - z_0) = 0$$

The equation of a plane can also be determined by specifying (1) two vectors and a point (Prob.

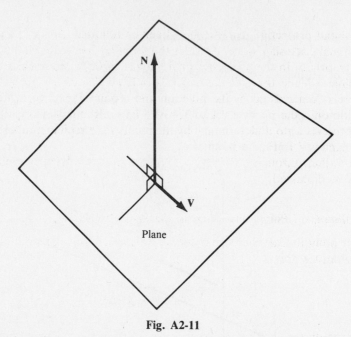

Fig. A2-11

A2.10) and (2) three points (Prob. A2.11). Using vector notation, we can write the distance D from a point $\bar{P}(\bar{x}, \bar{y}, \bar{z})$ to a plane as

$$D = \frac{[n_1(\bar{x} - x_0) + n_2(\bar{y} - y_0) + n_3(\bar{z} - z_0)]}{\sqrt{n_1^2 + n_2^2 + n_3^2}} \qquad \text{or} \qquad D = \frac{|\mathbf{N} \cdot \overline{\mathbf{P}_0 \bar{\mathbf{P}}}|}{|\mathbf{N}|}$$

where $\mathbf{N} = n_1 \mathbf{I} + n_2 \mathbf{J} + n_3 \mathbf{K}$ is a normal vector to the plane and $P_0(x_0, y_0, z_0)$ is a point on the plane.

A2.4 HOMOGENEOUS COORDINATES

The Two-Dimensional Projective Plane

The *projective plane* was introduced by geometers in order to study the geometric relationships of figures under perspective transformations.

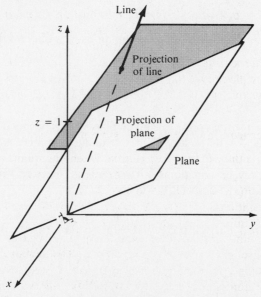

Fig. A2-12

The two-dimensional projective plane $\mathbf{P}_3$ is defined as follows:

In three-dimensional Cartesian space, consider the set of all lines through the origin and the set of all planes through the origin. In the projective plane, a line through the origin is called a *point* of the projective plane, while a plane through the origin is called a *line* of the projective plane.

To see why this is "natural" from the point of view of a perspective projection, consider the perspective projection onto the plane $z = 1$ using the origin as the center of projection. Then a line through the origin projects onto a point of the plane $z = 1$, while a plane through the origin projects onto a line in the plane $z = 1$ (Fig. A2-12).

In this projection, lines through points $(x, y, 0)$ in the plane project to infinity. This leads to the notion of ideal points, discussed later.

Homogeneous Coordinates of Points and Lines of the Projective Plane

If (a, b, c) is any point in Cartesian three-dimensional space, this point determines a line through the origin whose equations are

$$
\begin{aligned}
x &= at \\
y &= bt \qquad \text{(where } t \text{ is a number)} \\
z &= ct
\end{aligned}
$$

That is, any other point (at, bt, ct) determines the same line. So two points, (a_1, b_1, c_1) and (a_2, b_2, c_2), are on the same line through the origin if there is a number t so that

$$
a_2 = a_1 t \qquad b_2 = b_1 t \qquad c_2 = c_1 t \tag{A2.1}
$$

We say that two triples, (a_1, b_1, c_1) and (a_2, b_2, c_2), are equivalent (i.e., define the same line through the origin) if there is some number t so that the equations (A2.1) hold. We write $(a_1, b_1, c_1) \sim (a_2, b_2, c_2)$. The equivalence classes of all triples equivalent to (a, b, c), written as $[a, b, c]$, are the points of the projective plane. Any representative (a_1, b_1, c_1) equivalent to (a, b, c) is called the *homogeneous coordinate* of the point $[a, b, c]$ in the projective plane.

The points of the form $(a, b, 0)$ are called *ideal points* of the projective plane. This arises from the fact that lines in the plane $z = 0$ project to infinity. In a similar manner, any plane through the origin has an equation $n_1 x + n_2 y + n_3 z = 0$. Note that any multiple $kn_1 x + kn_2 y + kn_3 z = 0$ defines the same plane.

Any triple of numbers (n_1, n_2, n_3) defines a plane through the origin. Two triples are equivalent, $(n_1, n_2, n_3) \sim (d_1, d_2, d_3)$ (i.e., define the same plane), if there is a number k so that $d_1 = kn_1$, $d_2 = kn_2$, and $d_3 = kn_3$. The equivalence classes of all triples, $[n_1, n_2, n_3]$, are the lines of the projective plane. Any representative (d_1, d_2, d_3) of the equivalence class $[n_1, n_2, n_3]$ is called the *homogeneous line coordinate* of this line in the projective plane.

The ambiguity of whether a triple (a, b, c) represents a point or a line of the projective plane is exploited as the Duality Principle of Projective Geometry. If the context is not clear, one usually writes (a, b, c) to indicate a (projective) point and $[a, b, c]$ to indicate a (projective) line.

Correlation between Homogeneous and Cartesian Coordinates

If (x_1, y_1, z_1), $z_1 \neq 0$ are the homogeneous coordinates of a point of the projective plane, the equations $x = x_1/z_1$ and $y = y_1/z_1$ define a correspondence between points $P_1(x_1, y_1, z_1)$ of the projective plane and points $P(x, y)$ of the Cartesian plane.

There is no Cartesian point corresponding to the ideal point $(x_1, y_1, 0)$. However, it is convenient to consider it as defining an infinitely distant point.

Also, any Cartesian point $P(x, y)$ corresponds to a projective point $P(x_1, y_1, z_1)$ whose homogeneous coordinates are $x_1 = x$, $y_1 = y$, and $z_1 = 1$. This correspondence between Cartesian coordinates and homogeneous coordinates is exploited when using matrices to represent graphics transformations. The use of homogeneous coordinates allows the translation transformation and the perspective projection transformation to be represented by matrices (Chaps. 6 and 7).

To conform to the use of homogeneous coordinates, 2×2 matrices representing transformations of the plane can be augmented to use homogeneous coordinates as follows:

$$\mathbf{AX} = \left(\begin{pmatrix} a & b \\ c & d \end{pmatrix} \begin{matrix} 0 \\ 0 \end{matrix} \\ 0 \quad 0 \quad 1 \right) \begin{pmatrix} x \\ y \\ 1 \end{pmatrix}$$

Finally, note that even though we have a correspondence between the points of the projective plane and those of the Cartesian plane, the projective plane and the Cartesian plane have different topological properties which must be taken into account in work with homogeneous coordinates in advanced applications.

Three-Dimensional Projective Plane and Homogeneous Coordinates

Everything stated about the two-dimensional projective plane and homogeneous coordinates may be generalized to the three-dimensional case. For example, if $P_1(x_1, y_1, z_1, w_1)$ are the homogeneous coordinates of a point in the three-dimensional projective plane, the corresponding three-dimensional Cartesian point $P(x, y, z)$ is, for $w_1 \neq 0$,

$$x = \frac{x_1}{w_1} \qquad y = \frac{y_1}{w_1} \qquad z = \frac{z_1}{w_1}$$

In addition, if $P(x, y, z)$ is a Cartesian point, it corresponds to the projective point $P(x, y, z, 1)$. Finally, 3×3 matrices can be augmented to use homogeneous coordinates:

$$\left(\begin{pmatrix} & & \\ & 3 \times 3 & \\ & & \end{pmatrix} \begin{matrix} 0 \\ 0 \\ 0 \end{matrix} \\ 0 \quad 0 \quad 0 \quad 1 \right)$$

Solved Problems

A2.1 Describe the space curve whose parametric equations are $x = \cos t$, $y = \sin t$, and $z = t$.

SOLUTION

Noting that $x^2 + y^2 = \cos^2 t + \sin^2 t = 1$ (see Fig. A2-13), we find that the x, y variables lie on a unit circle, while the z coordinate varies. The curve is a (cylindrical) spiral.

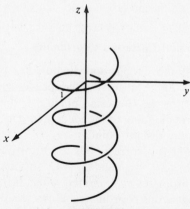

Fig. A2-13

A2.2 Find the equation of a sphere of radius r centered at the origin $(0, 0, 0)$.

SOLUTION

Let $P(x, y, z)$ be any point on the sphere. Then the distance D between this point and the center of the sphere is equal to the length of the radius r. The distance formula yields

$$\sqrt{(x-0)^2 + (y-0)^2 + (z-0)^2} = r \qquad \text{or} \qquad x^2 + y^2 + z^2 = r^2$$

This is the (implicit) equation of the sphere.

A2.3 Show that $\mathbf{V} \cdot \mathbf{V} = |\mathbf{V}|^2$ for any vector $\mathbf{V}$.

SOLUTION

If $\mathbf{V} = a\mathbf{I} + b\mathbf{J} + c\mathbf{K}$, then

$$\mathbf{V} \cdot \mathbf{V} = (a\mathbf{I} + b\mathbf{J} + c\mathbf{K}) \cdot (a\mathbf{I} + b\mathbf{J} + c\mathbf{K}) = a^2 + b^2 + c^2 = |\mathbf{V}|^2$$

A2.4 Let $\mathbf{V}_1 = 2\mathbf{I} - \mathbf{J} + \mathbf{K}$ and $\mathbf{V}_2 = \mathbf{I} + \mathbf{J} - \mathbf{K}$. Find (a) the angle between $\mathbf{V}_1$ and $\mathbf{V}_2$, (b) a vector perpendicular to both $\mathbf{V}_1$ and $\mathbf{V}_2$, and (c) a unit vector perpendicular to both $\mathbf{V}_1$ and $\mathbf{V}_2$.

SOLUTION

(a) We use the formula

$$\cos\theta = \frac{\mathbf{V}_1 \cdot \mathbf{V}_2}{|\mathbf{V}_1||\mathbf{V}_2|}$$

Now

$$|\mathbf{V}_1| = \sqrt{2^2 + (-1)^2 + (1)^2} = \sqrt{6} \qquad |\mathbf{V}_2| = \sqrt{1^2 + 1^2 + (-1)^2} = \sqrt{3}$$

and

$$\mathbf{V}_1 \cdot \mathbf{V}_2 = (2)(1) + (-1)(1) + (1)(-1) = 0$$

Thus $\cos\theta = 0$, and so $\theta = 90°$. So the vectors are perpendicular.

(b) The vector $\mathbf{V}_1 \times \mathbf{V}_2$ is perpendicular to both $\mathbf{V}_1$ and $\mathbf{V}_2$. So

$$\mathbf{V}_1 \times \mathbf{V}_2 = \begin{vmatrix} \mathbf{I} & \mathbf{J} & \mathbf{K} \\ 2 & -1 & 1 \\ 1 & 1 & 1 \end{vmatrix} = \begin{vmatrix} -1 & 1 \\ 1 & 1 \end{vmatrix}\mathbf{I} - \begin{vmatrix} 2 & 1 \\ 1 & 1 \end{vmatrix}\mathbf{J} + \begin{vmatrix} 2 & -1 \\ 1 & 1 \end{vmatrix}\mathbf{K} = -2\mathbf{I} - \mathbf{J} + 3\mathbf{K}$$

(c) Since $\mathbf{V}_1 \times \mathbf{V}_2$ is perpendicular to both $\mathbf{V}_1$ and $\mathbf{V}_2$, we find a unit vector having the direction of $\mathbf{V}_1 \times \mathbf{V}_2$. This is

$$\mathbf{U}_{\mathbf{V}_1 \times \mathbf{V}_2} = \frac{\mathbf{V}_1 \times \mathbf{V}_2}{|\mathbf{V}_1 \times \mathbf{V}_2|}$$

From part b, we have

$$|\mathbf{V}_1 \times \mathbf{V}_2| = \sqrt{(-2)^2 + (-1)^2 + (3)^2} = \sqrt{14}$$

So

$$\mathbf{U}_{\mathbf{V}_1 \times \mathbf{V}_2} = \frac{-2}{\sqrt{14}}\mathbf{I} - \frac{1}{\sqrt{14}}\mathbf{J} + \frac{3}{\sqrt{14}}\mathbf{K}$$

A2.5 Find the equation of the line passing through two points $P_0(x_0, y_0, t_0)$ and $P_1(x_1, y_1, z_1)$.

SOLUTION

To find the equation of a line, we need to know a point on the line and a vector having the direction of the line. The vector determined by P_0 and P_1, $\overline{P_0P_1}$ clearly has the direction of the line (see Fig. A2-14), and point P_0 lies on the line, so with direction vector

$$\overline{P_0P_1} = (x_1 - x_0)\mathbf{I} + (y_1 - y_0)\mathbf{J} + (z - z_0)\mathbf{K}$$

and point $P_0(x_0, y_0, z_0)$, the equation is

$$x = x_0 + (x_1 - x_0)t \qquad y = y_0 + (y_1 - y_0)t \qquad z = z_0 + (z_1 - z_0)t$$

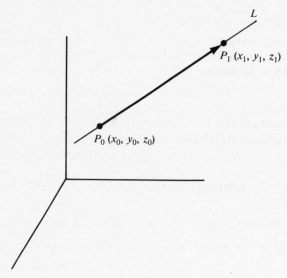

Fig. A2-14

A2.6 Find the equation of the line passing through $P_0(1, -5, 2)$ and $P_1(6, 7, -3)$.

SOLUTION

From Prob. A2.5, the direction vector is

$$\overline{P_0P_1} = (6 - 1)\mathbf{I} + [7 - (-5)]\mathbf{J} + (-3 - 2)\mathbf{K} = 5\mathbf{I} + 12\mathbf{J} - 5\mathbf{K}.$$

Using point $P_0(1, -5, 2)$, we have $x = 1 + 5t$, $y = -5 + 12t$, and $z = 2 - 5t$.

A2.7 Let line segment L_1 be determined by points $P_1(a_1, b_1, c_1)$ and $P_2(a_2, b_2, c_2)$. Let line segment L_2 be determined by points $Q_1(u_1, v_1, w_1)$ and $Q_2(u_2, v_2, w_2)$. How can we determine whether the line segments intersect?

SOLUTION

The parametric equations of L_1 are (Prob. A2.5)

$$x = a_1 + (a_2 - a_1)s$$
$$y = b_1 + (b_2 - b_1)s$$
$$z = c_1 + (c_2 - c_1)s$$

The equations of L_2 are

$$x = u_1 + (u_2 - u_1)t$$
$$y = v_1 + (v_2 - v_1)t$$
$$z = w_1 + (w_2 - w_1)t$$

Equating, we find

$$(u_2 - u_1)t - (a_2 - a_1)s = a_1 - u_1$$
$$(v_2 - v_1)t - (b_2 - b_1)s = b_1 - v_1$$
$$(w_2 - w_1)t - (c_2 - c_1)s = c_1 - w_1$$

Using the first two equations, we solve for s and t:

$$t = \frac{(b_1 - v_1)(a_2 - a_1) - (a_1 - u_1)(b_2 - b_1)}{(a_2 - a_1)(v_2 - v_1) - (b_2 - b_1)(u_2 - u_1)}$$

$$s = \frac{(b_1 - v_1)(u_2 - u_1) - (a_1 - u_1)(v_2 - v_1)}{(a_2 - a_1)(v_2 - v_1) - (b_2 - b_1)(u_2 - u_1)}$$

We now substitute the s value into equation L_1 and the t value into equation L_2. If all three corresponding numbers x, y, and z are the same, the lines intersect; if not, the lines do not intersect. Next, if both $0 \le s \le 1$ and $0 \le t \le 1$, the intersection point is on the line segments L_1 and L_2, between P_1 and P_2 and Q_1 and Q_2.

A2.8 Show that the equation of a plane has the implicit form $Ax + By + Cz + D = 0$, where A, B, and C are the components of the normal vector.

SOLUTION

The equation of a plane with normal vector $\mathbf{N} = A\mathbf{I} + B\mathbf{J} + C\mathbf{K}$ and passing through a point $P_0(x_0, y_0, z_0)$ is

$$A(x - x_0) + B(y - y_0) + C(z - z_0) = 0 \quad \text{or} \quad Ax + By + Cz + (-Ax_0 - By_0 - Cz_0) = 0$$

Calling the quantity $D = (-Ax_0 - By_0 - Cz_0)$ yields the equation of the plane:

$$Ax + By + Cz + D = 0$$

A2.9 Given the plane $5x - 3y + 6z = 7$: (a) find the normal vector to the plane, and (b) determine whether $P_1(1, 5, 2)$ and $P_2(-3, -1, 2)$ are on the same side of the plane.

SOLUTION

Write the equation in implicit form as $5x - 3y + 6z - 7 = 0$

(a) From Prob. A2.8, the coefficients 5, -3, and 6 are the components of a normal vector, that is, $\mathbf{N} = 5\mathbf{I} - 3\mathbf{J} + 6\mathbf{K}$.

(b) Let $f(x, y, z) = 5x - 3y + 6z - 7$. The plane has two sides, R^+ where $f(x, y, z)$ is positive and R^- where $f(x, y, z)$ is negative. Now for point $P_1(1, 5, 2)$, we have

$$f(1, 5, 2) = 5(1) - 3(5) + 6(2) - 7 = -5$$

and for point $P_2(-3, -1, 2)$,

$$f(-3, -1, 2) = 5(-3) - 3(-1) + 6(2) - 7 = -7$$

Since both $f(1, 5, 2)$ and $f(-3, -1, 2)$ are negative, P_1 and P_2 are on the same side of the plane.

A2.10 Find the equation of a plane passing through the point $P_0(1, -1, 1)$ and containing the vectors $\mathbf{V}_1 = \mathbf{I} - \mathbf{J} + \mathbf{K}$ and $\mathbf{V}_2 = -\mathbf{I} + \mathbf{J} + 2\mathbf{K}$ (see Fig. A2-15).

SOLUTION

To find the equation of a plane, we need to find a normal vector perpendicular to the plane. Since $\mathbf{V}_1$ and $\mathbf{V}_2$ are to lie on the plane, the cross product $\mathbf{V}_1 \times \mathbf{V}_2$ perpendicular to both $\mathbf{V}_1$ and $\mathbf{V}_2$ can be chosen to be the normal vector $\mathbf{N}$ (see Fig. A2-15). So

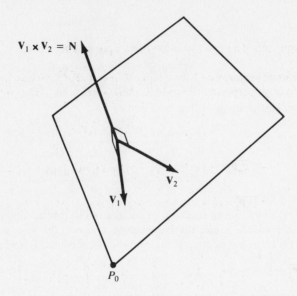

Fig. A2-15

$$\mathbf{N} = \mathbf{V_1} \times \mathbf{V_2} = \begin{vmatrix} \mathbf{I} & \mathbf{J} & \mathbf{K} \\ 1 & -1 & 1 \\ -1 & 1 & 2 \end{vmatrix} = \begin{vmatrix} -1 & 1 \\ 1 & 2 \end{vmatrix} \mathbf{I} - \begin{vmatrix} 1 & 1 \\ -1 & 2 \end{vmatrix} \mathbf{J} + \begin{vmatrix} 1 & -1 \\ -1 & 1 \end{vmatrix} \mathbf{K} = -3\mathbf{I} - 3\mathbf{J} + 0\mathbf{K}$$

So with $\mathbf{N} = -3\mathbf{I} - 3\mathbf{J}$ and the point $P_0(1, -1, 1)$, the equation of the plane is

$$-3(x - 1) - 3[y - (-1)] + 0(z - 1) = 0 \qquad \text{or} \qquad -3x - 3y = 0$$

Finally, $x + y = 0$ is the equation of the plane. This is an example of a cylinder surface, since z is a free variable and $y = -x$.

A2.11 Find the equation of the plane determined by the three points $P_0(1, 5, -7)$, $P_1(2, 6, 1)$, and $P_2(0, 1, 2)$ (see Fig. A2-16).

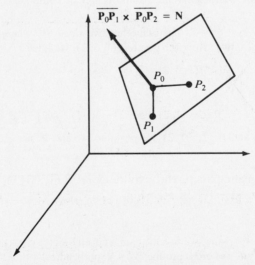

Fig. A2-16

SOLUTION

To find the equation of a plane, we must know a point on the plane and a normal vector perpendicular to the plane.

To find the normal vector, we observe that the vectors $\overline{\mathbf{P_0P_1}}$ and $\overline{\mathbf{P_0P_2}}$ lie on the plane, and so the cross product will be a vector perpendicular to both these vectors and so would be our choice for the normal vector; that is,

$$\mathbf{N} = \overline{\mathbf{P_0P_1}} \times \overline{\mathbf{P_0P_2}}$$

Now

$$\overline{\mathbf{P_0P_1}} = (2-1)\mathbf{I} + (6-5)\mathbf{J} + (1-(-7))\mathbf{K} = \mathbf{I} + \mathbf{J} + 8\mathbf{K}$$

and

$$\overline{\mathbf{P_0P_2}} = (0-1)\mathbf{I} + (1-5)\mathbf{J} + (2-(-7))\mathbf{K} = -\mathbf{I} - 4\mathbf{J} + 9\mathbf{K}$$

So

$$\overline{\mathbf{P_0P_1}} \times \overline{\mathbf{P_0P_2}} = \begin{vmatrix} \mathbf{I} & \mathbf{J} & \mathbf{K} \\ 1 & 1 & 8 \\ -1 & -4 & 9 \end{vmatrix} = \begin{vmatrix} 1 & 8 \\ -4 & 9 \end{vmatrix}\mathbf{I} - \begin{vmatrix} 1 & 8 \\ -1 & 9 \end{vmatrix}\mathbf{J} + \begin{vmatrix} 1 & 1 \\ -1 & -4 \end{vmatrix}\mathbf{K} = 41\mathbf{I} - 17\mathbf{J} - 3\mathbf{K}$$

So $\mathbf{N} = 41\mathbf{I} - 17\mathbf{J} - 3\mathbf{K}$, and with point $P_0(1, 5, -7)$, the equation of the plane is

$$41(x-1) - 17(y-5) - 3[z-(-7)] = 0 \qquad \text{or} \qquad 41x - 17y - 3z + 23 = 0$$

A2.12 Show that the equation of the plane that has x, y, and z intercepts $A(a, 0, 0)$, $B(0, b, 0)$, and $C(0, 0, c)$, respectively, is (see Fig. A2-17) $x/a + y/b + z/c = 1$.

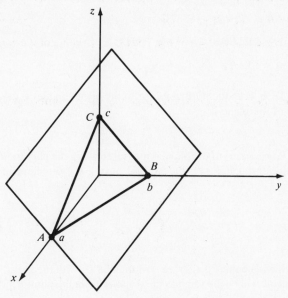

Fig. A2-17

SOLUTION

As in Prob. A2.11, we form the vectors $\overline{\mathbf{AB}} = -a\mathbf{I} + b\mathbf{J}$ and $\overline{\mathbf{AC}} = -a\mathbf{I} + c\mathbf{K}$. The normal vector to the plane is then

$$\mathbf{N} = \overline{\mathbf{AB}} \times \overline{\mathbf{AC}} = \begin{vmatrix} \mathbf{I} & \mathbf{J} & \mathbf{K} \\ -a & b & 0 \\ -a & 0 & c \end{vmatrix} = \begin{vmatrix} b & 0 \\ 0 & c \end{vmatrix}\mathbf{I} - \begin{vmatrix} -a & 0 \\ -a & c \end{vmatrix}\mathbf{J} + \begin{vmatrix} -a & b \\ -a & 0 \end{vmatrix}\mathbf{K} = bc\mathbf{I} + ac\mathbf{J} + ab\mathbf{K}$$

The equation of the plane with this normal vector and passing through $A(a, 0, 0)$ is

$$bc(x - a) + ac(y - 0) + ab(z - 0) = 0 \qquad \text{or} \qquad bcx + acy + abz = abc$$

Dividing both sides by abc, we have $x/a + y/b + z/c = 1$.

A2.13 Find the distance from a point $P_1(x_1, y_1, z_1)$ to a given plane (see Fig. A2-18).

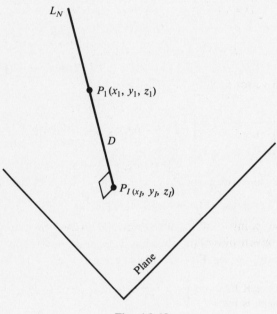

Fig. A2-18

SOLUTION

Let $\mathbf{N} = n_1\mathbf{I} + n_2\mathbf{J} + n_3\mathbf{K}$ be the normal vector to the plane, and let $P_0(x_0, y_0, z_0)$ be any point on the plane. The equation of the plane is

$$n_1(x - x_0) + n_2(y - y_0) + n_3(z - z_0) = 0$$

The distance D from $P_1(x_1, y_1, z)$ to the plane is measured along the perpendicular or normal to the plane.

Let L_N be the line through $P_1(x_1, y_1, z_1)$ and having the direction of the normal vector $\mathbf{N}$. The equation of L_N is

$$L_N: \quad \begin{aligned} x &= x_1 + n_1 t \\ y &= y_1 + n_2 t \\ z &= z_1 + n_3 t \end{aligned}$$

We first find the intersection point $P_I(x_I, y_I, z_I)$ of the line L_N with the plane. The distance from the point $P_1(x_1, y_1, z_1)$ to the plane will be the same as the distance from the point $P_1(x_1, y_1, z_1)$ to the intersection point $P_I(x_I, y_I, z_I)$.

Substituting the equations of the line L_N into the equation of the plane, we find

$$n_1(x_1 + n_1 t - x_0) + n_2(y_1 + n_2 t - y_0) + n_3(z_1 + n_3 t - z_0) = 0$$

Solving for t, we have

$$t = -\frac{n_1(x_1 - x_0) + n_2(y_1 - y_0) + n_3(z_1 - z_0)}{n_1^2 + n_2^2 + n_3^2}$$

Calling this number t_I, we find that the coordinates of P_I are

$$x_I = x_1 + n_1 t_I \qquad y_I = y_1 + n_2 t_I \qquad z_I = z_1 + n_3 t_I \qquad (A2.2)$$

The distance D from $P(x_1, y_1, z_1)$ to $P_I(x_I, y_I, z_I)$ is

$$D = \sqrt{(x_I - x_1)^2 + (y_I - y_1)^2 + (z_I + z_1)^2}$$

From equation (A2.2), we obtain

$$x_I - x_1 = n_1 t_I \qquad y_I - y_1 = n_2 t_I \qquad z_I - z_1 = n_3 t_I$$

Substitution into the formula for D yields

$$D = \sqrt{(n_1 t_I)^2 + (n_2 t_I)^2 + (n_3 t_I)^2} = |t_I| \sqrt{n_1^2 + n_2^2 + n_3^2}$$

or, substituting for t_I

$$D = \frac{|n_1(x_1 - x_0) + n_2(y_1 - y_0) + n_3(z_1 - z_0)|}{\sqrt{n_1^2 + n_2^2 + n_3^2}}$$

We can rewrite this in vector form by observing that

$$|\mathbf{N}| = \sqrt{n_1^2 + n_2^2 + n_3^2}$$

and that $(x_1 - x_0, y_1 - y_0, z_1 - z_0)$ are the components of the vector $\overline{P_0 P_1}$. So

$$D = \frac{|\mathbf{N} \cdot \overline{P_0 P_1}|}{|\mathbf{N}|} = \frac{d}{|\mathbf{N}|}$$

where $d = |\mathbf{N} \cdot \overline{P_0 P_1}|$.

A2.14 Find the intersection point of a line segment determined by two points $P_1(x_1, y_1, z_1)$ and $P_2(x_2, y_2, z_2)$ and a given plane.

SOLUTION

Let $\mathbf{N} = n_1 \mathbf{I} + n_2 \mathbf{J} + n_3 \mathbf{K}$ be the normal vector to the plane and $P_0(x_0, y_0, z_0)$ a point on the plane. The equation of the plane is then

$$n_1(x - x_0) + n_2(y - y_0) + n_3(z - z_0) = 0$$

The equation of the line determined by P_1 and P_2 is

$$x = x_1 + (x_2 - x_1)t \qquad y = y_1 + (y_2 - y_1)t \qquad z = z_1 + (z_2 - z_1)t$$

Substituting these equations into the equation of the plane, we have

$$n_1[x_1 + (x_2 - x_1)t - x_0] + n_2[y_1 + (y_2 - y_1)t - y_0] + n_3[z_1 + (z_2 - z_1)t - z_0] = 0$$

Solving for t, we find

$$t = -\frac{n_1(x_1 - x_0) + n_2(y_1 - y_0) + n_3(z_1 - z_0)}{n_1(x_2 - x_1) + n_2(y_2 - y_1) + n_3(z_2 - z_1)}$$

Calling this number t_I, we find that the intersection point $P_I(x_I, y_I, z_I)$ is

$$x_I = x_1 + (x_2 - x_1)t_I \qquad y_I = y_1 + (y_2 - y_1)t_I \qquad z_I = z_1 + (z_2 - z_1)t_I$$

If $0 \le t_I \le 1$, the intersection point lies on the line segment between P_1 and P_2. Otherwise, the intersection is on the extended line.

Note that the number t_I can be written in vector form as

$$t_I = -\frac{\mathbf{N} \cdot \overline{P_0 P_1}}{\mathbf{N} \cdot \overline{P_1 P_2}}$$

A2.15 Find the projection $\mathbf{V_p}$ of a vector $\mathbf{V}$ onto a given plane in the direction of the normal vector $\mathbf{N}$.

SOLUTION

From Fig. A2-19, by the definition of (head-to-tail) vector addition (see App. 1), we have

$$\mathbf{V_p} + k\mathbf{N} = \mathbf{V} \qquad \text{or} \qquad \mathbf{V_p} = \mathbf{V} - k\mathbf{N}$$

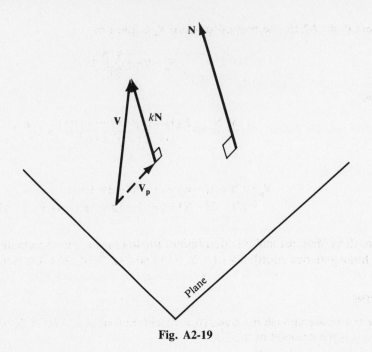

Fig. A2-19

To find the number k, we use the fact that $\mathbf{V_p}$ lies on the plane, so $\mathbf{N}$ is perpendicular to $\mathbf{V_p}$, i.e., $\mathbf{V_p} \cdot \mathbf{N} = 0$. So

$$0 = \mathbf{V_p} \cdot \mathbf{N} = \mathbf{V} \cdot \mathbf{N} - k(\mathbf{N} \cdot \mathbf{N}) \qquad \text{or} \qquad k = \frac{\mathbf{V} \cdot \mathbf{N}}{\mathbf{N} \cdot \mathbf{N}} = \frac{\mathbf{V} \cdot \mathbf{N}}{|\mathbf{N}|^2} \qquad (\text{since } \mathbf{N} \cdot \mathbf{N} = |\mathbf{N}|^2)$$

Then

$$\mathbf{V_p} = \mathbf{V} - \left(\frac{\mathbf{V} \cdot \mathbf{N}}{|\mathbf{N}|^2} \right) \mathbf{N} \qquad\qquad (A2\text{-}3)$$

A2.16 Let a plane be determined by the normal vector $\mathbf{N} = \mathbf{I} - \mathbf{J} + \mathbf{K}$ and a point $P_0(2, 3, -1)$.

(a) Find the distance from point $P_1(5, 2, 7)$ to the plane.

(b) Let a line segment be determined by $P_1(5, 2, 7)$ and $P_2(-2, 1, 0)$. Find the intersection with the plane.

(c) Let $\mathbf{V} = 2\mathbf{I} + 3\mathbf{J} - \mathbf{K}$ be a vector. Find the projection of $\mathbf{V_p}$ (in the direction of the normal) onto the plane.

SOLUTION

(a) The vector $\overline{P_0 P_1} = 3\mathbf{I} - \mathbf{J} + 8\mathbf{K}$. From Prob. A2.13 we have

$$D = \frac{|\mathbf{N} \cdot \overline{P_0 P_1}|}{|\mathbf{N}|} = \frac{|(1)(3) + (-1)(-1) + (1)(8)|}{\sqrt{(1)^2 + (-1)^2 + (1)^2}} = \frac{12}{\sqrt{3}} = 4\sqrt{3}$$

(b) With $\overline{P_0 P_1} = 3\mathbf{I} - \mathbf{J} + 8\mathbf{K}$ and $\overline{P_1 P_2} = -7\mathbf{I} - \mathbf{J} - 7\mathbf{K}$, from Prob. A2.14, we have

$$t_I = -\frac{\mathbf{N} \cdot \overline{P_0 P_1}}{\mathbf{N} \cdot \overline{P_1 P_2}} = -\frac{(1)(3) + (-1)(-1) + (1)(8)}{(1)(-7) + (-1)(-1) + (1)(-7)} = -\frac{12}{-13} = \frac{12}{13}$$

Since $0 \le t_I \le 1$, the intersection point is on the line segment between P_2 and P_1; furthermore, the intersection point is

$$x_I = x_1 + (x_2 - x_1)t_I = 5 + (-7)\tfrac{12}{13} = -\tfrac{19}{13}$$
$$y_I = y_1 + (y_2 - y_1)t_I = 2 + (-1)\tfrac{12}{13} = \tfrac{14}{13}$$
$$z_I = z_1 + (z_2 - z_1)t_I = 7 + (-7)\tfrac{12}{13} = \tfrac{7}{13}$$

(c)   From Prob. A2.15, the projection vector $\mathbf{V_p}$ is given by

$$\mathbf{V_p} = \mathbf{V} - \left(\frac{\mathbf{V} \cdot \mathbf{N}}{|\mathbf{N}|^2}\right)\mathbf{N}$$

Now

$$\frac{\mathbf{V} \cdot \mathbf{N}}{|\mathbf{N}|^2} = \frac{(2)(1) + (3)(-1) + (-1)(1)}{(1)^2 + (-1)^2 + (1)^2} = \frac{-2}{3}$$

So

$$\mathbf{V_p} = (2\mathbf{I} + 3\mathbf{J} - \mathbf{K}) - (-\tfrac{2}{3})(\mathbf{I} - \mathbf{J} + \mathbf{K})$$
$$= (2\mathbf{I} + 3\mathbf{J} - \mathbf{K}) - (-\tfrac{2}{3}\mathbf{I} + \tfrac{2}{3}\mathbf{J} - \tfrac{2}{3}\mathbf{K}) = \tfrac{8}{3}\mathbf{I} + \tfrac{7}{3}\mathbf{J} - \tfrac{1}{3}\mathbf{K}$$

A2.17 (a) What three-dimensional line determines the homogeneous coordinate point $(1, 5, -1)$? (b) Do the homogeneous coordinates $(1, 5, -1)$ and $(-2, -10, -3)$ represent the same projective point?

SOLUTION

(a)   The line passes through the origin $(0, 0, 0)$ and the Cartesian point $(1, 5, -1)$. So $x = t$, $y = 5t$, and $z = -t$ is the equation of the line.

(b)   The homogeneous coordinates represent the same projective point if and only if the coordinates are proportional, i.e., there is some number t so that $-2 = (1)t$, $-10 = (5)t$, and $-3 = (-1)t$. Since there is no such number, these coordinates represent different projective points.

Answers to Supplementary Problems

Chapter 1

1.39 Precision relates to the number of decimal places an input device can use to represent data. For example, if the thermometer in Prob. 1.2 could record temperatures between 00 and 99 degrees only, it would have two-place precision.

1.40 A high degree of coding error occurs because the sampling rate is too slow.

1.41

(a) $$\int_0^1 [12 \sin (t) + 3 \cos (2t)] \, dt - \sum_{i=0}^{239} \frac{12 \sin (i/240) + 3 \cos (2i/240)}{240}$$

(b) $$\int_0^1 [12 \sin (5t) + 3 \cos (10t)] \, dt - \sum_{i=0}^{239} \frac{12 \sin (5i/240) + 3 \cos (2i/240)}{240}$$

(c) $$\int_0^1 [12 \sin (50t) + 3 \cos (100t)] \, dt - \sum_{i=0}^{239} \frac{12 \sin (50i/240) + 3 \cos (100i/240)}{240}$$

(d) $$\int_0^1 [12 \sin (500t) + 3 \cos (1000t)] \, dt - \sum_{i=0}^{239} \frac{12 \sin (500i/240) + 3 \cos (1000i/240)}{240}$$

1.42 There are 525 raster lines on the standard CRT. Since the screen is refreshed at 60 Hz, it takes $\frac{1}{60}$ s to complete one full raster scan cycle. Due to top and bottom overscan, 23% (10% + 13%) of the raster lines are not displayed. Therefore only approximately $(1 - 0.23) * 525$ raster lines will be displayed. Thus, it takes 2 raster lines to represent each scan line. Consequently, it will take $\frac{2}{60}$ s = 2 raster lines/scan line $*$ $\frac{1}{60}$ s for each scan line to be displayed. Similarly, due to horizontal overscan, only 70 percent of each raster line is displayed. To find the time required to reach the coordinates of the light pen we define the following variables:

$$V = \text{time spent on top vertical overscan} = 0.1(\tfrac{1}{60}) = 0.00167 \text{ s}$$
$$L = \text{time to write each full line} = \tfrac{2}{60} * \tfrac{1}{525} = 0.0000635 \text{ s}$$
$$H = \text{time spent on left horizontal overscan} = 0.2 * L = 0.0000126 \text{ s}$$
$$P = \text{time in viewable area} = 0.7 * \tfrac{1}{60} * \tfrac{1}{525} = 0.0000222 \text{ s}$$

Therefore, the time T taken to reach the location (x, y) of the light pen would be

$$T = V + L * (y - 1) + H + P * x/200$$

(*Note:* Since L represents the number of full lines written, 1 must be subtracted from the y coordinate.) The time needed to reach each of the screen coordinates is:

(a) $T = V + L * (y - 1) + H + P * x$
$= 0.00167 + 0.0000635 * (80 - 1) + 0.0000126 + 0.0000222(\frac{137}{200})$
$\cong 0.006714 \text{ s}$

(b) $T = V + L * (y - 1) + H + P * x$
$= 0.00167 + 0.0000635 * (190 - 1) + 0.0000126 + 0.0000222(\frac{580}{200})$
$\cong 0.013744 \text{ s}$

(c) $T = V + L * (y - 1) + H + P * x$
$= 0.00167 + 0.0000635 * (195 - 1) + 0.0000126 + 0.0000222(\frac{28}{200})$
$\cong 0.013999 \text{ s}$

1.43 As the computer steps through display memory, it is already keeping track of the byte currently being displayed. This then means the computer can locate the light pen by storing the location of the byte being displayed when the pen senses the passing of the electron beam.

1.44 Graphics work generally requires a high degree of concentration. The acoustic tablet is so noisy that users find it distracting. In addition, ambient noise (which will create errors) is difficult to filter out.

1.45 Generally a graphics system designer will compare initial cost, cost per kilobyte, access time (the speed at which the data can be retrieved), cost of storage medium, the expected life of the storage device, the expected life of the storage medium, and the capacity of the device.

1.46 The relationship between voltage, amperage, and resistance is described by the equation $V = I * R$, where $V =$ volts, $I =$ current, and $R =$ resistance. Therefore, the length of the wire can be found as follows: $V = 1$ volt at the end of the wire and $I = 1$ A. Solving for R, we obtain

$$R = \frac{V}{I} = \frac{1}{1} = 1$$

The resistance per foot of wire was given as $0.05 \ \Omega/\text{foot}$. Therefore, solving for number of feet yields

$$\text{Number of feet} = \frac{R}{R \text{ per foot}} = \frac{1}{0.05} = 20 \text{ ft}$$

1.47 One start bit, 7 data bits, then 1 stop bit.

1.48 The graphics programmer is concerned with addressing capacity for two reasons. First, most graphics systems require an enormous amount of memory to be reserved for display memory, graphics data, and graphics subroutines. Second, the amount of memory the processor can address directly will greatly affect the speed at which the computer will respond.

1.49 The size of each page is equal to the amount of memory the computer's processor can address directly. Therefore, a computer with an 8-bit address width has pages 2^8 or 256 bytes long.

1.50 The word size of a processor determines the maximum number of commands in the processor's instruction set. Word size also determines the number of bits the computer can operate on at one time and the precision of the computer's calculations. Therefore, the word size of a computer's processor limits the number of machine language instructions the graphics programmer has available as well as the speed and precision with which the computer will work.

1.51 The range of integer values that can be expressed directly by a processor is equal to $\pm 2^{2^{W-1}}$, where W is the word size in bits. Therefore,

(*a*)
$$2^{(2*4-1)} - 1 = \pm 127$$
(*b*)
$$2^{(2*8-1)} - 1 = \pm 32,767$$
(*c*)
$$2^{(2*16-1)} - 1 = \pm 2,147,483,652$$

Chapter 2

2.36 See Fig. 2-1.

2.37 Cathode-ray tube.

2.38 The CRT is an analog device because its output is continuous.

2.39 An electron beam will bend when it passes through either an electrostatic or a magnetic field.

2.40 A phosphor's life is dependent on both the intensity and exposure time to a high energy-electron beam.

2.41 A very thin horizontal line displayed on an interlaced raster scan CRT may only be refreshed once every $\frac{1}{30}$ s. This is because the interlacing technique splits the raster line pattern into two separate patterns consisting of half the origin raster lines each. As a result the horizontal line would not be refreshed often enough to prevent flicker.

2.42 None. However, if no additional computer memory were employed, 48 percent of the picture would be lost.

2.43 Each pixel on the screen of a CRT used in the United States is usually refreshed once every $\frac{1}{30}$ s when interlacing is employed. Therefore, a phosphor with $\frac{1}{30}$-s persistence would virtually eliminate flicker. In addition, the phosphor would stop its phosphorescence the instant the electron beam passed on the next refresh cycle.

2.44 Since vertical overscan accounts for about 20 percent of the raster lines, the total number of visible raster lines will be 420 lines [525 lines × (0.100–0.20)]. Dividing the height of the visible screen by the number of visible lines will give an approximate spot with the spots just touching. In this case

$$\frac{7 \text{ in}}{420 \text{ raster lines}} = 0.017 \text{ in per raster line}$$

2.45 Most humans have a visual perceptual threshold of under $\frac{1}{30}$ s. Therefore, the flickering on and off of the image takes place too quickly for them to see. A small group of people have visual perceptual thresholds of $\frac{1}{40}$ s or faster. These people will always see a flickering image.

2.46 Least-significant bit.

2.47 The MSB represents 2 to the seventh power.

2.48 The LSB represents 2 to the zeroth power.

2.49

(a)		(b)		(c)	
1100	= 0CH	1111	= 0FH	0110	= 06H
+0011	= 03H	+ 1111	= 0FH	+0011	= 03H
1111	= 0FH	11110	= IEH	1001	= 09H

2.50

(a)		(b)		(c)	
1010	= 0AH	1011	= 0BH	1111	= 0FH
−0011	= 03H	−0001	= 01H	−0001	= 01H
0111	= 07H	1010	= 0AH	1110	= 0EH

2.51

$$
\begin{array}{r}
1010 = 0\text{AH} \\
1000 = 08\text{H} \\
\hline
0000 \\
0000 \\
0000 \\
1010 \\
\hline
1010000 = 50\text{H}
\end{array}
$$

2.52 Dividing by 2 is the same as single right shift in binary. Therefore, 0111/0010 = 0011.1. Dividing by 8 is the same as three right shifts in binary. Therefore, 0111/1000 = 0000.111.

2.53 1. Locate the starting address of the line that is to represent the y coordinate. In this case, line 2 starts at address 02H (0010 binary).

2. Right-shift the binary value equivalent to the *x* coordinate three times (this is the same as dividing by 8), then add the integer portion of this result to the result from step 1: 14 decimal = 00001110 binary. Right-shifting three times yields 00000001.11 binary. Adding the integer portion of this result to the result from step 1:

$$00000010 = 02H\text{—from step 1}$$
$$\underline{+00000001} = 01H\text{—}x \text{ integer value after right-shifting three times}$$
$$00000011 = 03H\text{—address of byte that will represent the pixel}$$

3. The remainder from step 2, 14 modulo 8 = 6, is stored as 0110 binary, which is 06H. Therefore, we want to light the sixth pixel from the MSB:

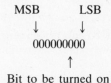

MSB   LSB

↓   ↓

000000000

↑

Bit to be turned on

4. OR the result from step 3 (00000100) with the present value of the address found in steps 1 and 2 (address 03H), and place the result in that address:

$$00000000 = 00H\text{—value stored at address 03H}$$
$$OR\ 00000100 = 04H\text{—value found in step 3}$$

2.54 1. The memory map is not sequential, so a lookup table (Table 2-3) must be developed. In Table 2-3, *y* = 8, so the first point is located on the line starting at address 0400H.

2. Right-shift the *x* value three times, and add the integer portion of the result to the result from step 1: 25 decimal = 19H = 00011001 binary; three right shifts yields 00000011.001. The integer portion is 00000011 = 03H. Add the result to the address found in step 1:

$$0400H$$
$$\underline{+0003H}$$
Address which will represent point $0403H$

3. The remainder from step 2, 25 modulo 8, is 1 decimal (00000001 binary). According to the lookup table (Table 2-1), the value to be ORed is 0100000 binary.

4. OR the value found in step 3 (01000000 binary) with the byte found in steps 1 and 2:

$$00000000 \text{ value of address 0403H}$$
$$\underline{OR\ 01000000} \text{ value found in step 4}$$
$$01000000 \text{ value to be stored at address 0403H}$$

2.55 The dimensions of a CRT are always given as width-to-height dimensions; therefore, to find the aspect ratio, we need only to identify the lowest common denominator and divide to find the aspect ratio: (*a*) the lowest common denominator for 15 and 10 is 5; so

$$3 = \frac{15}{5} \begin{matrix} \leftarrow \text{CRT width} \\ \leftarrow \text{Lowest common denominator} \end{matrix} \qquad 2 = \frac{10}{5} \begin{matrix} \leftarrow \text{CRT height} \\ \leftarrow \text{Lowest common denominator} \end{matrix}$$

Thus, the aspect ratio 3:2; (*b*) the lowest common denominator for 4 and 4 is 4; so

$$1 = \frac{4}{4} \begin{matrix} \leftarrow \text{CRT width} \\ \leftarrow \text{Lowest common denominator} \end{matrix} \qquad 1 = \frac{4}{4} \begin{matrix} \leftarrow \text{CRT height} \\ \leftarrow \text{Lowest common denominator} \end{matrix}$$

So thus, the aspect ratio is 1:1; (*c*) the lowest common denominator for 24 and 18 is 6; so

$$4 = \frac{24}{6} \begin{matrix} \leftarrow \text{CRT width} \\ \leftarrow \text{Lowest common denominator} \end{matrix} \qquad 3 = \frac{18}{6} \begin{matrix} \leftarrow \text{CRT height} \\ \leftarrow \text{Lowest common denominator} \end{matrix}$$

Thus, the aspect ratio is 4:3.

2.56 To fit the data to the memory map, the coordinates must be scaled, preferably by a power of 2, so that they are in the range of values allowed in the memory map. In this case, we divide by 2: $900/2 = 450$ and $520/2 = 260$.

2.57 Plasma displays are relatively thin or flat; are generally lighter than CRTs because the coils and magnets required for the CRTs deflection yoke are not used; and have memory—that is, once a gas cell has been lit, it will remain lit until it is specifically turned off; therefore, a memory map is not always required.

2.58 Liquid crystal displays have very low power requirements, depend on ambient light (therefore, the higher ambient light levels are, the clearer the LCD will appear), are lightweight compared to CRTs, and are relatively thin.

2.59 Liquid crystal displays may be viewed only from a restricted angle, are difficult to read at low ambient light levels, and respond relatively slowly (thus, animation is restricted).

2.60 Memory-tube displays offer very high resolution at a relatively low cost per display and do not require display memory.

2.61 Animation is difficult because once one pixel is lit, the entire screen must be cleared and rewritten to change the single pixel. The phosphor used in memory-tube displays glows at a low level, thus requiring dim ambient lighting.

Chapter 3

3.20

(a)

$y = 4x + 3$	x
11	2
31	7
7	1

(b)

$y = 1x + 0$	x
2	2
7	7
1	1

(c)

$y = -3x - 4$	x
-10	2
-25	7
-7	1

(d)

$y = -2x + 1$	x
-3	2
-13	7
-1	1

3.21

1. Compute the initial values. Prior to passing the variables to the line plotting routine, we exchange x and y coordinates, (x, y) giving (y, x).

$$dx = y_1 - y_2 \qquad Inc_1 = 2 * dy$$
$$dy = x_1 - x_2 \qquad Inc_2 = 2 * (dy - dx) \qquad d = Inc_1 - dx$$

2. Set (x, y) equal to the lower left-hand endpoint and x_{end} equal to the largest value of x. If $dy < 0$, then $y = x_2$, $x = y_2$, $x_{end} = y_1$. If $dx > 0$, then $y = x_1$, $x = y_1$, $x_{end} = y_2$.

3. Plot a point at the current (y, x) coordinates. Note the coordinate values are exchanged before they are passed to the plot routine.

4. Test to determine whether the entire line has been drawn. If $x > x_{end}$, stop.

5. Compute the location of the next pixel. If $d < 0$, then $d = d + Inc_1$. If $d \geq 0$, then $d = d + Inc_2$, $y = y + 1$.

6. Increment x: $x = x + 1$.

7. Prior to plotting, the (x, y) coordinates are again exchanged. Plot a point at the current (x, y) coordinates.

8. Go to step 4.

3.22

1. Set the initial values: (x_1, y_1) = start of line; (x_3, y_3) = end of line; m = slope = $(y_3 - y_1)/(x_3 - x_1)$; a = length of dash; c = length of blank.

2. Test to see whether the entire line has been drawn. If $x_1 > = x_3$, stop.

3. Compute end of dash:
$$x_2 = x_1 + a$$
$$y_2 = y_1 + a*m + b$$

4. Send (x_1, y_1) and (x_2, y_2) to the line routine and plot dash.

5. Compute the starting point of the next dash:
$$x_1 = a + c + x_1$$
$$y_1 = m*(a + b) + y_1 + c$$

6. Go to step 2.

3.23 (a) Scan converting points P_1 and P_2 if necessary, we suppose that (x_1, y_1) and (x_2, y_2) are already integers. Using the notation of Fig. 3-3, the coordinates of the bottom pixel at any step i are denoted $S_i(x_i, y_i)$ and those of the top pixel are $T_i(x_i, y_i + 1)$. The actual coordinates of the line $y = mx + b$ are $A_i(x_i, \bar{y}_i)$, where $\bar{y}_i = mx_i + b$. The distance s_i from the bottom pixel to the actual line coordinates is calculated as $s_i = \bar{y}_i - y_i$. The distance t_i from the top pixel to the actual line coordinates is $t_i = (y_i + 1) - \bar{y}_i$. The decision variable is

$$d'_i = s_i - t_i = (\bar{y}_i - y_i) - [(y_i + 1) - \bar{y}_i] = 2\bar{y}_i - 2y_i - 1 = 2(mx_i + b) - 2y_i - 1$$

We wish to express all of these variables incrementally in terms of the previously plotted pixel (which may have been a top or bottom pixel) denoted as $P'_{i-1}(x'_{i-1}, y'_{i-1})$. Then, because the slope is between 0 and 1, the next bottom pixel $S_i(x_i, y_i)$ satisfies

$$x_i = x'_{i-1} + 1 \qquad y_i = y'_{i-1}$$

and so,
$$d'_i = 2(mx'_{i-1} + m + b) - 2y'_{i-1} - 1$$

Similarly, we can write the decision variable d'_{i+1} as,

$$d'_{i+1} = 2(mx'_i + m + b) - 2y'_i - 1 \tag{1}$$

Then
$$d'_{i+1} - d'_i = 2[m(x'_i - x'_{i-1}) - (y'_i - y'_{i-1})]$$

Since the slope m satisfies $0 \le m \le 1$, then at each step the horizontal pixel increment satisfies $x'_i = x'_{i-1} + 1$. So,

$$d'_{i+1} - d'_i = 2[m - (y'_i - y'_{i-1})]$$

If at step i the plotted pixel P'_i is the top pixel T_i (meaning that $d'_i \ge 0$) then $y'_i = y'_{i-1} + 1$ and so,

$$d'_{i+1} - d'_i = 2(m - 1)$$

On the other hand, if the plotted pixel P'_i is the bottom pixel S_i (meaning $d'_i < 0$) then $y'_i = y_{i-1}$ and so,

$$d'_{i+1} - d'_i = 2m$$

Finally, writing $m = dy/dx$ and introducing the new decision variable, $d_i = (dx)*d'_i$ whose sign is the same as that of d'_i (since dx is positive in our case), we can multiply both equations by dx and we have

$$d_{i+1} - d_i = \begin{cases} 2(dy - dx) & \text{if } d_i \ge 0 \\ 2dy & \text{if } d_i < 0 \end{cases}$$

This is the incremental computation performed by Bresenham's algorithm. Noting that $y'_1 = mx'_1 + b$, then after multiplying eq. (1) by dx, the initial value d_2 can be written as $d_2 = 2dy - dx$.

(b)
$$d_i = \qquad D(s_i) \qquad + \qquad D(t_i)$$
$$= (x_{i-1} + 1)^2 + (y_{i-1})^2 - r^2 + (x_{i-1} + 1)^2 + (y_{i-1} - 1)^2 - r^2$$

If it is assumed that the circle is centered at the origin, then at the first step $x = 0$ and $y = r$ (see Fig. S-1). Therefore

$$d_i = \qquad D(S_i) \qquad + \qquad D(T_i)$$
$$= (0+1)^2 + r^2 - r^2 + (0+1)^2 + (r-1)^2 - r^2$$
$$= \qquad 1 \qquad + \qquad 1 \quad + r^2 - 2r + 1 - r^2$$

Collecting terms, we have $d_i = 3 - 2r$.

3.24   See Fig. S-2. Solving for $\theta = \pi/4$:

$$x = 2\cos(\pi/4) + 0 = 1.414 \qquad y = 1\sin(\pi/4) + 0 = 0.7071$$

Solving for $\theta = 3\pi/4$:

$$x = 2\cos(3\pi/4) + 0 = -1.414 \qquad y = 1\sin(3\pi/4) + 0 = 0.7071$$

Solving for $\theta = 5\pi/4$:

$$x = 2\cos(5\pi/4) + 0 = -1.414 \qquad y = 1\sin(5\pi/4) + 0 = -0.7071$$

Solving for $\theta = 7\pi/4$:

$$x = 2\cos(7\pi/4) + 0 = 1.414 \qquad y = 1\sin(7\pi/4) + 0 = -0.7071$$

3.25   (a)   Step 3 should be changed to read

$$x = a * \cos(\theta) - b * \sin\left(\theta + \frac{\pi}{4}\right) + h$$
$$y = b * \sin(\theta) + a * \cos\left(\theta + \frac{\pi}{4}\right) + k$$

    (b)   Step 3 should be changed to read

$$x = a * \cos(\theta) - b * \sin\left(\theta + \frac{\pi}{9}\right) + h$$
$$y = b * \sin(\theta) + a * \cos\left(\theta + \frac{\pi}{9}\right) + k$$

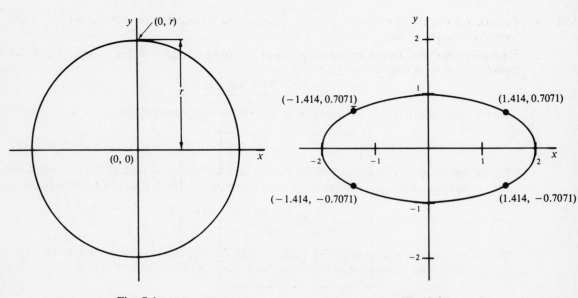

Fig. S-1   **Fig. S-2**

(c) Step 3 should be changed to read

$$x = a * \cos(\theta) - b * \sin\left(\theta + \frac{\pi}{2}\right) + h$$

$$y = b * \sin(\theta) + a * \cos\left(\theta + \frac{\pi}{2}\right) + k$$

Note that rotating an ellipse $\pi/2$ requires only that the major and minor axes be interchanged. Therefore, the rotation could also be accomplished by changing step 3 to read

$$x = b * \cos(\theta) \qquad y = a * \sin(\theta)$$

3.26 1. Set initial variables: a = radius, (h, k) = coordinates of sector center, θ_1 = starting angle, θ_2 = ending angle, and i = step size.

2. Plot line from sector center to coordinates of start of arc: plot (h, k) to $(a * \cos(\theta_1) + h, a * \sin(\theta_1) + k)$.

3. Plot line from sector center to coordinates of end of arc: plot (h, k) to $(a * \cos(\theta_1) + h, a * \sin(\theta_2) + h)$.

4. Plot arc.

3.27 When a region is to be filled with a pattern, the fill algorithm must look at a table containing the pattern before filling each pixel. The correct value for the pixel is taken from the table and placed in the pixel examined by the fill algorithm.

3.28 1. Assuming standard ASCII code is used to represent each character, scan the keyboard to see whether a key has been pressed. When a key is pressed, subtract 41H (the hexadecimal ASCII code value for A) from the value of the key just pressed.

2. Multiply the result from step 1 by 8 (the number of bytes representing each character) and add it to the starting address of the alternate character set table.

3. Copy the contents of the address found in step 2 and the contents of the next 7 bytes to the desired portion of display memory.

3.29 The human brain tends to compensate for deficiencies in models. For example, although the cube shown in Fig. S-3 is lacking the visual cue, convergence, it is perceived as a cube. When the method of aliasing is inconsistent, the brain either cannot decode the model or can decode it only with difficulty because there is no one rule that can be learned to compensate for the inconsistencies of the models.

3.30 1. Initialize (a) y to 0, (b) the active edge list to empty, and (c) the edge list of c cells (where c is the vertical resolution of display memory) to empty.

2. For each nonhorizontal edge, link the values $1/m (=\Delta x/\Delta y)$, x_A, y_{max} to cell y_{min}, where y_{min} is the minimum y value of edge E_i and x_A is its x coordinate.

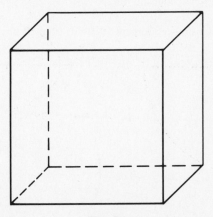

Fig. 5-3

3. Increment y by 1.
4. If y is greater than c, stop.
5. Add all edges linked to cell y to the active edge list and delete all edges for which $y \geq y_{max}$.
6. Sort the edges in the active edge list by minimum x value.
7. Fill the pixels between and including each pair of edges in the active edge list.
8. Increment each x_A by $1/m$.
9. Go to step 3.

Chapter 4

4.19

$$R_\theta = \begin{pmatrix} \cos\theta & -\sin\theta \\ \sin\theta & \cos\theta \end{pmatrix} \quad \text{and} \quad R_{-\theta} = \begin{pmatrix} \cos(-\theta) & -\sin(-\theta) \\ \sin(-\theta) & \cos(-\theta) \end{pmatrix} = \begin{pmatrix} \cos\theta & \sin\theta \\ -\sin\theta & \cos\theta \end{pmatrix}$$

Also

$$R_\theta \cdot R_{-\theta} = \begin{pmatrix} \cos\theta & -\sin\theta \\ \sin\theta & \cos\theta \end{pmatrix} \begin{pmatrix} \cos\theta & \sin\theta \\ \sin\theta & \cos\theta \end{pmatrix}$$

$$= \begin{pmatrix} (\cos^2\theta + \sin^2\theta) & (\cos\theta\sin\theta - \sin\theta\cos\theta) \\ (\sin\theta\cos\theta - \cos\theta\sin\theta) & (\sin^2\theta + \cos^2\theta) \end{pmatrix} = \begin{pmatrix} 1 & 0 \\ 0 & 1 \end{pmatrix}$$

Therefore, R_θ and $R_{-\theta}$ are inverse, so $R_{-\theta} = R_\theta^{-1}$. In other words, the inverse of rotation by θ degrees is a rotation in the opposite direction.

4.20 Magnification and reduction can be achieved by a uniform scaling of s units in both the X and Y directions. If $s > 1$, the scaling produces magnification. If $s < 1$, the result is a reduction. The transformation can be written as

$$(x, y) \mapsto (sx, sy)$$

In matrix form, this becomes

$$\begin{pmatrix} s & 0 \\ 0 & s \end{pmatrix} \begin{pmatrix} x \\ y \end{pmatrix} = \begin{pmatrix} s & x \\ s & y \end{pmatrix}$$

(a) Choosing $s = 2$ and applying the transformation to the coordinates of the points A, B, C yields the new coordinates $A'(0,0)$, $B'(2,2)$, $C'(10,4)$.

(b) Here, $s = \frac{1}{2}$ and the new coordinates are $A''(0,0)$, $B''(\frac{1}{2}, \frac{1}{2})$, $C''(\frac{5}{2}, 1)$.

4.21 The line $y = x$ has slope 1 and y intercept $(0,0)$. If point P has coordinates (x, y), then

$$M_L \cdot P = \begin{pmatrix} 0 & 1 \\ 1 & 0 \end{pmatrix} \begin{pmatrix} x \\ y \end{pmatrix} = \begin{pmatrix} y \\ x \end{pmatrix} \quad \text{or} \quad M_L(x, y) = (y, x)$$

4.22 The rotation matrix is

$$R_{45°} = \begin{pmatrix} \dfrac{\sqrt{2}}{2} & -\dfrac{\sqrt{2}}{2} & 0 \\ \dfrac{\sqrt{2}}{2} & \dfrac{\sqrt{2}}{2} & 0 \\ 0 & 0 & 1 \end{pmatrix}$$

The translation matrix is

$$T_{\mathbf{I}} = \begin{pmatrix} 1 & 0 & 1 \\ 0 & 1 & 0 \\ 0 & 0 & 1 \end{pmatrix}$$

The matrix of vertices $[A \ B \ C]$ is

$$V = \begin{pmatrix} 1 & 0 & 1 \\ 0 & 1 & 1 \\ 1 & 1 & 1 \end{pmatrix}$$

(a)

$$T_{\mathbf{I}} \cdot R_{45°} = \begin{pmatrix} \dfrac{\sqrt{2}}{2} & -\dfrac{\sqrt{2}}{2} & 1 \\[2mm] \dfrac{\sqrt{2}}{2} & \dfrac{\sqrt{2}}{2} & 0 \\[2mm] 0 & 0 & 1 \end{pmatrix} \quad \text{and} \quad T_{\mathbf{I}} \cdot R_{45°} \cdot V = \begin{pmatrix} \left(\dfrac{\sqrt{2}}{2}+1\right) & \left(-\dfrac{\sqrt{2}}{2}+1\right) & 1 \\[2mm] \dfrac{\sqrt{2}}{2} & \dfrac{\sqrt{2}}{2} & \sqrt{2} \\[2mm] 1 & 1 & 1 \end{pmatrix}$$

So the transformed vertices are $A'\left(\dfrac{\sqrt{2}}{2}+1, \dfrac{\sqrt{2}}{2}\right)$, $B'\left(-\dfrac{\sqrt{2}}{2}+1, \dfrac{\sqrt{2}}{2}\right)$, and $C'(1, \sqrt{2})$.

(b)

$$R_{45°} \cdot T_{\mathbf{I}} = \begin{pmatrix} \dfrac{\sqrt{2}}{2} & -\dfrac{\sqrt{2}}{2} & \dfrac{\sqrt{2}}{2} \\[2mm] \dfrac{\sqrt{2}}{2} & \dfrac{\sqrt{2}}{2} & \dfrac{\sqrt{2}}{2} \\[2mm] 0 & 0 & 1 \end{pmatrix} \quad \text{and} \quad R_{45°} \cdot T_{\mathbf{I}} \cdot V = \begin{pmatrix} \sqrt{2} & 0 & \dfrac{\sqrt{2}}{2} \\[2mm] \sqrt{2} & \sqrt{2} & \dfrac{3\sqrt{2}}{2} \\[2mm] 1 & 1 & 1 \end{pmatrix}$$

The transformed coordinates are $A''(\sqrt{2}, \sqrt{2})$, $B''(0, \sqrt{2})$, and $C''(\sqrt{2}/2, 3\sqrt{2}/2)$. From this we see that the order in which the transformations are applied is important in the formation of composed or concatenated transformations (see Fig. S-4). Figure S-4(b) represents the image of Fig. S-4(a) after application of the transformation $T_{\mathbf{I}} \cdot R_{45°}$; Fig. S-4(c) represents the same image after the transformation $R_{45°} \cdot T_{\mathbf{I}}$.

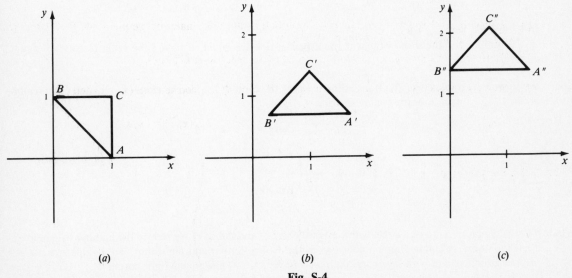

(a)   (b)   (c)

Fig. S-4

4.23 To determine the coordinates of the displaced object from the observer's point of view, we must find the coordinates of the object with respect to the observer's coordinate system. In our case we have performed an object translation T_v and a coordinate system translation $\bar{T}_v$. The result is found by the composition $\bar{T}_v \cdot T_v$ (or $T_v \cdot \bar{T}_v$):

$$\binom{x}{y} \mapsto \binom{x+a}{y+b} \mapsto \binom{x+a-a}{y+b-b} = \binom{x}{y}$$

So the coordinates have remained the same.

4.24 We express the general form of an equation in the $x'y'$ coordinate system as $F(x', y') = 0$. Writing the change of coordinate transformation in equation form as

$$x' = q(x, y) \qquad y' = r(x, y)$$

and substituting this into the expression for F, we find

$$F(q(x, y), r(x, y)) = 0$$

which is an equation in xy coordinates.

Chapter 5

5.16 From Prob. 5.1 we need only identify the appropriate parameters.

(a) The window parameters are $xw_{min} = 0$, $xw_{max} = 1$, $yw_{min} = 0$, and $yw_{max} = 1$. The viewport parameters are $xv_{min} = 0$, $xv_{max} = 199$, $yv_{min} = 0$, and $yv_{max} = 639$. Then $s_x = 199$, $s_y = 639$, and

$$W = \begin{pmatrix} 199 & 0 & 0 \\ 0 & 639 & 0 \\ 0 & 0 & 1 \end{pmatrix}$$

(b) The parameters are the same, but we map the lower left corner of the window $(0, 0)$ to the lower left corner of the viewport $(0, 639)$. So

$$W = \begin{pmatrix} 199 & 0 & 0 \\ 0 & 639 & 639 \\ 0 & 0 & 1 \end{pmatrix}$$

5.17 If $s_x = s_y$, then

$$\frac{xv_{max} - xv_{min}}{xw_{max} - xw_{min}} = \frac{yv_{max} - yv_{min}}{yw_{max} - yw_{min}} \qquad \text{or} \qquad \frac{yw_{max} - yw_{min}}{xw_{max} - xw_{min}} = \frac{yv_{max} - yv_{min}}{xv_{max} - xv_{min}}$$

Inverting, we have $a_w = a_v$.

    A similar argument shows that if the aspect ratios are equal, $a_w = a_v$, the scale factors are equal, $s_x = s_y$.

5.18 We form N by composing (1) a translation mapping the center $(1, 1)$ to the center $(\frac{1}{2}, \frac{1}{2})$ and (2) a scaling about $C(\frac{1}{2}, \frac{1}{2})$ with uniform scaling factor $s = \frac{1}{10}$, so

$$N = S_{1/10, 1/10, C} \cdot T_v, \qquad \text{where } \mathbf{v} = -\tfrac{1}{2}\mathbf{I} - \tfrac{1}{2}\mathbf{J}$$

$$= \begin{pmatrix} \frac{1}{10} & 0 & \frac{9}{20} \\ 0 & \frac{1}{10} & \frac{9}{20} \\ 0 & 0 & 1 \end{pmatrix} \begin{pmatrix} 1 & 0 & -\frac{1}{2} \\ 0 & 1 & -\frac{1}{2} \\ 0 & 0 & 1 \end{pmatrix} = \begin{pmatrix} \frac{1}{10} & 0 & \frac{2}{5} \\ 0 & \frac{1}{10} & \frac{2}{5} \\ 0 & 0 & 1 \end{pmatrix}$$

5.19 Let the clipping region be a circle with center at $O(h, k)$ and radius r. We reduce the number of candidates for clipping by assigning clipping codes as in the Cohen-Sutherland algorithm. To do this, we use the circumscribed square with lower left corner at $(h - r, k - r)$ and upper right corner at $(h + r, k + r)$ to preprocess the line segments. However, we now have only two clipping categories—not displayed and candidates for clipping. Next, we decide which line segments are to be displayed. Since the (nonparametric) equation of the circle is $(x - h)^2 + (y - k)^2 = r^2$, the quantity $K(x, y) = (x - h)^2 + (y - k)^2 - r^2$ determines whether a point $P(x, y)$ is inside, on, or outside the circle. So if $K \leq 0$ for both endpoints P_1 and P_2 of a line segment, both points are inside or on the circle and so the line segment is displayed. If $K > 0$ for either P_1 or P_2 or both, we calculate the intersection(s) of the line segment and the circle. Using parametric representations, we find (App. 1, Prob. A1.24) that the intersection parameter is

$$t_I = \frac{-S \pm \sqrt{S^2 - L^2 C}}{L^2}$$

where $L^2 = (x_2 - x_1)^2 + (y_2 - y_1)^2$
$S = (x_1 - h)(x_2 - x_1) + (y_1 - k)(y_2 - y_1)$
$C = (x_1 - h)^2 + (y_1 - k)^2 - r^2$

If $0 \leq t_I \leq 1$, the actual intersection point(s) $I(\bar{x}, \bar{y})$ is (are)

$$\bar{x} = x_1 + t_I(x_2 - x_1) \qquad \bar{y} = y_1 + t_I(x_2 - x_1)$$

So, if $K > 0$ for either P_1 or P_2 (or both), we first relabel the endpoints so that P_1 satisfies $K > 0$. Next we calculate t_I. The following situations arise:

1. $S^2 - L^2 C < 0$. Then t_I is undefined and no intersection takes place. The line segment is not displayed.

2. $S^2 - L^2 C = 0$. There is exactly one intersection. If $t_I > 1$ or $t_I < 0$, the intersection point is on the extended line, and so there is no actual intersection. The line is not displayed. If $0 < t_I < 1$, the segment $\overline{P_1 I}$ is clipped. If $K \leq 0$ for point P_2, the segment $\overline{IP_2}$ is displayed since it lies in the circle. If $K > 0$ for P_2, the line $\overline{IP_2}$ is not displayed.

3. $S^2 - L^2 C > 0$. Then there are two values for t_I, t_I^+, and t_I^-. If $0 < t_I^-, t_I^+ \leq 1$, the line segment $\overline{I^+ I}$ is displayed and the segments (assuming $t_I^+ > t_I^-$) $\overline{P_1 I^-}$ and $\overline{I^+ P_2}$ are clipped. If only one value, say, t_I^+, satisfies $0 < t_I \leq 1$, there is one actual intersection and one apparent intersection. If $K \leq 0$ for P_2, then $\overline{P_1 I^+}$ is clipped and $\overline{I^+ P_2}$ is displayed. If $K > 0$ for P_2, then $\overline{P_1 P_2}$ is not displayed (it is, in this case, tangent to the circle). If any combination of $t_I^+, t_I^- \geq 1$ or $t_I^+, t_I^- \leq 0$, then $\overline{P_1 P_2}$ is not displayed.

5.20 Following the logic of the Sutherland-Hodgman algorithm as described in Prob. 5.13, we first clip the "polygon" $P_1 P_2$ against edge $\overline{AB}$ of the window:

1. $\overline{AB}$. We first determine which side of $\overline{AB}$ the points P_1 and P_2 lie. Calculating the quantity (see Prob. 5.12), we have

$$\bar{C} = (x_2 - x_1)(y - y_1) - (y_2 - y_1)(x - x_1)$$

With point $A = (x_1, y_1)$ and point $B = (x_2, y_2)$, we find $\bar{C} = 6$ for point P_1 and $\bar{C} = 7$ for point P_2. So both points lie on the left of $\overline{AB}$. Consequently, the algorithm will output both P_1 and P_2.

2. $\overline{BC}$. Setting point $B = (x_1, y_1)$ and $C = (x_2, y_2)$, we calculate $\bar{C} = 11$ for point P_1 and $\bar{C} = -1$ for point P_2. Thus P_1 is to the left of $\overline{BC}$ and P_2 is to the right of $\overline{BC}$. We now find the intersection point I_1 of $\overline{P_1 P_2}$ with the extended line $\overline{BC}$. From Prob. A2.7 in App. 2, we have $I_1 = (4\frac{11}{16}, 3\frac{5}{8})$. Following the algorithm, points P_1 and I_1 are passed on to be clipped.

3. $\overline{CD}$. Proceeding as before, we find that $\bar{C} = 2$ for point P_1 and $\bar{C} = 6\frac{7}{8}$ for point I_1. So both points lie to the left of $\overline{CD}$ and consequently are passed on.

4. $\overline{DA}$. Setting point $D = (x_1, y_1)$ and $A = (x_2, y_2)$, we find $\bar{C} = -3$ for P_1 and $\bar{C} = 10$ for I_1. Then P_1 lies to the right of $\overline{DA}$ and I_1 to the left. The intersection point of $\overline{P_1 I_1}$ with the extended edge $\overline{DA}$ is $I_2 = (\frac{5}{16}, 2\frac{3}{18})$. The clipped line is the segment $\overline{I_1 I_2}$.

Chapter 6

6.9 From Prob. 6.2, we identify the parameters

$$\mathbf{V} = a\mathbf{I} + b\mathbf{J} + c\mathbf{K} = \mathbf{I} + \mathbf{J} + \mathbf{K}$$
$$|\mathbf{V}| = \sqrt{a^2 + b^2 + c^2} = \sqrt{1^2 + 1^2 + 1^2} = \sqrt{3}$$
$$\lambda = \sqrt{b^2 + c^2} = \sqrt{1^2 + 1^2} = \sqrt{2}$$

Then

$$A_V = \begin{pmatrix} \dfrac{\sqrt{2}}{\sqrt{3}} & \dfrac{-1}{\sqrt{2}\sqrt{3}} & \dfrac{-1}{\sqrt{2}\sqrt{3}} & 0 \\[2ex] 0 & \dfrac{1}{\sqrt{2}} & \dfrac{-1}{\sqrt{2}} & 0 \\[2ex] \dfrac{1}{\sqrt{3}} & \dfrac{1}{\sqrt{3}} & \dfrac{1}{\sqrt{3}} & 0 \\[2ex] 0 & 0 & 0 & 1 \end{pmatrix}$$

6.10 From Prob. 6.5, $A_{V,N} = A_N^{-1} \cdot A_V$. We find A_V first. From Prob. 6.2 we identify the parameters $|V| = \sqrt{3}$, $\lambda = \sqrt{2}$, $a = 1$, $b = 1$, $c = 1$. So

$$A_V = \begin{pmatrix} \dfrac{\sqrt{2}}{\sqrt{3}} & \dfrac{-1}{\sqrt{2}\sqrt{3}} & \dfrac{-1}{\sqrt{2}\sqrt{3}} & 0 \\[2ex] 0 & \dfrac{1}{\sqrt{2}} & \dfrac{-1}{\sqrt{2}} & 0 \\[2ex] \dfrac{1}{\sqrt{3}} & \dfrac{1}{\sqrt{3}} & \dfrac{1}{\sqrt{3}} & 0 \\[2ex] 0 & 0 & 0 & 1 \end{pmatrix}$$

For A_N^{-1}, we have $|N| = \sqrt{6}$, $\lambda = \sqrt{5}$, $a = 2$, $b = -1$, and $c = -1$. So

$$A_N^{-1} = \begin{pmatrix} \dfrac{\sqrt{5}}{\sqrt{6}} & 0 & \dfrac{2}{\sqrt{6}} & 0 \\[2ex] \dfrac{2}{\sqrt{5}\sqrt{6}} & \dfrac{-1}{\sqrt{5}} & \dfrac{-1}{\sqrt{6}} & 0 \\[2ex] \dfrac{2}{\sqrt{5}\sqrt{6}} & \dfrac{1}{\sqrt{5}} & \dfrac{-1}{\sqrt{6}} & 0 \\[2ex] 0 & 0 & 0 & 1 \end{pmatrix}$$

Note that $V' = A_{V,N} \cdot V = A_N^{-1} \cdot A_V \cdot V = \sqrt{2}\, I - \dfrac{\sqrt{2}}{2} J - \dfrac{\sqrt{2}}{2} K$ so that $V' = \dfrac{\sqrt{2}}{2} N$. In other words, the image of V under $A_{V,N}$ is not the vector N, but a vector that has the direction of N.

6.11 This follows from comparing the matrices A_V^{-1} with A_V^T from Prob. 6.2.

6.12 If we place vectors V and N at the origin, then from App. 2, $V \times N$ is perpendicular to both V and N. If θ is the angle between V and N, then a rotation of $\theta°$ about the axis L whose direction is that of $V \times N$ and which passes through the origin will align V with N. So $A_{V,N} = R_{\theta,L}$.

6.13 As in the two-dimensional case in Chap. 4, we reduce the problem of scaling with respect to an arbitrary point P_0 to scaling with respect to the origin by translating P_0 to the origin, performing the scaling about the origin and then translating back to P_0. So

$$S_{s_x,s_y,s_z,P_0} = T_{-P_0}^{-1} \cdot S_{s_x,s_y,s_z} \cdot T_{-P_0}$$

Chapter 7

7.16 From Prob. 7.5, we need to evaluate the parameters (a, b, c), (n_1, n_2, n_3), (d, d_0, d_1) to construct the transformation. From the equations in Prob. 7.6, part b [denoting the principal vanishing points as $P_1(x_1, y_1, z_1)$, $P_2(x_2, y_2, z_2)$, and $P_3(x_3, y_3, z_3)$], we find $a = x_2$ (or x_3), $b = y_1$ (or y_3), and $c = z_1$ (or z_2). Also

$$n_1 = \frac{d}{x_1 - a} \qquad n_2 = \frac{d}{y_2 - b} \qquad n_3 = \frac{d}{z_3 - c}$$

To find d, d_0, and d_1, we note (App. 2, Prob. A2.13) that the distance D from the point $C(a, b, c)$ to the plane can be expressed as $D = |d|/|\mathbf{N}|$, where $|\mathbf{N}|$ is the magnitude of $\mathbf{N}$. Since we need only find the direction of the normal $\mathbf{N}$, we can assume $|\mathbf{N}| = 1$. Then $d = \pm D$. The choice $\pm$, based on the definition of d in Prob. 7.5, is dependent on the direction of the normal vector $\mathbf{N}$, the reference point R_0, and the center of projection C. Since these are not all specified, we are free to choose, and we shall choose the $+$ sign, that is, $d = D$. Finally

$$d_1 = n_1 a + n_2 b + n_3 c \quad \text{and} \quad d_0 = d + d_1$$

7.17 We use the coordinate matrix $\mathbf{V}$ constructed in Prob. 7.1 to represent the unit cube.

(a) From Problem 7.14, the isometric projection matrix Par is applied to the coordinate matrix $\mathbf{V}$:

$$Par \cdot \mathbf{V} = \begin{pmatrix} 0 & \sqrt{\dfrac{2}{3}} & \dfrac{3}{2}\sqrt{\dfrac{2}{3}} & \dfrac{1}{2}\sqrt{\dfrac{2}{3}} & \sqrt{\dfrac{2}{3}} & \dfrac{1}{2}\sqrt{\dfrac{2}{3}} & \dfrac{3}{2}\sqrt{\dfrac{2}{3}} & 2\sqrt{\dfrac{2}{3}} \\ 0 & 0 & \dfrac{\sqrt{2}}{2} & \dfrac{\sqrt{2}}{2} & 0 & \dfrac{-\sqrt{2}}{2} & \dfrac{-\sqrt{2}}{2} & 0 \\ 0 & 0 & 0 & 0 & 0 & 0 & 0 & 0 \\ 1 & 1 & 1 & 1 & 1 & 1 & 1 & 1 \end{pmatrix}$$

This is the matrix of the projected vertices, which can now be read off (see also Fig. S-5).

$$A' = (0, 0, 0) \qquad\qquad E' = \left(\sqrt{\dfrac{2}{3}}, 0, 0\right)$$

$$B' = \left(\sqrt{\dfrac{2}{3}}, 0, 0\right) \qquad F' = \left(\dfrac{1}{2}\sqrt{\dfrac{2}{3}}, -\dfrac{\sqrt{2}}{2}, 0\right)$$

$$C' = \left(\dfrac{3}{2}\sqrt{\dfrac{2}{3}}, \dfrac{\sqrt{2}}{2}, 0\right) \qquad G' = \left(\dfrac{3}{2}\sqrt{\dfrac{2}{3}}, -\dfrac{\sqrt{2}}{2}, 0\right)$$

$$D' = \left(\dfrac{1}{2}\sqrt{\dfrac{2}{3}}, \dfrac{\sqrt{2}}{2}, 0\right) \qquad H' = \left(2\sqrt{\dfrac{2}{3}}, 0, 0\right)$$

(b) To produce a dimetric drawing, we proceed, as in part (a), by using the dimetric transformation Par from Prob. 7.15. Choosing the projection ratio of $\frac{1}{2}:1:1$ (i.e., $l = \frac{1}{2}$), we have

$$Par = \begin{pmatrix} \dfrac{\sqrt{2}}{3} & \dfrac{\sqrt{14}}{6} & \dfrac{\sqrt{14}}{6} & 0 \\ 0 & \dfrac{\sqrt{2}}{2} & \dfrac{-\sqrt{2}}{2} & 0 \\ 0 & 0 & 0 & 0 \\ 0 & 0 & 0 & 1 \end{pmatrix}$$

The projected image coordinates are found by multiplying the matrices Par and $\mathbf{V}$:

$$Par \cdot \mathbf{V} = \begin{pmatrix} 0 & \dfrac{\sqrt{2}}{3} & \dfrac{2\sqrt{2}+\sqrt{14}}{6} & \dfrac{\sqrt{14}}{6} & \dfrac{\sqrt{14}}{3} & \dfrac{\sqrt{14}}{6} & \dfrac{2\sqrt{2}+\sqrt{14}}{6} & \dfrac{\sqrt{2}+\sqrt{14}}{3} \\ 0 & 0 & \dfrac{\sqrt{2}}{2} & \dfrac{\sqrt{2}}{2} & 0 & \dfrac{-\sqrt{2}}{2} & \dfrac{-\sqrt{2}}{2} & 0 \\ 0 & 0 & 0 & 0 & 0 & 0 & 0 & 0 \\ 1 & 1 & 1 & 1 & 1 & 1 & 1 & 1 \end{pmatrix}$$

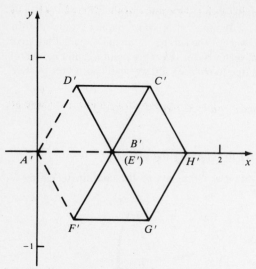

Fig. S-5

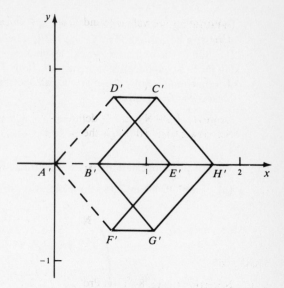

Fig. S-6

The image coordinates are (see Fig. S-6)

$$A' = (0, 0, 0)$$

$$E' = \left(\frac{\sqrt{14}}{3}, 0, 0\right)$$

$$B' = \left(\frac{\sqrt{2}}{3}, 0, 0\right)$$

$$F' = \left(\frac{\sqrt{14}}{6}, \frac{-\sqrt{2}}{2}, 0\right)$$

$$C' = \left(\frac{2\sqrt{2} + \sqrt{14}}{6}, \frac{\sqrt{2}}{2}, 0\right)$$

$$G' = \left(\frac{2\sqrt{2} + \sqrt{14}}{6}, \frac{-\sqrt{2}}{2}, 0\right)$$

$$D' = \left(\frac{\sqrt{14}}{6}, \frac{\sqrt{2}}{2}, 0\right)$$

$$H' = \left(\frac{\sqrt{2} + \sqrt{14}}{3}, 0, 0\right)$$

7.18   Since the planes we seek are to be located at the origin, we need only find the normal vectors of these planes so that orthographic projections onto these planes produce isometric projections. In Prob. 7.14, we rotated the xyz triad first about the x axis and then about the y axis to produce an isometric projection onto the xy plane. Equivalently, we could have tilted the xy plane (and its normal vector $\mathbf{K}$) to a new position, thus yielding a new view plane which produces an isometric projection with respect to the (unrotated) xyz triad. Using this approach to find all possible view planes, we shall use the equations from Prob. 7.14 to find the appropriate rotation angles. From the equations

$$\sin^2 \theta_x - \cos^2 \theta_x = 0 \quad \text{and} \quad \cos^2 \theta_y = \tfrac{1}{2}[\sin^2 \theta_y + 1]$$

we find the solutions

$$\sin \theta_x = \pm\frac{\sqrt{2}}{2}, \quad \cos \theta_x = \pm\frac{\sqrt{2}}{2} \quad \text{and} \quad \sin \theta_y = \pm\sqrt{\frac{1}{3}}, \quad \cos \theta_y = \pm\sqrt{\frac{2}{3}}$$

From Chap. 6, Prob. 6.1, part b, the matrix that produces the tilting is

$$R_{\theta_{x,\mathbf{I}}} \cdot R_{\theta_{y,\mathbf{J}}} = \begin{pmatrix} \cos \theta_y & 0 & \sin \theta_y \\ \sin \theta_x \sin \theta_y & \cos \theta_x & -\sin \theta_x \cos \theta_y \\ -\cos \theta_x \sin \theta_y & \sin \theta_x & \cos \theta_x \cos \theta_y \end{pmatrix}$$

Applying this to the vector $\mathbf{K} = (0, 0, 1)$, we find the components of the tilted vector to be

$$x = \sin \theta_y \qquad y = -\sin \theta_x \cos \theta_y \qquad z = -\cos \theta_x \cos \theta_y$$

Substituting the values found above, we have eight candidates for the normal vector $\mathbf{N} = x\mathbf{I} + y\mathbf{J} + z\mathbf{K}$, where

$$x = \pm\sqrt{\frac{1}{3}} \qquad y = \pm\sqrt{\frac{1}{3}} \qquad z = \pm\sqrt{\frac{1}{3}}$$

However, both $\mathbf{N}$ and $-\mathbf{N}$ define normals to the same plane. So we finally have four solutions. These are the view planes (through the origin) with normals

$$\mathbf{N}_1 = \sqrt{\frac{1}{3}}(\mathbf{I} + \mathbf{J} + \mathbf{K}) \qquad \mathbf{N}_3 = \sqrt{\frac{1}{3}}(\mathbf{I} - \mathbf{J} + \mathbf{K})$$

$$\mathbf{N}_2 = \sqrt{\frac{1}{3}}(-\mathbf{I} + \mathbf{J} + \mathbf{K}) \qquad \mathbf{N}_4 = \sqrt{\frac{1}{3}}(\mathbf{I} + \mathbf{J} - \mathbf{K})$$

Chapter 8

8.10 Referring to Fig. 8-7 (and Prob. 8.4), we call $\overline{\mathbf{CR}}$ the vector having the direction of the line from the center of projection C to the window corner R. Similarly, we call $\overline{\mathbf{CL}}$ the vector to the window corner L. Then:

1. *Top plane*—determined by the vectors $\mathbf{I_p}$ and $\overline{\mathbf{CR}}$ and the reference point R_f
2. *Bottom plane*—determined by the vectors $\mathbf{I_p}$ and $\overline{\mathbf{CL}}$ and the reference point L_f
3. *Right side plane*—determined by the vectors $\mathbf{J_q}$ and $\overline{\mathbf{CR}}$ and the reference point R_f
4. *Left side plane*—determined by the vectors $\mathbf{J_q}$ and $\overline{\mathbf{CL}}$ and the reference point L_f
5. *(Hither) front plane*—determined by the (view plane) normal vector $\mathbf{N}$ and the reference point P_f
6. *(Yon) back plane*—determined by the normal vector $\mathbf{N}$ and the reference point P_b

8.11 Suppose that the plane passes through point $R_0(x_0, y_0, z_0)$ and has a normal vector $\mathbf{N} = n_1\mathbf{I} + n_2\mathbf{J} + n_3\mathbf{K}$. Let the points $P_1(x_1, y_1, z_1)$ and $P_2(x_2, y_2, z_2)$ determine a line segment. From App. 2, the equation of the plane is

$$n_1(x - x_0) + n_2(y - y_0) + n_3(z - z_0) = 0$$

and the parametric equation of the line is

$$x = x_1 + (x_2 - x_1)t \qquad y = y_1 + (y_2 - y_1)t \qquad z = z_1 + (z_2 - z_1)t$$

Substituting these equations into the equations of the plane, we obtain

$$n_1[x_1 + (x_2 - x_1)t - x_0] + n_2[y_1 + (y_2 - y_1)t - y_0] + n_3[z_1 + (z_2 - z_1)t - z_0] = 0$$

Solving this for t yields the parameter value t_I at the time of intersection:

$$t_I = -\frac{n_1(x_1 - x_0) + n_2(y_1 - y_0) + n_3(z_1 - z_0)}{n_1(x_2 - x_1) + n_2(y_2 - y_1) + n_3(z_2 - z_1)}$$

We can rewrite this using vector notation as

$$t_I = -\frac{\mathbf{N} \cdot \overline{R_0 P_1}}{\mathbf{N} \cdot \overline{P_2 P_1}}$$

The intersection points $I(x_I, y_I, z_I)$ can be found from the parametric equations of the line:

$$x_I = x_0 + (x_2 - x_1)t_I \qquad y_I = y_0 + (y_2 - y_1)t_I \qquad z_I = z_0 + (z_2 - z_1)t_I$$

If $0 \le t_I \le 1$, the intersection point I is on the line segment from P_1 to P_2; if not, the intersection point is on the extended line.

Chapter 9

9.9   Referring to Fig. 7-10 in Chap. 7, we define a vertex list as

$$V = \{ABCDEFGH\}$$

and an explicit edge list is:

$$E = \{\overline{AB}, \overline{AD}, \overline{AF}, \overline{BC}, \overline{BG}, \overline{CD}, \overline{CH}, \overline{DE}, \overline{EF}, \overline{EH}, \overline{FG}, \overline{GH}\}$$

The cube can be drawn by drawing the edges in list E. Referring to Prob. 9.2, we note that a typical polygon, say, P_1, can be represented in terms of its edges as

$$P_1 = \{\overline{AB}, \overline{AD}, \overline{BC}, \overline{CD}\}$$

9.10   The knot set can be represented as $t_0, t_0 + L, t_0 + 2L, \ldots$. On the interval $t_i = t_0 + (i-1)L$ to $t_{i+2} = t_0 + (i+1)L$, we have

$$B_{i,1}(x) = \frac{x - [t_0 + (i-1)L]}{(t_0 + iL) - [t_0 + (i-1)L]} B_{i,0}(x) + \frac{[t_0 + (i+1)L] - x}{[t_0 + (i+1)L] - (t_0 + iL)} B_{i+1,0}(x)$$

On the interval $[t_i, t_{i+1}]$, that is, $t_0 + (i-1)L \le x \le t_0 + iL$, we have $B_{i,0}(x) = 1$ and $B_{i+1,0}(x) = 0$. On the interval $[t_{i+1}, t_{i+2}]$, that is, $t_0 + iL \le x \le t_0 + (i+1)L$, we have $B_{i,0}(x) = 0$ and $B_{i+1,0}(x) = 1$. Elsewhere both $B_{i,0}(x) = 0$ and $B_{i+1,0}(x) = 0$. So

$$B_{i,1}(x) = \begin{cases} \dfrac{x - t_0 + (i-1)L}{L} & \text{on} \quad t_0 + (i-1)L \le x \le t_0 + iL \\[2ex] \dfrac{t_0 + (i+1)L - x}{L} & \text{on} \quad t_0 + iL \le x \le t_0 + (i+1)L \\[2ex] 0 \quad \text{elsewhere} \end{cases}$$

9.11   From the definition of a B-spline, $B_{i,3}(x)$ is nonzero only if $t_i \le x \le t_{i+4}$. In terms of the given knot set, this equates to $i \le x \le i + 4$. With $x = 5.5$, $B_{i,3}(5.5)$ is nonzero for $i = 2, 3, 4,$ and 5. Now

$$B_{i,3}(5.5) = \frac{(5.5) - i}{(i+3) - i} B_{i,2}(5.5) + \frac{(i+4) - (5.5)}{(i+4) - (i+1)} B_{i+1,2}(5.5)$$

or

$$B_{i,3}(5.5) = \frac{(5.5) - i}{3} B_{i,2}(5.5) + \frac{i - (1.5)}{3} B_{i+1,2}(5.5)$$

Starting with $i = 2$,

$$B_{2,3}(5.5) = \frac{3.5}{3} B_{2,2}(5.5) + \frac{0.5}{3} B_{3,2}(5.5)$$

Now $B_{2,2}(x)$ is nonzero if $2 \le x \le 5$. Thus $B_{2,2}(5.5) = 0$, and so $B_{2,3}(5.5) = (0.5/3) B_{3,2}(5.5)$. Because $B_{3,2}(x)$ is nonzero for $3 \le x \le 6$, we find that

$$B_{3,2}(5.5) = \frac{(5.5) - 3}{5 - 3} B_{3,1}(5.5) + \frac{6 - (5.5)}{6 - 4} B_{4,1}(5.5)$$

Now $B_{3,1}(x)$ is nonzero if $3 \le x \le 5$. So $B_{3,1}(5.5) = 0$. Now $B_{4,1}(x)$ is nonzero if $4 \le x \le 6$. Thus

$$B_{3,2}(5.5) = \frac{0.5}{2} B_{4,1}(5.5)$$

Now

$$B_{4,1}(5.5) = \frac{(5.5) - 4}{5 - 4} B_{4,0}(5.5) + \frac{6 - (5.5)}{6 - 5} B_{5,0}(5.5)$$

Since $B_{4,0}(x)$ is nonzero if $4 \le x \le 5$, we find that $B_{4,0}(5.5) = 0$. So

$$B_{4,1}(5.5) = \frac{0.5}{1} B_{5,0}(5.5)$$

However, $B_{5,0}(x) = 1$ if $5 \le x \le 6$. So $B_{5,0}(5.5) = 1$, $B_{4,1}(5.5) = 0.5(1) = 0.5$, and $B_{3,2}(5.5) = (0.5/2)(0.5) = 0.25/2$, and finally

$$B_{2,3}(5.5) = \frac{0.5}{3} \left(\frac{0.25}{2} \right) = \frac{0.125}{6} = 0.0208333$$

The computations for $B_{3,3}(5.5)$, $B_{4,3}(5.5)$, and $B_{5,3}(5.5)$ are carried out in the same way.

Chapter 10

10.28 The properties of parallel projection can be used to simplify calculations if the objects to be projected are transformed into "new objects" whose parallel projection results in the same image as the perspective projection of the original object.

10.29 Since the Z-buffer algorithm changes colors at a pixel only if $Z(x, y) < Z_{buf}(x, y)$, the first polygon written will determine the color of the pixel (see Prob. 10.7).

10.30 A priority flag could be assigned to break the tie resulting in applying the Z-buffer algorithm.

10.31 A system that distinguishes 256 depth values would require one byte of memory ($2^8 = 256$) to represent each z value. Thus $1 \times 512 \times 512 = 256K$ of memory would be needed.

10.32 The scan-line method can take advantage of (a) scan-line coherence, (b) edge coherence, (c) area coherence, and (d) spatial coherence.

10.33 Scan-line coherence is based on the assumption that if a pixel belongs to the scan-converted image of an object, the pixels next to it will (most likely) also belong to this object.

10.34 Since this figure is a polygon, we need only find the maximum and minimum coordinate values of the vertices A, B, and C. Then

$$\begin{array}{ll} x_{min} = 0 & x_{max} = 2 \\ y_{min} = 0 & y_{max} = 2 \\ z_{min} = 1 & z_{max} = 2 \end{array}$$

The bounding box is shown in Fig. 10-27.

10.35 Horizontal line segments ($y_{min} = y_{max}$) lie on only one scan line; that is, there is no need to find the intersection with the scan line.

10.36 We search the z coordinates of the vertices of the polygon for the largest value, z_{max}. The depth of the polygon is then z_{max}.

10.37 Area coherence is exploited by classifying polygons with respect to a given screen area as either a surrounding polygon, an intersecting polygon, a contained polygon, or a disjoint polygon. The key fact is that a polygon is not visible if it is in back of a surrounding polygon.

10.38 When using a hidden-surface algorithm to eliminate hidden lines, we set the fill color of the polygons, determined by the lines, to the background color.

10.39 By using the extents of the objects in a picture, we need only solve the intersection equations for those objects whose extents are pierced (intersected) by a given ray.

Chapter 11

11.34 (*a*) Currently the 100 users are paid $3,500,000/year:

$$(100 \text{ users}) \times \$35,000/\text{user} = \$3,500,000$$

The average worker works 250 eight-hour days each year (after weekends, holidays, and vacation) or 720,000,000 s. The total time per year lost due to errors may be found as follows:

$$\text{Seconds lost per year} = 100 \text{ users} \times \frac{250 \text{ errors}}{\text{user}} \Big/ \text{day} \times \frac{250 \text{ days}}{\text{year}} \times \frac{10 \text{ s}}{\text{error}} \text{ canceling units}$$

$$= 62,500,000 \text{ s/year lost due to errors}$$

Therefore, the current cost of errors is

$$\frac{\$3,500,000}{\text{year}} \times \frac{62,500,000 \text{ s}}{720,000,000 \text{ s/year}} = \$303,819/\text{year}$$

(*b*) Since the routine will cost $50,000 to develop, the time required for the system to pay back would be found as follows. The routine will reduce errors by 10 percent; therefore, savings per year are

$$0.10 \times 303,819 = \$30,382/\text{year}$$

Therefore

$$\text{Pay back} = \frac{50,000}{30,382} = 1.65 \text{ years}$$

11.35 One of the most common mistakes is to leave the user with no visible information indicating how the current system configuration can be exited. For example, a user may use a menu to put the system in a mode that accepts text from the keyboard. After the selection is made, the menu disappears, leaving the user with no obvious method for returning to graphics mode. Another common mistake is making messages too terse. For example, an error message may state "illegal operator" after the user has entered the following:

$$y = 2 * x + 3 \ \& \ 4$$

where "&" is an illegal character. A better response would be to move the cursor to the ampersand and allow the user to either change the character or delete the entire entry.

11.36 The system displays two types of inconsistency. First, similar information (the request for coordinate data) is displayed in two different display areas. It is better to consistently display similar information in the same screen location. The second inconsistency is between the actual wording of the two prompts. Since the same type of information is required, the same prompt should be used.

11.37 The user is redundantly warned to stop in four ways: (1) The color red is associated with stopping, (2) an octagon is associated with stopping, (3) the tone signals the user to be alert to some type of important information from the system, and (4) the printed word STOP indicates that the user should stop.

11.38 Information types can be tied to display locations. For example, if one area is consistently used for error messages only, the printing of any message will indicate to the experienced user that an error was made. This will often allow the experienced user to ignore the specific message and simply react to the error and take corrective action.

11.39 The old saying "Actions speak louder than words" is literally true when attempting to reduce operator workload. A well-designed system can "look" for specific user activities that indicate that the user would like the system to perform specific tasks, thereby shifting the need to take action from the user to the computer. For example, rather than force the user to select a text mode when text is desired, the graphics computer program should recognize that keyboard activity indicates the user's desire to enter text.

11.40 No, the computer's actual information structure can be completely different from the user's perception of the information structure. All that is required is that the system not behave unexpectedly.

11.41 Storing information directly in display memory makes coding relatively simple because a linked information structure does not have to be generated. This frees the programmer from the need to keep track of any dynamic changes in the information structure.

11.42 Since the objects stored in display memory only are not dynamically linked, the computer system does not have to search the information list and interpret what it finds prior to reacting to the user's request.

11.43   1.   Let E = error factor, sw = user pointing indicator = 0, $x = x$ stylus location, $y = y$ stylus location, $x_i = x$ location of object i, $y_i = y$ location of object i.

      2.   Read the location of the input stylus (magnetic pen, mouse, light pen, or whatever $x - y$ input device is being used):
$$x = \text{stylus } x \text{ position} \qquad y = \text{stylus } y \text{ position}$$

      3.   Compare the location of the stylus with the centroid location of each of the objects on the display plus or minus the error factor E. If $x - E \geq x_i$ and $x + E \leq x_i$ and $y - E \geq y_i$ and $y_i \leq y + E$ then $sw = 1$ highlight object i. (Note: E is used to describe a bounding box surrounding the object.)

      4.   Check to see if user wants to "pick up" highlighted object. If $sw = 1$, set object centroid = to x, y.

      5.   Continue to display the object at the stylus coordinates until user indicates new location of object by setting $sw = 0$.

11.44 Some examples are (1) development of headings, labels, and borders for charts; (2) creation of an electronic slide show, (3) development of animated lettering and symbols for television titles, and (4) weather map generation.

11.45 A viewgraph is similar to a standard slide transparency, except that it is much larger (usually $8\frac{1}{2} \times 11$ in) and designed for showing on an overhead projector.

11.46 When a freehand line is drawn, each point must be independently defined and saved. This requires a lot of computer time and memory and should thus be avoided.

11.47 Character font describes the style of lettering.

11.48 Point size is a term used in typography to describe the size of characters.

11.49   1.   Since there are no headings given, the program would skip the heading routine and proceed to the next step.

      2.   Total data

$$\begin{array}{r} 100 \\ 50 \\ \underline{50} \\ 200 \end{array}$$

      3.   Find percent of the total for each data class:
$$A = \tfrac{100}{200} = 0.50 \qquad B = \tfrac{50}{200} = 0.25 \qquad C = \tfrac{50}{200} = 0.25$$

      4.   Convert to radians to find the portion of the circle to be represented for each data class:

$$A = 0.50 * 2\pi = \pi \qquad B = 0.25 * 2\pi = \frac{\pi}{2} \qquad C = 0.25 * 2\pi = \frac{\pi}{2}$$

      5.   Plot sectors where θ_1 = starting angle, θ_2 = ending angle: (a) for A, plot a sector with $\theta_1 = 0$ and $\theta_2 = \pi$; (b) set $\theta_1 = \theta_2$ to get new starting angle for B; (c) next, set $\theta_2 = \theta_1 + \pi/2 = \pi + \pi/2 = 3\pi/2$; (d) plot sector B with $\theta_1 = \pi$ and $\theta_2 = 3\pi/2$; (e) set $\theta_1 = \theta_2$ to get new starting angle for C; (f) next, set $\theta_2 = \theta_1 + \pi/2 = 3\pi/2 + \pi/2 = 2\pi$; (g) plot C with $\theta_1 = 3\pi/2$ and $\theta_2 = 2\pi$.

11.50 After step 5, a command to draw a rectangle would be required. Thus, the rectangle would be divided proportionally with respect to the total amounts making up the detailed slice.

11.51 There would be no change. Only the axis labeling would differ.

11.52 Refer to Fig. S-7. Step of Prob. 11.29 is modified so that the rectangles for each data subclass A, B, C are placed one on top of the other (stacked) before proceeding to the next tick mark.

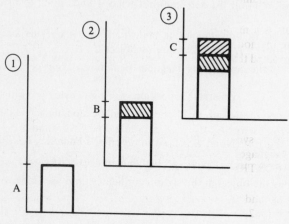

Fig. S-7

11.53 Let $2w$ be the width of a bar and y be its altitude. Assuming that there are two bars per cluster, for each tick mark a rectangle would be drawn at $(xt - w, y)$ to (xt, y). A second rectangle would be drawn at (xt, y) to $(xt + w, y)$ (see Fig. S-8).

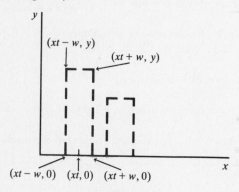

Fig. S-8

11.54 The x and y coordinates would be exchanged.

11.55 1. Divide the number of people in each city by the value of each full picture:

$$\text{City A} \rightarrow \frac{1000}{100} = 10$$

$$\text{City B} \rightarrow \frac{850}{100} = 8.5$$

2. Plot pictures:

Key ☇ = 100 people
City A ☇ ☇ ☇ ☇ ☇ ☇ ☇ ☇ ☇ ☇
City B ☇ ☇ ☇ ☇ ☇ ☇ ☇ ☇ ۶

11.56 Computer-aided design.

11.57 Computer-aided manufacture.

11.58 Computer-integrated manufacturing (CIM). However, CIM implies that the entire system is coordinated with management activities by an overseeing computer system.

11.59 It is a description of the number and type of components used to build a specific part.

11.60 Finite element analysis is a method of simulation which allows a designer to simulate the mechanical behavior of a structure by modeling it as a finite number of simpler components (elements) whose states can be more easily computed than would be possible by directly simulating the behavior of the structure as a whole.

Chapter 12

12.34 Since GKS consists of a syntax for stringing together specifically defined procedures, it may be implemented in any language as an enhancement. For example, GKS is commonly implemented in C, BASIC, COBOL, FORTRAN, and PASCAL.

12.35 The elements in the X and Y arrays represent Cartesian coordinates. For example, in the arrays $X = (1, 3, 7, 9)$ and $Y = (5, 2, 10, 14)$, the coordinates $(1, 5)$, $(3, 2)$, $(7, 10)$, and $(9, 14)$ are represented.

12.36 The elements in the X and Y arrays represent Cartesian coordinates. For example, with the use of the data from Prob. 12.7, a POLYMARKER $(5, X, Y)$ command would result in Fig. S-9 if the POLYMARKER attribute value were set to 3.

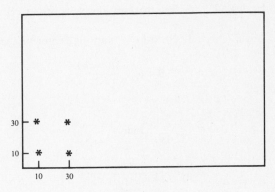

Fig. S-9

12.37 The FILL command always closes figures by connecting the first and last points in the X and Y arrays. Therefore, if the FILL AREA index is set to the hollow fill attribute value, θ, a square will be drawn.

12.38 (a) The POLYLINE attributes that can be changed are color, solid, dash type, and stroke width.

    (b) The attributes of POLYMARKER that can be changed are color and marker type.

    (c) The attributes of FILL AREA that can be changed are fill pattern, pattern size, skew of the pattern in both the x and y directions, and pattern color(s).

12.39 Some TEXT attributes that can be changed are color, character orientation, direction of printing, order of printing, font, character height, character width, spacing between characters, slant, and stroke width (see Fig. S-10).

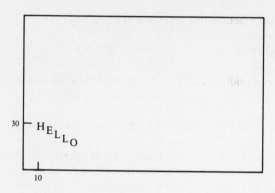

Fig. S-10

12.40 See Fig. S-10.

12.41 See Fig. 12-5(*c*).

12.42 See Fig. 12-5(*a*).

12.43 See Fig. 12-5(*b*).

12.44 None; GKS is designed such that it is independent of the actual implementation.

12.45 The same routine described in Chap. 3 would be used, except the plot command could be replaced with POLYMARKER.

12.46 For the slice that is to be exploded, change the location of its center.

12.47 1. After each slice is drawn (Prob. 12.20, step 4), find the center of each sector. Let

$$\theta = \theta_1 + \frac{(\theta_2 - \theta_1)}{2}$$

Then

$$x = \frac{\text{radius}}{2} * \cos \theta$$

$$y = \frac{\text{radius}}{2} * \sin \theta$$

2. Print label (*i*):

$$\text{TEXT}(x, y, \text{label (i)})$$

12.48 1. Set window:

$$\text{SET WINDOW } (1, 1979, 1983, 0, 300)$$

2. Generate axes.

3. Set starting values of variables:

$$x = 1979$$
$$y = 0$$

4. Check to determine whether last value has been plotted:

$$\text{If } x > 1982 \text{ then stop}$$

5. Plot rectangle ($w = \frac{1}{2}$ width of bar):

$$X(1) = x - w$$
$$X(2) = x + w$$
$$Y(1) = 0$$
$$Y(2) = \text{sales value (i)}$$
$$\text{Rectangle } (X, Y)$$

Refer to Prob. 12.18.

6. Increment counter.

7. Go to step 4.

12.49 Assuming that each cluster had two values, step 5 would be modified as follows ($w =$ width of bar):

1.	$X(1) = x - w$
2.	$X(2) = x$
3.	$Y(1) = 0$
4.	$Y(2) = $ value of first data value in cluster
5.	Rectangle (X, Y)
6.	$X(1) = x$
7.	$X(2) = x + w$
8.	$Y(1) = 0$
9.	$Y(2) = $ value of second data value in cluster
10.	Rectangle (X, Y)

12.50 Assuming that each stack was composed of two values, step 5 would be modified as follows ($w = \frac{1}{2}$ width of the bar):

1.	$X(1) = x - w$
2.	$X(2) = x + w$
3.	$Y(1) = 0$
4.	$Y(2) = $ value of first data value in stack
5.	Rectangle (X, Y)
6.	$Y(1) = Y(2)$ (since bars are to be stacked)
7.	$Y(2) = Y(1) + $ value of second data value in stack
8.	Rectangle (X, Y)

12.51

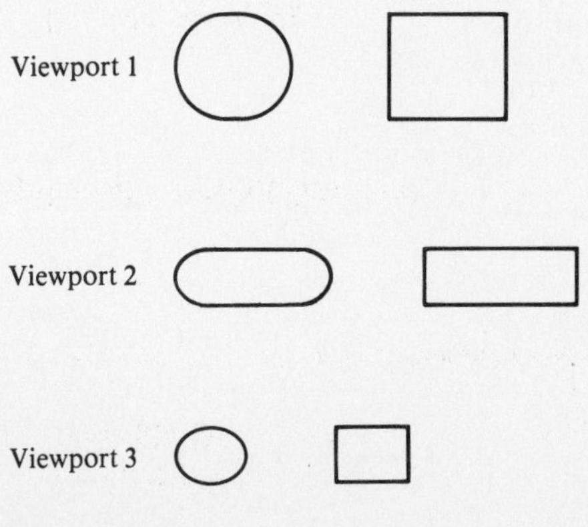

12.52 The figures will appear distorted because the aspect ratio of each viewport is not 1 to 1. Therefore, each move in the y direction is not equal to each move in the x direction.

12.53 Segments allow objects to be manipulated by simply referring to the segment number. As a result, segments can be translated, rotated, panned, and zoomed.

12.54 Segments are removed with the DELETE SEGMENT (n) command.

12.55 (*a*)   To move the square, first set the center of movement at the square center:

$$fx = 50 \qquad fy = 50$$

Next, set the translation vector

$$tx = 20 - 50 = -30 \qquad ty = 20 - 50 = -30$$

Set $r = 0$, $sx = sy = 1$, switch $= 0$ (for world coordinates). Evaluate the matrix with the EVALUATE TRANSFORMATION MATRIX (fx, fy, tx, ty, r, sx, sy, switch, MATRIX) command. Then apply the transformation set SEGMENT TRANSFORMATION (1, MATRIX).

(*b*)   To rotate the square $\frac{1}{2}\pi$, set the center of rotation

$$fx = 50 \qquad fy = 50$$

Set the rotation value

$$r = \frac{\pi}{2}$$

Set $tx = ty = 0$, $sx = sy = 0$, and switch $= 0$. Evaluate the matrix with the EVALUATE TRANS-FORMATION MATRIX (fx, fy, tx, ty, r, sx, sy, switch, MATRIX) command. Then apply the rotation with the SET SEGMENT TRANSFORMATION (1, MATRIX) command.

(*c*)   To double the size of the square, set $sx = 2$ and $sy = 2$, $fx = fy = 50$, $r = 0$, $tx = ty = 0$, and switch $= 0$. Next, evaluate the transformation matrix with the EVALUATE TRANSFORMATION MATRIX (fx, fy, r, tx, ty, sx, sy, switch, MATRIX) command. Finally, apply the scaling matrix with the SET SEGMENT TRANSFORMATION (1, MATRIX) command.

12.56 No, the system can be set up such that each user has an independent work space until the user's segment is merged with the entire model.

12.57 The GKS standard is constantly evolving. Therefore, the head designer should obtain a current copy of the GKS standard from ANSI.

Index

Acoustic tablet, 7
Active edge list, 68, 195, 196, 214
A/D (analog-to-digital) conversion, 2, 20–23
  amplification, 2, 5
  conversion, 2, 3
  quantization, 2–4
    aperture time, 4
    coding error, 4
    sample rate, 4
  sensing, 2, 3
Additive modeling, 172
Aliasing, 69, 78
Alignment transformation, 119–122, 124
Amplitude uncertainty, 4
Analog, 1, 20, 32
Analog input devices, 1, 5, 20
Analog-to-digital conversion (see A/D conversion)
Angle measurement between vectors, 261, 267, 301
Anode, 43
Anticyclic spline condition, 176
Aperture time, 4, 23
Approximation, 172, 177–179
  Bézier–B-spline, 178
  Bézier-Bernstein, 177
Area coherence, 194, 212
Artistic creation, 229
ASCII (American Standard Code for Information Interchange), 8, 15–16, 27
Aspect ratio, 42, 99, 114
Axis, 231, 241, 249
Axonometric projections, 130

B-splines, 174, 185–187
  interpolation, 175
Bar chart, 231, 241
  clustered, 231
  horizontal, 231
  simple, 231, 241
  stacked, 231
  vertical, 231
Base conversion, 272, 287–289
Basic objects, 229
Basis (blending) functions, 172
  B-splines, 174
  Bernstein polynomials, 174
  Hermite cubic polynomials, 173
  Lagrange polynomials, 173
Bernstein polynomials, 174
Bézier-Bernstein approximation, 177
Bézier-Bernstein surfaces, 180
Bill of materials, 243
Binary numbers, 271, 286–289
Bit (cognitive), 271, 286

BITBLT (raster operational graphics) (raster op), 69, 78
Blanking (see Shielding)
Blending functions (see Basis functions)
Boundary block transfer, 68, 78
Boundary fill, 66, 76
Bounding box, 194, 198, 202, 212
Bresenham's circle algorithm, 60–61, 74, 79
Bresenham's line algorithm, 57, 72–73, 79
Brevity, 224, 235
Burning, phosphor, 34
Byte, 271, 286

Cabinet projection, 131, 145
CAD (computer-aided design), 233
CAD/CAM (computer-aided design–computer-aided manufacturing), 233
Canonical clipping, 155
Cartesian coordinates:
  correlation with homogeneous coordinates, 299
  three-dimensional, 290
  two-dimensional, 260
Cathode, 43
Cathode ray tube (CRT), 30, 32
Cavalier projection, 131, 145
Center of projection, 127, 149
Charting, 230–233
  bar, 231, 241
  line, 232, 242
  pictogram, 231, 241
  pie, 230, 240, 241
Chunking, 224, 235
CIM (computer-integrated manufacturing), 233
Circle, equation of:
  nonparametric, 275, 276
  parametric, 263, 277
Clamped spline, 176
Clipping:
  general, 114
  lines (see Line clipping)
  points, 100
  polygons, 102–104
  three-dimensional, 153–156
  two-dimensional, 80–104
Clipping categories, 101, 109
Clipping planes, 154
  back (yon), 154
  front (hither), 154
Clock speed, 19, 30
Coding error, 4, 23
Cohen-Sutherland line clipping algorithm, 101, 109, 154, 167

Coherence, 194
  area, 194, 212
  edge, 194, 211
  scan-line, 194, 223
  spatial, 194, 212
Command-data list (display file), 226–228, 236, 237, 244
Communications devices, 15
Compatibility, 224
Composing functions, 118–119, 270, 284
Compressed-memory storage, 12, 25–27
Computer-aided design (CAD), 233
Computer-aided design–computer-aided manufacturing (CAD/CAM), 233
Computer ergonomics, 224
Computer-integrated manufacturing (CIM), 233
Conductive coating, 44
Consistency, 225
Control electrode, 32, 46, 47
Control points, 177
Convex polygon, 102
Coons surfaces, 181, 187
Coordinate system:
  Cartesian coordinates, 260
  homogeneous, 298–300
  left-handed, 260
  polar coordinates, 263
  right-handed, 260
  three-dimensional, 290
  two-dimensional, 260
Coordinate transformations, 80, 82, 94–95, 117–118
  inverse, 84
  matrix description, 85, 118
  reflection (*see* Reflection)
  rotation (*see* Rotation)
  scaling (*see* Scaling)
  translation (*see* Translation)
  viewing transformations (*see* Viewing transformations)
Coprocessor system, 17
Cross product, 296, 301
Cross-section curves, 181
CRT (cathode ray tube), 30, 32
Current transformation, 87, 96, 119
Curve design, 172
Curve segments, 172
Curved surfaces, 172
  design of, 179
Curves, equations of, 291–292
  explicit form, 292
  implicit form, 292
  nonparametric, 292, 300
  parametric, 292–293
Cyclic spline condition, 176
Cylinder surfaces, equations of, 294

Decimal numbers, 271, 286–289

Deflection yoke, 33, 47
Depth buffer algorithm (*see* Z-buffer algorithm)
Depth comparison, 190, 205
Depth value, 192
Designing, 233
Digital, 1, 20, 32
Digital camera, 11
Digital input devices, 1, 5, 20
Dimetric projection, 131, 148
Direct addressing, 18, 29
Direct clipping, 155
Direction of projection, 130, 131, 142
Display device, 32
Display file (*see* Command-data list)
Display memory only information structures, 226–227
Display-memory storage, 12
Display processing unit, 17
Display space, 191, 208
Display transform, 191
Distance from a point to a plane, 306, 308
Distance formula, 273, 291
Dot product, 266, 279, 280, 295
Drafting, 233
Drawing, 229
Dropping out, 18

Echo, 15
Edge coherence, 194, 211
Edge list, 67, 195
  (*See also* Active edge list; Explicit edge listing)
Editing, 227
  basic, 229
  global, 237, 238
  local, 237, 238
Electron gun, 32, 46
Endpoint codes, 101, 108, 154, 157
Ergonomics, 224
Explicit edge listing, 171, 189
Explicit vertex list, 171, 185
Exploded pie chart, 230, 241
Extent, 100, 194, 198, 202, 212, 223

Finite-element analysis, 233
Fit, 42
Flexibility, 223, 235
Flicker, 18, 34
Floating-point operations, 19
Flood fill, 66, 76
Flooding gun, 44, 51
Fluorescence, 34, 37
Fluorescent cells, 43
Focusing electrode, 33
Font, 243
Frame buffer, 29
Functions (mapping, operator, transformations), 269–271

Functions (*continued*):
  composition of, 270
  domain, 269
  graph of, 270
  inverse, 270
  matrix, 269, 285
  range, 269
  (*See also* Composing functions)

Geometric forms and models, 170–189
  curved surface, 172
  curved surface patch, 172, 179, 181
  lines, 170
  points, 170
  polygonal net (mesh), 171
  polygons, 170
  polyhedron, 172
  polylines, 170
  quadric surfaces, 182
  wireframe, 171
Geometric transformations, 80, 115–117
  matrix description, 85, 118
GKS (graphics kernel system), 14, 244–259
GKS attributes, 245–247
GKS clipping, 249
GKS input, 250
GKS primitives:
  FILL AREA, 244
  POLYLINE, 244
  POLYMARKER, 244
  TEXT, 244
GKS segment transformations, 250
GKS segments, 249–250
GKS viewport, 247–248
GKS window, 247–248
Glass box technique, 233
Graphics kernel system (*see* GKS *entries*)
Graphics storage devices, 11
Graphics storage formats, 11, 12
Graphics transformations:
  composite, 85, 118–119
  coordinate, 80, 82, 94–95, 117–118
  current transformation, 87, 96, 119
  geometric, 80, 115–117
  homogeneous coordinates, 85–86, 298–300
  instance transformations, 86, 95–96, 119
  inverse, 82
  matrix description, 85, 118–119
  three-dimensional, 115–148
  two-dimensional, 80–97
Guiding nets, 179–180
  Bézier–B-spline surfaces, 180
  Bézier-Bernstein surfaces, 180

Hermitian cubic polynomial interpolation, 175
Hexadecimal numbers, 271, 286–289
Hidden-line elimination, 202

Hidden-surface problem, 190
Homogeneous coordinates, 85–86, 298–300
  ideal points, 299
  lines, 299
  points, 299, 309
Homogeneous form of a matrix, 86, 118
  GKS, 250
Horizon line, 140
Human factors, 224

Icon, 224, 225
Ideal points, 299
Image-only storage, 12
Image transformations, 149
Indirect addressing, 18, 29
Information recoding, 224, 235
Information storage, 14
  display memory only, 226, 227
  information structures, 226–228
  (*See also* Command-data list)
Input devices, 1, 5, 20
  analog, 1
    joystick, 5, 6
    mouse, 5, 6
    paddle control, 5, 6
    trackball, 5, 6
  digital, 1
    keyboard, 6, 8, 24
    light pen, 6–7, 23, 24
    magnetic pens and tablets, 6, 7, 24
    touch-sensitive screen, 7–8, 24
  GKS input, 250
  strobe, 2
Inside-outside test of view volumes, 167
Inside test for polygons, 103
Instance, 227, 228, 237, 238
Instance transformation, 86, 95–96, 119
Instancing, 80, 86
Instruction set, 19, 30
Interlacing, 34, 47
Interpolating surface patches, 181
  Coons surfaces, 181, 187
  lofted surfaces, 181, 189
Interpolation, 172, 175–176
  Hermitian cubic, 175
  Lagrange polynomial, 175
  spline, 175
Intersections, computation of, 108, 168, 169, 281, 302, 307, 308,
Inverse function, 270
Inverse matrix, 269
Isometric projection, 131, 147, 148

Joystick, 5, 6

Keyboard, 6, 8, 24
Knots (nodes), 172, 173, 185, 187

Lagrange polynomials, 173
  interpolation, 175
Law of Cosines, 261
LCD (liquid crystal display), 24, 43–44, 51
Left-right test, 103, 154
Light pen, 6–7, 23, 24
Line, equation of:
  nonparametric, 262, 273
  parametric, 263, 277, 280, 281, 292, 297, 301, 302
Line chart, 232, 242
Line clipping, 101–102, 154
  (*See also* Cohen-Sutherland line clipping algorithm; Midpoint subdivision clipping algorithm)
Line segment, 170
Linear blending, 181, 189
Liquid crystal, 24, 44
Liquid crystal display (LCD), 24, 43–44, 51
Lofted surfaces, 181, 189
Lofting, 181, 189
Lookup table, 39–40, 50

Magnetic pen and tablet, 6, 7, 24
Mathematical surfaces, 203
Mathematics of projection (*see* Projection)
Matrices, 267–269, 282–289
  addition of, 268
  concatenation (*see* Matrix concatenation)
  homogeneous form, 86, 118
  identity, 269
  inverse, 269
  multiplication (*see* Matrix multiplication)
  scalar multiplication, 268
  transpose, 268
Matrix concatenation, 86, 118–119, 268
  (*See also* Matrix multiplication)
Matrix multiplication, 86, 268
  composition of matrix functions as equivalent to, 118, 270, 285
Memory mapping (plotting a point), 36, 49
Memory pages, 18, 29
Memory-tube display, 44, 51
Midpoint subdivision clipping algorithm, 103, 109, 154
Modeling, 170
  additive, 172
  solid, 172
  subtractive, 172
Modem (modulator-demodulator), 16
Mouse, 5, 6
Multilevel structures, 87
Multiview projection, 130

NAPLPS (North American Presentation-Level Protocol-Level Syntax), 16–17, 27–29
Natural spline, 176
Nested instances, 87

Nested structure, 227, 228, 238
Nibble, 271, 286
Nodes (*see* Knots)
Normal vector, 297, 303
Normalization transformation, 98, 105, 114
Normalized device coordinate system (NDCS), 98
Normalized display space, 191
Normalized perspective to parallel transform, 191, 206
Normalized viewing coordinate system, 156
Normalizing transformation for canonical view volumes, 155, 161–167
Number systems, 271–272
  binary, 271, 286–289
  decimal, 271, 286–289
  hexadecimal, 271, 286–289

Object coordinate space, 86
Object transformations, 149
Objects, 229, 237, 238
  basic, 229
  specialized, 229
  user-defined, 229
Oblique projection, 130, 144
Ohm's law, 6, 23
Operator workload, 225
Orientation (right- and left-handed), 260, 290
Orthographic projections, 130
Overscan, 36, 47, 48
Overstrike, 70, 78

Paddle control, 5, 6
Painter's algorithm, 196–199, 217
Parallel projection, 130–132, 142–148
  axonometric, 130
  cabinet, 131, 145
  cavalier, 131, 145
  dimetric, 131, 148
  isometric, 131, 147, 148
  multiview, 130
  oblique, 130, 144
  orthographic, 130
  trimetric, 131
Parallel transmission, 15, 27
Parallel vectors, 296
Parametric equations, 263
  circles, 263, 277
  curves, 292–293
  lines, 263, 277, 280, 281, 292, 297, 301, 302
  surfaces, 293–295
Pattern filling, 79
Persistence, 34, 47
Perspective to parallel transform, 190, 205
Perspective anomalies, 129
  perspective foreshortening, 127, 129
  topological distortion, 129, 134
  vanishing points, 129, 138
  view confusion, 129

Perspective foreshortening, 127, 129
Perspective projection, 127–130, 135, 136
  one principal vanishing point, 139
  three principal vanishing points, 139, 148
  two principal vanishing points, 139, 140
Phosphorescence, 34, 47
Phosphors, 33, 47
Phosphorus coating, 33
Physical device coordinate system (PDCS), 98
Picket fence problem, 70–71
Pictogram, 231, 241
Picture creation, 86
Pie chart, 230, 240, 241
Planar polygon, 170
Planes, equations of, 293, 297, 303–305
Plasma display, 43, 51
Plotter, 45, 52
  drum, 45–46, 52
  flatbed, 45, 52
Plotting a point (memory mapping), 36, 49
Plotting resolution for graphing, 270
Point clipping, 100
Point size, 243
Pointillism, 55
Polar coordinates, 263
Polarized film, 44
Polygon, 170
Polygon clipping, 102–104
Polygon list, 195, 213
Polygon listing, 171, 185
Polygon scan conversion (fill), 66–68, 77
Polygonal net (mesh), 171–172
Polyhedron, 172
  faces of, 172
  hidden surfaces of, 221
Polyline, 170
  GKS, 244
Polymarker, 244
Polynomial, 172
  piecewise, 172
Polynomial basis functions, 173
Positively oriented polygons, 102
Potentially visible polygon list (PVPL), 200
Presentations, 229–233
Primitive, 44
Principal vanishing points, 127, 138, 148
Printers, 46
  character, 46
  dot-matrix, 46
Priority, 257
Priority algorithm, 196–199, 217
Processing devices, 17
  single processor, 17
  two processors, 17
Processor addressing capacity, 18, 24
  direct addressing, 18
  indirect addressing, 18

Projection, 127–132, 143
  center of, 127, 149
  classification of, 128
  direction of, 130, 131, 142
  (See also Parallel projection; Perspective projection)
Projection of a vector onto a plane, 307, 308
Projection box technique, 233
Projection plane (see View plane)
Projective plane, 298

Quadric surfaces, 182–184
  equations of, 182–184, 294
Quantizing, 4

Random access (vector) CRT, 44
Raster operational graphics (raster op) (BITBLT), 69, 78
Raster scan, 32, 33
Ray tracing, 202, 220
Reflection, 82, 84
  three-dimensional, 124–126
  two-dimensional, 82, 92–93, 97
Refresh, 30, 34, 47
Region filling, 65–68, 76–77
Representations, 171
  explicit edge listing, 171
  explicit vertex list, 171
  polygon listing, 171
Resolution, 42
Response time, 223, 235
Rotation, 83, 118
  three-dimensional, 116–117, 122–123
  two-dimensional, 81, 88–90, 95, 97

Sampling rate, 4, 23
Scaling, 83
  homogeneous, 82
  magnification, 82
  reduction, 82
  three-dimensional, 116, 126
  two-dimensional, 81, 85, 90–91, 97
Scan conversion, 56
  circles, 58–61, 73–74
  ellipses, 61–63, 74–75
  lines, 56–58, 71–73
  points, 56
  polygons, 66–68, 77
  rectangles, 65, 75
  sectors and arcs, 64–65, 75
Scan-line algorithms, 193, 210
  for hidden surface removal, 195
Scan-line coherence, 194, 223
Screen projection plane, 156
Seed, 66
Serial transmission, 15, 27
Shearing transformation, 94, 162, 165

Shielding (blanking), 36, 48, 99, 113
Side of a plane, 294, 303
Single processor system, 17
Slide show, 229
Snow, 18
Solid modeling, 172
Sort buffer algorithm (*see* Z-buffer algorithm)
Spatial coherence, 194, 212
Splines, 175–176
    anticyclic, 176
    clamped, 176
    cubic, 176
    cyclic, 176
    natural, 176
Spot size, 36
Squareness, 42
Standard perspective projection, 129, 132, 134
Stereotypic user expectations, 235
Storage formats, 11, 12, 24–27
    compressed-memory, 12, 25–27
    display-memory, 12
    image-only, 12
    information (*see* Information storage)
Strobe, 2
Subdivision algorithms, 199–201, 218
Subpicture, 86
Subtractive modeling, 172
Surface patch, 172
    (*See also* Interpolating surface patches)
Surfaces, equations of, 293–295
    cylinder surfaces, 294
    explicit form, 293
    implicit form, 293
    nonparametric, 293
    parametric, 293–295
    planes, 293
    quadric surfaces, 182, 294
    sphere, 301
Sutherland-Hodgman polygon clipping algorithm, 103, 110–112, 114

Three-dimensional transformations, 115–148
Three-dimensional viewing, 149
Tick marks, 231, 241
Tilting transformation, 119
Touch-sensitive screens, 7–8, 24
Trackball, 5, 6
Transducer, 5
Transformations (*see* Functions)
Transforming curves and surfaces, 182
Translation, 83
    matrix form, 85
    three-dimensional, 115
    two-dimensional, 81
Translation vector, 333

Trimetric projection, 131
Two-dimensional transformations, 80–95
    composite, 85
    GKS, 250
    matrix description, 85

Unequal intensity, 70
Unit vector, 295, 301
Up vector, 150
User interface, 224, 235, 236

Vanishing points, 127, 129, 138
Vector components, 265, 279, 295
Vector (random access) CRT, 44
Vector devices, 44–46
Vectors, 264–267, 279–281, 295–298
    addition, 265
    angle measurement between, 261, 267, 301
    cross product, 296
    dot (scalar) multiplication, 266, 295
    length, 266, 295
    normal, 297, 303
    orthogonal, 266, 280, 296, 301
    parallel, 296
    unit, 295, 301
Vertex list, 170
    explicit, 171, 185
View plane, 127, 149, 150
View plane coordinate system, 150, 157, 158
View plane normal, 127
View reference point, 127
View volume, 149, 153, 161, 169
Viewgraphs, 229
Viewing transformations:
    normalization transformation, 98
    three-dimensional, 149–153, 157
    two-dimensional, 98–99, 105
Viewport, 98, 149
    GKS, 247–248, 256, 257
Virtual display device, 98
Visible polygon face, 222

Window, 98, 153
    GKS, 247–248, 257
Wireframe model, 171
Word size, 19, 30
Workstation, 250
Workstation transformation, 98, 105, 114
World coordinate system (WCS), 98, 157
Wright algorithm for mathematical surfaces, 204

Z buffer, 192, 207, 208, 222, 223
Z-buffer algorithm (depth buffer algorithm), 192–193, 207, 208
Zero page, 19

Catalog

If you are interested in a list of SCHAUM'S
OUTLINE SERIES send your name
and address, requesting your free catalog, to:

SCHAUM'S OUTLINE SERIES, Dept. C
McGRAW-HILL BOOK COMPANY
1221 Avenue of Americas
New York, N.Y. 10020